Governing Financial Globalization

Over the last three decades, financial globalization has emerged as one of the principal governance challenges of the modern era. This book examines how globalization has led to the rise of multi-level global financial governance and assesses the analytical use of that concept within international political economy.

This volume unpacks the increasingly complex patterns of governance and authority associated with financial globalization by discussing a range of complementary case studies, including:

- The everyday life of global finance;
- Macroeconomic policy;
- European Union banking regulation;
- IMF policy in Asia;
- The City of London's financial markets;
- The New International Financial Architecture.

Governing Financial Globalization contends that the concept of multi-level governance can provide a fruitful way of identifying sources of power and authority in, and enhancing our understanding of, the increasingly complex field of monetary and financial governance in a globalizing world. This interdisciplinary volume combines insights from political science, economics, geography, sociology and social anthropology. It will appeal to all academics working on the social and political aspects of finance and economic organization more generally.

Andrew Baker is a lecturer at the School of Politics and International Studies at Queen's University Belfast.

David Hudson is an ESRC Postdoctoral Fellow in the Department of Political Science and International Studies at the University of Birmingham.

Richard Woodward lectures in the Department of Politics and International Studies at the University of Hull.

RIPE series in global political economy

Series editors

Louise Amoore   *University of Newcastle, UK*
Randall Germain   *Carleton University, Canada*
Rorden Wilkinson   *University of Manchester, UK and Wellesley College, US*

Formerly edited by Otto Holman, Marianne Marchand and Marianne Franklin
(University of Amsterdam), and Henk Overbeek (Free University, Amsterdam)

The RIPE series editorial board

Mathias Albert (Bielefeld University, Germany), Mark Beeson (University of Queensland, Australia), A. Claire Cutler (University of Victoria, Canada), Marianne Franklin (University of Amsterdam, the Netherlands), Stephen Gill (York University, Canada), Jeffrey Hart (Indiana University, USA), Eric Helleiner (Trent University, Canada), Otto Holman (University of Amsterdam, the Netherlands), Marianne H. Marchand (University of Amsterdam, the Netherlands), Craig N. Murphy (Wellesley College, USA), Robert O'Brien (McMaster University, Canada), Henk Overbeek (Vrije Universiteit, the Netherlands), Anthony Payne (University of Sheffield, UK) and V. Spike Peterson (University of Arizona, USA).

This series, published in association with the *Review of International Political Economy*, provides a forum for current debates in international political economy. The series aims to cover all the central topics in IPE and to present innovative analyses of emerging topics. The titles in the series seek to transcend a state-centred discourse, and focus on three broad themes:

- The nature of the forces driving globalization forward;
- Resistance to globalization;
- The transformation of the world order.
- The series comprises two strands:

The RIPE Series in Global Political Economy aims to address the needs of students and teachers, and the titles will be published in hardback and paperback. Titles include:

Transnational Classes and International Relations
Kees van der Pijl

Gender and Global Restructuring:
Sightings, Sites and Resistances
Edited by Marianne H. Marchand and Anne Sisson Runyan

Global Political Economy
Contemporary Theories
Edited by Ronen Palan

Ideologies of Globalization
Contending Visions of a New World Order
Mark Rupert

The Clash within Civilisations
Coming to Terms with Cultural Conflicts
Dieter Senghaas

Global Unions?
Theory and Strategies of Organized Labour in the Global Political Economy
Edited by Jeffrey Harrod and Robert O'Brien

Political Economy of a Plural World
Critical Reflections on Power, Morals and
Civilizations
Robert Cox with Michael Schechter

**A Critical Rewriting of Global
Political Economy**
Integrating Reproductive, Productive and
Virtual Economies
V. Spike Peterson

Contesting Globalization
Space and Place in the World Economy
André C. Drainville

**Global Institutions and
Development**
Framing the World?
Edited by Morten Bøås and Desmond McNeill

**The Political Economy of European
Integration**
Theory and Analysis
Edited by Erik Jones and Amy Verdun

**Global Institutions,
Marginalization, and Development**
Craig N. Murphy

Routledge/RIPE Studies in global political economy is a forum for innovative new research
intended for a high-level specialist readership, and the titles will be available in hardback
only. Titles include:

1   Globalization and Governance*
*Edited by Aseem Prakash and
Jeffrey A. Hart*

2   Nation-States and Money
The Past, Present and Future of National
Currencies
Edited by Emily Gilbert and Eric Helleiner

**3   The Global Political Economy of
Intellectual Property Rights**
The New Enclosures?
Christopher May

4   Integrating Central Europe
EU expansion and Poland, Hungary and
the Czech Republic
Otto Holman

**5   Capitalist Restructuring,
Globalisation and the Third Way**
Lessons from the Swedish Model
J. Magnus Ryner

**6   Transnational Capitalism and
the Struggle over European
Integration**
Bastiaan van Apeldoorn

7   World Financial Orders
An Historical International Political
Economy
Paul Langley

**8   The Changing Politics of Finance
in Korea and Thailand**
From Deregulation to Debacle
Xiaoke Zhang

**9   Anti-Immigrantism in Western
Democracies**
Statecraft, Desire and the Politics of
Exclusion
Roxanne Lynn Doty

**10   The Political Economy of
European Employment**
European Integration and the
Transnationalization of the
(Un)Employment Question
Edited by Henk Overbeek

**11   Rethinking Global Political
Economy**
Emerging Issues, Unfolding Odysseys
*Edited by Mary Ann Tétreault, Robert A.
Denemark, Kenneth P. Thomas and Kurt Burch*

Governing Financial Globalization

International political economy
and multi-level governance

Edited by Andrew Baker, David Hudson and Richard Woodward

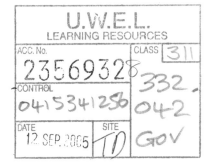
 Routledge
Taylor & Francis Group

LONDON AND NEW YORK

First published 2005
by Routledge
2 Park Square, Milton Park, Abingdon, Oxon OX14 4RN

Simultaneously published in the USA and Canada
by Routledge
270 Madison Avenue, New York, NY 10016

Routledge is an imprint of the Taylor & Francis Group

Typeset in Baskerville by Taylor & Francis Books Ltd
Printed and bound in Great Britain by Antony Rowe Ltd, Chippenham,
Wiltshire

British Library Cataloguing in Publication Data
A catalogue record for this book is available from the British Library

Library of Congress Cataloging-in-Publication Data
A catalog record for this title has been requested.

ISBN 0–415–34125–6

Contents

Illustrations

Figures

Contributors

Andrew Baker is a lecturer in the School of Politics and International Studies, Queen's University Belfast. His book *The Group of Seven: Finance Ministries, Central Banks and the Politics of Global Financial Governance*, will be published by Routledge next year.

Philip G. Cerny is Professor of Global Political Economy at Rutgers University, Newark, New Jersey. He previously taught at the Universities of York, Leeds and Manchester in the United Kingdom and has been a visiting professor or visiting scholar at Harvard University, Dartmouth College, the Fondation Nationale des Science Politiques (Paris), and New York University. He is the author of *The Politics of Grandeur: Ideological Aspects of de Gaulle's Foreign Policy* (1980) and *The Changing Architecture of Politics: Structure, Agency, and the Future of the State* (1990).

Emiliano Grossman is a research fellow at the Centre de recherches politiques de Sciences Po (CEVIPOF) in Paris. He has worked on economic interest groups and European integration. His current research deals with the institutional and political determinants of financial liberalization in Europe.

David Hudson is currently an ESRC Postdoctoral Fellow in the Department of Political Science and International Studies at the University of Birmingham. His research focuses on globalization and financial markets, and the development of a social theory of prices.

Paul Langley is Lecturer in International Political Economy at Northumbria University. He is author of *World Financial Orders: An Historical International Political Economy* (Routledge/RIPE Series, 2002). He is currently working on a manuscript entitled *The Everyday Life of Global Finance: Saving and Borrowing in Britain and America*.

Susanne Soederberg is an Associate Professor of Global Political Economy in Development Studies at Queen's University, Kingston, Canada. She is the author of *The Politics of the New International Financial Architecture: Reimposing Neoliberal Dominance in the Global South* (Zed Books, 2004).

Ben Thirkell-White is a lecturer in the School of International Relations, University of St Andrews. His research concentrates on the governance of finance, particularly in middle-income countries. He is currently completing a book which is to be published by Palgrave: *The IMF and the Politics of Financial Globalisation: From the Asian Crisis to a New International Financial Architecture?*

Richard Woodward is Lecturer in Political Economy at the University of Hull. He is currently writing up his doctoral thesis on the governance of financial markets in the City of London and undertaking research into the role of the OECD in global governance.

Foreword

Few conferences merit the publication of one book, let alone two. But this is the second volume that has grown out of a conference held at the Political Economy Research Centre (PERC) at the University of Sheffield in June 2001 on the theme of multi-level governance. PERC has always seen its role as providing a space in which interdisciplinary work in the social sciences can flourish and in which scholars from different traditions and with different commitments can engage and learn from one another. It seemed to the organizers that the notion of multi-level governance, which had then just begun to enter the wider and increasingly fashionable discussion of changing forms of governance, from its origins as part of the debate about the unique nature of the European Union, would be likely to benefit from this form of interdisciplinary dissection. Accordingly, the conference aimed to bring together scholars with an interest in governance from several different disciplines and sub-disciplines, notably political science, law, international political economy, public policy, geography, economics and sociology. I think all those who were present would acknowledge that it succeeded in this ambition, for the discussion was consistently lively and indeed sometimes challenging in relation to the different perspectives brought forward.

As already indicated, one book emanating from the conference – edited by Ian Bache and Matthew Flinders and simply entitled *Multi-Level Governance* – has already been published (in early 2004) by Oxford University Press. It sets out the main competing approaches to the study of governance presented to the conference. But Andrew Baker, David Hudson and Richard Woodward noticed that many of the papers delivered in Sheffield in June 2001 sought to apply the concept of multi-level governance to the area of money and finance, and they decided that it would be worthwhile bringing these analyses together in a further conference volume. Their decision is fully vindicated by the quality of the chapters that follow. These range over conceptual issues, such as the undermining of old understandings of territory affected by the new circuits of money and the problems of accountability posed by the internationalization of finance, and then explore a series of interesting case studies of monetary and financial governance, running from European banking policy to the role of the International Monetary Fund in the Asian financial crisis, and to the (intriguingly titled) 'everyday life of global finance'.

The editors themselves make sure that the big questions, as seen from a broader international political economy (IPE) perspective, are raised at the outset and brought back for summary discussion at the end. In their Introduction they set the context for the book by introducing the notions of globalization and globality and explaining how the arguments raised by these terms of debate serve to challenge many existing conceptions of power and authority in the contemporary world order. They propose multi-level governance as a potentially helpful alternative framework of understanding, but instantly move on to acknowledge and debate some of its theoretical, practical and methodological shortcomings. In particular, they draw attention to the difficulty of identifying discrete levels within systems of multi-level governance – what they call the problem of the 'L' in MLG. All in all, the collection coheres extremely effectively and constitutes an excellent illustration of the kind of interdisciplinary work which is still so badly needed and which PERC, amongst other centres and bodies, seeks to support.

Anthony Payne
Co-Director
The Political Economy Research Centre
University of Sheffield

Acknowledgements

The idea of this volume was first mooted at a conference held by the Political Economy Research Centre (PERC) at the University of Sheffield: *Multi-Level Governance: Interdisciplinary Perspectives*, 28–30 June 2001. We would like to thank the staff and directors of PERC for having the foresight and prescience to organize the conference. At that conference a number of the papers in the area of IPE seemed to have a similar take on both the potential and the limitations of multi-level governance. Moreover, these papers complemented one another very well. Together, as a collection, these papers seemed to constitute a more potent contribution to the existing literature than as standalone individual pieces. We certainly felt that, together, these papers could further understanding of the relevance of notions of multi-level governance for the study of IPE and global governance. We hope the finished product goes some way towards meeting this goal and makes a thought-provoking contribution to the study of financial and monetary governance in an era of globalization.

As editors we wish to thank the contributors to the volume for their cooperation and efficiency, which on the whole made the editing of this volume a surprisingly agreeable task. We also wish to thank one anonymous reviewer who gave us a particularly thoughtful and penetrating commentary on each of the individual chapters, and more importantly on the volume as a whole. Randall Germain, as the editor of the *RIPE studies in Global Political Economy* series, has been supportive throughout, and we hope that what we have produced reflects favourably on this excellent series and the bold inter-disciplinarity that has enabled RIPE as a journal to challenge academic boundaries and to make an enormous contribution to the development of IPE, over the first decade of its existence. Heidi Bagtazo and Grace McInnes of Routledge were unfailingly helpful and professional throughout the process of preparing this manuscript, providing advice right through from the initial submission of our proposal up to completion of the final manuscript. We also wish to record our gratitude to Tony Payne, the co-director of PERC, who showed a generosity of spirit and great efficiency in agreeing to write the foreword to this volume. Colleagues at our various institutions have also proved helpful in reading and commenting on drafts of various chapters. In particular we would like to thank Matthew Watson, Simon Lee, Lee McGowan and Stefan Andreasson. Of course, any remaining omissions and errors are our responsibility alone.

Andrew Baker, David Hudson and Richard Woodward
April 2004

Part I

1 Introduction

Financial globalization and multi-level governance

Andrew Baker, David Hudson and Richard Woodward

Financial globalization has emerged as one of the principal governance challenges over the last two decades. National and international policy-makers regularly debate and refer to financial globalization in an assortment of settings and arenas. With increasing frequency, academics have also debated the significance of financial globalization, its merits or otherwise, and the challenges it poses to those charged with governing financial affairs (see amongst others Cerny 1993a, 1998a; Helleiner, 1994; Kapstein 1994; Cohen 1996; Eichengreen 1996, 1999; Germain 1997; Pauly 1997; Soros 1998; Eatwell and Taylor 2000; Kaiser, Kirton and Daniels 2000; Andrews, Henning and Pauly 2002; Bryant 2003; Underhill and Zhang 2003). The priorities of this volume are to concentrate analysis upon, and attempt to unpack the increasingly complex patterns of, governance and authority associated with 'globalization'.

Reductions in direct controls and taxation on financial transactions, the elimination of longstanding restrictions on financial intermediaries, the expansion of lightly regulated offshore financial centres, the introduction of new technologies, and the emergence of new innovative financial products have all combined to speed the movement of finance capital across borders. Moreover, politically engineered processes of marketization and de-regulation in the financial services sector have served to erase the distinction between financial markets on the one hand and the international monetary and exchange rate regime on the other. Whereas, at one time, the two were distinct, with the latter considered the preserve of governments and the former segmented by national economic space, sector and self-regulating cartels, today macroeconomic management problems and exchange rate issues are bound up with financial markets. Large private financial institutions can instantaneously move vast amounts of speculative and investment capital across political jurisdictions and market segments, often within a single company structure (Underhill 1997b). These developments mean that the regulation and supervision of financial sectors directly affects the ways and rate at which capital can be moved across and within borders and financial institutions, therefore influencing exchange rates, the financing options of governments and the general stability of the financial sector (Underhill 1997b).

The developments described above are often referred to in a form of shorthand as financial globalization. Recent financial crises engulfing Mexico

(1994), East and South Asia (1997–98), Brazil and Russia (1999) and Argentina (2001–2) have impoverished millions as their jobs and savings have been swept away. Similarly, in the United States, the corporate scandal involving Enron decimated the life savings of many of its employees and imperilled the retirement incomes of millions of workers whose pension funds had seen fit to invest in the collapsed energy giant. In other words, global finance and financial globalization are not simply a phenomenon existing out there, a vicarious experience divorced from our everyday lives. Our everyday lives and the prosperity of citizens throughout the world are indelibly connected to the vicissitudes of global financial markets (Langley, Chapter 5 of this volume). For these reasons the development of effective mechanisms to govern money and finance continues to feature prominently on the political agenda at both national and international levels.

In this volume we are not concerned with debating the extent and scope of 'financial globalization', or whether it can be reversed, but rather with the governance challenges it produces, different actors' perceptions of these challenges, the responses they are subsequently drawing and how those responses are operating in practice. Recent developments in financial governance are also challenging conventional approaches to analysing governance and authority in political science and international relations. We contend in this volume that the concept of multi-level governance provides a fruitful line of enquiry for identifying sources of power and authority and enhancing our understanding of the increasingly complex field of monetary and financial governance under conditions of 'financial globalization'.

As the Foreword by Tony Payne at the start of the book indicates, the volume originated out of an interdisciplinary conference on multi-level governance at the Political Economy Research Centre at the University of Sheffield, in the summer of 2001. It became apparent that a number of those presenting papers on monetary and financial governance shared similar insights, not only on how multi-level governance might be usefully developed and where its weaknesses lay, but also on future research trajectories in International Political Economy (IPE). Together as a collection of essays, those assorted insights constitute a much more potent contribution to the existing literature than as standalone papers.

This introductory chapter highlights four themes and purposes, which reverberate through the remainder of the book. First, we demonstrate why existing analytical frameworks in IPE and their conceptualizations of governance and authority no longer suffice under conditions of globalization. Second, we advance multi-level governance as an alternative analytical framework that has the potential to address some of these problems and contribute to a fuller understanding of monetary and financial governance. Third, while championing multi-level governance as an improvement over previous analytical frameworks, we acknowledge that existing scholarship pertaining to multi-level governance suffers from a number of methodological, theoretical and practical flaws. We consequently seek to identify ways in which multi-level governance can be refined to strengthen its appeal. This is linked to a fourth, and final, theme which is the presentation of a series of contemporary case studies demonstrating the utility (or otherwise) of the multi-level governance framework to monetary and financial issues and how empirical research can contribute to the conceptual development of multi-level governance and to the study of governance processes and IPE more generally.

Globalization and financial governance

Globalization remains an overused and under-specified concept. All too often it is invoked as a portmanteau term claiming to describe or explain the myriad of changes witnessed over recent decades (Higgott and Reich 1998). The use of the term globalization to capture these processes and tendencies has not gone unchallenged with a series of critical interventions showing that much analysis is in danger of mixing up hyperbole with substance (Boyer and Drache 1996; Berger and Dore 1996; Hirst and Thompson 1999; Walter *et al.* 1999; Watson 1999; Held *et al.* 1999; Scholte 2000). The empirical case against 'the often wildly exaggerated and wilfully extrapolated claims made in the name of globalization' is clearly very important (Hay and Marsh 2000b: 2–3). However, our intention here is not to enter into details of this debate, but instead to emphasize the collective challenge that these and other processes represent to received ideas of regulation, authority and governance. In short, we would emphasize that 'globalization', while involving material changes, is also a diverse discourse or social construction that has strategically changed the mental context of governing as much as the material one (Hay and Rosamond 2002; Rosamond 2003). And in that sense, and even if not necessarily in others, it remains absolutely crucial to acknowledge the significance of the term globalization for developments in governance.

Though the controversy surrounding the concept rumbles on, there is some agreement that governance refers to the institutions, mechanisms or processes backed by political power and/or authority that allow an activity or set of activities to be controlled, influenced or directed in the collective interest (Rosenau 1992, 1995, 1997, 2000; Commission on Global Governance 1995; Malpas and Wickham 1995; Hirst 1997; Mathiason 1998; Held *et al.* 1999). Recent experiences, whether they be monetary integration in Europe or a succession of contagious financial crises, have suggested that the nation state as a political entity based on territoriality and sovereignty, while by no means a passive actor, appears unable (or unwilling) adequately to dispense monetary and financial governance functions. Certainly, in response to the challenges posed by more interconnected monetary and financial systems, the actors involved in monetary and financial governance have diversified, while the relationships between them have become more complex. These developments pose conceptual challenges for academics working on financial and monetary issues relating to how to explain and analyse increasingly complex governance processes, as well as how to think about changing patterns of power and authority.

Globalization, IPE and concepts of power and authority

The emergence of International Political Economy as a recognizable (inter-) discipline in the early 1970s was largely born of frustration with existing work in the fields of International Relations (IR) and international economics. Mainstream IR research centred upon the causes and consequences of interstate war, sidelining consideration of economic matters and their impact on international political relations. Meanwhile international economics was castigated for its reliance on elegant models depicting economic behaviour taking place in a political vacuum. Strange (1970) remarked that IR and international economics suffered from 'a case of mutual neglect' and developed a compelling case for the creation of IPE as a disciplinary space in which to investigate how the political and economic domains interact, overlap and synchronize in the international domain. However, IPE is emphatically not, as some seem to believe (see, for example, Spero 1977) a mere subdiscipline of IR. From the outset IPE sought to promote itself as 'open field' (Strange 1996a) drawing on the contributions and concerns of classical political economy from the eighteenth century to the present, and willing to embrace interventions and insights from a whole range of perspectives (gender, environmentalism, culture, development, civilizations) and disciplines (politics, economic, sociology, history, geography, anthropology) (see Palan 2000b; Underhill 2000a; Gills 2001).

Despite IPE's rich and diverse ancestry, and reservations about IR theory, a lot of work in IPE continues to rely on the assumptions of mainstream IR scholarship. These assumptions, which have important ramifications for the way we think about the notion of governance, were always problematic but have been further exposed by the intensification of global interconnectedness. As has already been intimated, the last decade has seen the emergence of a voluminous literature detailing the causes and consequences of financial globalization and offering prescriptions for its effective governance. One of the central contentions of this volume is that the notion of globalization, whether it is employed as a theoretical construct or as a means of describing an empirical reality, has fatally undermined conventional approaches to IPE and their understandings of governance and authority.

Governance, global finance and the erroneous territorial assumptions of IR

The analytical assumption which unites mainstream theories of IR is that states are the main actors in world affairs and are the sole repository of power and authority. As a consequence governance was deemed the exclusive preserve of governments where 'state territoriality sets the spatial parameters within which governance is encountered' (Woodward, Chapter 3 of this volume). As Cox (1992: 161) notes, the term 'international relations' 'embodies certain assumptions about global power relations that need to be questioned', especially as it 'implies the Westphalian state system as its basic framework'. It assumes we are interested only in inter*national* political processes, that is to say relations between states, and to explain how and under what conditions states can work together to mitigate the anarchical tendencies of the international system. He goes on to argue that the state system is not, and indeed never was, an adequate framework for conceptualizing world politics because states constitute just one of the many strands of power and authority that, woven together, produce the fabric of global relations.

In contrast, one of the novelties of globalization, whether it is used to describe a process or an end condition, is that it is suffixed with an '*ation*' rather than a '*nation*' (see Woodward 2003, and Chapter 3 of this volume). While inter*national* frameworks are imbued from the outset with the notion that states are the only source of power and authority in the global political system, 'globalization as an "ation" makes no prior hypothesis about the main actors or the dominant patterns of world politics', (Woodward 2003: 310) but instead regards the delineation of these patterns as a matter for empirical investigation. When viewed through the lens of globalization, therefore, governance has appeared to some authors to consist of a range of competing and overlapping 'structures of authority' (Rosenau 1997) including, but not reducible to, the state and involving inter-relationships between a mix of public and private bodies, in which there may be no obvious hierarchy or command structure.

Of course, no serious scholar of IPE today would deny the continuing importance of states in the governance of money and finance. Unquestionably, national settings do remain relevant where monetary and financial governance are concerned (Cohen 1998; Bryant 2003). National money forms and national financial markets persist. Similarly, as the chapters by Baker, Woodward and Cerny in this volume make clear, central banks, national treasuries and national regulatory agencies continue to reach key monetary and financial decisions. None the less, the idea that the world, especially in the economic domain, is best conceptualized as a system of states is increasingly at odds with the world as it is experienced and observed. The notion of 'globalization' has given analytical expression to these practical concerns. As Strange (1996a) argued, we have witnessed a diffusion of power and authority from the state. In this respect, contemporary forms of authority are as complex as they ever were, appearing to some to be analogous to medieval times (Bull 1977; Kobrin 1998; Cerny, Chapter 2 of this volume). Moreover, recently there has been a growing recognition of the increase in private authority in the IPE literature (Sinclair 1994b; Cutler *et al.* 1999a; Higgott *et al.* 2000; Hall and Biersteker 2002). Private governance is proving particularly prevalent in areas characterized by rapid change, where leaden-footed governments have been unable, or unwilling, to maintain an effective regulatory framework. It is therefore not surprising that it is in the esoteric and arcane world of global finance that private structures of governance have been most evident, as authority is in part subcontracted out from the state.

Structural power and authority

However, before we investigate further how power and authority are no longer exercised solely by states in the monetary and financial field and the conceptual challenges flowing from this, we need to say a few words on what we mean by the terms power and authority. Our basic position is that if power is about a *capacity* to act, authority is about the (perceived) *right* to act. Therefore, it is quite possible to have power without authority, and to have authority but relatively little power.

It is well established in the critical IPE literature that international monetary relations are characterized by the exercise of structural power, whereby actors influence the choice of others without appearing to put pressure on them, through the possession of key strategic resources that shape the wider structures within which states and corporate enterprises relate to one another (Strange 1994). One such example of structural power is the impact of US interest rate decisions, or movements in the value of the dollar on the world economy more generally, allowing the United States a greater degree of autonomy in its macroeconomic policy and allowing it to deflect economic adjustment costs onto other states. Other examples include the decisions by US authorities to let the dollar float, to liberalize their capital account and de-regulate financial markets in the 1970s that transformed the international financial system (Helleiner 1994). The location of the deepest and most liquid financial markets in the United States has also created what some see as a powerful Dollar–Wall Street Regime, or a Wall Street–Treasury axis, that is able to steer international monetary and financial outcomes in US interests (Wade and Veneroso 1998; Gowan 1999). A considerable number of authors consequently agree that the United States enjoys structural power in international monetary and financial relations (Helleiner 1994; Strange 1994; Germain 1997; Gowan 1999; Seabrooke 2001). While there is no doubt that structural power is important for monetary and financial governance, we would contend that this is not the same thing as authority.

Authority has a number of qualities and characteristics that make it quite distinct from structural power, although authority can be used as a form of power. Structural power comes from the possession of certain material, informational and procedural resources and is not reliant on the consent or acceptance of other actors. It shapes outcomes irrespective of the decisions of other actors and can be used unintentionally, as well as intentionally. Authority, on the other hand, emerges from the discharge of specific duties in accordance with a specific office or title, and is frequently, but not always, related to the possession of critical expertise by the office- or title-holder (Aykens 2002). Unlike power, authority rests on consent and an actor's recognition that a proposal, or the decision of another actor, should be complied with. This means that authority also rests on trust and persuasion, rather than on coercion or simple structural capability, and it is therefore associated with legitimacy (Lukes 1987; Hurd 1999; Hall and Biersteker 2002). Of course, authority varies across time in accordance with the track record of particular individuals and institutions and the credibility they are able to build up with their peers, based on their ability to forward convincing explanations of and solutions to particular events and problems. Whether an actor possesses authority is primarily a function of whether others believe their statements and actions to be truthful and credible, and this in turn means authority must be continuously nurtured through personal performance (Aykens 2002).

Authority is a particularly important concept where monetary and financial issues are concerned, because of their technical character. For example, the familiarity of the personnel of finance ministries, central banks, regulatory agencies and private financial institutions with various sophisticated economic models, enables them to forward sophisticated analyses of various financial and monetary developments and, on the basis of this, advocate specific policy recommendations. Those wishing to dispute the analyses of these actors have to use similarly technical sophisticated economic analyses and discourses. With many interested parties not possessing this technical expertise, finance ministries, central banks, regulatory agencies (both national and transgovernmental) and private industry interests have found it easy to monopolize financial governance on the grounds of their technical supremacy. Technical expertise, therefore, contributes to the authority of finance ministries, central banks, regulatory agencies and private financial institutions, but it also insulates monetary and financial governance from wider public debates, despite the fact that monetary and financial governance is an issue of utmost public interest.

Distinguishing authority from structural power is conceptually important in the study of IPE, because it enables us to understand that the conduct of global financial governance consists of more than the simple exercise of power, but also involves interactions based on the construction of technical arguments by actors operating at numerous levels, or across discrete but overlapping social spaces. Of course, definitions of valid technical knowledge can be shaped by structural power resources relating to professional norms in the field of economics and the recruitment practices of policy-making agencies and financial firms, but we also need to acknowledge that it is possible to have a considerable degree of technical authority, while possessing relatively little in the way of structural power resources.

Four categories of authority in global financial governance

Once we take a broad view of authority, and associate it with competencies and expertise as discussed above, there is no reason to equate authority with a narrowly statist conception of legitimacy. Instead it becomes important to look at existing *de facto* sources of authority. Claims to authority vary over time, space and issue area. Recent surveys of global financial governance have tended to support the idea that the field is now administered by a plethora of structures of authority (see for example Scholte 1997, 2002a;

Woods 2001). In addition to the state, this literature identifies at least four further categories of structures of authority which come together to govern global finance: international multilateral institutions, transgovernmental regulatory networks, regional regulatory cooperation, and finally private authority including, but not reducible to, 'the market'. So, first, the most conspicuous response of states to the difficulties of managing global financial markets has been to intensify international cooperation on monetary and financial issues. This has been achieved through the creation of formal multilateral financial institutions, notably the International Monetary Fund (IMF) (see Pauly 1997; Broughton 2000; Stiglitz 2002), the World Bank, the Organization for Economic Cooperation and Development (OECD), and a growing number of informal and less institutionalized collaborative arrangements embodied in the 'gaggle of G's' (G7, G8, G10, G20, G22, G24, G30) striving for global financial stability (Culpeper 2000; Baker 2000a, 2003, forthcoming). These bodies, whose roles have steadily expanded, are charged with delivering a more stable financial order through resolving and responding to financial crises, the formulation of codes of good practice on regulatory and macroeconomic matters, and effective surveillance of the global financial system (see chapters by Baker (Chapter 6) and Soederberg (Chapter 10) in this volume). Second, recent years have seen the profusion of what Slaughter (1997), following Keohane and Nye (1977), terms 'transgovernmental networks' of regulators. Unlike the multilateral financial institutions, whose membership consists of states, transgovernmental regulatory networks are composed of national regulatory agencies working in a given specialist area of financial governance. These networks seek to develop and disseminate standards of international best practice which national regulators should adhere to when developing and policing their domestic regulatory structures. The first transgovernmental network, the Basle Committee for Banking Supervision (BCBS), was created in 1974 to oversee the regulation of international banking. Since then the principle of transgovernmentalism has extended into the realm of securities with the creation of the International Organization of Securities Commissions (IOSCO) in 1984. Similarly the insurance industry is now increasingly subject to the influence of transgovernmental rules after the founding, in 1994, of the International Association of Insurance Supervisors (IAIS).

Third, the last decade has seen the rise of authority structures linked to regional financial spaces, most notably in the European Union (EU) (see Grossman, Chapter 7 of this volume). This has already spawned a new currency (the Euro), new regulatory structures (including a raft of Directives from the European Commission) and has acted as a catalyst for new forms of regulatory cooperation among national authorities via the Committee of European Securities Regulators (CESR). Though it has been bedevilled by the horse-trading that characterizes EU decision-making, the Financial Services Action Plan (FSAP), due to be completed by 2005, appears to be bringing the dream of a single market for financial services ever closer, which may be both the cause and the consequence of the relocation of political authority to the European level.

The fourth strand of authority emanates from the private sector. Within the critical IPE literature this is often highlighted as the most important contemporary challenge to democratic accountability and authority. Finance, it is suggested, enjoys a structural power or hegemonic position within societal decision-making structures (Lukes 1974; Gill and Law 1989; Strange 1994). However, while intuitively very appealing, theoretically speaking it is also the most 'slippery' of the new locations of authority. It is too often characterized by broad, sweeping terms such as 'neo-liberalism', the 'Washington Consensus', 'globalization', or some compound of the above. However, often taking their cue from the rich work of Antonio Gramsci (1971) or Karl Polanyi (1944) (on which, see Birchfield 1999), there have been a number of useful attempts to specify the authority of the market, for example, the 'new constitutionalism', 'disciplinary neo-liberalism' (Gill 1995), the 'embedded financial orthodoxy' (Cerny 1994b). In this shift towards embedding the new constitutionalism it is vitally important to identify the agents implied within this process. A number of industry associations have sought to promulgate and disseminate international best practice standards, which are then policed on a self-regulating basis by the industry concerned. This trend is most pronounced in the global securities industry where the collective proclamations of the World Federation of Stock Exchanges (FIBV) (created in 1961 as the International Federation of Stock Exchanges), the International Securities Market Association (ISMA) created in 1969, and the International Council of Securities Associations (ICSA) formed in 1988 now constitute a sophisticated and elaborate framework of rules governing global securities transactions (see Filipovic 1997). Similarly, international standards for auditing and accounting have been developed primarily by private sector organizations. The International Accounting Standards Board (ISAB) (formerly the International Accounting Standards Committee (IASC)), a body constituted by professional accountancy organizations, was created in 1973 and is charged with continuing to develop global rules for financial reporting. In Europe, private arrangements for governing auditing date back to the 1950s and the establishment of the Union Europeenne des Experts Comptables Economiques et Financiers (UEC). Private authority is also beginning to colonize areas which were previously the exclusive domain of the state. In the area of money laundering, for example, twelve leading international private banks in conjunction with Transparency International launched the Wolfsberg Anti-Money Laundering Principles in October 2000, setting down the policies, procedures and principles that should underpin the governance of private banking relationships. Technical expertise, especially in an area as specialized as global finance, is a deep source of legitimacy: for instance, the role of credit rating agencies (Sinclair 2000a). There is also a significant role for cultural patterns in the acceptance of financial hegemony (Harmes 2001a; Langley, Chapter 5 of this volume).

The diffusion of authority and the inadequate response of IR

The diffusion of authority in the global political system, coupled with the recognition that '"international" no longer embraces much of what transpires across national boundaries' (Rosenau 2000: 171) led to a series of analytical innovations in IR theory, including work on transnational relations (Keohane and Nye 1972; Strange 1976), interdependence (Keohane and Nye 1977) and regime theory (Krasner 1983). Unfortunately, these frameworks clung dogmatically to the notion that states were the main actors and continued to conceptualize authority and governance too narrowly. Though states remain critically important, these frameworks fail to recognize that authority is diffused among a myriad of overlapping actors, which come together to govern the global financial system. However, the recognition that governance of global money and finance is more complex than traditional frameworks suggest is only the first step. We need to find and develop alternative frameworks that are capable of grappling with 'the global' and gaining some analytical purchase on this complexity. In turn this will enable us to discern the patterns of authority that characterize financial and monetary governance, and to assess the implications of these patterns of governance for power, authority and democracy in the financial and monetary domain. It is against this background of complexity that commentators began to speculate about the possibility of referring to, and conceptualizing, governance as multi-level.

Multi-level governance: states, markets and 'global' political economy

The application of multi-level frameworks to organize and classify social phenomena for systematic analysis is well-established practice in the social sciences. Traditional approaches to IR and IPE, for example, assume that there are two discrete fields or 'levels' of analysis, each governed by different assumptions, exhibiting different tendencies and thus susceptible to interpretation using different analytical tools (see Waltz 1959; Singer 1961). First, there is the international level or the 'level of the international system' (Singer 1961: 80–2), which, because of the absence of an overarching authority, is considered to be anarchical with outcomes governed by the distribution of power among states. Secondly, there is the domestic level or the 'level of the national state' (Singer 1961: 82–9), at which a central authority is responsible for making, implementing and enforcing a rule-based political system. The international level has generally been the preserve of scholars associated with IR and IPE who have tended to ignore the national level or at least to make assumptions that render it irrelevant to analysis, by assuming that all national-level systems are fundamentally the same and react in the same way to international-level stimuli for example. Similarly the domestic level has generally been the preserve of comparative politics scholars who treat the international level as given, believing national political systems to be insulated from the vagaries of international-level politics. However, it was recognized that this rigid separation of the domestic and international levels was somewhat arbitrary, and several theoretical frameworks have been propounded to illuminate the intimate entanglement between the domestic and international levels, ranging from Rosenau's (1969) conception of 'linkage politics' and Keohane and Nye's (1972, 1977) work on 'transnationalism' and 'complex interdependence' to Putnam's elucidation of 'two level games' (Putnam 1988).

Unquestionably, each of these frameworks has injected greater nuance into the study of IR and IPE, expanding the range of variables used to explain international behaviour. Nevertheless each of these approaches suffers from a number of analytical flaws. First, as we have already noted, they continue to assert that the state is the basic unit of analysis. Second, they assume that there are only two levels of human community. Finally, and most importantly for our purposes, they perpetuate the dichotomy between domestic and international levels, treating them as two separate, if related, realms. In other words, the domestic or international level remains the dependent variable with these frameworks aiming to explain the domestic determinants of international politics or the international determinants of domestic politics. However, the rapid advance in the extensity, intensity, and velocity of human interaction has blurred the 'Great Divide' (Clark 1999) between the domestic and international levels to the point of meaninglessness (see, for example, Agnew and Corbridge 1995; Ferguson and Mansbach 1996; Rosenau 1997; Ferguson and Barry Jones 2002). While splitting the world into domestic and international spheres may be analytically convenient, it is also a gross distortion. A key contention here is that the world needs to be examined holistically as encapsulated in the notion of 'globality'. Yet, on the other hand, it is vitally important not to fall prey to any form of universalistic holism. Therefore what is required is an analytical framework capable of gaining some purchase on the totality of political relationships in the world through recognizing a range of actors at many different levels; and it is this void that multi-level governance is seeking to fill.

Until now, multi-level governance has been employed most extensively in connection with the study of the EU to reflect the diffusion of decision-making competencies across several levels of government (see, for example, Marks *et al.* 1996a; Marks *et al.* 1996b). Unfortunately, in IPE, though the idea of governance being multi-levelled or multi-layered is often conjured with (see, for example, Scholte 2002a; Payne forthcoming), the questions of what it means to talk of multi-level governance, or what analytical purchase can be obtained from its application, have rarely been probed in any depth. One creditable exception to this is the model of multi-level governance outlined by Hirst and Thompson in their book *Globalization in Question* (1999: Chapter 7). They argue that the governance of the global economy is possible at five interdependent levels: (1) agreements between the G3 (the US, EU and Japan); (2) international regulatory agencies; (3) regional trade and investment blocs; (4) nation-states; and (5) subnational regions (see Table 1.1). This depiction of governance being provided by a series of hierarchically arranged territorial containers is certainly contestable (see Woodward, this volume). Nevertheless it is a useful departure point for a discussion of multi-level governance because it is both a concrete expression of the 'club sandwich' or 'layer cake' allusions made by authors seeking to construct the multi-level analogy and it highlights the advantages and disadvantages of existing approaches to multi-level governance.

Table 1.1   Governance by governments

Group of 3 (European Union, North America, Japan)
International Regulatory Authorities (WTO, IMF, World Bank etc.)
Regional-level Governance (EU, APEC etc.)
National-level Governance
Subnational-level Governance

Source: Adapted from Hirst and Thompson (1999).

The merits of the existing multi-level governance literature

Existing formulations of multi-level governance such as the one above have four principal advantages over existing frameworks. First, like all analytical frameworks seeking to impose order on a disordered world, they present a simplified account. Nevertheless it is a more nuanced framework than either state-centred approaches, or analyses that present globality as an undifferentiated space devoid of topography or shape. Multi-level governance gives expression to the idea that there are many interacting authority structures at work in the emergent global political economy.

Second, there is an open-endedness about MLG frameworks. Unlike some of the inward-looking baronies that characterize IR/IPE, they have no preconceived ideas about which authority structures constitute the main actors, or what the causal relationships amongst them are, but instead regard these questions as matters for empirical investigation. As such they provide a means of ordering and organizing analysis, a mental map for navigating increasingly complex and diffuse structures of authority. Though they may be imperfect, they are still more nuanced than the perspective advanced by state-centric or hyperglobalist analysis.

Third, multi-level governance does not rely on a capricious separation of the domestic and international spheres of activity. Multi-level governance recognizes that human interaction and human communities exist at a number of different levels that do not fit into neat containers labelled domestic and international. Fourth, multi-level governance not only preserves a central role for public authority, in particular the authority of the state, but also recognizes that state authority is enmeshed in dense webs of governing arrangements that are dependent on the actions, strategies and decisions of other governments, supranational, transnational and sub-state actors (Cerny, Chapter 3 of this volume). In other words, it sensitizes us to the idea that public authority takes a multiplicity of forms with decision-making competencies spread across a number of levels.

The shortcomings of existing multi-level governance literature

Nonetheless, the current multi-level governance literature has five principal shortcomings, which not only impede its potential application to monetary and financial affairs, but also inhibit our understanding of global political economy and the contemporary nature of monetary and financial order. The first problem highlighted by a number of contributors to this volume is that so far multi-level governance has dealt solely with formal, public structures of authority (see the chapters by Woodward, Hudson and Baker). In other words, the study of multi-level governance has been hijacked by state-centred approaches that have habitually conflated multi-level governance with multi-level government (Jordan 2001). Indeed Porter (2002: 2) has gone as far as to state that 'multi-level governance refers to a particular subset of contemporary governance arrangements in which decision-making authority is distributed across more than one level of relatively autonomous *public sector institutions*' (emphasis added). It is unclear how private, market and other non-territorial forms of authority fit into such a framework. Though this oversight may be justifiable in certain contexts, it cannot be justified with regard to the study of monetary and financial governance where, as this chapter has already established, private and market forms of governance have proliferated. Multi-level governance is a more nuanced analytical framework but it only illuminates part of the complexity associated with monetary and financial governance. More seriously, by failing to sufficiently disassociate itself from the existing orthodoxy, multi-level governance as it is presently conceived is open to the charge that it is an anodyne development of, rather than a replacement for, established state-centred frameworks.

A second serious flaw stems from the problems associated with the term 'level' (the 'L' in MLG), and the way levels are used in the existing multi-level governance literature. One such problem arises from the propensity of existing multi-level governance literature to cast levels in purely territorial terms. This arises from the tendency to view authority as the exclusive preserve of governments, which is consequent upon their control of a given territorial space. However, these 'spaces of places' models (see Cohen 1998; Woodward, Chapter 3 of this volume) are ill-suited to understanding an area of global political economy which is increasingly characterized by the prevalence of private and market structures of authority that transcend established territorial boundaries and might be said in certain cases to be de-territorialized, or supraterritorial (Scholte 2000; Ferguson and Barry Jones 2002: 1). The authority of these actors neither derives from, nor is constrained by, Westphalian coordinates. That is to say territoriality is overlain by functional, sectional and socially-oriented spatial forms that do not fit elegantly into established territorial containers. The existing MLG literature also pays scant attention to whether, and how, coherent levels can be identified. For example, Table 1.1 suggests that the notion of a level is invoked to describe an agglomeration of actors that operate at and over the same spatial scale. Unfortunately, these sharp delineations cannot be sustained in practice because the whole notion of a level is susceptible to the allegation that it arbitrarily divides subject matter into 'convenient boxes' (Amin and Palan 2002). Furthermore, in certain cases actors might be said to belong simultaneously to a number of different levels, to perform different roles at different levels and for there to be a divergence between the level at which their authority might be said to exist and the level at which it impacts. There also appears to be an inbuilt assumption that all actors appearing at the same level are identical and respond to external stimuli in the same way, yet states have different power resources in global politics, different internal structures, and this may impact on their behaviour and approaches to governance and regulation in different ways (Weiss 1998).

A third shortcoming arises from the persistent confusion and ambiguity surrounding the use of the terms actors and levels in MLG literature. In this introduction, governance has been defined in actor-oriented terms, that is to say that we have looked to the agency of certain authoritative actors to govern money and finance. However, this leaves us with a series of awkward questions to consider. What happens to these actors when they are viewed in terms of levels? Do they forgo their agency or is it their agency that sustains the level to which they belong? Are levels now actors imbued with agency? That is to say, have levels become authoritative actors? Not wishing to impose conformity on our contributors, these questions will be pursued in more detail in individual chapters.

Fourth, approaches to multi-level governance continue to be obsessed by hierarchy. Multi-level governance has generally focused 'upon the division of powers and competencies between various levels of political authority' (O'Brien 2002: 5), privileging relationships between different vertical layers of authority at the expense of examining horizontal relationships among actors at a given level. In many ways this is not surprising. The very idea of levels and levels of analysis is imbued with hierarchical implications. However, as the chapters by Grossman and Woodward demonstrate, horizontal relationships between different actors at the same level are sometimes crucial to the delivery of effective governance and may offer important clues as to how different levels are constructed. Moreover, different levels or social spaces often interact or cut across with one another in complex ways that are not strictly hierarchical.

Finally, the existing multi-level governance literature is devoid of normative analysis. Multi-level governance appears to prioritize the question of *whether* the world can be governed but conveniently skates over the thorny questions of *who* governs, the values that should underpin governance, and the *interests* that should be represented. The context in which multi-level governance has become popularized is important here. In an era where national governments are widely perceived to be losing control over the global economy, it appears a common-sense response to be concerned with the question of whether governance is possible and to suggest that devolving political authority upwards in order to operate at the same 'levels' as a globally integrated economy is a plausible solution to the problem. However, this leaves little room to consider, to take just one example, the democratic implications of devolving responsibility for governance to other levels. In contrast to the emancipatory potential and political progressivism implicit in so much of the work on multi-level governance in EU studies, it is argued that, just because relations between different arenas are becoming more intertwined and inter-related, eroding hierarchical command structures and creating more complex bargaining relations between competing and overlapping authorities, this does not necessarily result in more socially progressive and democratically oriented outcomes. For further discussion see the chapters by Cerny (2), Thirkell-White (8), Soederberg (10) and Baker (6).

Aims and structure of this volume

Aims and themes

There are five recurring themes and related aims in this volume. First, despite the popularity of the term 'multi-level governance', little rigorous work has been conducted on the precise nature and meaning of the concept, resulting in a continued ambiguity surrounding its definition and purpose. The literature applying MLG in a meaningful fashion is meagre across the social sciences and there is a near-total absence in the field of IPE. Therefore the first aim of this volume is systematically to apply multi-level governance to the area of money and finance and to consider the conceptual challenges arising from it. In particular, to what extent is financial and monetary governance multi-levelled? What is meant by this? What, if any, analytical insights can be gained from applying the notion of multi-level governance to money and finance? What are the principal levels involved in the governance of money and finance? How do these different levels interact? Can multi-level governance help us understand what drives policy in the areas of money and finance, who holds authority, and what are the implications of this for democracy and the notion of public purpose?

There is a general dissatisfaction with multi-level governance as it has been so far developed. As we have already demonstrated, particular concern surrounds the concept of a 'level' with its continued reliance on territory, its inability to come to terms with non-territorial authority structures, and whether and how levels might be identified. The second aim of the volume is to examine how multi-level governance might be developed so as to enhance our understanding of how the current monetary and financial order is constituted and maintained, and how IPE might proceed to illuminate patterns of governance, power and authority in the emerging global political economy. The contributors to this volume seek actively to pursue the issue of how markets and market actors might be integrated into multi-level analytical frameworks, although they reach different answers as to how, and to what extent, this might be achieved. Notably, we follow the lead of Geoffrey Underhill and others who have reacted against the orthodoxy that states and markets are based on contrasting logics. Instead we start from the position that states and markets constitute integrated ensembles of governance that can be thought to represent a state–market condominium (Underhill 2000a). The volume will also specifically engage with and seek to refine the idea of a level. Here 'levels' will be defined as discrete socially constructed spaces or settings, as systems of social interactions with their own distinguishable logics that are distinct from other social spaces and systems of social interaction, although they may be influenced by them, such as, for example, financial market*places* (see Hudson, Chapter 4 of this volume). These social spaces have their own distinct social purpose and role in the formulation and implementation of policy and, in this case, the reproduction of monetary and financial discipline. A number of authors also question whether levels should be discarded altogether in favour of 'dimensions' (Baker, Chapter 6), 'domains' (Woodward, Chapter 9) or 'concentric models' (Smith 1997).

With the exception of Grossman, the contributors to this volume suggest both that multi-level governance exists and that generally there is more of it. The third aim of the volume is to assess why this is the case and whether the trend will endure. In identifying specific agents and their roles in forwarding various globalizing tendencies, the contributors are adding to our concrete under-standing of globalization. It represents an exercise in process tracing that is so often absent from discussions of globalization. In this sense we see the chapters as part of the movement towards treating globalization as an *explanandum* rather than the *explanans* (Hay and Marsh 2000b; Rosenberg 2000).

The fourth theme is that multi-level governance is an analytic framework capable of describing an empirical reality, but it falls short of being a theoretical construct capable of explanation. Multi-level frameworks are useful in that they provide a means of ordering and organizing open-ended empirical analysis, but ultimately deriving explanations from the framework is fraught with problems. This is not necessarily a problem as long as it is explicitly acknowledged. We see a multi-level perspective as a contextual variable, describing the shape and struc-ture of the political topography within which agents interact, and which in turn they affect with their interaction. In this sense multi-level governance is a place to begin from, and one that sensitizes the student to likely patterns of behaviour and influence. However, within this multi-level framework it is then necessary to operationalize theoretical frameworks to explain outcomes (see Hudson, Chapter 4 of this volume, on the case of markets).

The final theme is that, despite the sometimes revolutionary changes to the global economy in the past three decades, the state still has a leading role in financial and monetary governance, and that multi-level governance helps us to decode how its role has evolved alongside the globalizing tendencies it has nurtured. An explicit focus of this volume is state–market, and indeed market–market, interactions, as part of the overall pattern of multi-level governance in the financial and monetary domain. Moreover, it is argued that such analysis helps to shed light on the nature of financial markets, the behaviour that characterizes them and the social and political consequences of such behaviour. These issues are integral to the continued stability, sustainability and legitimacy of the global system, the continued role and authority of the state and non-state actors, and the implications of this for legitimate democratic governance. The final question explored in this volume therefore draws on the findings of the various chapters. If we are to talk about the multi-level governance of money and finance and apply this analytical approach to monetary and financial issues, what does this tell us about changing patterns of authority and democracy in the contemporary global order?

We return to these five themes in the conclusion. In light of the different arguments and case studies presented by our contributors, we suggest some concrete and backed answers to these themes. Naturally, different authors emphasize different themes, and there is not necessarily a consensus even when the emphasis is the same. We have no desire to impose any false uniformity on the various chapter conclusions. Nevertheless, it is clear to us that there are a number of points of convergence that we can usefully emphasize. This allows us to point to a number of potentially useful research programmes based upon the arguments developed within this volume. But first, we turn to the individual chapters.

Structure of the volume

The volume is divided into three parts. The other three chapters that make up Part I deal with the conceptual, analytical and theoretical issues arising from the study and application of multi-level governance. More specifically, the individual chapters by Cerny, Woodward and Hudson, respectively take up the challenges of theorizing the changing structure of authority within multi-level governance from a historical perspective; theorizing the geography of multi-level governance; theorizing the market within the political economy of multi-level governance. Part II presents a broad cross-section of different examples of multi-level financial governance. The case studies allow for the development of a much richer notion of the multi-level governance of finance and money. These include a look at the reproduction of 'global finance' in everyday life (Langley); the setting of macro-economic policy (Baker); European banking (Grossman); the nature of the IMF's interventions (Thirkell-White); the City of London (Woodward); and the Global Financial Architecture (Soederberg). Part III of the volume contains our conclusions by way of those of the various contributors.

In Chapter 2 Philip Cerny provides the historical context. He describes the evolution of a complex ongoing process, over two centuries in duration, that has characterized the rise of multi-level financial governance. According to Cerny this process involves actors facing sets of constraints and opportunities stemming from resources, rules of the game, institutional structures and informal practices that have been put in place over time by others. The different 'levels' in this process involve different (if overlapping and interconnected) sets of actors and exhibit different structural, or institutional, characteristics, making it crucial to be able to examine at the same time (a) the *endogenous* characteristics of each level (the 'inside'), (b) the *exogenous* environment in which that level exists (the constellation of levels 'outside') and, perhaps most importantly, (c) the various and complex linkages and interactions that *cut across and link* the levels. Cerny identifies three major ramifications for financial system governance associated with what he refers to as the current phase of re-globalization: a transformation in the character of financial systems in general, domestic and transnational, public and private, as public goods; a shift in the nature of nation–state–level economic interventionism towards the 'competition state' and/or the 'regulatory state'; and the locking-in of a complex 'neo-medieval' form of governance of global finance, in effect generating a range of more complex and asymmetric levels. He argues that global finance today is a patchwork of hierarchies, markets and networks, stabilized and governed by institutional *bricolage*, market-led innovation, crisis and response. Moreover, this alters the fundamental logic of accountability of 'modern' liberal democracy – a phenomenon that is overwhelmingly restricted to the nation-state level. On the one hand, certain kinds of traditional non-market values associated with the nation-state are increasingly 'off-limits' to the (national) democratic political process. On the other hand, political actors are searching for ways of reinventing public and social values to make them more effective given the complex constraints and opportunities of multi-level governance.

In the third chapter Richard Woodward expands upon many of the observations made in this introduction with regard to the limitations of the existing multi-level literature, and argues the case for the introduction of a spatial element to the analyses, emphasizing the importance of IPE's continued engagement with geographers. In particular, Woodward argues that the existing multi-level governance literature suffers from an excessive reliance on 'spaces of places' models that allows territoriality to set the parameters in which governance is encountered. These models are ill-suited to global financial markets characterized by complex, overlapping structures of authority, many of which are not reducible to territorial coordinates. A non-territorial spatial element to analysis is vital. Woodward argues that adjustments to the existing literature on multi-level governance are essential but queries whether this can be achieved within the framework of levels, as they are conventionally understood.

In Chapter 4 David Hudson builds upon this analysis, arguing that IPE suffers from myopia over the dynamics of financial markets which represents a severe impediment to the analysis of finance. This short-sightedness can be overcome, he argues, by a heterodox reading of the multi-level governance literature requiring that IPE step beyond its current claims to inter-disciplinarity to embrace insights from geography, sociology and anthropology. This allows us to identify financial marketplaces as the key missing elements in analyses of financial governance. The multi-level framework emphasizes how finance is not simply an inchoate and shapeless global space but a complex network of spaces. It is within these spaces, marketplaces, that, for instance, the price dynamics of financial markets can be better understood. It is a sustained interdisciplinary lens that allows the structuring of market outcomes to be comprehended.

The case studies in Section II seek to apply the multi-level framework, assess its relevance, to put the earlier criticisms into a concrete context and to ask whether these cases suggest ways in which multi-level governance can be improved. This section opens with a chapter by Paul Langley. In this important chapter Langley develops a sustained analysis of the observation made at the outset of this chapter about the linkages between 'global finance' and the level of our everyday lives. In making his argument he seeks to challenge some of the unhelpful dualisms prevalent in IPE. In particular, Langley takes issue with those who identify dichotomies between the 'real' and financial economies and national and global economies. The result, he argues, is that global finance comes to be depicted as existing 'out there', divorced from our daily existence overlooking the complex interlinkages between the local and the global, i.e. the impact global finance has upon our everyday lives and the restructuring of our everyday practices that sustain global finance and allow it to flourish.

In Chapter 6 Andrew Baker examines the case of multilateral surveillance and macroeconomic policy. Baker demonstrates the limitations of explaining macroeconomic outcomes in terms of a traditional two-level game (Putnam, 1988). Contemporary macroeconomic policy, he argues, is dominated by the concept of credibility, which involves public authorities engaging in a continuous, ongoing form of coded communication with an audience of global investors – most notably the foreign exchange market. This is an emerging form of diplomacy which takes us beyond the simple inter-governmentalism many assume to characterize international monetary relations. A more interactive three-dimensional relationship is at work in holding the current macroeconomic and exchange rate regime and its constituent ideas in place. Moreover, a three-dimensional analytical framework can usefully be applied in explanations of contemporary macroeconomic governance. Such a framework demonstrates that authorities are becoming more accountable to non-citizens, their peers and the markets, than they are to electorates in the formulation of their macroeconomic policies.

In Chapter 7, Emiliano Grossman examines the emergence of a distinct European level of banking policy through the lens of multi-level governance. Such a lens brings the interaction between national, regional and global standards in banking regulatory policy into sharp focus. It also helps draw out more clearly some of the overlapping and complementary developments at these various levels, the process by which the work of different authorities produces both consensus and conflict, and the dynamic relationship between the processes of globalization and Europeanization. Grossman's contribution differs from other chapters in two important ways. First, in contrast to the chapters by Hudson and Baker, he suggests that the need to incorporate the market as a distinct level of analysis is less pressing in the case of banking regulation. This is because banking regulation has a long-standing tradition of corporatism, consisting of more explicit ensembles of integrated state–market governance, which in turn are increasingly being reproduced at the European level with obvious threats for national regulatory practice. Second, in contrast to the chapters by Woodward, Soederberg, Thirkell-White and Baker, he argues that, while there is continued diversity in national arrangements, the persistent trend in European banking regulation is for less rather than more multi-level governance, as banking regulation is increasingly being centralized at the European level.

Ben Thirkell-White's focus in Chapter 8 is the role played by the IMF in middle-income countries during the Asian financial crisis. The IMF's appeals to good governance and the use of conditionality are examined in terms of legitimacy and their intrusive nature. However, the IMF's intrusive role cannot be explained within a simple intergovernmental framework. Despite increasing engagement with civil society the outcomes resulting from IMF conditionality reflect transnational financial market preferences and seem to be serving to undermine democratic arrangements in middle-income countries. Importantly, however, these outcomes were the result of multi-level interactions involving a diverse range of actors and authorities. Thirkell-White applies Hooghe and Marks's distinction between type I (formal) and type II (informal) multi-level governance to the IMF's role in Korea and Indonesia. On the basis of these cases he argues that there is a need for more formal type I governance in which the role of the Fund is more tightly defined and specified in work-out programmes, if undemocratic outcomes are to be avoided.

In Chapter 9 Richard Woodward then assesses the applicability of existing frameworks of multi-level governance to the City of London. He suggests that the City has developed an emergent multi-level system of governance in a conventional spaces of places sense. However, the case study of the City of London brings into sharp relief the shortcomings of existing frameworks, not least their ignorance of non-state structures of authority, the problems of identifying levels and the relations within and between them and the inability of such a framework to *explain* the changes in the City of London over the past three decades.

In Chapter 10, the final case study chapter, Susan Soederberg looks at one of the salient contemporary financial governance issues of modern times, namely the form of the global financial architecture. This chapter considers the debates surrounding the review of financial institutional architecture, the difficulties of reform and efforts at institutional innovation. It also illustrates why recent reform efforts have been nothing more then incremental adjustments to the existing architecture. The fundamental intellectual premises (neo-liberal Washington consensus) that underpin the current financial order have been strengthened and reinforced rather than challenged as a consequence of the proposals that emerged in the aftermath of the Asian financial crisis. By looking at two initiatives – the Financial Stability Forum (FSF) and the Reports on Observance of Standards and Codes (ROSCs) – Soerderberg illustrates how neo-liberal discipline is being maintained by an emerging multi-level governance structure.

In the final section of the volume we develop our conclusions. The concluding chapter refers back to the various cases and examines the relationships between market structures and practices, institutional forms, salient ideas and wider societal preferences, discussing what the application of multi-level governance frameworks contributes to our understanding of these matters. In particular, we consider the main issues highlighted in this introduction. Is multi-level governance a suitable analytical lens through which to view contemporary structures of financial governance? Why is there 'more' multi-level governance, and will this trend be sustained? How, if at all, can the notion of multi-level governance be refined to overcome the shortcomings in the existing literature? Are overlapping multi-level governance structures enhancing market power and interests at the expense of public interests, is this contributing to a democratic deficit in the field of money and finance, and what are the implications of this for the exercise of power and authority in the contemporary monetary and financial order? And, finally, can multi-level governance ever be a genuine explanatory theory, or will it remain an analytical framework?

2 Power, markets and accountability

The development of multi-level
governance in international finance

Philip G. Cerny[1]

Introduction

The politics of financial governance in the contemporary world are the product
of a complex process of historical evolution that is still ongoing. In this process,
actors face sets of constraints and opportunities – the distribution of resources,
rules of the game, institutional structures, informal practices and the like – that
have been put in place over time by others. Yet those structural conditions are
never seamless and are more or less open to manipulation and change by both
accident and design (Cerny 1990, 2000a). In this context, the role of the nation-
state in financial governance is both a historical 'given' and profoundly
problematic. This chapter will outline certain aspects of the development of
financial governance over the past couple of centuries – at the ebb and flow
of earlier forms of internationalization, twentieth-century nationalization and
now globalization – as a political phenomenon, as actors seek to use finance and
money in order to pursue power and shape development, and as the constraints
and opportunities provided by financial resources and systems in turn shape
those political changes. Obviously in such a limited space it will be necessary to
schematize these developments. Much could be added, and some parts of the
analysis will be contested. Nevertheless, I hope that the 'big picture' presented
here will stimulate analysis and provoke debate on these profound transformations in the global political economy.

The concept of multi-level governance will be used here to mean not only
how different kinds of political institutions overlap, co-exist and conflict in the
same social space but also how political and economic institutions and processes
– mainly banks and markets for 'securities' (e.g. bonds, shares and other financial
instruments) – interact and shape each others' development. Complex structures
are continually forming and re-forming: from networks of 'international financial centres' (Germain 1997) in 'world cities', to what Lenin and Hilferding
called 'finance capital', i.e. interlocking networks of banks, governments and
industry to promote industrialization; to sub-state, state and supranational (especially regional) regulatory processes; to 'self-regulating markets' (Polanyi 1944)
and transnational 'webs of governance' (Cerny 2002); and ultimately to the
patchy emergence of an 'international financial architecture' with the growing

role of the International Monetary Fund, the World Bank, the World Trade Organization and other international regimes. These changes are all driven by every economic actor's need for money as the unifying infrastructure of all economic assets and processes, whether as a unit of account, a store of value, a medium of exchange or a source of man-made credit for new ventures and growth – the 'infrastructure of the infrastructure' (Cerny 1993b, 2000b).

At the same time, the concept of multi-level governance is not merely a description of the changing playing field of the global political economy but also an analytical framework that identifies key variations and disjunctions as well as similarities and connections amongst the processes at work. Different 'levels' will involve different (if overlapping and interconnected) sets of actors, and will exhibit different structural or institutional characteristics, making it crucial to be able to examine at the same time (a) the *endogenous* characteristics of each level (the 'inside'), (b) the *exogenous* environment in which that level exists (the constellation of levels 'outside') and, perhaps most importantly, (c) the various and complex linkages and interactions that *cut across and link* the levels. Sometimes we are in the presence of different (if linked) institutional levels that can be identified by their more or less formal organizational characteristics; sometimes we are focusing on different (if linked) populations of actors; and sometimes we are looking at cross-cutting processes and quite specific material phenomena that differentiate our particular constellation – in this case, the provision of money and finance – from others within the wider 'political economy'.

With regard to this wider question, the structuration and manipulation of financial governance are crucial components of both political-institutional change and economic change, shaping the development of capitalism and modern society across the globe. Those intertwined processes of change in a more and more cross-cut and interdependent world derive from the need to construct *political* mechanisms to cope with the potential (and often very real) volatility and the uneven distributive consequences of financial market expansion – to control and stabilize financial systems and to ensure that the 'invisible hand' of capitalism operates in the public interest rather than leading to war and social strife. This quest for an institutional framework – not only to tame capitalism but also to *capture its benefits* by making it work more effectively and efficiently – first led to the emergence and consolidation of the modern nation-state and the international states system themselves as medieval and early post-feudal institution-building proved inadequate to the task, but there has always been a massive transnational and international dimension to this process (Kindleberger 1984; Spruyt 1994). In this sense, there has always been a crucial element of multi-level governance in finance, both domestic and international. Today, however, that process is developing a more institutionally intricate, if still somewhat fragmented, structure across borders. Old and new 'regulatory' processes, both within and across borders, are therefore crystallizing in new patterns in a more open and interdependent world, and it is necessary to analyse these developments both in and of themselves and in the context of wider changes in the global political economy.

In the eighteenth and nineteenth centuries, European – mainly competing British and French – capitalism spread around the globe. This process was characterized not only by military imperialism and colonization but also by the development of new international and transnational mechanisms to finance trade, commodity production and industrialization. International and transnational mechanisms developed to finance that expansion, especially the Gold Standard, backed up by the powerful alliance of London's financial markets and the British state (Ingham 1984; Eichengreen 1996). But at the same time, late-developing industrial states and new actors such as national corporate interests, trade unions and political parties of both right and left – remember, this was an age of emerging liberal democracy in the leading capitalist states – sought to consolidate capitalism at a national level, reinforced by the Second Industrial Revolution and the large-scale mass production industries that all 'modern' industrial societies had to possess (Reich 1983). This required massive investments that in most rapidly industrializing countries (except to some degree the United States: Cerny 2000c) required extensive government coordination and intervention.

The competitive drive of elites and masses alike towards rapid, domestically-led industrialization led in the late nineteenth and early twentieth centuries to a breakdown of relatively open international financial governance and a protectionist, nationalist response – including increasing state regulation and support for domestic sources of investment – that lasted through the 1930s and contributed to the causes of both World Wars, reinforced paradoxically by both Stalinism and Nazism on the one hand and the emergence of liberal democratic industrial welfare states on the other (Polanyi 1944; Kindleberger 1973; Strange 1986). By the middle of the twentieth century, what John Gerard Ruggie has called the 'regime of embedded liberalism' blended the freeing of trade with the maintenance of capital controls to insulate the welfare state from 'hot money' – destabilizing speculative cross-border capital flows (Ruggie 1982; Helleiner 1993).

But today the pressures of financial globalization – or 're-globalization', as I will call it below – are increasingly straining the capacity of states and state actors to control the forces that have been unleashed. States are caught in a dense web of diverse and often conflicting pressures, cross-cutting structures, institutional developments, and the strategies and *ad hoc* tactics employed by economic, political and social actors to cope with the problems of growth and change. In this sense, globalization is currently leading to a 'messy' and interpenetrated world political context in which new institutions, practices and projects jostle with old, creating new questions of how to organize political power, accountability and market structures themselves. This is sometimes called a 'neo-medieval' world (e.g. Minc 1993; Cerny 1998b) – i.e. one of overlapping and cross-cutting jurisdictions, competing authorities, economic restructuring, changing social and political coalitions and attempts to develop new institutional strategies (Spruyt 1994). Thus the inherently multi-level nature of finance itself and the problem of controlling and stabilizing it are increasingly being tackled in complex and sometimes contradictory ways by the development of multi-level institutional processes, practices and rapidly evolving strategies ostensibly for putting money at the service of society.

This chapter will look mainly at four aspects of financial governance: national systems; international and transnational regimes; public sector governance structures; and private sector governance structures. Each of these can in some ways be thought of as a 'level' of governance in abstract terms. However, it is the interactions and relationships among these categories that constitute the complex levels that really concern us. How does the dynamic interaction among states, regimes, public and private sectors in a globalizing world lead to the development of new kinds – and new 'levels' – of governance? We will look first at how national financial systems – systems rooted in the growth of the nation-state as the organizing principle of world (and domestic) politics – emerged and consolidated in the eighteenth–twentieth centuries, and how those 'embedded' systems still to a large extent form the core of financial governance today despite the pressures of internationalization and globalization. Then it will examine how those pressures are not only challenging the capacity of national financial systems to control and stabilize global finance, on the one hand, but also triggering major transformations, both strategically devised and *ad hoc*, in the wider (global?) institutions and practices of financial governance today, on the other.

I will argue that, taken together, these changes have three major ramifications for financial system governance: a transformation in the character of financial systems in general, domestic and transnational, public and private, as public goods; a shift in the nature of nation-state-level economic interventionism towards the 'competition state' and/or the 'regulatory state'; and the locking-in of a complex 'neo-medieval' form of governance of global finance, in effect generating a range of more complex and asymmetric levels. Global finance today is a patchwork of hierarchies, markets and networks, stabilized and governed by institutional *bricolage*, market-led innovation, crisis and response; it may be a learning process, but it is also one of trial and error. Furthermore, these changes alter the fundamental logic of accountability of 'modern' liberal democracy – a phenomenon that is overwhelmingly restricted to the nation-state level. Certain kinds of traditional non-market values and policies that in the 'modern' nation-state have been in the domain of national governments are increasingly 'off-limits' to the (national) democratic political process, while political actors are searching for ways of reinventing public and social values to make them more effective given the complex constraints and opportunities of multi-level governance.

The historical background: embedding national financial systems

Multi-level governance and the early modern system

Multi-level financial governance is nothing new in principle. However, until recently history seemed to be a process of centralizing key aspects of financial governance in the nation-state. In contrast, in the Middle Ages, the Renaissance and the Absolutist periods, monarchs and the nobility could raise relatively little in the way of taxes compared to governments today except levies in kind from peasants and some customs duties on trade. They depended on loans from bankers and wealthy people for their wars and other political projects, loans which were often not repaid. Early international or 'translocal' trade (Spruyt 1994) in Europe – and increasingly across the world as the Age of Discovery gave way to European empires (Pomeranz and Topik 1999) – was financed by a combination of state monopolies like the Dutch and British East India Companies, on the one hand, and extensive private international banking networks centred mainly on Amsterdam and London (Germain 1997; Kindleberger 1984), on the other. But while the tentacles of these private networks (which were also often public monopolies too) extended across the globe, they were vulnerable to events both at home and abroad that limited their capacity both to extend credit and to guarantee the value of money.

Paradoxically, it was the centralization of financial governance in the nation-state that enabled an international financial system to develop too. Only in the nineteenth century, after Britain, in particular, had developed a more centralized domestic financial system overseen by the Bank of England (established in 1694), did there develop a genuine international financial and monetary system, a complex structure often identified by an over-simple label – the Gold Standard. That system was itself rooted in convoluted forms of collaboration between the state and the private sector – what Geoffrey Ingham has called the 'City of London/Bank of England/Treasury nexus'. While the British currency, the Pound Sterling, was stabilized and its value guaranteed in gold – a commodity seen for centuries by many as having some sort of intrinsic or natural value beyond artificial currencies – London merchant banks developed a system for extending credit to traders across the world and guaranteeing payment, even (especially!) for so-called 'third party trade', i.e. where there was no British party to the transaction and no commodities passed through Britain or its Empire (Ingham 1984; Germain 1997).

Although Britain was only for a relatively short time the Industrial Revolution's 'workshop of the world', essentially from the late eighteenth to the mid-nineteenth centuries (Hobsbawm 1969), London was the world's financial centre and in some ways has become so again today. It is far and away the most internationalized of the major financial centres – neither New York nor Tokyo, even though these are much more heavily capitalized, comes close in terms of the proportion of international transactions. This all came about not because of the power of the British state – although that played a crucial back-up role – nor because of British financial clout *per se* – the French and others had a lot of monetary resources too – but because of the system itself in which the national and the international, the public and the private, were inextricably intertwined. Trading in money, the reliability of payment at agreed prices across the world, and indeed the *creation* of money through the extension of credit, have always depended upon the predictable value of money and what is called the 'safety and soundness' of the markets and institutions that ensure such outcomes. The openness and liquidity of the financial markets in London, not only the merchant banks and the commodity and stock exchanges but also famously including the development of shipping insurance through Lloyd's of London, made London powerful because it was at the hub of a financial system whose spokes reached right around the world and that was protected and fostered by the British state.

The consolidation of financial governance in the modern nation-state

The first half of the twentieth century, in contrast, was a time of the nationalization and politicization of money. Late industrializing nation-states, in their search for rapid development, increasingly attempted to *internalize* financial governance in order to reduce their dependence on once all-pervading British economic – and political – hegemony. In the first place, the British-led system eventually became overly sclerotic and deflationary. The system, although backed up by an increasingly liberal democratic British state as the political reforms of the nineteenth century were consolidated, depended not on the government so much as on the willingness of market actors to accept certain norms about how financial markets ought to work and how the financial system could oil the wheels of industrialization, capitalist development and the increasing internationalization of production, trade and finance. But, as Karl Polanyi has so notably described, the international financial system with the Gold Standard at its core became increasingly rigid (Polanyi 1944). In particular, governments with chronic balance of payments deficits had actually to ship gold abroad to their creditors, leading to a decrease in the domestic money supply, deflation, austerity, slump and popular unrest, and governments increasingly resorted to other methods in order to avoid such consequences – especially trade protectionism. Indeed, demands for democratization and social reform were inextricably intertwined during key periods with the downside of the Gold Standard and demands for protection – and inflation.

Expanding the money supply, and thus financing growth, also became dependent on the *amount* of gold available in the world. Slumps in the 1890s in the United States and elsewhere were partly attributable to an insufficient money supply – read gold supply – and the issue of gold became the centrepiece of incredibly contentious politics (Degen 1987). The 1896 US presidential election occurred in the shadow of what was then called the 'Great Depression' of 1893, a label that was later to be transposed to the 1930s. Farmers, workers and more marginal sections of the middle class, who tended to vote for the Democratic Party, had over previous decades become more radical as banks and financiers were blamed for the lack of money and credit in the economy and growing debt resulting from deflation. When prices (and wages) are going down, people's existing debts become more and more burdensome, whereas when prices are going up, those debts shrink in proportion to income. Inflation was therefore seen as a cure for, not a cause of, monetary ills.

These groups in the US in particular had been calling for some time for the adoption of a silver standard, like China, because there was simply a lot more silver in the world than gold; gold was deflationary, silver inflationary. Their champion was William Jennings Bryan, a firebrand orator who headed the Populist Party, a radical breakaway, and whose followers took over the 1896 Democratic Convention and nominated Bryan for President. At the same time, however, William McKinley, who became the Republican Party nominee, was a champion of the Gold Standard. The United States was not on the Gold Standard *de jure* but had been operating a *de facto* gold standard since 1879. Bryan's acceptance speech at the convention became one of the most notable oratorical landmarks of American history, foreshadowing the debate between conservative 'trickle down' theories and Keynesian demand management theories of economic policy. Known as the 'Cross of Gold Speech', the key section was:

> Upon which side will the Democratic Party fight; upon the side of the 'idle holders of idle capital' or upon the side of the struggling masses? . . . There are those who believe that if you will only legislate to make the well-to-do prosperous, their prosperity will leak through on those below. The Democratic idea, however, has been that if you legislate to make the masses prosperous, their prosperity will find its way up through every class which rests upon them. . . . You come to us and tell us that the great cities are in favour of the gold standard; we reply that the great cities rest upon our broad and fertile prairies. Burn down your cities and leave our farms, and your cities will spring up again as if by magic; but destroy our farms and the grass will grow in the streets of every city in the country. . . . [W]e will answer their demand for a gold standard by saying to them: You shall not press down upon the brow of labour this crown of thorns, you shall not crucify mankind upon a cross of gold.

In fact, McKinley, elected President with the support of big business and Wall Street as well as other conservative constituencies, was saved from further deflation by the discovery of new sources of gold in the Yukon, Alaska, Colorado and South Africa. The money supply expanded and this set the political stage for the US officially to adopt the Gold Standard in the Currency Act of 1900 (usually known as the Gold Standard Act). The rest of the period up to the First World War was a time of rapidly increasing trade and prosperity in many parts of the world (Degen 1987). Economic internationalization increased as trade and capital flows as a proportion of Gross Domestic Product (GDP) reached heights only regained in the 1980s. An expanding gold supply temporarily stemmed demands for inflation and protection.

Imperialism, mass politics and technological change

However, this period was also a time of the late expansion of empires, the 'Scramble for Africa' and increasing confrontation amongst the European powers. This pattern soon extended to the United States, especially after it too became a colonial power in the wake of the Spanish–American War of 1898, extending American power even to the Far East with the takeover of the Philippines and the declaration by Secretary of State John Hay in 1899–1900 that the United States favoured an 'Open Door' policy giving all the colonial powers the right to intervene in China (Williams 1972). President Theodore Roosevelt, who as Vice President acceded to office on the assassination of McKinley in 1901, had previously been Secretary of the Navy and championed the expansion of American sea power around the world to rival Britain.

Thus three linked factors had already altered the underpinnings of the system by 1914 when the First World War broke out – imperialism, the mushrooming of social and political demands for state intervention in the domestic economy, and technological change. Financial governance was progressively subordinated to the conjunction of these three factors within the expanding, bureaucratizing and increasingly democratic/populist nation-state itself. The first factor was imperial expansion, which instead of spreading liberal, bourgeois international capitalism, as Marx had predicted, instead led to intense zero-sum political, military and economic competition across the world amongst the major empires. Marxism itself changed for good when Lenin in 1917 published his celebrated pamphlet *Imperialism, the Highest Stage of Capitalism*, bringing national empires and imperial nation-states – and the seemingly inevitable conflicts between them – back to the centre of the politics of international economics and finance. But you didn't have to be a Marxist or a Leninist to see such clashes as the core of a new – statist, mercantilist and realist – world politics. Diplomats, bureaucrats, politicians, interest groups and indeed mass publics alike grasped this new reality.

At the same time, the nature of national economies was changing too. Britain and the United States had, for quite different but connected reasons, developed as liberal democracies as well as capitalist societies and states. The liberal British political tradition, traceable back to constitutional monarchy, the English Civil War and even the Magna Carta, was embedded in the culture and practices of the British polity and was transferred in somewhat different form to the American Constitution. But Britain was also a polity that had developed during the First Industrial Revolution, when the newest technology of the time still meant that production could be developed incrementally, in modular fashion, with the addition of new machines and workers as in a textile mill. This did not require huge amounts of capital, which could thus be obtained through local banks, wealthy individuals and retained profits (Hobsbawm 1969).

Rather than trying to conquer her neighbours, as was the geopolitical fate of 'continental' powers, Britain tried to keep a balance of power in Europe while increasingly extending her economic empire not only directly but also increasingly at arms' length, through 'informal' rather than 'formal' imperial control, to embrace new sources of raw materials and markets. The United States, in contrast, developed on a continental imperial scale, with huge internal markets and raw material resources but also with investment finance imported from Britain. Nevertheless, by the time the US started to extend its economic empire outside North America, it followed the informal model and developed it further through the Open Door Policy which called for the European powers to open their China trade to each other – or at least to American trade and finance – rather than setting up exclusive, protectionist 'concessions' in major Chinese cities. The US eventually extended this approach to Latin America and other parts of the world, including the British Empire itself (Williams 1972; Gardner 1976).

At the same time, however, significant technological innovations appeared in the late nineteenth and twentieth centuries that altered the nature of industrial development and international as well as domestic competition. What Alfred Chandler Jr has called the 'modern industrial enterprise' was at that point just emerging from the so-called Second Industrial Revolution. Instead of relatively small, competing firms, as in the textile industry, that could raise and use financial capital easily and locally, the railways (especially in the US with its great distances), steel, weapons manufacture, chemicals, oil and other new heavy industries operated through the exploitation of huge economies of scale in large integrated factories, requiring increasingly large and well trained managerial superstructures ('scientific management') and depending upon larger and larger markets for their mass produced products (Chandler 1992; Reich 1983). Chandler argues that only the United States had a large enough market, enough domestically produced raw materials and enough capital for this process to take place within a liberal, market-led context. In other rapidly industrializing countries, states and state–bank–industry complexes ('finance capital' – Lenin) developed huge industrial cartels along with imperial markets and raw material sources to organize and manage the process. (Britain, however, a First Industrial Revolution power in relative decline, was both liberal and imperial.) It is a matter of historical debate, however, whether the American non-cartellized model was the result of market size *per se* or of anti-trust legislation, which broke up several large monopolies and oligopolies after 1890.

Financial governance and the Second Industrial Revolution

Indeed, the paradigm Second Industrial Revolution firm was American – the Ford Motor Company. Henry Ford's plant at River Rouge outside Detroit, Michigan, became by far the largest factory in the world. It had the first-ever moving assembly line, introduced in 1913, and the most specialized workers, who were given significantly higher wages to ensure their loyalty at a time of growing trade union activity. Production was standardized; as Ford himself said of the Model T, the firm's only mass product from 1908 to 1927: 'You can have any color, as long as it's black.' Indeed, Stalin wanted Soviet factories to be like Ford's. Second Industrial Revolution industries required huge amounts of capital to finance these developments and the extensive sunk costs such fixed capital entailed. Raising and deploying these huge amounts of capital altered the fundamental market logic of both domestic and international finance. In the US, it was possible for competing Second Industrial Revolution firms to raise this sort of capital, as in the automobile industry where General Motors, Chrysler and others competed with Ford. In other countries, it was not, and governments stepped in to help. (Britain, again, was a partial exception, as its head start in industrialization, foreign investment and imperialism meant that it never really experienced a full-blown Second Industrial Revolution.)

There were several ways such capital could be raised, separately or in some combination. In the first place, firms could sell stock to the public or to other firms. Crucial to this development was an organizational innovation called the 'limited liability company', developed during the nineteenth century and first legalized in New York State. This organizational form meant quite simply that stockholders, officially the owners of the company, could only stand to lose as much as the value of their stock was worth. If a company went bankrupt with huge debts, they would therefore not stand to lose their livelihoods, houses, etc., to pay off the creditors. Interestingly, the insurance firms that make up Lloyd's of London have until recently always continued to use unlimited liability, which meant that their members could make unlimited profits but could also lose everything; in the 1990s some changes were made in the wake of various disasters that ruined a number of well-known 'names' (as Lloyd's investors are called).

The limited liability company, once attacked by Adam Smith for potentially taking the entrepreneurial dynamism out of capitalism, proved to be its most important driving force. This is because it can attract whole classes of new, mainly small and medium investors – the new and rapidly growing middle classes of modern capitalism – who would otherwise be deterred by the risks of unlimited liability. The British and American economies have relied on stock markets for far more of their capital-raising activities than have other major economies. In a seminal comparative work, John Zysman characterizes them as 'arms' length financial systems' in which the suppliers of capital are kept out of direct involvement with managing the firm, permitting the kind of separation of ownership from control that is seen as the basis of the modern corporate system (Zysman 1983; Berle and Means 1932).

However, outside Britain and the US, two other methods of raising these large amounts of capital were generally preferred – long-term bank finance, and state investment financed through taxation. In economic terms, this was because the countries in which these firms were located did not have access to broad and liquid stock markets and therefore to mass-based sources of investment; and/or because they were building from scratch, did not have the existing industrial base and retained earnings to draw upon, and moreover faced stultifying cheap import competition, especially from Britain; and/or because their internal consumer and intermediate goods markets were too small for the kind of mass sales that would make such firms profitable by themselves. In political terms, dominant social and political groups in those countries wanted to accelerate and promote development in the national interest while retaining the power to control that process for themselves – while paradoxically at the same time workers wanted to protect their jobs from international competition. An unholy alliance of business, labour and the state – often called 'corporatism', with its mid-twentieth-century variant called 'neocorporatism' – generally supported state and bank-led industrialization behind protectionist barriers. Industrialization came to be seen as a public good. International finance lost its domestic constituency.

The first of these methods involved expanding debt finance rather than market finance, i.e. setting up or supporting large banks that would take a leading role in supplying big loans. In return, the banks usually retained some element of strategic influence or even control over the development of the firms in order to boost the industrialization process. The second involved government subsidization and often direct or indirect control – including setting up of new or nationalized industries in the public sector. Usually there was some combination of the two, with a state–bank–industry nexus (Lenin and Hilferding's 'finance capital') promoting heavy industry – different forms of what Zysman called a 'credit-based financial system' (Zysman 1983). This frequently, but not always, involved some sort of cartellization, i.e. price fixing and/or agreed carving-up of markets amongst different firms. Germany and Japan used different versions of this approach in the late nineteenth century, with France fluctuating between weak versions of both. At the same time, industry and the state were themselves each becoming increasingly bureaucratized as well as more closely intertwined (Weber 1968).

In the twentieth century, this approach was sometimes also linked with different versions of state planning, with Soviet-style Communist systems being the most extreme versions and post-Second World War French 'indicative planning' the most market-friendly. But usually such interventionism was more *ad hoc*, dependent upon the perceived needs of the particular industrial sector and the economic and political climate of the time. Often it was undertaken in response to democratic demands for economic growth, trade union integration, public service provision and the like, coming from the political Left as well as from the political Right with its corporate allies. Indeed, such interventionism became part of a 'Postwar Consensus' in Western Europe and Japan, accepted reluctantly by the United States and celebrated in managerial education and in such books as John Kenneth Galbraith's *The New Industrial State*, which appeared just as the model was entering its long-term decline (Galbraith 1967).

Finance and the changing capitalist state

Therefore state financial interventionism was a key element in the development of a more national form of capitalism in the first half of the twentieth century – in reaction to both economic and technological developments and political pressures and practices on both Right and Left. Neo-Marxists like Joachim Hirsch in the 1970s argued that, because individual capitalists and firms are concerned only with profits, competition and the survival of their own firms, they cannot be relied upon to develop the systemic structures and processes that are necessary to stabilize and expand the system as a whole. In other words, capitalism requires a state – based on 'extra-economic coercion' – to make it work. The state, he wrote, is the 'ideal collective capitalist' – not the mere instrument of capitalists but the crucial institutional structure that makes capitalism itself viable and expanding (Hirsch 1978).

Politically, this sort of intertwining of state and capital has been at the core of a whole range of scholarly debates about the nature of the modern capitalist state, usually seen as starting with Andrew Shonfield's masterpiece *Modern Capitalism* (Shonfield 1965). In the 1970s and 1980s it led to extensive and sophisticated debates both within the Weberian tradition of economic sociology and within Marxism and neo-Marxism. For example, the rather eclectic school of thought called the 'New Institutionalism' (or just 'institutionalism') in Political Science, Sociology, History and Economics and that has been so influential since the 1980s starts from the premise that these different styles of state–industry imbrications have become so 'embedded' in the very institutions, practices, norms and public perceptions of what states do – and what they should do – that globalization (financial or otherwise) is either relatively impotent or is shaped and exploited by states and state actors in fundamentally contrasting ways in different types of nation-state, national society and national economy (Hall and Taylor 1996).

In this literature, of which Zysman's *Governments, Markets and Growth* (1983) is a key early example, the distinction between financial market systems and credit-based financial systems is a crucial, pivotal reflection of the divergence between different forms of capitalism, embedded and locked in at the national level. On the one hand, there is the internationalist, globalizing, liberal, financial market-based Anglo-American (or 'Anglo-Saxon') model that is attempting to expand to the rest of the world. However, it is often asserted, such a development is politically and socially destabilizing, undermining forms of labour organization, political culture and social values that are still vibrant and locked in. Germany, Austria and Scandinavia, on the other hand, are usually seen as the paradigmatic examples of the alternative phenomenon, often called 'organized' or 'concerted' capitalism (Crouch and Streeck 1997; Hall and Soskice 2001). Some writers include a more statist version based either on Japan or on France (or both) (Schmidt 2002). Whether firm-led or state-led, however, concerted capitalism is the product of systematic and mutually reinforcing organizational linkages between the two focusing on and further embedding national-level political and economic structures and processes.

Furthermore, such writers argue, the Anglo-Saxon model may not be all that economically efficient, either. National economies and their state superstructures can be extremely efficient at nurturing a whole range of industries that either retain Second Industrial Revolution characteristics or that benefit from close proximity – 'economies of agglomeration' – and develop network effects (synergies) whereby different firms learn from each other and interact in a positive-sum game under the benevolent hand of the state – and of social democratic values. This is what was meant by British Chancellor of the Exchequer Gordon Brown's reference to 'post-neoclassical endogenous growth theory' in the late 1990s. Thus the role of the state in promoting economic development and growth through financial intervention and support – and in linking that with political values – is still seen as critical in an age of globalization.

On the other hand, a different range of scholars, usually those who give explanatory priority to globalization in their analyses, emphasize convergence rather than divergence – and usually see financial globalization as the key independent variable driving such convergence, up to a point. Less sophisticated versions of this perspective simply suggest the 'end of geography' (O'Brien 1992) or the coming of a 'borderless world' (Ohmae 1990). More sophisticated versions focus on three interconnected developmental trends. The first of these is financial globalization, the core problematic of this book. The second is the argument that industrial structures are changing fundamentally, becoming more fragmented and flexible again, primarily because of technological change. And the third is that liberal values and market norms – what is called 'neoliberalism' in Europe (although that word often has somewhat different connotations in the United States[2]) – are superseding the kinds of national political solidarity that characterized Second Industrial Revolution state interventionism.

Neoliberalism and financial governance

The result of the interaction of these three trends is that neoliberal forms of institutional change are 'overdetermined', or in other words that there are several different kinds of independent variable – economic/financial, institutional/structural and political/cultural – driving globalization towards neoliberal outcomes. These different variables develop along different lines at different speeds, however, so there is still room for a certain amount of divergence *within* convergence (Hülsemeyer 2003; Soederberg, Menz and Cerny, forthcoming). In the rest of this chapter, I will explore these changes and consider their implications for financial globalization and multi-level governance.

Taken together, these changes have three major implications for financial governance. In the first place, the character of financial systems as public goods is changing fundamentally, with knock-on effects on the character of public goods more generally. In the second place, following on from the previous point, the role of the state is both decreasing and increasing as more and more states shift from the kind of interventionism associated with the Postwar Consensus to that of a 'competition state' and/or 'regulatory state'. And finally, in determining the outcomes of political processes – what Harold Lasswell once famously called 'Who gets what, when, and how?' – I will argue that multi-level processes are leading to the locking-in of a complex, asymmetric, 'neo-medieval' form of governance of global finance. As the nation-state becomes increasingly entwined and enmeshed in cross-cutting webs of governance, the international financial system is becoming more and more multi-level and structurally complex, giving different kinds of actors new roles to play and carving out new spaces – in terms of market structures expanding their tentacles within and across national spaces and/or expanding roles for the various structures and processes that make up the 'new international financial architecture' (Armijo 2002).

This form of governance goes beyond a simple multi-level framework to high-light an even deeper complexity. In what is an increasingly uneven process of pluralizing the politics of finance, it empowers a range of actors operating within and through overlapping and intertwined financial 'fiefdoms', thereby not only promoting neoliberalism but also creating spaces for distinctive responses and varieties of neoliberalism to develop. These changes alter the fundamental logic of accountability of 'modern' liberal democracy by placing certain kinds of now traditional non-market values and policies 'off-limits' to the political process, especially at the national level. Nevertheless, the challenge for the future will be to find ways of manipulating and shaping these processes in order to reinvent and reinsert public and social values despite this lack of formal accountability.

The re-globalization of finance and financial governance in the twenty-first century

The United States and the re-globalization of financial governance

Just as the globalization of finance has roots going back to the Renaissance (Kindleberger 1984) and the embedding of national financial systems over-lapped with the Gold Standard, so the processes that are going on today reach back into history too. On the one hand, of course, as Robert Gilpin has pointed out, 'the logic of the market system is to expand geographically and to incorpo-rate more and more aspects of a society within the price mechanism, thus making domestic matters subject to forces external to the society' (Gilpin 2002: 26). On the other hand, the alternative to market logic is the logic of authority or 'the authoritative allocation of values' (and resources), which is at the core of politics (Easton 1953). Although in the modern world the latter has usually been seen as referring to the state, values and resources can be authoritatively allocated at a number of different levels, even within the private sector, as the multi-level governance thesis in this book emphasizes. In this context, financial *re*-globalization, as I am calling the recent process, can be traced back to the 1930s, paradoxically just as the nationalization and politicization of finance – what Polanyi called the 'Great Transformation' – were taking place (Polanyi 1944).

The key to understanding this paradoxical situation in the 1930s is to look at the role of the United States in the international financial system. The interwar period was basically a period, as I have said, of monetary and financial nation-alization. The British role in maintaining the Gold Standard was fatally undermined by the First World War, the transformation of Britain from a cred-itor to a debtor nation (mainly war debts to the US), financial crises in Germany, France and elsewhere and the breakdown of the postwar policy of demanding reparations from Germany for the costs of the war, and the shocks resulting from the Wall Street crash of 1929 (Kindleberger 1973; Simmons 1994). The slightly more flexible post-First World War successor to the Gold

Standard, the Gold Exchange Standard, was left behind after 1931 and currencies were subjected to rounds of competitive devaluation in order to try to maintain national competitiveness.

At the same time, the United States, which had bankrolled the Allies after the first devastating phases of the war, quickly weathered a brief postwar downturn and embarked on the Roaring Twenties, marked by rapid economic expansion fuelled by a popular stock market boom – despite the failure of reparations and the inability or unwillingness of other powers to pay their war debts. The US thus turned inwards (except with regard to Latin America), and after the 1929 Wall Street Crash, when the Depression began to bite in the early thirties, the main reaction was one of protectionism and blaming America's problems on external causes. The Smoot-Hawley tariff of 1930 and the New Deal under President Franklin D. Roosevelt, who succeeded Herbert Hoover in 1933, looked to emulate the late industrializers with their state-led, domesticist approaches, including agricultural subsidies, support for industry, the newly expanding welfare state, even a stab at corporatism in the National Industrial Recovery Act, and proto-Keynesian 'pump priming' and macroeconomic demand management. The money supply, however, was not sufficiently expanded and American financial markets and banks were subjected to a whole new system of regulations which curtailed the kind of independent role they had played since the Civil War and which they would not again play until the 1970s.

Kindleberger (1973) has called this period a 'hegemonic interregnum', a gap between British leadership in stabilizing and running the international monetary system and the emergence with the Second World War of what the Americans saw as their own 'reluctant leadership' – a new hegemonic phase with the United States playing the financial stabilizer. Nevertheless, the seeds were sown in the 1930s for that reluctant leadership or new American hegemony. Two developments in 1934–35 were at the root of this transformation. The first was the Reciprocal Trade Agreements Act. Representing the main victory of the 'internationalist' faction in the Administration of Franklin Delano Roosevelt, the RTAA legalized the authority of the Executive Branch – with powers delegated by Congress – to set up a network of free trade agreements all with a 'Most Favoured Nation Clause', i.e. extending the benefits of any new agreements to existing partners (Gardner 1964). The second was a ban on domestic private gold trading and the statutory linking of the dollar to a gold value that would last until the late 1960s – $35 an ounce. Thus the dollar succeeded sterling as the anchor of a revamped Gold Exchange Standard, setting the stage for the 1944 Bretton Woods Agreement and the dollar standard of the postwar world.

The Administration went down this internationalizing road because of the experience of the first few years of the New Deal, which, despite all the economic and social reforms, did not cure the Depression. Domestic reflation and industrial promotion were not enough. Since the late nineteenth century, American domestic markets, for all their size, were too small to absorb all America's surplus agricultural production (the largest in the world since the 1860s) and industrial production (the largest in the world since the 1880s). The balance shifted to those groups within the Administration who believed that only internationalization – an end to zero-sum, so-called 'beggar-thy-neighbour' policies in international trade and monetary policy – could 'solve' the problems causing the Depression by promoting exports and foreign investment that would boost profits at home. A combination of a larger interventionist role for the state at home plus the promotion of a more open international economy, what John Gerard Ruggie (1982) would later call 'embedded liberalism', had its roots in this transformation of the New Deal.

Postwar reforms of financial governance

Just as with regard to security policy the Second World War convinced American elites and mass publics alike that American national security could never again be guaranteed through isolationism but that American security required a secure international system under American leadership (Yergin 1977), so they were also won over to a belief in the need for internationalizing Open Door capitalism itself to provide expanding markets and new investment opportunities. This did not mean merely promoting economic growth through expanding international trade, although that was perhaps the most salient element of the change. It also meant putting the dollar at the heart of a postwar system that would not only stabilize the value of international money, as the Gold Standard was supposed to have done, but also provide sufficient liquidity to the international economy to promote a virtuous circle of growth and avoid the deflationary effects of the Gold Standard. The complex negotiations and agreements that constituted the Bretton Woods System attempted to reconcile those goals (Gardner 1980).

Of course, those goals were only reconcilable up to a point. As other countries became more prosperous there was plenty of liquidity around, especially in the form of dollars exported through American overseas defence expenditure (from the Korean War Boom, to the expansion of US multinational corporations, to inflationary spending on the Vietnam War) and through the chronic US balance of payments deficit after 1958 (Block 1977; Odell 1982). Those dollars were increasingly recycled through the budding Eurodollar market in London and came to be seen by Europeans as swelling the world money supply – the US 'exporting inflation' to other countries through an overly strong dollar protected by the maintenance of its gold value at $35 an ounce. For a decade from the late fifties to the late sixties, successive US Administrations rejected the possibility of devaluing the dollar, which they felt would destabilize the system, while European governments increasingly called for this to be done. The 'dollar glut' or 'dollar overhang' eventually led the Nixon Administration to withdraw the dollar from the Bretton Woods exchange rate system in 1971 – 'closing the gold window' (Gowa 1983).

Managing the global financial system after 1971: crisis and adjustment

The result was to prove revolutionary for the international financial system. Although the dollar has remained the 'top currency' (Strange 1986; Cohen

2004a), exchange rates amongst the major financial powers had by 1973 shifted from a semi-fixed or managed system – the 'adjustable peg' – as represented by Bretton Woods to a floating exchange rate system. Despite interventions and attempts to set up 'target zones' by various governments (especially the French in the early 1980s) and the fixing of their currencies to the dollar by various developing countries, the major players became the various firms and traders in the currency markets themselves. Whereas in the 1950s only a small fraction of international capital movements was private sector flows, by the mid-1990s only a small fraction was public sector flows.

Attempts to fix the value of currencies by governments have increasingly led to crises that have damaged and transformed whole economies, from the forced withdrawal of sterling from the European Exchange Rate Mechanism (the precursor of the euro) in September 1992, to the Mexican crisis of 1994, the Asian and Russian crises of 1997–98 and the Argentinian crisis of 2001–2, among others. Even the role of the dollar is increasingly questioned today, both inside and outside the United States (Cohen 2004a). While most American administrations over the past twenty years have pursued a 'strong dollar' policy, the current financial bear market and quasi-recession since 2000 have led the Bush Administration to 'talk the dollar down' on the international exchanges.

The main beneficiary has been the new euro, which weakened against the dollar when it was first introduced but has recently risen above its first issue level. Indeed, the euro corporate bond market is now larger than the US equivalent and the European bond market as a whole has in just three years grown from about a third of the size of the American bond market to being almost as large. Although financial predictions are notoriously unsafe, it would seem that international investors, the mainstay of American financial strength since the 1980s – enabling the United States to maintain a huge balance of trade and payments deficit while keeping the dollar strong (something that economic theory says is abnormal and bound to deteriorate, as has been happening in late 2003 and early 2004) – may for the moment at least be shunning the US in favour of a newly-strong euro. Of course, a stock and bond market upturn in the US, which to some extent has been happening since 2002 (although some analysts think the bear market is still with us), might attract those investors back.

One of the reasons those investors might be attracted back is the character of the American financial system itself. A key aspect of this is the openness of the American system generally. The evolution of that system since the 1960s – despite the austere regulatory and general financial environment of the thirties, forties and fifties, when US securities markets were generally stagnant – has significantly reinforced and expanded its 'financial market system' character. Domestic reforms of the 1960s, 1970s and 1980s focused on what was inaccurately called 'deregulation', although this really involved the adoption of more pro-market, pro-competitive regulations, rather than simply a 'bonfire of controls' (Moran 1991; Cerny 1991). But these domestic reforms, in an international environment of mushrooming capital flows and increasing financial interpenetration – reinforced by the political programmes and huge electoral victories of Margaret Thatcher in the United Kingdom and Ronald Reagan in the United States – has led financial market actors across the world to see the American financial market model as the wave of the future.

Regulatory convergence and institutional change: 'trading up'?

This has for the most part remained the case across the world even in the current slump. *Pro*-market regulations – seen as structural reforms – rather than old-style interventionism are increasingly thought to be the only way to create systems where hyperinflation and financial crises can be controlled and economies stabilized. Despite attempts to moderate and tinker with financial marketization by key member states of the European Union, for example, the European Commission has increasingly taken the stance that completion of the single market for capital flows and financial services requires significant moves towards American- and British-style market regulations, corporate governance norms, state withdrawal from industrial subsidies, a more open takeover code, greater disclosure and transparency practices and investor protection. In Southeast Asia, in Korea, in Argentina, in Mexico, and increasingly in other areas of the world by-passed or disadvantaged by financial globalization, neoliberal domestic financial regulatory reform is steadily if unevenly gaining ground. Even in Japan, hit by economic stagnation for more than a decade and more recently by deflation, the financial system is gradually being streamlined, banks shaken out and restructured, corporate governance reformed along American lines, unprofitable companies occasionally (increasingly?) being allowed to go bankrupt, and financial markets being re-regulated according to pro-market prescriptions (Cerny 2004).

In the meantime, a second aspect of this change is a move not towards increasingly unsupervised markets, what some economists call 'competition in laxity', but if anything an increasingly complex pro-market re-regulation of the American system. To the extent that the American model is actually a model, its lessons are somewhat different from the ones usually associated with financial globalization, liberalization and deregulation. The US is strengthening and expanding its statutory regulations, becoming increasingly what Michael Moran, writing mainly about Britain, calls a 'regulatory state' (Moran 2002).

Some years ago, University of California political scientist David Vogel, writing about environmental regulation, made a distinction between the 'Delaware Effect' and the 'California Effect' (Vogel 1995). The US state of Delaware, in a number of issue areas including finance, has developed a track record for creating a highly permissive regulatory environment, seeking to attract firms and economic activities to the state through deregulation and competition in laxity. California, by way of contrast, has developed a highly complex and weighty superstructure of environmental and other regulations. Vogel argues that firms and economic actors do not simply seek permissive environments but also want to ensure not only stability but also high standards of market behaviour amongst their counterparties as well as a strong legal system to provide sanctions for opportunistic or fraudulent behaviour. Thus it is not the presence or absence of regulations *per se* that counts, but what kind of regulations they are. These actors, like international traders in the nineteenth century looking to the City of London for financial services, want a stable, predictable but expansionary pro-market system for price discovery, contracts, bargaining and the like.

These developments reflect a wider set of behavioural trends in both domestic and international capitalism, a kind of dialectic between pushing the edge of the institutional envelope by innovators and entrepreneurs in expanding sectors, on the one hand, and the desire of such actors at a later stage to lock in their first-mover gains through government support and regulation, on the other. Debra Spar has written a particularly cogently argued and thorough book applying this framework to waves of technological development, *Pirates, Prophets and Pioneers: Business and Politics Along the Technological Frontier*. In chronicling the development of information and communications technology from early global exploration, to telegraphy, to Microsoft and cyberspace, she demonstrates how new innovations at first undermine existing regulatory and other interventionist systems as 'pirates, prophets and pioneers' jostle to take advantage. But once they have succeeded and their industries have become more mature, they actively lobby governments for regulations to stabilize conditions. In Spar's analysis, however, it is always the governments of states that provide those regulatory conditions (Spar 2001).

Institutional innovation and multi-level governance

In today's multi-level governance, in contrast, especially with regard to financial markets, such a dialectic is more far-reaching, cutting across borders and leading to institutional innovations that are international, transnational, translocal and global. It is not merely the governments of states that provide the increasingly critical public good of pro-market, 'California Effect' regulation. Of course, states are still at the core of such a multi-level regulatory system. But cities and city-regions are also crucial, as Saskia Sassen argues (Sassen 2003). And probably the most salient level involves international regimes. The World Bank and the International Monetary Fund, interestingly enough, shifted in the 1990s from simply promoting the liberalization of capital controls and domestic economies to giving priority to getting effective financial regulatory systems up and running before opening up vulnerable domestic economies to global capital flows (for a controversial take on this, see Stiglitz 2002). This is what is often called the move from the 'Washington Consensus' of the late 1980s (Williamson 1990b) to a 'Post-Washington Consensus' today. Finally, the core of the attraction of the World Trade Organization today is not simple pressure to reduce trade barriers and open up domestic economies to international competition but rather the dispute settlement mechanism, which increasingly provides a quasi-legal forum for negotiating reciprocal forms of liberalization – and using sanctions to enforce them.

As mentioned earlier, these changes also mirror changes in the United States itself. Despite attempts by the current Bush Administration to loosen regulations on industry and finance, a series of critical events has put the ball back in the court of the re-regulators. Indeed, pressures for increasingly stringent pro-market re-regulation have been at the forefront of American political and economic debates for the past decade. In one of the best books on this subject, Arthur Levitt, Chairman of the Securities and Exchange Commission from 1992 to 2001, has chronicled his efforts to improve transparency, corporate governance and investor protection in the complex world of Washington lobbies, bureaucracies and Congressional politics (Levitt 2002).

The legacy of those efforts looked as if it would be eroded when President George W. Bush appointed an accountancy industry lawyer, Harvey Pitt, to succeed Levitt in 2001. But, as so often happens, Pitt became locked into pursuing certain not too dissimilar structural changes himself, especially when the huge fraud and accounting scandals involving major firms like Enron, WorldCom, Arthur Andersen, etc., broke in 2001. Pitt was forced by the Sarbanes-Oxley Act of 2002 to set up another statutory body under the aegis of the SEC, the Public Accounting Oversight Board, to supervise the previously self-regulating accountants. Furthermore, the ongoing campaign by New York State Attorney General Elliot Spitzer to penalize the biggest financial services firms for falsely touting stocks in return for non-auditing services has further highlighted the way the bull market of the 1980s and 1990s created huge opportunities for market abuse. Pitt was forced to resign because of his various stumbles and was replaced in 2003 by William Donaldson, who is seeking to streamline the overly complex regulatory system and reassert the SEC's authority.

The reaction, therefore, is not deregulation as such, but more and more pro-market re-regulation. These trends are not confined to national financial services markets either, nor are they confined to statutory regulation. Self-regulation and mixed, public–private forms of regulation are being reshaped too. One of the most important developments at the time of writing involves ongoing negotiations between the US private sector-based Financial Accounting Standards Board (FASB) and the mainly British-based International Accounting Standards Board (IASB) to come up with harmonized, convergent norms and indeed organizational templates, not just for accounting standards *per se* but for corporate governance more widely. There are two sorts of issues here. The first is the nature of regulation itself. While American-style regulation involves the writing of complex rules that cover as many eventualities as possible, British accounting standards are called 'principle-based' standards and do not depend on detailed rules. Two competing cultures exist, with British sceptics believing that the American approach merely creates more and more loopholes for opportunists to exploit while American sceptics believe that principles-based accounting standards would be difficult to apply to complex and detailed cases. Nevertheless, the negotiations are proceeding and look likely eventually to succeed.

Securitization and multi-level governance

Indeed, I have argued elsewhere that the most important developments in financial governance are taking place in private and mixed public–private venues, as the concept of markets themselves merges into wider institutional analytical frameworks (Cerny 2000b and 2002) – a key contention of all of the authors represented in this book. A central element in this process is 'disintermediation', which Levitt describes as 'cut[ting] out the middlemen' (Levitt 2002: 189). Bank-led and state-led credit-based systems are based on the principle that decisions on how to allocate capital are not made by the investors themselves but by bankers and bureaucrats. Those who deposit money in a bank and/or who pay their taxes do not themselves determine to what end use their money is put – intermediaries do. But the impact of increasing international capital flows, floating exchange rates and the mushrooming of currency markets, the heady expansion of securities markets since the 1980s, the marketization of financial services themselves, and the development of a range of financial innovations, especially derivatives markets, asset-backed securities markets, commercial paper, etc., are all pushing in this direction. In other words, the expansion of financial markets themselves, even within the banking sector (and the state!) has led to a process which I have called (in line with some financial market analysts) 'securitization' (Cerny 2000b).

'Securitization' in this broad sense means that the allocation of capital increasingly follows financial market techniques for the trading of securities, i.e. that the investor is supposed to make the basic decision as to where to invest while the 'broker' merely follows instructions. In other words, the investor is the 'principal' and the broker merely his or her 'agent'. Of course, it doesn't quite work this way in practice except for large investors; small investors usually do not have the time or expertise to instruct brokers on details, although they may outline broad parameters. And most smaller investors invest through mutual funds where the composition of the portfolio is determined by the managers, although there is choice between a range of different types of funds. Nevertheless, active investors can manage their portfolios if they develop a basic expertise; indeed, about half of Levitt's book consists of crucial basic tips on how to do this (Levitt 2002).

Securitization is usually guided by a particular set of theoretical principles, which have become dominant in financial markets, based on the concept of 'portfolio diversification'. In other words, investors, unlike banks and states, should protect themselves against catastrophic losses by holding a number of different and contrasting kinds of securities, balancing different kinds of risks and potential returns. They must 'hedge' as well as 'speculate'. This is the financial market version of limited liability, although it does not involve direct statutory protection but rather active management. Efficient portfolio diversification is, however, important not only to individual investors but to how financial market systems themselves work. Like limited liability, it attracts much wider and more diverse classes of investors into the system. In other words, it creates the possibility – in an expanding market, at least – of bringing more investment funds into the system itself.

Banks in many countries, and state bureaucracies all over the world, are limited by their deposit and tax bases respectively. When asked why he robbed banks, the mid-twentieth-century American bank robber Willie Sutton – the last of a dying breed? – said: 'Because that's where the money is.' But in a world of relatively disintermediated and securitized financial markets with the possibility of reallocating capital anywhere in the world, financial markets – not traditional banks and especially not states – are where the money is. Banks can of course combine different kinds of financial services – depending on the national regulatory environment they exist in – and become significant market players. Indeed, as banks adjust to a securitized world, their role is no longer that of traditional intermediaries but of market players in their own right, adapting to and reinforcing the securitization process. But states, in contrast, quickly bump up against the limits of their tax bases and, especially (but not exclusively!) in poorer and developing countries, have all too often resorted to printing money as a way of creating new investment – leading to hyperinflation and the repeated bailing out of underinvested failing industries. Such an outcome penalizes the poor more than the rich, as low wages are sticky and welfare systems underfunded in such circumstances. Lower-middle-class households are relatively the worst penalized, as they lose the value of any investments they have and become rapidly downwardly mobile.

Multi-level governance and neoliberal politics

In this context, then, political actors of all kinds are increasingly accepting neoliberal financial restructuring, the marketization of financial systems and adjustment to the demands of global capital as crucial public goods. Although reactions are always filtered through different domestic political and social systems, especially where those systems are well embedded and accepted by mass publics as well as elites, the 'safety and soundness' of financial systems have become the bottom line of contemporary politics in the developing world as well as in the developed world. While the politics of neoliberalism involve the acceptance of financial market liberalization, regulatory convergence, privatization and the like, political demands for social protection, equity and welfare are still strong and growing stronger as the result of a range of critiques of globalization. Democratic accountability, although still almost exclusively organized through national jurisdictions, requires political actors to play both sides of the street – to accept the 'disciplines' or constraints of financial globalization while increasingly seeking ways to re-inject the social into an otherwise predominantly neoliberal world. This means operating on a number of different playing fields at the same time, attempting to manipulate the specific patterns of opportunities and constraints on each while reconciling the outcomes with both financial globalization and domestic demands – not an easy task.

For example, when Luis Ignacio Lula da Silva was elected President of Brazil in 2002, many market actors – and some political actors in the developed world, most notoriously the then US Secretary of the Treasury Paul

O'Neill – feared that his socialist principles would lead him to reassert the kind of state-and-bank-led model that had characterized Brazil under regimes of both Left and Right for decades, from Getulio Vargas in the 1930s to the military regime of the 1970s and their successors until the 1990s. The domesticist development model they had copied from late industrializers such as Germany and Japan put domestic finance at the core of both the import substitution and the later export promotion models of industrialization. Only with the election of the former Marxist, turned neo-liberal, Fernando Henrique Cardoso to the Presidency in 1994 were a marketized financial system and the institutional conditions thought to be required for it (budget surpluses, price stability, an independent central bank, openness to foreign portfolio as well as direct investment, etc.) effectively adopted.

Da Silva, however, confounding some market expectations, has continued and even reinforced those policies, while stressing the need to complement them with targeted campaigns against poverty and hunger. Indeed, Da Silva has taken those campaigns to the alternative World Social Forum in Porto Alegre as well as to the establishment World Economic Forum in Davos. Neoliberal approaches to financial governance, he believes, need to be counterbalanced by international-level social measures. The recently elected President of Argentina, Néstor Kirchner, a former statist/populist on the left of the Peronist Justice Party, has declared his solidarity with Da Silva in seeking ways to combine multi-level, neoliberal forms of financial governance – recognizing that 'that's where the money is' in today's world – with more systematic and globally coordinated forms of compensation for the losers from globalization. Whether such a balancing act can succeed in the medium or long run is still unclear. Financial crises still loom, and responses, whether in terms of national politics, international regimes, public sector governance processes or private sector 'self-regulatory' processes (not to mention the overlap and interaction among these categories), are still at the trial-and-error stage.

Conclusions

Multi-level financial governance is often a more complex, circular and interpenetrated process than the label would at first suggest. It involves the globalization of financial markets and the crystallization of a range of formal and informal transnational and transgovernmental institutions, networks and private regimes. These webs of governance are at the heart of both political and economic change today. Although no one set of institutions or processes possesses anything like holistic, sovereign 'authority', they all engage in 'the authoritative allocation of values' and resources and enmesh national governments in webs of financial and political power. It involves nation-states, epistemic communities and non-governmental organizations, transnational and transgovernmental policy networks, multinational firms, international and transnational markets, and more traditional intergovernmental regimes like the World Bank, the International Monetary Fund and the World Trade Organization. The last of these, for example, increasingly shares elements of pooled sovereign authority with its member states – both donors and recipients of funding – as well as drawing in and co-opting private sector actors, both firms and NGOs.

It certainly still involves states. Although states have been shedding some of their mid-twentieth-century interventionist functions, the demands of the 'competition state' and the 'regulatory state' are raising the profile of pro-market, neoliberal regulatory standards and testing whether the 'California Effect' will be more important in shaping future political responses and economic decisions than the previously dominant image of the 'Delaware Effect'. Furthermore, although there has not been space to go into them here, it involves both subnational and international regional bodies, from development agencies to the European Union, which must adapt to the imperatives of raising funds through market mechanisms rather than being over-dependent on taxation or bank debt. It also involves many new groups of actors and interests, whether small investors, multinational corporations or small businesses, etc., seeking to cash in in the way their predecessors cashed in on limited liability companies, but always subject to the vagaries of markets. Different states still diverge among their approaches to financial governance, but that divergence is everywhere bound up in a process of coping with and adapting to the pressures of globalization (Lütz 2002).

The national state in developed capitalist countries has had and continues to have a privileged strategic position, stemming from its long institutionalization and embeddedness, as lead regulator of financial institutions and markets. However, this position does not stem from the essence or property of 'sovereignty' or 'autonomy' as such, i.e. from some sort of elemental indepen-dence from other actors, institutions and processes. Rather, it stems from the very *inter*dependence of those actors and institutions themselves. It results from the state's 'crossroads' position in a complex *network* of actors, institutions and processes – nodes of power and authority – from the local to the global (Cerny 1990: 85–110). This also has always been true to some extent. But the dense, cross-cutting linkages characteristic of markets and other transnational structures and processes today is transforming that crossroads position itself. The state is increasingly stuck at the crossroads, faced with a much larger and more complex road network to deal with. It must share and coordinate more and more of its regulatory power with those other nodes. The state becomes less a sovereign, more an enforcer of rules that must dovetail with the wider trends of financial globalization and the proliferation of transnational interests – not so much a strategic controller as a traffic cop.

Of course, this process also involves losers from globalization, who still must be compensated through some sort of political process if stability – and even, if one dare say it, democracy – is to be maintained and extended. Finally, multi-level financial governance requires political creativity to knit the levels together. The upside of multi-level financial governance is flexibility. Indeed, the flexibi-lization of governance in general is the main consequence of globalization, financial or otherwise. The downside includes a lack of coordination amongst levels and actors; the alienation of people and groups who do not identify cultur-ally or individually with aspects of this more complex world; the potential undermining of established institutions which have developed a certain *acquis* and effectiveness over time and which operate poorly in more complex condi-tions; and the marginalization of certain countries and groups of people who systematically lose out. Sub-Saharan Africa stands out as the main region seem-ingly unable to cope with the imperatives of neoliberal globalization at all these levels, primarily because it is ensnared in both a 'commodity trap'[3] of concen-trating on producing commodities whose prices on world markets continue to decline, and a socio-political trap of state failure and endemic social conflict caught in a vicious circle.

Nevertheless, social, political and economic actors are increasingly learning to live with globalization and trying to develop strategies and tactics for shaping it in the future. There may be opportunities for creative political action that the old nation-states, with their Second Industrial Revolution corporate and state bureau-cracies, would have stifled in the so-called 'Golden Age' of the mid-twentieth century. Indeed, finance for investment can be obtained from a wider range of sources and in a greater range of types potentially suited to different uses. While there may be no 'ideal collective capitalist' in such a world, multi-level governance provides a greater range of points of access to complex political as well as economic processes, new possibilities for expanding the 'public good' of financial stability and liquidity across the world – despite the frequently painful financial crises that mark this transition – and new opportunities to capture the benefits of globalization for a wider range of constituencies. In this context, the multi-level governance of global finance does not merely produce constraints in terms of complexity, 'messiness' and a lack of broad accountability, but may also generate significant new potential opportunities in terms of flexibility and growth.

Notes

1 I would particularly like to thank Andrew Baker, Paul Cammack and Susanne Lütz for their helpful and detailed comments on an earlier draft of this chapter.
2 There are two differences to specify. On the one hand, the word 'liberal' as a political label in the United States means something similar to 'moderate social democratic', whereas in Europe it means support for free market capitalism – what in the US is called 'classical liberalism' or 'nineteenth-century liberalism'. Therefore, whereas 'neoliberalism' is often used in US politics and journalism to mean a kind of moderate social liberalism adjusted for globalization, in Europe in contrast (and in European – and indeed some North American – political economy terminology) neoliberalism means economic Thatcherism or Reagonomics – i.e. 'conservatism' in US terms. On the other hand, in International Relations theory, Robert O. Keohane has used the term neoliberal in an institutionalist sense to mean the development of international regimes and the development of more durable forms of international cooperation based on absolute gains and transaction cost savings (Keohane 1984) – as distinct from the dominance of zero-sum relative gains in the 'neorealism' of such writers as Kenneth Waltz (Waltz 1979). In this chapter, 'neoliberal' and 'neoliber-alism' are used in the European sense of free market or classical liberalism.
3 See online at www.unctad.org (accessed 1 July 2004).

3   Money and the spatial challenge

Multi-level governance and the 'territorial trap'

Richard Woodward

The progressive intensification of globalizing tendencies in recent years has exacerbated the difficulties of managing global financial affairs. This has spawned a vast and perpetually expanding literature on the causes and consequences of financial globalization and the possibilities of governance (see Introduction, this volume). Traditional approaches to IPE have assumed the provision and maintenance of the basic infrastructure pertaining to the governance of financial activity to be the responsibility of the state and state-based international organizations. However, the popular view of globalization, informed by what Held *et al.* (1999: 3–5) refer to as the 'hyperglobalization thesis', suggests we now inhabit a 'borderless world' (Ohmae 1990) where social, economic and political processes are organized on a global scale and in which the power and authority of states are diffused to regional, global, market and private actors. Under these circumstances the state's propensity to define and deliver the requisite functions of financial and monetary governance are curtailed or eliminated (Ohmae 1995; Strange 1996a; Greider 1997; Friedman 2000). This extreme version of globalization is now widely regarded, at least in academic circles, as epistemologically and empirically suspect. From a methodological standpoint the claims of the hyperglobalizers rest upon false dichotomies of the social realm, in particular between the state and 'the global' (Amoore *et al.* 1997; Brenner 1998, 1999; Clark 1999). That is to say the state and the global are conceived as fundamentally opposed forms of social and political organization, leading to the misguided conclusion that the consolidation of globalizing tendencies must necessarily have a negative impact upon the state's capacity to govern those tendencies. Equally, at the empirical level, reports of the demise of the nation-state have been greatly exaggerated (see Herz 1957, 1976). Indeed under conditions of contemporary globalization the nation-state has flourished with over 100 new sovereign states coming into existence over the past 40 years.

For these reasons recent globalization literature inveighs against notions of state obsolescence, suggesting the divide between the state and the global is illusory, and demonstrating the state's continued importance to global financial governance. In the first place, whilst not denying that there have been powerful changes in the state's external environment, the hyperglobalizers ignore the extent to which the state has been a critical agency responsible for unleashing and entrenching globalization, particularly in the financial realm, as part of a sustained political venture (Helleiner 1994; Strange 1986, 1998; Palan and Abbott 1996; Pierre 2000b; Peck 2001). Second, the hyperglobalizer's stance is contingent upon static and absolute conceptualizations of statehood and sovereignty, distracting attention from the more complex transformations in the role of the state under conditions of contemporary globalization (Evans 1997; Rosenau 1997; Brenner 1999; Haslam 1999; Held *et al.* 1999; Jayasuriya 1999, 2001; Slaughter 2000; E.S. Cohen 2001; Peck 2001). Instead, critics argue for the adoption of a more historically sensitive disposition, recognizing statehood and sovereignty not as immutable objects but as dynamic categories whose attributes 'continuously evolve' (Cerny 1999a: 1; E.S. Cohen 2001) alongside the globalizing tendencies they contest and nurture. States constantly refurbish the object and mechanisms of governance, discarding some functions while replenishing and accumulating others. Rather than a simple process of state retreat, there is an ongoing process of state transformation.

Despite the persistence of the state, some commentators have suggested that an exclusive focus on its role has led to a misleading oversimplification of the contemporary structures of financial governance. This research points to a profusion of regulatory mechanisms whose power and authority is not necessarily dependent upon the legitimacy conferred by the public sphere. These 'spheres of authority' (Rosenau 1997) supplement and, on occasion, supplant the roles previously executed by the state, generating a kaleidoscopic mosaic of governance mechanisms for the emergent global financial system (Rosenau 1997, 2004; Scholte 1997, 2002a; Woods 2001). These observations imply that the state is neither a necessary nor a sufficient condition for governing globalization, signposting the possibility of 'governance without government' (Rosenau and Czempiel 1992). The exposure of the complexity associated with global financial governance led to demands for new analytical frameworks capable of reflecting and interpreting this labyrinth of authority structures. Multi-level governance offered a plausible response to this call for theoretical innovation. In International Relations (IR) and International Political Economy (IPE), the multi-level governance[1] approach remains in its infancy (see, for example, Yarborough and Yarborough 1994; Hirst and Thompson 1999). This chapter's central contention is that these emergent theories, though superficially attractive, suffer from a number of methodological, theoretical and practical flaws deriving from an excessive reliance upon state-centred understandings of political geography inherited from the disciplinary orthodoxies of IR and IPE. Conceptions of multi-level governance in IR and IPE are dominated by what Cohen (1998) calls 'spaces of places' models, which are infatuated by the role of the state. These models assume govern*ance* to be synonymous with govern*ment*, delineating political space and authority according to the territorial coordinates established by the state. Thus state territoriality sets the spatial parameters within which governance is encountered and exercised. This conceptualization, it is argued, has some utility in that it points to the possibility of governance taking place on a variety of territorial scales or 'levels'. The problem is that it fails to capture the intricacies associated with the structures of authority in the contemporary global economy, many of which are not amenable to the spatial assumptions of state-centred epistemologies. Therefore spaces of places models alone are not a sound basis for the development of a generalizable framework of multi-level governance. Spaces of places models need to be complemented by an analysis of non-state spheres of authority understood as 'spaces of flows' (Cohen 1998). The spaces of flows perspective recognizes that some spheres of authority are deterritorialized, meaning that they derive their power and authority from, and exercise their power and authority over, functional or social as opposed to territorial spaces. The strength of this approach is its appreciation of sites and structures of governance that cut across, exist within and cascade through territorial levels. The problem is that the spaces of flows blueprint ignores or marginalizes structures of power and authority grounded in territorial space, so, like the spaces of places model, it represents an incomplete narrative on contemporary financial governance. Cohen's (1998: 23) solution to this dilemma is to introduce a fresh concept, 'the authoritative domain', that recognizes, reconciles and synthesizes territorial and non-territorial elements of power and authority into a single overarching governance condominium. This alerts us to the fact that governance is a multi-level phenomenon in that it originates and is encountered at spatial scales of varying extent. Nevertheless, the presence of non-territorial structures of authority means that these levels should not define our understanding of governance. While authoritative domains provide some useful insights into the nature of contemporary arrangement for the governance of money and finance, a number of residual problems remain. In particular, the question of whether the concept of a 'level', indelibly connected with notions of hierarchy and territory, is sufficiently nuanced to understand and interpret non-territorial structures of authority, urgently needs to be addressed. It is the contention of this chapter that there are analytical limitations associated with the idea of a level that should be explicitly acknowledged when the multi-level governance framework is invoked and, moreover, that these limitations may necessitate levels to be radically rethought or even abandoned completely.

Spaces of places: governance by government

Despite its claims to interdisciplinarity it remains the case that a lot of work in IPE continues to be heavily influenced, some would say inhibited, by the assumptions of mainstream IR scholarship (see Introduction, this volume). Embedded into orthodox theories of IR and IPE is a political geography that divides the globe up into hermetically sealed packages of land, each governed by a sovereign whose authority is absolute, exclusive and indivisible. Political space is based on notions of place, and notions of place are dominated to an overwhelming extent by the territoriality of the state. There is no political space other than the state and no political space between states. The state has 'captured' (Taylor 1994, 1995) political space, prompting Walker (1995: 29) to

observe that 'because states are, other forms of politics cannot be'. This conflation of political authority with the state had important implications for
conceptualizations of governance in IR and IPE. In short, states and relations
between states were considered necessary and sufficient conditions for governance. At the heart of this model was the belief that govern*ance* was dispensed
solely by govern*ments* or institutions sanctioned or constructed by government.
Indeed the term 'governance' was absent from the realist vocabulary. As
Rosenau (2000: 168, 170) explains, mainstream accounts proceed on the basis
that the authority of the state 'is so predominant that inquiry must begin and
end with assessment of how that authority is exercised', with a consequence that
'the vast majority of IR scholars have had no need to develop or use the concept
of governance in the analysis of world affairs'. Governance as it is now understood was an enduring feature of the international environment, but it was
deemed to be undertaken by the institutional apparatus of the state, i.e. government, and was not considered a distinct and separate phenomenon warranting
its own label.

This 'spaces of places' discourse has pervaded the development of multi-level
governance in IPE.[2] These models with their emphasis on hierarchically-ordered
territorial containers are a development of, rather than a replacement for, the
established mindset. Hirst and Thompson's (1999) framework of multi-level
governance exemplifies the approach. They outline a generally applicable model
of multi-level governance based upon territorial scales of varying extensity (see
Table 3.1). Sites and structures of governance are understood entirely by the
territorial scale at which they exist and operate. On this basis they argue that
governance operates at five levels in the global economy. At the apex of the
structure are the agreements between the G3 nations to coordinate, manage and
stabilize macroeconomic policies. Beneath this are the international regulatory
agencies. In the case of global finance this incorporates the major components of
the international financial architecture; the international financial institutions
(International Monetary Fund, World Bank and increasingly the World Trade
Organization under the rubric of the General Agreement on Trade in Services)
and the international networks of experts and standard-setting bodies such as the
International Organization of Securities Commissions (IOSCO) and the
International Association of Insurance Supervisors (IAIS). The third level
consists of regional instruments of governance such as the initiatives launched by
the European Union and the Asia-Pacific Economic Cooperation forum (APEC).
States constitute the fourth level of governance. The final level refers to governance undertaken by sub-state actors or those whose impact is at a sub-state
level. The five levels are interdependent. Inadequate governance in one level can
be offset by effective governance structures in other levels. Similarly, ineffective
governance in one level can undermine effective governance in other levels.
Global governance requires capable structures to be in place at all five levels.

The derivation of the spaces of places model of multi-level governance from
traditional state-centred theories brings with it the advantages and disadvantages
associated with such approaches. The benefits are that it offers a clear, straight-

Table 3.1 Governance by governments

Group of 3 (European Union, North America, Japan)
International Regulatory Authorities (WTO, IMF, World Bank etc.)
Regional-level Governance (EU, APEX etc.)
National-level Governance
Subnational-level Governance

Source: Adapted from Hirst and Thompson (1999).

forward and parsimonious conceptualization of multi-level governance. It imposes a modicum of order on an increasingly complex world and interprets multi-level governance in a manner consistent with the liberal internationalist order with which we are familiar. Furthermore, it serves to highlight that globalization is not causing the creation of a single global space but a reconfiguration and rearticulation of territoriality resulting in differentiated territorial spaces (Brenner 1998). Finally, it emphasizes the continuing importance of the state in regulating and providing the legal and social infrastructure required for the operation of financial markets. However, these benefits are outweighed by a number of theoretical and practical drawbacks.

First, this theory relies excessively upon territorial notions of space and its most visible manifestation, the state. This is demonstrated in part by the labels (inter*national*, sub*national*) ascribed to the levels in the model (see Taylor 1996). While state centrism is eroded by the observation that sites and structures of authority are identifiable at levels above and below the state, it is re-imposed by the belief that governance is only possible via the application of public sources of authority that depend ultimately upon the state. This illustrates Taylor's (2000: 1105) misgivings about the current predilection for emphasizing territorial re-scaling which 'can be a means for preserving a statist agenda with its conventional geographic mosaic of territories'. States have proved a remarkably resilient and successful means of organizing political space. Nonetheless, theories predicated exclusively on state-centred accounts of spatiality are snared by what Agnew (1994, 1998) terms the 'territorial trap'. The territorial trap refers to three geographical assumptions that underpin state-centred social science theory: first, that states are considered to exercise absolute and exclusive power over a specific territory; second, that the domestic and the foreign realms are distinct entities subject to different rules and modes of behaviour; finally, that 'the boundaries of the state define the boundaries of society such that the latter is contained by the former' (Agnew 1998: 49). Agnew is insinuating that social science has

> . . . privileged some spatial forms, particularly, but not only, the sovereign territoriality of statehood, over all others. Rendering these forms as fixed over time, without any possibility of historical reconstitution, essentially

eliminated temporal change along with spatial variation other than between homogeneous blocks of territorial space . . .

(Agnew 1996: 1929).

The spatiality of the state is so dominant and socially ingrained that states are frequently elevated to the status of naturalized units of political space defying historical change. The problems stemming from this approach with regard to multi-level governance are threefold; i) states are incorrectly assumed to be a fixed and eternal form of political organization; ii) all entities in the same level are assumed to be alike; and iii) it precludes spheres of authority predicated on alternative spatialities. The first two problems will be dealt with in this section, the final one in the next section on spaces of flows.

The reification of the state raises significant questions about the suitability of the spaces of places template as a basis for theories of multi-level governance. In the 1970s and 1980s research into international governance in IR and IPE underwent some analytical progression (Kratochwil and Ruggie 1986; Rosenau 2000). Work upon transnationalism (Keohane and Nye 1972; Strange 1976), interdependence (Keohane and Nye 1977) and regimes (Krasner 1983) injected greater nuance into understanding of international governance. Nevertheless, the state continued to be the prime unit through which international governance was appraised. The reluctance of IR and IPE seriously to interrogate their epistemological and ontological foundations produced widespread dissatisfaction among critical geographers and political scientists (see, for example, Rosow 1994; Taylor 1996; Guzzini 1998; Cerny 1999b; Youngs 1999). Critical scholars disputed the contention that the state should always be centre-stage in understanding and explaining social phenomena. Territorial arrangements are primarily 'geographical expression(s) of social power' (Cohen 1998: 14; c.f. Kratchowil 1986; Ruggie 1993c; Anderson 1996; Hudson 1998; Agnew 1999; Cutler 1999a). Consequently states and the states system are contingent upon an historically specific constellation of power and authority. A redistribution of social power could severely weaken the link between statehood, sovereignty and territoriality, gradually making way for alternative conceptualizations of political space, and challenging the presupposition that states are inviolable features of our physical and imagined landscape (Carr 1981; Agnew 1994, 1996; Bull 1977; Kobrin 1998; Brenner 1999; Hirst 2001). For some, the present round of globalization is providing exactly this kind of reconfiguration of power and authority, problematizing the notion of the state as the naturalized container in which economic, social and political activities take place (Brenner 1998). States are not necessary and sufficient constituents of the global system, suggesting they are not necessary and sufficient conditions for governance across differing historical contexts. The ramifications for spaces of places conceptions of multi-level governance are significant. These models assume that the prevailing mode of territorial organization will persist, concealing both the fluidity and historical contingency of territorial arrangements. The levels in these models are presented as immutable, absolute and pre-ordained. By doing so, the spaces of places edifice runs the risk of generating an inflexible model that re-imposes the structural determinism of existing methodologies.

The second set of problems arises from the neat characterization of levels. There is an unwritten assumption that because the actors in the levels are demarcated by similar territorial spaces, they must exhibit a high degree of homogeneity. They are viewed as having identical institutional architectures, responding to stimuli in the same way, to be unaffected by their position in the global order and dispensing governance functions through the same means. States are often taken to be identical monolithic entities. However, comparative analyses of states' institutional apparatus have revealed substantial differences consequent upon their social and historical specificity (Weiss 1998; Gray 1999). The present era of globalization has not resulted in states converging on a model of capitalist accumulation but has 'encouraged a spectrum of adjustment strategies' (Held *et al.* 1999: 9; see also Palan and Abbott 1996) involving a plethora of governance mechanisms as states attempt to navigate and manage change. The state level might be territorially identifiable but this should not lead to the conclusion that all actors in the level are integrated in the system in the same way. Moreover, there is a tendency to superimpose the assumptions about the homogeneity of states and their interactions with other levels. The problem with this, as Anderson (1996: 139–40) observes, is 'political processes and institutions at different scales are likely to be qualitatively (not just quantitatively) different in their character and interrelationships (or lack of them)'. Other levels will also be heterogeneous and the nature of the relations between those actors is likely to diverge from the nature of relations among states. The orderly construction of levels proffered by Table 3.1 conceals considerable diversity, conflict and inconsistency.

The neat construction of levels also masks other more practical problems. Initially no consideration is given as to how these other neatly delineated levels might be identified in practice. There are no steadfast rules about the conditions which need to be present to determine whether a coherent 'level' can be said to exist. The international level covers a multitude of differentiated relationships. For instance, Hirst and Thompson's model differentiates between the G3, the international level and the regional level. It might be argued that G3 and regional agreements are by their very nature international and should therefore constitute part of the international level rather than a distinct level of their own. These problems are magnified further when consideration is given to the global level. As Cerny (1999b: 154) comments, 'just where the global "level" lies, how it is structured, or how tight its constraints are' remain unclear. Next, territorial scales are not as explicit or as exclusive as such a model describes. The spaces of places model depicts sharp distinctions between levels assembled in a hierarchy. Sites and structures of authority are limited to one territorial scale, precluding the possibility that the same agents may appear in more than one level. This seems absurd when the model is set out in such a way that lower levels constitute the basic building blocks of upper levels. Increasingly territorial scales are regarded as imbricated and intertwined. There may be incongruence between the spatial scale at which a structure of authority 'exists' and the scale at which its authority is operationalized and impacts. Moreover, agents occasionally perform different governance functions at different levels (see Woodward, Chapter 9 of this volume). Finally, there are also problems with the fixed hierarchical ordering of territorial scales. Where, for example, would a city with an important financial centre fit into such a model? Normal spatial referents would place the city in the sub-state level of governance. The burgeoning literature on world cities questions this assertion. It is accepted that cities are linked to their territorial pachyderms in key ways, but the virtual geography of a city's transactions and linkages are to some extent incompatible with the physical geography of its location (Beaverstock *et al.* 2000). This is not to deny that cities are grounded in a specific territorial context but to challenge conventional hierarchical orderings of territory. In short, these developments do not suggest 'that the emerging character of political identities is best thought of in terms of territorial levels or scales organized in a settled hierarchy' (Agnew 2000: 94). The arrangement of territorial scales is more complex than this model suggests and we have not yet begun to consider structures of authority from beyond the public domain.

Spaces of flows

If territorial coordinates could solely define political space, then multi-level governance by government would provide an eminently sensible framework for conceptualizing contemporary governance. However, as Kobrin (2002: 60) rightly observes, 'while all forms of political organization occupy geographic space . . . that does not mean that they are *territorial* systems of rule' (emphasis in original). The contradictions and ambiguities which the governance by government approach conveniently suppresses are being exposed by the decaying territorial model and exacerbated by globalizing tendencies.

Globalization is distinct from the international focus preceding it because it is an 'ation' not a 'nation'. Inter*national* relations and related levels of analysis (sub*national*, trans*national*, supra*national*) are imbued with the assumption that states are the sole means through which political space is conceived and political authority exercised and understood. In contrast globalization, as the 'ation' suffix attests, does not assume the prior existence of nation-states, pointing to the possibility that political space can be structured in alternative ways and that political authority is not the sole preserve of the state (Woodward 2003 and Introduction, this volume). This is the basis for the development of spaces of flows models of governance. They emphasize deterritorialized sites and structures of authority founded upon functional, or 'sovereignty free' (Rosenau 1990), notions of space defined by 'networks of transactions or relationships' (Cohen 1998: 21). Their spatiality is incompatible with customary Westphalian coordinates as they operate above, beneath, within and across the spaces defined by territory.

Detaching political authority from its state-centred moorings led many scholars to pursue surrogate sources of authority with renewed vigour. The role played by private and non-state sources of authority was resurrected as a pertinent avenue of inquiry (see Cutler 1995; Cutler *et al.* 1999a; Higgott *et al.* 2000, Ronit and Schneider 2001; Hall and Biersteker 2002).[3] Private sources of authority are not original, but their importance was overshadowed by mainstream research's excessive focus on public authority structures (Murphy 2000; Cutler 1999a; Cutler *et al.* 1999b). Arguably the breadth and depth of non-state governance structures, particularly in economic and financial matters, is greater than ever before. A number of actors have been identified and studied as agencies of private governance, including credit rating agencies (Sinclair 1994a, 1999, 2000a; King and Sinclair 2001) and the various codes of conduct drawn up by business and professional associations (Cutler 1999b; Bennett 2000; Haufler 1999, 2000; Ronit and Schneider 1999).

The structures of governance envisaged by spaces of flows models are more fragile, ephemeral and amorphous than those formulated by the spaces of places thesis. This perspective makes the case that governance is administered by a complex cast of ceaselessly changing performers. Spaces of flows theories have the advantage of more accurately reflecting the disaggregated nature of authority in the modern global system. They promote the idea that economic activities are receptive to governance by actors from outside the public sphere. Their intervention signifies that the exclusivity accorded to territory in the spaces of places model is misguided. Fitting governance into a territorial straitjacket omits structures of authority located in a non-territorial context. Indeed the more radical versions of the spaces of flows thesis turn the governance by government thesis on its head, rejecting the notion that government has a role to play in financial and monetary governance.

The problem with the deterritorialized approach is that it understates the continued significance of territorial modes of governance. These theories are derived from the same genus as the hyperglobalist species of globalization. It is assumed that the territorial spaces of places model has already been or is in the process of being entirely displaced by deterritorialized spaces of flows with the concomitant extinction of the state. There is a general sentiment that state-oriented notions of politics 'appear to account for less and less of contemporary patterns of power and authority in an era of globalization' (Pierre 2000b: 5). However, most commentators continue to assert a role, albeit diminished to varying degrees, for the state. Many point to the fact that territorially-based authority provides the 'scaffolding' (Brenner 1999) of governance, which supports the continued expansion of global activity. The legal and institutional prerequisites upon which economic accumulation depend are still the preserve of the state. International agreements designed to harmonize and formalize norms of behaviour across national boundaries have encouraged cross-border economic activity by reducing the risks associated with it. The point is that networks, even though they may appear to operate in an ethereal realm, are constructed not only of flows but also of *nodes*. Cities have been described as spaces of places in a space of flows (Taylor 2000: 1113). In other words, although globalization does not automatically assume the state to be a permanent element of authority in the global system, that does not mean that states and relations among states can be disregarded. Globalization and accompanying notions of globality are signifying that the state is just one of many threads of authority which, woven together, constitute the fabric of global relations.

Authoritative domains and the levels problematic

The realization that many forms of authority in the financial arena are better conceptualized as non-territorial spaces of flows raises a dilemma: namely, can these authority structures be reconciled with established frameworks of multi-level governance predicated on territoriality? The simplest and most popular solution to this puzzle is to deny that it exists. This chapter has detailed two methods of achieving this. One is to adopt the position of the hyperglobalizers and argue that we already inhabit a post-modern global economy where globalization has dissolved the state and public sources of authority rendering territorial levels of authority irrelevant to the analysis. The second is to maintain that rigid dichotomy between the state, public and territorial forms of authority on the one hand and the market, private and non-territorial forms of authority on the other and to treat them as two separate if related spheres of activity. For example Rosenau (1990: 247, emphasis added) identifies the co-existence of two broad groups of actors – 'sovereignty free' and 'sovereignty bound' – 'the result is a paradigm that neither circumvents nor negates the state-centric model but posits sovereignty-bound and sovereignty-free actors as inhabitants of *separate worlds that interact in such a way as to make their co-existence possible*'. Similarly John Gerard Ruggie (1993c: 172) sees 'a decentred yet integrated space-of-flows, operating in real time, which exists alongside the spaces-of-places that we call national economies'. The adoption of such a stance, as Gamble (2000: 110) observes, is problematic because 'one of the difficulties in discussing economic governance is the assumption that the economy belongs to the private sphere and governance to the public, and that economic governance is therefore concerned with the relationship between the economy and the state, how the state *governs* the economy' (emphasis in original). By assuming that governance is the exclusive preserve of public authority they deny the possibility that the market or the private sphere can act authoritatively. In this way they can justify the continued focus on how public forms of authority derived from territory govern markets and the private sphere, and preserve the appeal of existing territorial understandings of levels.

A more fruitful way of proceeding is to build on Underhill's (2000a: 818, 821) exhortation to dispense with the depiction of the relationship between political authority and markets as one of 'interdependent antagonism' and to recognize instead that they are part of the 'same integrated ensemble of governance, a state–market *condominium*' (emphasis in original). Cohen's (1998: 23) notion of 'authoritative domain' is one example of such an approach. This concept is a hybrid combining 'transactions and territoriality – the functional dimension as well as the physical – in a single amalgam of use and authority'. It contains the idea that financial governance is shared by authority structures with territorial and non-territorial elements and that the importance of these components varies across differing spatial and temporal contexts. Some authority structures are firmly tethered to a specific territorial arena, whereas others have slipped territorial anchors and operate in spaces defined largely by social convention. Moreover, these structures of authority are not coterminous with conventional understandings of territorial space. The boundaries suggested by the spaces of places model are constantly in flux, being blurred by governance structures operating across and within them. This suggests new authority structures being superimposed on conventional territorial approaches.

The implications for multi-level governance are significant. Authoritative domains do not deny the fact that governance takes place on the territorial scales referred to by the spaces of places model. However, we are reminded that territoriality is overlain and occasionally overrun by functional, sectional or socially oriented spatial forms. Territory, and particularly the territoriality of the state, are *partially constitutive but not definitive* of the spatial frameworks of analysis (Taylor 1996: 1926). Sites and structures of authority are not placeless, but authority cannot be discerned solely by reference to territory. The state and forms of authority based on the state, are not entirely by-passed, but the extent of their authority is qualified in important ways.

Social and financial relations that do not reflect conventional geographical contexts have always punctured the watertight territorial containers implied by places of spaces models. Peck (2001: 450) echoes the widely held opinion that 'the old notion of national states as "containers", linked unproblematically with territorially bounded chunks of space and an associated set of territorially bound social processes, is both theoretically and politically defunct'. Similarly, Gamble (2000: 113) argues 'markets, hierarchies and networks are not containable within tight, territorially defined, political jurisdictions'. The state and territoriality are not impervious containers but act more like unique colanders immersed in the icy waters of the 'global'. They place some limits on the extent and exercise of governance but also allow currents of authority to pervade and percolate through them. Under these circumstances it is not a case of entirely abandoning spaces of places and levels but of recognizing their limitations. Anderson (1996: 151) develops a metaphor of an adventure playground to describe the overlapping and multi-level nature of contemporary governance with its 'mixture of constructions, multiple levels, and encouragement of movement – up, down, sideways, diagonally, directly from high to low, or low to high – [that] captures the contemporary mixture of forms and process much better than the ladder metaphor'.

Conclusion

In IPE the development of coherent models of multi-level governance is still in its infancy. This chapter has argued that models of multi-level governance offer a constructive and original route to understanding governance of the global economy but that existing models are defective. Most seriously the irrepressible focus upon state-centred, public and territorially defined sources of authority conceals or distorts the role played by private, hybrid and non-territorial mechanisms of governance. Cohen's idea of authoritative domains draws our attention to the existence and importance of the role played by non-territorial structures and their interaction with conventional territorially-based sources of authority. Private governance will, on occasion, conform to the territorial spaces of the state. However, these structures of authority are not *always* amenable to interpretation through the hierarchically ordered territorial levels and spaces reflected in spaces of places model. When plotting patterns of multi-level governance, states and territorial coordinates remain central points of reference. What authoritative domains point to is that territory should be one of many coordinates; it should not define our map. Authoritative domains are messy and poorly defined, but this is arguably justified given the fragmented and disjointed world they are attempting to elucidate and comprehend.

Conceptions of multi-level governance pursued through the idea of authoritative domains provide a reasonable way of classifying contemporary governance. However, there are a number of questions which need to be addressed by future research. First, authoritative domains remain vague and undertheorized. More work is needed to assess how territorial and non-territorial authority interacts to produce authoritative domains and how these domains can be identified. Second, research is required to investigate how the various levels intersect and overlap and how (if at all) they interrelate or could be made to interrelate to form an integrated model of global governance. Indeed, conditions of rapid change raise the question of whether a generalizable model of multi-level governance is possible or desirable. Finally, the mosaic of governance implied by authoritative domains suggests that the difficulties of identifying and clarifying coherent notions of levels should be addressed. As Hirst and Thompson (1999: 193; c.f. Benz 2000) readily concede, 'appropriate concepts of economic governance, capable of recognizing the five interdependent levels of activity from world markets to regions, have hardly begun to develop'. The problems of identifying coherent levels has led one commentator to speculate as to whether

> . . . the very idea of political systems having 'levels' may need to be discarded since it produces thought dominated . . . by formal institutions operating along vertical or horizontal axes . . . it may be more relevant to think in terms of 'concentric' models of territorialized governance which overlap and are connected to other models . . .

> (Smith 1997: 727).

The etymological linkages of levels of analysis with realist IR and IPE theories mean that multi-*level* governance may well connote hierarchy and rigid levels. Smith appears to be hinting at the possibility of marginalizing political 'levels' in favour of less tangible conceptions of political space. This could mean a shift towards notions of multi-*layered* governance, which simply indicates the idea that governance is administered simultaneously by innumerable structures of authority working in concert.[4] The danger is that theories of multi-level governance end up becoming so nuanced and methodologically demanding that they end up simply being descriptions of how the world – rather than a theoretical model of the world – can be explained and understood. The challenge for IPE scholars is to refine theories of multi-level governance that overcome the rigidity, inflexibility and historic specificity of the spaces of places model, and to attempt to generate models capable of explaining and understanding the complex patterns of governance that characterize the modern global economy.

Notes

1   Multi-level governance has elsewhere been referred to as multi-layered governance (Held *et al.* 1999: 62–77) and multi-tiered governance (Martin and Pearce 1999). These terms are normally used interchangeably but the conclusion of this paper will suggest that multi-level and multi-layered governance have subtly different connotations.

2   This also pertains to the arena in which the concept of multi-level governance has been most widely debated and developed, the European Union (EU). The EU is often invoked as the exemplar of multi-level governance and has been the basis for much theorizing in recent years (Scharpf 1997, 2001; Smith 1997; Martin and Pearce 1999; Benz 2000; Brugue, Goma and Subirats 2000; Ekengren and Jacobsson 2000; Sutcliffe 2000; Reigner 2001). The problem is that research has tended to focus on relations between nation-states (the inter*governmental* approach – which conceptualizes the EU as a single level of intergovernmental relations arguably denying the EU's claim to be a multi-level polity) or on relations between different levels of govern*ment* (subsidiarity). The study of multi-level governance in the EU has been hijacked by state-centred methodologies, with multi-level govern*ance* habitually conflated with multi-level govern*ment* (Jordan 2001). Krasner (2001) also questions whether the study of governance in the EU yields suitable evidence. He argues that the EU is a case-specific ensemble of authority structures rather than the basis for a generalizable model of multi-level governance. Similar deficiencies to those encountered in work on multi-level governance in the EU can also be identified in research into multi-level governance in federal states, which again focus on links between different levels of govern*ment* (see, for example, Stilwell and Troy 2000; Painter 2001).

3   Indeed it could be argued that references to 'non-state actors' serve to emphasize the privileged status of the state in IR and IPE.

4   It is noticeable that many scholars are increasingly referring to the multi-layered as opposed to multi-level nature of economic and financial globalization and governance (see, for example, Scholte 2002a: 13; Johnston 2001: 687).

4 Locating and understanding the marketplace in financial governance

IPE, interdisciplinarity and multi-level governance

David Hudson

Introduction

While it is now a commonplace for the International Political Economy (IPE) literature to make the observation that it is not a case of states versus markets, the full implications of this insight have not always been developed. In this chapter I explore how the notion of multi-level governance might help us realize the full potential of a political economy of financial governance, rather than just the politics of financial governance.[1] I do so from a position that sees both state and market as an integrated ensemble of governance (Underhill 2000b). Unhappy with the structural and economistic understandings of the market, which are often to be found in IPE, I travel elsewhere, specifically to the economic sociology, human geography and social anthropology literatures. While far less parsimonious, they offer a far fuller understanding of what markets are, and as such offer a stepping-off point for more creative thinking about financial governance – from an integrated state–market perspective.

The chapter proceeds in three parts before outlining conclusions. The first part, 'Governance', asks in what sense can we speak of financial governance? Is this structure of governance multi-level, and what might we mean by this? It approaches these questions by drawing attention to the popularity of global governance for International Relations (IR) and IPE before moving onto the concept of multi-level governance. I suggest that the notion of multi-level governance helps sensitize the IPE and global governance literature to the variety of levels of governance; this is against the implicit notions of global space devoid of topography or shape. In contrast to the narrowly political frameworks of multi-level governance that currently abound, it is necessary to move towards incorporating the economic too. Moreover, it is argued that it is essential to explicitly incorporate the market as a 'level' of financial governance. The second part, 'Different notions of financial governance', identifies how the existing IPE literature has explored the concept of financial governance to date.[2] It identifies two possible notions of financial governance but argues that both are limited by their tendency to think of governance as an object of analysis rather than a mode or framework of enquiry. Financial markets and marketplaces are focused upon as the key missing elements in the theorization of financial governance. This is because the dynamics generated by market outcomes both govern our market societies and have to be governed through regulation. In order to develop an understanding of how these financial dynamics are generated, the lenses of economic sociology, human geography and social anthropology are used to develop an anatomy of financial markets. The spatiality of the market and the causal mechanisms behind market dynamics are analysed so as to show that, although outcomes may be global, they are the result of the social practices of market trading which are highly localized in origin. This suggests that marketplaces are discrete spaces in the structure of governance. Finally, the third part, 'Towards an anatomy of "global" finance', outlines a corresponding research methodology for investigating marketplaces. It also concludes by outlining some key questions and issues opened up by this alternative framework, making a number of suggestions as to how this should fit into a financial governance research programme.

Governance

As a concept, governance – in common with so many others – is something of a product of its time.[3] As Gerry Stoker notes, its roots are 'various', from institutional economics to Foucauldian analyses, from international relations to public administration (Stoker 1998: 18). Nevertheless, despite their different histories these various roots and routes of governance share the understanding that 'the world of governing is changing' (Stoker 1998: 26). Hence, in our era of apparently perpetual flux it has emerged as an alternative way of theorizing contemporary authority structures, and how they are undergoing transformation (Rosenau 1992: 1–3).

As most who have explored the concept agree governance can, and indeed does, have a variety of possible meanings (Rhodes 1996: 652; Stoker 1998: 17). Nevertheless, one thing is made clear, and that is, 'Current use does not treat governance as a synonym for government' (Rhodes 1996: 652). Thus, as Rhodes (1996: 652–3) stipulates, 'governance signifies a change in the meaning of government, referring to a new process of governing; or changed condition of ordered rule; or the new method by which society is governed'. More specifically Jan Kooiman (1993: 258) outlines how governance 'can be seen as the pattern or structure that emerges in a socio-political system as "common" result or outcome of the interacting intervention efforts of all involved actors. This pattern cannot be reduced to one actor or group of actors in particular.'

While providing a useful definition of governance to be carrying on with, these brief discussions also highlight a couple of issues that are important to the way that governance has, and indeed has not, been analysed hitherto. First, as Rhodes argued governance signifies a new process or method of governing. There are a variety of ways that this novelty is manifest. However, from a political economy perspective one of the most significant is how governance blurs the boundaries between the public and private sectors (Stoker 1998: 17). Or, in terms more familiar to IPE, governance blurs the boundaries between state and market. This is the first issue to bear in mind. The second is that it should be clear that, in all of these definitions, the implicit manner of talking about governance is as an *object of analysis*, as a description or statement about how the world is. Yet there is often some conceptual slippage here because governance often becomes a *mode of analysis* or theoretical framework. For instance, Stoker (1998: 18) notes that the 'value of the governance perspective rests in its capacity to provide a framework for understanding changing processes of governing'. While I do not disagree with Stoker's point, I think that it is both important and useful to keep the distinction between these two clear. This is because these two different conceptual uses of governance – as an object of analysis and as a framework for analysis – serve to define and to delimit one another. The more specific argument here is that governance as a framework for analysis has served to construct governance as an object of analysis. This is a consequence of disciplinary discourses and is considered in more detail below.

Global governance

Perhaps unsurprisingly, within IR/IPE it has become increasingly popular to couple the concept of governance to the word global (Rosenau and Czempiel 1992; Commission on Global Governance 1995; O'Brien *et al.* 2000; Scholte 2000: ch. 6). There is a variety of interwoven reasons why governance is a particularly useful concept for those concerned with political analysis of world order.[4] Intellectually speaking it is arguable that the end of the Cold War and the 'globalization of world politics' have undermined the disciplinary trajectory of IR more than any other of the social sciences (Cerny 1996; Baylis and Smith 1997; Clark 1999; Youngs 1999). That is, until surprisingly recently, the mainstream of IR has been comfortable with the knowledge that the international relations of 'high' politics have provided a clear and justifiable research programme. These events, or at least the shifting mindsets of scholars engaged in this field, have meant the need to reassess (see, for example, Walker 1993; Kofman and Youngs 1996; Hay and Marsh 2000b).

Global governance, properly conceived, should operate in a situation without an overarching or external structure of centralized authority, viz. government (Rosenau 1992: 7–8; O'Brien *et al.*: 2). Although governance can, and in virtually all cases should of course, still include nation-state governments as a key element within these shifting structures of authority (Rosenau 1992: 4; Underhill 2000b). Nevertheless, there should be no ultimate authority; in short, 'governance without government'. This of course is familiar – *ad nauseam* – to students of IR/IPE as 'anarchy': the absence of overarching authority (see Ashley 1988; Walker 1993). However, as Alexander Wendt (1992) argued in his seminal article, anarchy is indeed what states make of it. The basis of his argument is that anarchy is an institution itself rather than the absolute absence of institutional structures. A global web of linkages and flows of economic, political and cultural artefacts is thus seen to ameliorate the political 'emptiness' – as traditionally conceived – of this space

(Rosenau, 1992: 4, 7–8). Key here, then, is the observation that authority is ceasing to lie solely within the purview of government.[5] Now the structures of authority in the current world order are arguably much broader, encompassing actors, institutions and structures beyond states and intergovernmental organizations. This is, of course, hardly novel to the globalization thesis, but was also one of the main thrusts of 'complex interdependence' (see Keohane and Nye 1977; Ohmae 1990, 1995; Hirst and Thompson 1999; Held *et al.* 1999; Scholte 2000): that new issues and new actors were both spawned and empowered through the advent of new communications technologies and economic integration.[6] Nevertheless, it is clear that all the talk of globalization has served to embed these arguments yet deeper into IR/IPE than before. Indeed, the majority of ongoing research in contemporary IR/IPE is all about explaining these structures and how they might govern the behaviour of states, firms, pressure groups and such like as they operate in and across national territories. As a movement to straddle this either/or of government/anarchy, it becomes obvious why global governance has developed as such a key and increasingly popular concept within the remit of IR.

But why, we might ask, multi-level governance? The need for such a prefix, by way of distinguishing it as a particular approach to the study of governance, appears superfluous. This is because governance surely implies that it is an approach that takes structures of authority to be disaggregated or multi-level anyway? Governance clearly marks the analytical shift away from treating authority structures as embodied within a single institution to one that sees a variety of actors linked through networks. However, the problem with much of the literature on global governance, along with IR/IPE more generally, is that it settles with an understanding of world politics which (over)emphasizes the global level of institutionalization. Too often, in accounting for global governance, the appropriate layer of institutional analysis is deemed to be the supra- or inter-governmental bodies such as the United Nations (UN), the World Trade Organization (WTO), the Bank of International Settlements (BIS), or the International Monetary Fund (IMF).

Global governance is often posited as a way of going beyond the state, or incorporating the state into a broader framework. As such it is often portrayed as inhabiting some conceptually superior ground. However, there is a real danger that increased emphasis upon macro-level dynamics may obfuscate the socially grounded processes which ultimately produce politics. That is, political outcomes, although they manifest themselves as global, are produced and indeed experienced at a variety of locales, or levels. More simply, institutions are not just global or statist. Instead there is an infinite number of levels which rely upon grounded social relations to produce them. So it may be that the rubric 'multi-level' could act as a useful metaphorical device in guiding analysis. I argue that the analytical space which the concepts of multi-level governance and global governance open up are of considerable utility, especially if thought through together. Thus it should be emphasized that the notion of global governance is as much to do with smaller spatial scales as it is with the global. As Youngs (1999: 97) argues, thinking globally 'does not mean, of course, that global space can come to be considered as some kind of homogenous, undifferentiated mass; quite the reverse'. Similarly Taylor *et al.* (1995) outline how '[g]lobal change does not in any sense make other geographical scales disappear, quite the reverse in fact: the rise of "globalization" coincides with a simultaneous affirmation of "localization" as places both of control (e.g. world cities) and of resistance (e.g. new nationalisms).' So while, as Sassen argues, 'the major dynamics at work in the global economy carry the capacity to undo the particular form of the inter-section of sovereignty and territoriality embedded in the modern state', it does not render either of them unimportant, and nor does it render them in opposi-tion to one another. Rather, there can be said to be 'new geographies of power' (Sassen 1996: 5). So might the literature on multi-level governance help us to understand these new, layered geographies of power?

Multi-level governance

Peters and Pierre (2001a) have suggested that a 'baseline definition' of multi-level governance is:

> . . . it refers to negotiated, non-hierarchical exchanges between institutions at the transnational, national, regional and local levels . . . Taken one step further, the definition could be slightly expanded to denote relationships between governance processes at these different levels. Thus, multi-level governance refers not just to negotiated relationships between institutions at different levels but to a vertical 'layering' of governance processes at the different levels.
>
> (Peters and Pierre 2001a: 131–2)

However, the tempered promise of multi-level governance as a more flexible concept – and a useful one for IPE – is reflected in Peters and Pierre's closing sentence of the article, as well as the multi-level governance literature more generally. Here they state that the levels to be explored in multi-level governance are the formal institutions of authority at the state, regional and local levels. Thus, we might even want to suggest that multi-level governance seems some-thing of a misnomer. Instead of multi-level governance, a more appropriate label might be multi-level government. Perhaps it is only fair to expect that, when political scientists are talking amongst themselves, formal and often domestic institutions remain the focus for analysis. Yet, as was argued in the introduction, if one wants to study financial governance, then a rather different notion of multi-level governance is required. It needs to incorporate the move away from purely public spheres of authority.

This shift away from the state as the single 'container' of authority can be characterized as a twofold movement. First, as emphasized in multi-level governance approaches, is a vertical movement upwards to supra-national levels of authority and downwards to sub-national levels of authority. Second, there is also a sideways shift – whether purposively or not – to private actors (Strange 1996b). Therefore a political economy approach to governance means, as Geoffrey Underhill (2000b: 4) notes, 'overcoming orthodoxy and understanding markets and political authorities as part of the same, integrated ensemble of governance, not as contrasting principles of social organization'.

Having said this, in many ways neither account of the multiple levels of governance forgoes the possibility of including these 'missing' levels. But thinking of governance as 'multi-level' should help to operate against the more structural, and worse still agency-less, accounts of political power found in most 'global' analyses (though see Cerny 2000a; O'Brien 2000; Hay 2002). However, the fact that neither includes the rich variety of political (and social or economic) levels or spaces in an explicit manner says, first, much for disciplinary (political science and IR respectively) boundaries. But second, and of more immediate significance, it is a consequence of the manner in which governance is theorized. In short, that governance as a framework for analysis has constructed governance as an object of analysis in line with disciplinary assumptions. In order to go beyond these restricted understandings of governance, the chapter now outlines a more heterodox multi-level framework of analysis.

A framework for analysis: beyond the global and the inter-governmental

Governance as an object of study is delineated by the analyst's disciplinary givens. Consequently, to make multi-level governance a suitable framework for studying the IPE of financial governance, some kind of disciplinary synthesis is required. First, global governance benefits from multi-level governance because it reminds us to look at a variety of levels other than the 'global'. This is because, in the broadest terms, global change does not erode the significance of other spatial scales; on the contrary, it coincides with the affirmation of smaller scales. Second, multi-level governance has remained too concerned with examining formal institutions as the only significant nodes in the networks of governance. Thus, what is needed is a framework which recognizes not only a fluid range of scales, but also the significance of non-formal institutional or social nodes of authority. As Youngs (1999: 97) argues, 'thinking globally'

> . . . has increasingly come to be understood as thinking spatially. This does not mean, of course, that global space can come to be considered as some kind of homogenous, undifferentiated mass; quite the reverse. To think spatially is to take spatial dimensions of social relations seriously, to recognize that political, economic and cultural exchanges take place in different forms of social space and, together with structural influences, contribute to how that space is framed and perceived. Space is not just a blank backdrop to human relations; it is socially constituted, and must therefore be regarded as a contingent element of the dynamics of social relations, and directly relevant to considerations of agency/structure issues.

Given this social and spatial understanding of contemporary political structures, the analytical shift to governance is advantageous in that it transcends the tired old dualism of states and markets, which acts as a barrier to 'thinking spatially'. Authority and power can now be incorporated as flowing through a single system, which side-steps the ontological/methodological preoccupation with state authorities as the sole vessels of political action. Therefore, one must be willing to abandon state-centrism/governmentalism. Specifically, there is 'a need to expand the analytic terrain within which the social sciences examine some of these processes, that is to say, the explicit and implicit tendency to use the nation-state as the container of social, political and economic processes' (Sassen 1996: 28–9). Abandoning state-centrism is not abandoning analysing the state; instead it requires an 'understanding of the state as political space' (Youngs 1999: 2). This move forces a rethinking of the role of the state, and in Youngs's (1999: 95–6) view also demands an approach willing to embrace multidisciplinarity and borrowing. Youngs's 'political economy of spatiality' approach is a way of avoiding the reductionism of treating the state as a closed unit, and instead exploring and understanding its *and other spaces'* social and politico-economic construction and contestation (Youngs 1999: 6–11, 61–3, 115–16). This essentially involves:

> . . . a refusal to treat politics or political economy as static or abstract, and a determination to ground them: treating them as processes involving people operating within territorially defined and spatially structured circumstances, as articulated by discursive as well as more obviously material practices associated with power relations.
>
> (Youngs 1999: 54)

While the above has not been in contrast to some of the claims made by those who study multi-level and global governance, it differs in that it allows the analyst a more flexible approach to constructing the levels/spaces of governance. It side-steps the methodological trap produced by the unreflexive conflation of governance as a framework for analysis and as an object of analysis. Thus, in this section, the analysis of governance has also been represented as global and multi-level, but with a rather different understanding of the 'global' and 'multi-level' than normal. Treating the global as a process which includes a range of levels, and theorizing these levels as discursively and socially constructed, allows a more flexible and inclusive approach to multi-level governance. Before suggesting how this might apply to finance, the chapter considers how IPE has hitherto understood the issue of financial governance.

Different notions of financial governance

Over the past couple of decades the topic of finance has moved to a central position within the IPE literature (see Cohen 1996, 2002; Cerny 1998a). As with IPE more generally, the range of work on finance has been broad and eclectic. How has financial governance been understood in this literature? Following Roger Tooze (1984), Robert Gilpin (1987: 9) famously defined IPE as a set of questions. Similarly we can define IPE's understandings of financial governance in terms of two generic questions that it most often asks; and in doing so it is possible to identify two elements of financial governance – as an object of analysis. That is, most IPE approaches to financial governance inquire into one (or more usually both) of the following questions: (i) how can we appropriately regulate capital flows? and (ii) what are the effects of capital movements upon states, firms and civil society? The two different questions suggest quite different understandings of what financial governance is. For the former it is a case of the *governance **of** finance*, and for the latter *governance **by** finance*. Having outlined these two elements of financial governance, this part of the chapter will conclude by arguing that both are only accounts about finance, rather than analyses of finance. That is, even when both questions are addressed there remains a missing element to the analysis, and that is the market. IPE operates with a black-box understanding of the dynamics of financial markets because it too often begins with a pre-given, abstract and economistic concept of finance. This is not sustainable given that, in the two generic questions, this missing element – financial markets – is the very 'thing' that is to be governed and the thing that is governing. However, by drawing on the framework of the social and spatial understanding of multi-level governance suggested above, an alternative way of theorizing finance is proposed in part three.

Financial governance take 1: governance of finance

The first question is characterized by its classic approach to IPE and the state–market relationship. Here, the possibilities for, and the desirability of, market regulation by state authorities is debated (Eichengreen 1999; Kaiser *et al.* 2000; Eatwell and Taylor 2000; Webb 2000). In many ways this is remarkably close to the multi-level governance of intergovernmental relations that was considered above. States are deemed responsible for prudent regulation of capital within their borders; and for regulation of cross-border flows they are required to cooperate at a higher spatial level of authority, the inter- or supragovernmental level. So here the bulk of the literature focuses on, for the most part, the role of the IMF and that of the BIS (Giannini 2000) – though, of course, the role of states is still paramount. This is either through the forum of the G7/8, or unilaterally in the case of the more powerful, such as the United States, the United Kingdom, Japan and Germany (Bayne 2000; Webb 2000; Baker 2000a).

This literature has developed through an initial interest in the construction, role and ultimately the demise of the Bretton Woods system. The era of instability associated with the end of dollar convertibility and the move to flexible exchange rates reinvigorated the need for alternative approaches to regulating disruptive currency movements (ul Haq *et al.* 1996; Webb 2000). Similarly, the debt crisis may be viewed as a crucial catalyst in seeking to redress some of the power held by private finance. As the 1990s unfolded, far from a redress of power and this instability being abated, there appeared ever more need to rethink the structures of global financial regulation. Here the devastation wrought upon the Mexican, East Asian, Russian and Brazilian economies, not to mention societies, was warranted sufficiently disruptive to initiate a debate – both academic and practitioner – on what was rather grandly called the new International Financial Architecture (IFA) (Eichengreen 1999; Kaiser *et al.* 2000; Soederberg, Chapter 10 of this volume).

However, this apparent unity of purpose should not obscure the possible divergence of positions in how to respond appropriately to these developments. Perhaps most apparent here is the issue of whether markets are deemed to be in need of further liberalization, correcting or fundamentally re-regulating. This is clearly a debate which is ongoing in most areas of state–market analysis, and is hardly a new one. If, for instance, one is to think of someone who sees markets as inherently rational and naturally equilibrating, then the policy suggestions for the IFA would look rather more liberal than if one were to characterize markets as speculative and prone to disequilibria. It is to these questions that the chapter will return to in part three.

So essentially this first issue primarily concerns itself with addressing the possibility, desirability, feasibility and efficacy of a range of structures which political agents – often states – can erect around and within finance in order to maximize its efficiency and/or minimize its disruption. For instance, this involves investigations into intergovernmental bargaining, diplomacy, institutional design and fit, regulatory structures and suchlike. As well as some parts of IPE, such an approach is generally to be found in the IR literature and instances of area studies, especially the EU (see Grossman, Chapter 7 of this volume) and political science more generally. As such, this first question about financial governance leads to an understanding of governance that is best characterized as the *governance **of** finance*.

Financial governance take 2: governance by finance

While such investigations are in no doubt of the utmost importance, especially of late, there is also a second sense in which we may plausibly speak of financial governance. This second theme in the literature is one that identifies the increasing power and role of financial forces in shaping contemporary economic, political and social outcomes (Pauly 2000; Story 2000; Thirkell-White, Chapter 8 of this volume). This is often expressed in terms of the structural power of capital (Przeworski 1985; Gill and Law 1988). The power that capital is reputed to have over governments is by virtue of its mobility, in opposition to the rooted nature of territorially bound and confined governmental authorities. These insights have proved ever more popular and seemingly persuasive when taken up within the ambit of globalization. It is suggested that the technological advances, economic integration and liberalization associated with globalization have further empowered capital at the expense of state control and labour.

Capital mobility and financial restructuring – alongside Coca-Cola and the Internet – are often heralded as archetypal illustrations of globalization.

Consider a passage from Giddens's BBC Reith Lectures (1999), in which for him the biggest difference between the globalized and the pre-globalized world

> . . . is in the level of finance and capital flows. Geared as it is to electronic money – money that exists only as digits in computers – the current world economy has no parallels in earlier times. In the new global electronic economy, fund managers, banks, corporations, as well as millions of individual investors, can transfer vast amounts of capital from one side of the world to another at the click of a mouse. As they do so, they can destabilize what might have seemed rock-solid economies (as happened in East Asia . . .). I would have no hesitation, therefore, in saying that globalization, as we are experiencing it, is in many respects not only new, but revolutionary.

This sort of account is to be found in most analyses of political science, the business school literature and, perhaps crucially, in many media accounts. Although often highly impressionistic and unsophisticated in their use of data – what Andreas Busch (2000) terms their 'casual empiricism' – such accounts retain enormous influence over the contemporary political imagination. This may range from the erosion of the state itself (Ohmae 1990) to rather more plausible accounts about the more limited efficacy of (particular) macro-economic policies feasible for state authorities (Weiss 1998; Sassen 1996: ch. 2; Germain 1997; Pauly 2000), and the concurrent changing nature of the state (Cox 1986, 1987; Stopford and Strange 1991; Cerny 1997; Sassen 1996: 22–5).

While sometimes overstated, exaggerated and stylized, these accounts nevertheless do capture something of the dilemmas of accountability and control now faced by regulatory authorities. The concern here is that finance, by virtue of its prepotency, is shaping and governing societies in very particular ways. The credibility that is demanded of governments institutionalizes policies aimed at low inflation and fiscal restraint, reflecting market priorities at the expense of expansionary alternatives (see Baker, Chapter 6 of this volume). In terms of corporate governance we are witnessing the financialization of firm decision-making; the imposition of short-termist restructuring rather than decisions based upon longer-term production enterprise. And also, at the level of society, there is an increasing marketization of everyday life (see Langley, Chapter 5 of this volume). So this is the second sense in which we can speak of financial governance, and one best characterized as *governance **by** finance*. Indeed, as intimated above, the anti-democratic and disruptive nature of these flows has meant that the first type of study – concerning international cooperation and regulatory structures of governance – has become ever more urgent.

Reconsidering the orthodox understandings of global and multi-level governance, it is clear that these most closely correspond to the first type of financial governance. Here analysis centres on the way in which formal political authorities attempt to regulate, in various ways, capital movements. The second approach to the financial governance appears to fit less well into these understandings. It might be thought to be global, but it is difficult to locate any sense of what Rosenau calls 'purposive behaviour', short perhaps of an overriding capitalist logic. Yet I want to argue here that an adapted understanding of multi-level governance is better able to capture the structures of this thing called finance, this thing that states try to govern, and which in turn appears to govern the behaviour of states, firms and societies.

A missing lacuna: financial markets as a level of governance

Lest I be accused of some kind of literary apartheid, the point here is not necessarily that a piece of work must fall neatly into one or other of these two themes. So in this sense the typology is simply meant as a heuristic distinction. Indeed, most accounts tackle both of the questions of financial governance in that dealing with one inherently implies the other, and so there are many synergies between these two questions. Nevertheless, even when treating the two questions as part of a whole, there remains a lacuna. An analytical gap lies between the two notions of governance, a missing variable between the governance of finance and the governance by finance. There remains something that is not developed sufficiently by either question. What the bulk of the literature does is treat the two moments of financial governance – the agency of regulatory bodies, and the structure of financial capital – as a dualism, and as such the dynamic relationship between the two often remains unexplored.

The proposed solution here revolves around pointing towards a third sense in which it might be possible to think of the IPE of finance. This is an approach that does not so much attempt a synthesis of the two questions as point towards a missing element between the two, and an element which is only ever sketched within the margins: I am thinking here of financial markets (and their constitutive participants). The irony of this, though, is that this sketch is in many ways central to both analyses. In the former, financial markets are the *object of analysis*, the thing that is to be regulated, and in the latter they become the *subject of analysis*, the thing which does the structuring. The key problem with the role that is often attributed to the market in the governance process is that it is still treated and perceived as a structural given with actor-like qualities.[7] The history of IPE is such that it has developed by borrowing understandings of the market from either orthodox liberal economics, or from more critical Marxian political economy. When applied at the systemic level these assumptions have become embedded in IPE and it has failed to reassess these borrowed concepts. As Underhill (2000a) argues, we should see the state and the market as an integrated ensemble of governance, as a state–market condominium. The question then becomes one of understanding the actual and grounded process of how the ensemble interacts. The suggestion here is that a more heterodox version of multi-level governance is able to include the market; specifically, by treating the market as a space rather than just a level of governance. Once unpacked and rendered contingent and socio-economic, markets can be examined as a crucial node for the structures that make up finance more broadly.

So, perhaps counter-intuitively, I want to suggest that despite the amount of IPE scholarship relating to finance there has still been relatively little work done actually on finance; read financial markets. Instead, most analyses can lay claim to little more than being about finance. This difference goes deeper than mere lexical pluralism.[8] For instance, accounts which point to the contemporary power of finance and its effects, or those which debate the merits of various structures to regulate this power, are both analyses within the realm of finance, but do not necessarily integrate a sustained understanding of financial markets. So, while both speak *about* finance, they do not speak *of* it. Instead, to speak of finance would be to specify the 'it' which is to be regulated, or the 'it' which is shaping the political, economic and social environments in which governments, societies, firms and individuals operate, i.e. financial markets. My argument is that, aside from stylized or assumed specifications of this 'it', much of the IPE literature about finance does not have a particularly well-developed concept of financial structures and actors (for an exception, see Harmes 1998). This conceptual hole is a consequence of the inability to treat financial markets as an active part of the structures of governance.

It should be noted that this identification of the paucity of accounts of, for want of a better expression, the full structures of finance was not the result of being able to see the invisible. On the contrary, the ability to identify the lack of consideration given to financial markets is due to a number of accounts which have developed some understanding of it elsewhere. Crucially these accounts have for the most part been developed outside of IPE – economic sociology, human geography and economic anthropology – and will be considered below.

Towards an anatomy of 'global' finance

So, despite the claimed paucity of IPE accounts of financial markets, what are the main analytical characteristics attributed to them? It is possible to identify two distinct elements most commonly attributed to financial markets. First is a notion of finance as flows and movements of capital, often on a global scale – this is the capital mobility hypothesis. And second, there is a notion of finance whereby it is motivated by a particular dynamic, whether this be rational or speculative. The rest of the chapter will address these *spatial* and *causal* characteristics so commonly attributed to finance, and then seek to present an alternative understanding. This alternative understanding will be one which reinforces the advantage of thinking in terms of multi-level spaces of governance.

Element I: Spatiality

When looking at the spatiality of finance there are two rather different debates which could be had here. The first focuses on finance as mobile flows of capital, and therefore the question becomes one of whether financial flows really are as mobile as some might suggest? This is a debate that arises from the oft-assumed fully integrated and globally sensitive nature of 'round-the-clock-round-the-world' markets versus the more empirically-based analysis which would suggest that a globally integrated market is still far from existing (Hirst and Thompson 1999). While this is evidently an important debate, it is not one I wish to deal with here. The second question of spatiality is, even if flows are or were global, is this the only way to think about finance? The answer here is no! One way to illustrate this is to draw a distinction between money and finance; whereas money is treated as the actual stock or flow of capital, finance also includes the institutional bases of those flows. This shift in focus, from one that sees money as capital to one that finds it necessary to interrogate the institutional nature of the places that this money flows to, through and from, raises some rather different issues, most notably the importance of particular places in the financial system, for instance 'global cities' (see also Woodward on the City of London, Chapter 9 of this volume).

In contrast, the erosion of space is almost axiomatic to the bulk of discussion about globalization, and still crucial to – but usually more implicit within – discussions of finance. As Martin Albrow (1990) suggests: 'Globalization refers to all those processes by which the peoples of the world are incorporated into a single world society, global society.' While there is some movement towards a more differentiated understanding of globalization, the dominant tendency is nevertheless still one that emphasizes the contemporary meaningless of place, especially within non-specialist literatures and the press. Given the digitized and fluid nature of contemporary money forms, it is perhaps little surprise that these ideas appear to have the most force when speaking of finance. Arguably one of the most cited books, in title at least, illustrating such a thesis is Richard O'Brien's (1992) *Global Financial Integration: The End of Geography*. In it he outlines the manner in which modern communication technologies, and the concurrent deregulation which has accompanied their growth, allow for certain activities to relocate wherever they please. Thus, the nature of banking and finance – its reduction of money to digits upon a screen or in cyberspace – has heralded for O'Brien the 'end of geography'. While it must be said that O'Brien, echoing Spike Milligan, does not dismiss the assertion that 'everybody has to be some-where', what he is doing is denouncing the necessity of *particular* locations.[9] Hence, deregulation and technological and communications advances imply decentralization and spatial spread.

However, O'Brien, in line with much commentary upon globalization more generally, makes what appear to be two rather elementary errors. The first is empirical. If one is to inspect the hypothesis that financial globalization is associated with decentralization and the 'end of geography', the evidence rather suggests otherwise. In actuality, in many cases the dominant tendency is towards increased agglomeration (Sassen 2000). The second is rather more conceptual, and that is to assume that the erosion of space entails the end of place.

In addressing these errors it is possible to draw a couple of general insights from the literatures on economic and human geography. First, Sassen (2000: 6–12) points to the importance of material processes in the implementation of globalization. Here she underlines the importance of major organizing sites for managing the huge complexity of global operations. Evidently key here are financial structures (Sassen 1991). Sassen argues that the need for producer services – marketing, advertising, consulting, storage, cleaning, security, maintenance, transport, personnel, accounting, legal, technical – in close proximity overrides the possibility and pressures towards relocation. Second, it is also possible to identify a range of social reasons – as explored below – why centralization will not only occur within cities, but also within particular sections of cities, i.e. financial districts. So, if anything, we are actually witnessing what Sassen (2000: xiv) has termed the 'new geographies of centrality'. Rather than considering finance to be a global space devoid of topography or shape, the actual structures more resemble a network. Within this network, as with all networks, there are nodes which act as control centres, as sites for decision-making and transformatory practices – i.e. institutions.

The suggestion that finance must be increasingly conceptualized along these lines – as a mixture of multi-level and network governance – has a number of consequences. First, the need to trace and analyse these networks suggests that certain examples of work from geography and sociology could usefully be explored. This could be developed alongside the plethora of work that already exists tracing individual institutional character and histories. These institutions include organizational structures as diverse as intergovernmental organizations (IMF, BIS), government treasuries, central banks, investment banks and commercial banks. To this list it is possible to add private credit rating agencies, think tanks, and even academic bodies. Commenting upon Sinclair's (1994b) work on credit rating agencies, Sassen (1996: 16) notes how 'they have emerged as important governance mechanisms whose authority is not centred on the state'. We can see how these institutions operate as a connected whole in order to produce a system of rule. Each institution is linked through the flow of ideas and behaviour. The key points here become, first, how these fit together and how they are under continual contestation through their place within the network rather than simply being considered as self-contained; and second, that there is a particular node which remains, if assessed in these terms, desperately undertheorized. This node is the market itself. Although, as suggested here, IPE has neglected theorizing the market, somewhat amazingly so have economists themselves – a point which both Ronald Coase (1988) and Douglass North (1977) have argued. There have been some attempts to theorize the market, but they remain largely peripheral to IPE (see, for example, Block 1990; Swedberg 1994). Thus, it is the significance of the market itself that has been relegated by the other two approaches to financial governance.

Element II: Causality

The dominant understanding – certainly among economists – is that markets operate in line with the 'efficient markets hypothesis' (Fama 1970). In short, this means that traders are able to discount future rises or falls in prices, and as such will buy or sell accordingly, meaning that the market clears at the expected level (Jensen 1978). Under such conditions of efficiency it remains impossible for traders to make capital gains. Central to this hypothesis is the assumption of rational expectations. Under such an assumption, actors are considered fully able to predict future events based upon current knowledge, absent random non-systematic errors. Significantly, the foundation for actors' knowledge is the underlying value of the factors in the real economy, which the prices in the financial markets are said to represent. Thus, it is only the emergence of relevant 'news' about the economy which will cause a movement in prices as traders change their position accordingly – the so-called 'random walk'.

While there are many *conceptual* critiques of neoclassical assumptions in existence, the study of financial markets appears to reveal a specific example of a market institution further removed than most from the idealized mechanisms of supply and demand. So, the debate about the necessity of parsimonious models notwithstanding, there is significant contemporary and historical evidence that such assumptions are misplaced – in that they are not only unrealistic, but crucially that they result in misunderstanding the market (Friedman 1953). An alternative literature points to a rather different dynamic of price formation in financial markets. Drawing on a range of historical and empirical sources, a now significant body of work argues that financial markets are dominated by speculative motives (see, for example, Frankel 1996; Harvey 1999; Chancellor 1999).

An orthodox account of the relationship between the real and financial economy is that the latter reflects the former. If so, one would expect that the demand for portfolio investment would be similar to, and be guided by, the same preferences as FDI (Harvey 1999: 203–4). However, the large and persistent trade imbalances and currency price volatility suggests that this might not be the case. In an alternative understanding, prices begin to form in expectation of future market performance without regard for underlying fundamentals; at least, for a time. In this period, the price (and therefore the assumed value) of an asset becomes de-linked from the 'real' economy. Just such a situation was famously outlined by Keynes (1936 [1997]: 158) in his distinction between enterprise and speculation, where he reserved 'the term speculation for the activity of forecasting the market, and the term enterprise for the activity of forecasting the prospective yield of assets over their whole life'. While the latter was tied to the real economy and its performance, the former was analogous to a parlour game or a competition, where the successful were those who guessed correctly what the average guessing of the rest of the market actors was going to be. The problem, of course, was that moment when the real economy reasserted itself, when the bubble burst, when people realized that '@Home' was not actually worth more than Lockheed Martin, when investors no longer wanted to hold Thai baht.

It is not difficult to imagine how this debate over whether markets are inherently efficient or whether they are inherently prone to instability and speculation proceeds.[10] The difficulty with such a debate is that it is often an extreme one, with proponents taking partisan positions *based upon a raft of assumptions*, making any meaningful dialogue unlikely at best. However, the real difficulty here is not so much the adoption of partisan positions – far from it – but instead that these are based upon a particular formalism and assumptions about market outcomes.

Recalling the earlier call to think of multi-level governance as a 'political economy of spatiality', then it demands that the analyst explore the processes in and by which social practices are spatially embedded. This is in stark contrast to, say, the assumption of states as actors. Similarly, it is a problem here because the market, too, is a social institution, but is not granted any causal significance in such frameworks. That is, the space or node of the market just becomes an instance of whatever meta-narrative of financial behaviour happens to be held by the analyst. So here, institutions are mechanisms by which capital is allocated through a rational interpretation of data available, or by which institutions distribute capital according to a speculative dynamic. Thus, similar to the theory of the state as a unified actor, so to are we left with an anthropomorphized 'market as actor'. On the other hand, the advantage of a spatial approach is that it demands that these nodes be unpacked. That is, that what can often be treated as a singular body is actually simply a space within which there are a number of competing and contested practices and/or discourses. Significantly, for Keynes (1936 [1997]: 158) there was no need to expect one dynamic necessarily to dominate the other. In the end it was a matter of historical specificity, a matter for empirical investigation, and not one for formalism.

So, what follows argues for the continued importance of a geography of finance in line with Sassen's Global Cities, but also a more specific micro-geography embedded within this, including a theorizing of this space. In the foregoing discussion, the orthodox (equilibrium) and the heterodox (speculative) explanations of market outcomes both have a role for market actors, but not a particularly developed one. Although it might be argued that the latter takes a slightly more contextualized approach, it still retains a view of traders as bounded and sovereign actors. The alternative is one that places market actors – traders, speculators or investors – within a social context.

Theorizing the marketplace as a level of governance

In a not dissimilar analysis to Sassen's, Nigel Thrift (1994) is also interested in the continued, and perhaps increased, importance of global cities as control centres of the global economy. In his analysis, however, he places more emphasis upon the social rather than the material determinants of agglomeration. The need to be close to and part of the information, expertise and social interaction that are so key to financial markets and the deals that take place within them, forces serious participants to embed themselves within these networks (Adler and Adler 1984; Baker 1984; Clark and O'Connor 1997; Leyshon and Thrift 1997). Hence we see the formation of financial districts within these global cities (Amin and Thrift 1992). Consider Sassen's (2000: 95) otherwise passing comment about the desirability of being able to interact face-to-face in high-risk business meetings: 'Telecommunications cannot replace these networks. The complexity, imperfect knowledge, high risk and speculative character of many endeavours as well as acceleration in the circulation of information and in the execution of transactions heighten the importance of both personal contact and spatial concentration.' In attempting to develop this insight, Sassen draws a distinction between two types of information. The first is simply datum: facts and figures, which, thanks to the communications revolution, has been globalized. The second is interpretation, evaluation and judgement. This aspect of information is crucially the one which depends upon social proximity and access to social infrastructures.

The language and distinction here is uncannily similar to a rather more famous distinction made over twenty years ago by Clifford Geertz (1975) in his *Interpretation of Cultures*. Drawing on Wittgenstein and Weber, he argued that 'man is an animal suspended in webs of significance he himself has spun', these webs being cultural; and the aim of analysis should therefore be interpretative in search of the meaning of these webs – in short, ethnography (Geertz 1975: 5). He elaborates on the significance of meaning for understanding human interaction by drawing the distinction between 'thin' and 'thick description', with which Sassen's account is so resonant. He describes a situation where we might observe somebody exercising a rapid contraction of their eyelid. This, the physiological description, is Geertz's 'thin description', and while accurate it does little to impart much information to the observer. The poverty of such a description is illustrated if we imagine two people, one whose eye has just twitched and the other who has just winked. The understanding and significance of the difference can only emerge within an understanding of the wider webs of meaning within which the participants are enmeshed (Geertz 1975).[11] It is easy, then, to extrapolate this insight yet further, in so far as the wink may be executed in a slightly different manner – it may be conspiratorial, it may be flirtatious – and the same manner of winking may itself convey rather different meanings in different environments. Thus the important, if simple, point here is that the context – culture, the result of social interaction – becomes a crucial variable to examine.

In that culture is existent within our everyday lives, the financial markets are no different.[12] If anything, the financial markets depend upon this sort of information to a greater extent than whether we are worried about whether the person opposite us has just twitched or knowingly winked. Traders depend upon these social networks in order to make sense of the prevailing market mood. Market trends are therefore formed in line with the 'information' which flows along these links. As such, the analysis of market dynamics becomes a much more interpretative and local analysis than so much of the literature suggests. Therefore, this shift in level of analysis, from global down to local, is not so much a claim to a superior access to knowledge as an attempt to uncover some of the undertheorized aspects of financial markets. In doing so, the aim is to begin to tease out a number of different insights to those which are routinely presented; it also provides another aspect towards a more holistic account of 'global finance', one that seeks to understand its multi-layered character.

While, as suggested in these pages, it is felt that a holistic understanding of financial governance structures would be through a kind of mapping exercise identifying key spaces and linkages which structure the movement and distribution of money and credit, this is clearly a massive exercise. A possible alternative is that financial marketplaces have been highlighted as a particular level of the governance structures of finance in need of theorizing. This is justified upon three grounds, not necessarily mutually exclusive: first, that marketplaces are a critical element of the system and are therefore justifiable by virtue of their importance alone; second, that despite their obvious importance as strategic sites they have been unduly neglected in scholarship on the structures of international finance; third, that financial markets could be seen as a repository, either real or metaphorical, of global actors, structures and actions. In a sense, therefore, studying the marketplace might be a manner of understanding the broader structures. Taken individually or together these reasons provide a convincing, though hardly exhaustive, series of justifications for the study of financial marketplaces.

Research issues for the political economy of multi-level financial governance

Having developed the above arguments about what (research into) a financial system of multi-level governance might look like, it is now possible to point to some issues which look promising for future research in this vein.

Ideas and practices within institutions

Most of the institutions involved with global finance (states' treasuries, IMF, BIS) have already been blessed with a rich vein of literature upon them, their work and role. Key here are the dominant narratives about financial markets within these institutions. As the work of Wayne Baker (1984) makes clear, if markets are taken to be other than efficient, then the mindset informing their regulation must also shift in line with the more empirical studies of market dynamics presented. So, for instance, policy-makers must work with the effects upon trading that building or clearing systems have. As has been argued throughout, it is of utmost importance to recognize that these market structures are part of the ensemble of governance, and not simply as something external to be controlled.

However, it has been suggested that from a 'political economy of spatiality' perspective actual marketplaces as institutions have been relatively undertheorized. So key here is the need to study the ideas and behaviour of market actors such as traders, etc., within their social environment. Moreover, the specificity of environments suggests a move away from analyses, which treat finance as a homogenous whole. As Tony Porter (2001b) argues, there is a need to resist attempts to treat capital as a single structure. However, not only are there clearly different types of financial instruments and thus different regulatory regimes, but it is also significant that they are traded in rather different spaces, both geographically and socially. Consider for instance the difference between foreign exchange trading which is now an inter-bank market and is no longer done on a trading floor, and the trading environment for, say, equities, which still possess a concrete marketplace. Not only might one expect these different instruments to act rather differently just because they are different instruments, but also because of their institutional setting. Especially interesting would be the inter-subjective ideas within these markets, which help produce market dynamics, especially the existence of self-fulfilling trends within the market. Yet a conceptual distinction might need to be made between these endogenous dynamics to the marketplace and the interpretation of exogenous dynamics for the marketplace, for instance the role of news, media and economic data. So, while the argument that analyses which treat market actors as bounded, rational, sovereign atoms is surely wrong, then an analysis which argues that economics has nothing to say, and that actors are operating in a purely inter-subjective, self-socialized, and hermetically sealed environment is also missing the point – which leads to the second issue.

Ideas and practices between institutions

In tracing the form and content of these linkages it becomes more clear how the variety of governing institutions, both private and public, interact to produce a historically specific form of finance. Two examples seem most obvious. In relation to the previous point, the environment that the market is situated within and shaped by is derived to a large degree from the ideas held about it, especially within the other institutions of finance which set the regulatory agenda. Clearly the agenda that is followed structures the market through the form of these network relationships. Second, the role of particular sources of news and data, and how the markets are linked (because it is clearly not a simple correspondence relationship) to broader structures, is important in understanding how and why markets react as they do. This sort of interaction is captured by Andrew Baker's notion (Chapter 6 of this volume) of coded diplomacy between the markets and governments. However, as suggested in the above, this should not be seen as diplomacy with an abstract category, but instead with a particular social space.

Conclusions

The key point of this chapter has been that, when thinking about financial governance, there are many advantages to not only including but also opening the market up to analysis. Two alternative (but not competing) notions of what constitutes financial governance were identified. It was suggested that each 'moment' of governance led to a particular set of issues for the student of IPE, but that neither was completely satisfactory. This is because market outcomes are the product of a dialectical relationship between their political regulation and their socio-economic practices/structures. Too often the actual socio-economic process is taken as a given, especially within the macroscopic disciplines such as IR and IPE. This is why thinking of governance as an integrated state–market whole is such a radical challenge to IPE – if followed to its logical conclusion. The foregoing has argued that an adapted notion of multi-level governance proves instructive in this task. However, from a political economy perspective, the limitations of orthodox multi-level governance were quickly revealed.

In this respect, the process of assessing the strengths and weaknesses of an emergent concept such as multi-level governance is clearly aided through an interdisciplinary dialogue. This much is difficult to disagree with. However, in this chapter I have argued that developing better understandings of the world requires a further step: a thoroughgoing commitment to multidisciplinarity, taken to mean that any single study should be prepared to draw, at times heavily, from other disciplines. Moreover, this goes beyond IPE's normal claims to inter-disciplinarity (Strange 1970; Underhill 2000a). This is because the structures of financial governance were shown to be (significantly) spatial and social as well as political and economic. Thus, to develop this more holistic understanding, it is necessary to incorporate insights from, *inter alia*, human and economic geography, economic sociology and social and economic anthropology. Finally, a schematic set of questions were suggested for further research into financial marketplaces within the structures of financial governance. These involve opening up the black box of the market and understanding it as a more social and therefore contingent category than is regularly understood. And in turn there is, therefore, a need to rethink the role of the institutions of financial governance – both public and private – in terms of their *interaction with* the market *qua* a place of structuration or mediation instead of as an abstract and homogenous category.

Notes

1 An earlier version of this chapter was presented as a paper at the conference 'Multi-Level Governance: Interdisciplinary Perspectives' at the University of Sheffield, June 2001. I want to thank Andrew Baker, Matthew Watson, Ben Thirkell-White, Richard Woodward and an anonymous referee for their insightful, extensive and incredibly helpful comments on that earlier version – although, of course, the responsibility for any remaining shortcomings is mine alone.

2 Given that all voices must initially speak from somewhere, the following does so from within IPE. However, through the course of the account, the analysis attempts to re-orient itself in order to speak *to* IPE from elsewhere.

3 This is not, however, to say that the processes of governance themselves are partic-ularly new, only the mainstream and sustained analysis governance is now receiving. For good examinations of the historical dimension to global governance see Murphy (1994), Germain (1997) and Langley (2002a) for analyses applied to financial governance.

4 'World order' is used here in the sense used by Robert Cox (1986: 249, fn. 2) instead of the more common phrase 'international system'. This is to signify that there is no necessary sense of equilibrium in international patterns of behaviour, and that these patterns operate over a geographically limited space.

5 This, though, is not to mistake previous eras of government authority as absolute – on which point, see Krasner (1999) – but just that there is an observable change in the location of this authority.

6 Interestingly the development of IPE as a distinct discipline is particularly instructive here. As Cox (2000: 32) argues, the emergence of IPE was not only due to a demand to include issues and dimensions of power that were politico-economic rather than

just politico-military, but it was also an explicit challenge to the ossified categories and boundaries (both empirical and conceptual) of IR.

7   Financial markets are held to possess aggregate qualities. For some this means that 'markets' are able to engage in rational allocation through the price system, and for others that they are inherently irrational and speculative.

8   This usage of 'about' plays upon some of the word's multiple meanings: for instance to mean nearby, but without being in direct proximity to; around, in the sense of circumnavigating; and also as an approximation. All of these, it is argued, capture certain elements of this work.

9   Spike Milligan's comment was allegedly a reply to an acquaintance at a party who expressed surprise at meeting Milligan there.

10 For a particularly graphic example of such an exchange, see Soros (1998); Solow (1999a); Soros (1999); Solow (1999b).

11 The original distinction of thin and thick description is drawn from the Oxford philosopher Gilbert Ryle.

12 There is now a developing literature on the anthropology of financial markets that seeks to explore the role of culture within the markets. See, for instance, Adler and Adler (1984), Abolafia (1996), Kalthoff *et al.* (2000), Hasselström (2003).

Part II

5 The everyday life of global finance

A neglected 'level' of governance

Paul Langley

As an interdisciplinary field of study, International Political Economy (IPE) has established itself as one of the key academic avenues for inquiry into global finance. IPE scholars have done much to begin to develop an alternative understanding of global finance to that offered by the dominant neo-liberal mode of knowledge. Yet it is the contention here that, like the neo-liberal common sense present in mainstream economics, technocratic circles and the business press, the field of IPE has tended to overlook the ties that bind global finance and our everyday pension, investment, insurance, mortgage and consumer credit practices.[1] Global finance is, then, typically represented as existing 'out there' and somehow separate from our everyday lives. By contrast, this chapter reflects upon the significance of our everyday saving and borrowing practices in global finance. It is argued that revaluing the everyday has considerable implications for how global financial governance is understood. As such, the chapter contributes to the objective of this volume to consider global financial governance in a holistic manner as constituted by numerous and inter-related sets of authority relations across various 'levels', spaces and social settings.

The chapter begins by exploring why global finance tends to be bounded and differentiated from everyday financial practices. It suggests that popular dichotomies drawn between the financial/'real' economies and the global/national economies are central to the imaginary spatial enclosure of global finance from our everyday practices. Global finance becomes a discrete space that is defined as much by what it is not – it is not 'real' or national – as by what it is deemed to be. In the second part of the chapter I highlight the extent to which accounts of governance have followed from and reinforced this dominant representation of the social space of global finance. Global financial governance typically becomes limited to the institutions and agents that exercise authority within the assumed discrete and deterritorialized space of global finance. The third part of the chapter then moves to show that the restructuring of everyday practices is an essential constitutive feature in qualitative changes that are central to the emergence of global finance. With reference to illustrative examples of US and UK occupational pension and consumer credit practices, particular attention is paid to the contribution of the restructuring of these practices to disintermediation as a key qualitative change. It is not simply that global finance has consequences for everyday credit practices, but that global finance in part rests upon the restructuring of everyday life. In the final part of the chapter I turn my attention to rethinking global financial governance. I argue that the understanding of governance present in IPE that focuses exclusively on transnational institutions and elites is necessarily partial, as it neglects the dynamics of governance that extend through the everyday 'level' of global finance. More specifically, I elaborate an institutional-discursive conceptualization of governance. This leads me to underline the importance of neo-liberal governance principles, and the manner in which a transformation in the identities and practices of everyday actors is discursively framed as they self-govern their financial lives.

The social space of global finance

World finance has undergone a transformation that most observers date as beginning in the early 1970s and accelerating through the 1980s to the present. As with so many other areas of social life, the transformation of world finance has tended to be captured under the rubric of 'globalization'. International organizations, national governments, financiers and the business press are all apt to further a neo-liberal mode of knowledge of change, suggesting that contemporary finance has been marked by the unprecedented emergence of a genuinely integrated, twenty-four-hour global marketplace – that is, so-called 'global finance' (Langley 2002a: 1–3). Powered by innovations in information and telecommunications technologies and the assumed spread of universal market rationality, the inference is that the twenty-four-hour global marketplace for finance is 'spaceless' as it follows the sun from East to West. Whilst those creating, allocating, buying and selling financial instruments may be a very great distance from each other, they effectively behave as if they occupy the same market space.

As the work of Henri Lefebvre (1991) serves to reminds us, this portrayal of the space of global finance is of considerable political significance. What in Lefebvre's terms we may call the 'representation of space' of global finance acts as an important anchor point through which the dominant discourse and understanding of global finance is articulated, a 'tool in the exercise of control and authority' (Abbott 2002: 164). The portrayal of global finance as 'spaceless' (i.e. not territorial or able to be mapped) actually serves to endow global finance with particular qualities as a socially constructed spatial context. Global finance becomes a discrete spatial entity that is 'out there' somewhere, beyond the spaces of territory and everyday place. Drawing on Palan (1999: 59), global finance as a spatial entity is not subject to 'physical closure, which implies physical restrictions on the movement of people, goods, capital, and ideas', but to 'imaginary closure, or the processes that lead subjects to believe that they inhabit a closed entity'. For state policy-makers and representatives of the principal international organizations, these assumed spatial characteristics have enabled global finance to be portrayed as a powerful exogenous force. Neo-liberal policies of financial orthodoxy and structural adjustment are justified and legitimated, as the exogenous force of global finance is beyond control and does not permit alternatives.

The representation of global finance as occupying a bounded and discrete space has been partly challenged by research in IPE and across the social sciences. This research stresses the continuing importance to our understanding of global finance of the persistence of both diverse national financial systems (e.g. Moran 1991; Vogel 1996) and key financial centres as organizational spaces (e.g. Sassen 1999; Germain 1997). The result has been a considerably more nuanced reading of change that challenges the neo-liberal image of the emergence of a smooth and seamless global market for finance. Despite these interventions, however, there is still clearly a sense in which global finance is represented in IPE inquiry as 'out there', bounded and differentiated from other spaces. Of crucial importance here would appear to be the drawing of two imagined dichotomies – between the financial/'real' economies and the global/national economies – that, taken together, bound the space of global finance and fill it with particular meanings. Significantly, both dichotomies figure in the representations of the space of global finance present in the neo-liberal common sense and in IPE research.

The financial/'real' economies dichotomy

The drawing of an imagined dichotomy between the financial and 'real' economies is clearly not new. Such disaggregating of economy draws on a long lineage of thought that stretches back to Aristotle's distinction between the home economics of 'oikonomia' and the superfluous economics of 'chrematistics' (Langley and Mellor 2002: 54). Yet the finance/'real' economies dichotomy tends to be especially prevalent in representations of contemporary global finance. The dichotomy is a common feature of different long-standing approaches to political economy that, when brought to bear in our understanding of global finance, seems to find particular relevance.

The image of finance as separate from the 'real' economy is present in neo-liberal political economy as the dominant mode of knowledge of global finance. Here the key assumption that establishes this dichotomy is that finance is the use of holdings of money (as a store of value) in order to facilitate 'real' investment and exchange. Finance therefore serves to automatically equate saving and investment at a market-clearing rate of interest and maintain macroeconomic equilibrium (Guttmann 1994: 28). The current privileging of 'shareholder value' by corporate managers is one particular expression of this understanding of the relationship between finance and production (cf. Williams 2000), with the stock market coming to be identified as the key mechanism of capital allocation.

The assumed automatic and thereby near-mystical capacity of finance to create capital for 'real' investment helps to endow finance with an 'unreal' set of characteristics. The pace of recent innovations in financial instruments, the transformation of finance into computerized information flows, and the sheer complexity of transactions would seem to justify the belief that finance is 'unreal' and amazing. This is especially the case once finance is juxtaposed with the material 'reality' of everyday economic life. As Cox (1996: 181) highlights, differences in the perceived experience of social time – the mundane and relatively slow pace of the 'real' economy and the rapidity, volatility and speed of finance – also does much to imbue finance with this air of 'unreality'. Only experts and financiers appear able to populate this other, faster world. Under neo-liberal readings, financiers become the swashbuckling buccaneers and rocket scientists of our age. Only a web of recent and hugely influential theories from Economics – including the likes of portfolio theory, Modigliani-Miller, the efficient markets hypothesis, and asset pricing models – appear able to explain how finance mysteriously, yet efficiently and rationally, optimizes the allocation of capital for 'real' investment.

Whilst highlighting that the relationship between finance and the 'real' economy is not simply a positive one, the Marxist and Keynesian traditions of political economy tend to share and reinforce this dichotomy. For Marxist-derived analyses, finance becomes, at particular historical junctures, the speculative and parasitical realm of accumulation that is distinguished from the more fundamental sphere of production (e.g. Altvater 1997; Amin 1996). Important here is the effective triumph in Marxist theorizing of Hobson's use of the concept of 'finance capital', developed with reference to Britain, over that of Hilferding. For Hilferding, 'finance capital' referred not only to finance, but to the fusion of industrial and financial capital during the establishment of German monopoly capital at the turn of the last century (Brewer 1980: 83–6). Keynes, of course, did much to carry forward an essentially Marxist reading of the financial/'real' economies dichotomy. For Keynes, volatile and uncertain short-term international financial flows heighten uncertainty in the 'real' economy and encourage a convergence in macroeconomic policy that is inappropriate (Kirshner 1999: 315–16). The smooth functioning of the 'real' economy becomes dependent upon the use of capital controls to prevent the speculative excesses of finance. Whilst the Marxist and Keynesian reading of the relationship between finance and the 'real' economy remains largely marginalized at present, what is significant in our terms is that here too the financial/'real' economies dichotomy looms large in analysis.

The disagreement between traditions of political economy as to the nature of the relationship between the financial and 'real' economies is mirrored in IPE inquiry. Those following what, in Murphy and Tooze's (1991b) terms, we might call an 'orthodox IPE' approach tend to concur in the main with the neo-liberal view. Gilpin (1987: 306), for example, describes the function of international finance as being 'to transfer accumulated capital to the location where its marginal rate of return is highest and where it can ... be employed most efficiently'. Analysis, therefore, concentrates on the extent to which legal and institutional barriers and associated price and interest rate differentials can be said to be reducing in the context of an emerging global financial marketplace (see Dombrowski 1998: 4–5 for review). Meanwhile, what following Murphy and Tooze (1991b) we might call 'new IPE' tends to offer a Marxist- and/or Keynesian-derived reading. For instance, falling levels of corporate manufacturing profitability and increased interest rate and exchange rate volatility are held to have led to an 'investment strike' as capital concentrates on making returns from freely-operating finance (Allen 1994; Brenner 2001). Strange (1986) and Cox and Sinclair (1996: 179–83) similarly highlight a de-coupling of global finance from the 'real' economy since the mid-1970s as central to the emergence of what Strange calls 'casino capitalism'. By mirroring the disagreement between the traditions of political economy and aside from the obvious normative differences, then, those writing in IPE create a similar financial/'real' economies dichotomy in the spatial representation of global finance to that furthered by the neo-liberal common sense.

The global/national economies dichotomy

In the representation of global finance as a bounded and discrete space 'out there', the drawing of a dichotomy between global/national economies is also central. It would seem that the roots of this second dichotomy can be traced to a set of well-worn and deeply embedded paradigmatic ideas that serve to construct and sustain it. What these ideas share is a commitment to what Scholte terms 'methodological territorialism'.

> Methodological territorialism refers here to the practice of understanding the social world and conducting studies about it through the lens of territorial geography. Territorialist method means formulating concepts and questions, constructing hypotheses, gathering and interpreting empirical evidence, and drawing conclusions all in a territorial spatial framework. These habits are so engrained in prevailing methodology that most researchers reproduce them unconsciously.
>
> (Scholte 2000: 56)

The allure of methodological territorialism is indeed long-standing in Economics and the understanding of finance, extending well beyond its ongoing appeal in current neo-liberal macroeconomics.[2] As Jane Jacobs (1984: 31) highlights, the 'most formative and venerable assumption' that 'nations are the salient entities for understanding the structure of economic life' is some four centuries old, first informing the state-building 'bullionist' doctrines of the early mercantilist economists. As such, central dynamics in the consolidation of state–societies since the mercantilist period have been the ideology of economic nationalism (cf. Levi-Faur 1997), the establishment of the edifice of the national economy as an imaginary and regulatory construct (Cameron and Palan 1999), and the macroeconomic measurement of economic activity through systems of national accounts.

Against this background, the description of contemporary finance as 'global' comes to be seen as essential to the representation of its very particular spatiality. Under methodological territorialism, 'the state border as an economic boundary serves to separate and *create* the "domestic" and the "international" economies as discrete spaces' (Cameron and Palan 1999: 274, emphasis in original). For neo-liberal readings in particular, then, the use of the term 'global' implies that contemporary finance has become genuinely integrated into a single market to the extent that the territorialist spatial referent of 'international' (i.e. between nations) has been transcended and is no longer adequate (cf. Ghosh and Oritz 1997). Put another way, global finance is 'out there' beyond the national economy because it can no longer be described in territorialist terms as 'international'.

The designation of contemporary finance as 'global' performs a not dissimilar role in IPE and related social scientific analysis. For instance, Economic Geographer Andrew Leyshon (1996) talks of the emergence of a 'global financial space' that is 'post-national' in character. Meanwhile, for IPE scholar Benjamin Cohen (2001: 207), 'Currency deterritorialization is part and parcel of the accelerating globalization of world economic affairs'. Similarly, for Susan Strange (1988: 88–9), finance

> . . . is global in that all the major capital markets of the world are so closely linked together that in many respects they function as if they were one system. They react promptly and visibly to developments elsewhere in the system. The bankers and dealers in securities operate as though time zones were more significant than political frontiers . . .

Such are the assumed transnational qualities of global finance that some IPE scholars have questioned whether a 'paradigm shift' is required, away from the territorialist methods of mainstream Economics and International Relations (IR) (Cerny 1994a; Cohen 1996).[3]

In conjunction with the financial/'real' dichotomy, the global/national dichotomy is also important in bounding the space of global finance in terms of what it is not. Certain aspects of finance are deemed not to be part of global finance because they are 'real' and/or national. This has several sets of delimiting implications for IPE inquiry. First, a research agenda follows that, largely replicating the common sense assumptions of neo-liberal politicians and bureaucrats about the space of global finance, situates global finance as a bounded exogenous force that acts on national states and societies. Global finance is positioned in consequential relationships to the autonomy or otherwise of states' monetary and fiscal policy-making; the capacity of national financial systems to maintain their distinctive institutional arrangements; and the configurations of national social forces (see Cohen 1996 for review). Second, the subject matter of global finance is effectively ring-fenced. National and so-called 'retail' finance is divorced from global and so-called 'wholesale' finance. Only the latter becomes the proper focus of IPE inquiry. Scholte's (2000: 58–9) work is particularly illustrative and representative here. Whilst listing a range of financial activities including foreign exchange, offshore bank deposits, and securitized funds that are deemed to be global in character, he also asserts that 'many currencies, credit cards and other forms of money have restricted circulation within a given territorial space. Likewise, most people on earth today continue to hold their bank accounts locally' (p. 59). In short, global finance is positioned in a transnational space of its own that serves to bracket it off from other forms of finance.

Global financial governance

Accounts of global financial governance present in IPE provide an extremely illustrative example of how the dominant representation of the social space of global finance stands as an anchor point in the understanding of global finance. Explanations of global financial governance follow from and reinforce the dominant representation of the social space of global finance. Global financial governance becomes delimited to the institutions and agents that inhabit the bounded and discrete space of global finance.

Three broad theoretical approaches to understanding global financial governance are discernible in the IPE literature. First, for those who retain close theoretical links with IR and liberal economics, governance is primarily associated with the authority and policy-making of state institutions in the face of globalizing markets (Cohen 2000; Eichengreen 1999; see Woodward, Chapter 3 of this volume, for a critique). As Hudson notes in Chapter 4 of this volume, the concern here is with the governance of financial markets. Second, those following institutionalist approaches tend to focus their interest on the financial governance roles of international organizations – the International Monetary Fund (Pauly 1997), the Bank of International Settlements (Kapstein 1994), and the International Organization of Securities Commissions (IOSCO) (Porter 1993) – and their recent restructuring amidst the post-Asian crisis drive for a so-called 'new international financial architecture' (Germain 2001; Porter 2001a). Some have turned their attention to private business associations such as the International Primary Market Association, the International Securities Markets Association, and the International Federation of Stock Exchanges (Filipovic 1997), whilst others highlight more broadly the interaction between international organizations and so-called 'global civil society' (O'Brien *et al.* 2000). Institutionalists have also begun the important work of incorporating market institutions into their understanding of financial governance (Underhill 2000c; Cerny 2001; see also Hudson, Chapter 4 of this volume). Third, those IPE scholars writing in the tradition of historical materialism have done much to explicitly situate governance institutions in the social power relations of the global financial order. For instance, Soederberg (2001b) views financial governance institutions, centred on the G7 states and the 'Wall Street–Treasury–IMF complex' (Wade and Veneroso 1998), as legitimated by the neo-liberal ideals of the Washington-consensus and the outcome of the power and preferences of US-centred financial capital.

Current research in IPE leads us, then, to focus in the first instance on the bounded and contested institutional face of contemporary global financial governance. Elsewhere I have characterized this institutional face as taking a 'transnational multilateral' (Langley 2004) form. The notion of 'multilateralism' tends to be used in a state-centric manner by IR/IPE scholars to refer to the coordination of national policies by three or more states. Such state-centric notions are inadequate in the current era of transnational relations where a broad spectrum of public and private actors coalesce and compete across a wide-ranging institutional fabric. Whilst clearly an attempt to capture the distinctive practices of contemporary global governance, O'Brien *et al.*'s (2000) concept of 'complex multilateralism' alone also remains inadequate as multilateral institutions are interdependent with transnational market institutions in the structure of financial governance. Market authority rests not with the cumulative rational decisions of individuals that comprise the market according to neo-liberalism but, in view of the subjective, hierarchical, collective and socially embedded nature of financial markets, with the principal market networks that play a role in the organization of credit practices. In Cerny's (2001: 6, emphasis in original) terms, it is through transnationalization that 'markets are becoming more entrenched *not just as narrowly economic mechanisms*, but as quasi-political governance structures in their own right'. Such transnational networks are facilitated by information and communications technologies that enable coordination and control through an infrastructure of monitors and modems. Functional as opposed to national divisions within market networks and intra-institutional movements of capital and credit are representative of genuinely transnational management strategies. The furthering of market authority in contemporary financial governance has, however, remained interdependent with complex multilateral initiatives in crisis management, regulation and supervision.

Everyday saving and borrowing in global finance

In this section of the chapter I wish to challenge the forgoing account of the social space of global finance as a precursor to rethinking current IPE accounts of global financial governance. My starting point is the confluence of four key sets of theoretical insights. First, I reject neo-liberal and orthodox IPE conceptions of the subject matter of global finance as international capital flows (cf. Cohen 1996; Dombrowski 1998). I draw instead on theories that view money and finance as comprised of social relations and practices that arise from the very nature of credit as claims, obligations and 'promises to pay' (cf. Ingham 1996; Woodruff 1999). It follows that understanding global finance requires attention not only to the organization of actual promises to pay themselves (e.g. credit instruments, loan agreements, etc.) and their associated capital flows, but to the field of social relations and practices that make these possible.

Second, Held *et al.* (1999) observe that contemporary economic globalization is marked not only by the expanded reach of networks of production, finance and consumption across the globe, but also by an intensification and deepening of such interconnectedness within the richest state–societies of North America, Western Europe and Asia in particular. Put another way and drawing upon Bauman (1998), economic globalization has seen a step-wise growth in the real and perceived interconnections between 'the near' and 'the far'. The everyday social relations of 'the near' – 'primarily that which is usual, familiar and known to the point of obviousness; something seen, met, dealt or interacted with daily, intertwined with habitual routine and day-to-day activities' (Bauman 1998: 13) – increasingly and regularly extend way beyond the here and now. When placed alongside the first theoretical insight, the suggestion is that global finance not only involves the expanded reach of market networks to embrace, for instance, the so-called 'emerging markets' of Asia and Latin America. It is also a qualitative change that rests in part on a transformation in the everyday social relations and practices of credit in line with the 'far away' image of twenty-four-hour integrated financial markets. There are, in short, ties that bind global finance and the everyday.

A third key theoretical insight arises from the juxtaposition of the social theory of money with work on the comparative political economy of financial systems. Much of the social theory of money that draws on Marx, Simmel and Habermas holds that instrumental rationality and the capacity to transform social relations into an abstract and numerical equivalent are the key features of money. It follows that the spread of money is associated with the destruction and homogenization of social relations (Leyshon 1996: 63–5). At first blush, what is suggested is that a transformation in the everyday social relations and practices of credit in line with the 'far away' image of twenty-four-hour integrated financial markets is likely to lead to homogenization. However, comparative research into contemporary national financial restructuring suggests otherwise. As the relations and practices of credit have developed they have taken different institutional configurations across state–societies, including state-led (e.g. France), bank-based (e.g. Germany) and capital market (e.g. UK, USA) arrangements (cf. Zysman 1983). Contemporary restructuring has not realized convergence and homogenization, but is following divergent trajectories in contrasting contexts (Vogel 1996). More specifically, as Moran (1991: 121) highlights with regard to regulatory change, the processes of change are characterized by a 'diffusion' of practices from the US and UK. Global finance is predominantly centred in New York and London, and the 'far away' image of the twenty-four-hour global marketplace reflects the institutionalized capital market arrangements of the so-called Anglo-Saxon 'model'. Inquiry into the ties that bind the restructuring of everyday credit practices with the qualitative changes associated with global finance needs to recognize, then, that such restructuring will be by no means uniform in pace or extent, and is likely to be more pronounced in the Anglo-Saxon capital market state–societies (UK, USA, Canada, Australia, the Netherlands). There is clearly a sense in which the social space of global finance is primarily Anglo-Saxon.

Fourth, research into contemporary financial exclusion highlights that the intensification of global credit relations within Anglo-Saxon state–societies is extremely uneven. On the one hand, those market institutions that stand to profit from an expansion in everyday credit practices would appear likely to benefit from a deepening of credit relations to include those previously excluded from, for instance, consumer credit. On the other hand, however, such a deepening of credit relations is impeded as the previously excluded are deemed too 'risky' and unlikely to be able to meet any new obligations. The intensification of global credit relations has, then, been subject to considerable social stratification in general, a deepening or 'superinclusion' (Leyshon and Thrift 1996: 1150) within the upper and middle echelons of male white society (cf. Leyshon and Thrift 1995; Gill 1997b). The specific extent or otherwise of inclusion varies considerably across different sets of everyday credit practices for which risks are measured differently. The more inclusive dynamics of everyday banking practices contrast, for instance, with mutual fund saving practices. The everyday credit practices that primarily concern us here – that is, the structured sets of saving (i.e. occupational pensions) and borrowing (i.e. consumer credit) practices through which individuals and households become enmeshed in the claims and obligations of global credit relations – are largely the preserve of the superincluded in Anglo-Saxon state–societies.[4]

These theoretical insights suggest, then, that the story of global finance is not just a discrete tale of what is happening 'out there' and its consequences for states and societies. Rather, contemporary transformations in social relations and practices of the everyday are important constitutive features of global finance. The emergence of global finance has been 'lived' in the changing experiences of everyday credit practices. I explore this below with reference to disintermediation, a dynamic of qualitative change that is widely recognized to be central to the emergence of global finance.[5]

Disintermediation

'Disintermediation' is a change in the predominant forms of the credit instruments employed that is commonly identified as a significant feature of global finance. Since the Latin American debt crisis of the early 1980s in particular, the provision of credit to sovereign and corporate borrowers has been subject to 'disintermediation' (International Monetary Fund 1998a: Annex V). As the name suggests, disintermediation involves a shift from the directly intermediated creation of credit primarily in the form of bank loans to the more indirectly intermediated issuing of capital and equity market instruments. The sheer volume of disintermediated credit instruments dwarfs bank loans. Closely intertwined with disintermediation is 'securitization', that is, the 'bundling', pricing, and secondary trading of formerly illiquid claims and obligations arising from the creation of credit. The focus for securitization has been the displacement of the risks arising from outstanding claims and obligations, including exchange rate, interest rate and credit risks. Global finance has witnessed a rapid increase in practices that seek the displacement of such risks by hedging price fluctuations, utilizing an ever-widening range of derivatives instruments.

The emergence of the new world of disintermediated global finance has entailed important but uneven, unequal and incomplete changes in everyday saving and borrowing practices. The saving and borrowing practices of the superincluded in Anglo-Saxon state–societies have, in particular, undergone considerable restructuring that is an essential constitutive element in disintermediation. The saving practices of these groups increasingly circumvent the traditional intermediation role of commercial banks and provide for the ever larger amounts of accumulated capital that are the material basis for disintermediated credit creation. For example, by the late 1990s, over 50 per cent of US households held stocks as a result of one set of practices or another, up from 25 per cent in 1987 and only 3 per cent prior to the Wall Street Crash of 1929 (Harmes 2001b: 103). Two broad restructuring trends in saving practices are most significant. First, since the early 1980s mutual funds (unit trusts in the UK) that are invested in the capital and equity markets have tended to become a substitute for saving practices that formerly utilized high-interest bank accounts. 'Non-banks', such as retailers and corporations, have acted as high street and 'virtual' internet outlets for mutual funds, thereby encouraging this trend. According to Clayton (2000: 15), the assets of mutual funds in the US where this trend is most pronounced are now greater than those of US banks.

Second, since the economic crisis of early 1970s and the associated attack on the welfare state, occupational pension practices have come to play an increasingly central role in saving for retirement. In Gordon Clark's (2000: 17) terms, occupational pensions are 'eclipsing all other forms of private savings, and transforming the nature and structure of global financial markets'. He calls this the emergence of 'pension fund capitalism'. It has been estimated that pension funds held investment assets (stocks, shares, bonds, cash and property) to the value of $13,000 billion in 1999. Around 60 per cent of these assets or $7,800 billion were held for US policy holders, with those of Japanese policy holders worth $1,500 billion and UK policy holders $1,400 billion (Blackburn 2002: 6). To give this some perspective, according to OECD figures world GNP stands at $28,000 billion and the world-wide value of stock markets at $23,000 billion.

The constitutive importance of everyday practices to disintermediated and securitized global finance has not been limited to the savings side. Recent expansions in mortgage and consumer credit have both directly and indirectly enabled and been facilitated by disintermediation and securitization. In the US, securitized bonds derived from everyday borrowing have become a key growth area. While the value of bonds issued by US corporations grew from 13 per cent of GDP in 1980 to 18 per cent by 1997 and issues by financial firms rose from 3 per cent of GDP to 17 per cent over the same period, the growth in the value of issues of so-called asset-backed securities (credit card receivables and mortgages repackaged as bonds) climbed from non-existence in 1983 to 9 per cent of GDP by 1997 (Henwood 1998: 27). More indirectly, and given the intensified relations between everyday saving practices and global finance, rising stock markets across the G7 (except Japan) during the 1990s contributed to a sense of well-being that manifested itself in a borrowing binge. Across the G7 states, household liabilities as a percentage of household income rose from 53 per cent in 1985 to 74 per cent in 1996 (Clayton 2000: x). The 'average' American had eleven credit cards in 1999, up from seven in 1989 (Clayton 2000: 90). Whilst stock markets continued to rise, this level of outstanding obligations seemed sustainable and unproblematic.

The restructuring of the everyday credit practices of the superincluded has also been a constitutive feature in the re-articulation of risk that lies at the heart of the disintermediation trend. Under intermediated credit creation, the risks of a default on outstanding obligations by a borrower are, for instance, borne by the bank as maker of a loan. In contrast, under disintermediated relations, risks of a default or downturn are borne by investors as holders of the securities issued, not by the bank that arranges the issue. Recent changes in pension practices are particularly illustrative of the everyday dynamics of change (Harmes 2001b: 105–8; Cutler and Waine 2001). In broad terms, the decay of state-based 'pay as you go' (PAYG) pensions, whereby income is transferred from current workers to pensioners via taxation, is the erosion of a collectivist approach to the risks of saving for old age. More specifically, occupational pensions practices in the US and the UK have shifted since the 1980s and mid-1990s respectively away from defined-benefit or 'final salary' schemes to defined-contribution schemes. Under the former, risks were held by the employer as the value of a pension was predetermined and guaranteed regardless of the fund's performance. Under the latter, the value of a pension reflects the market value of the fund's investments at the time of retirement. The risks of saving for old age are individualized and held by the employee. At the same time, this individualization of risk feeds a generalization of risk in the sense that the collective fate of those nearing retirement becomes increasingly tied to the performance of disintermediated global finance.

Rethinking global financial governance

In this final section of the chapter I reflect upon the extent to which revaluing the everyday life of global finance has considerable implications for how IPE scholars understand global financial governance. As noted above, a particular account of governance tends to follow from the dominant representation of global finance as a bounded and differentiated space 'out there'. Global financial governance becomes limited to the institutions and agents of what I have called transnational multilateralism, to those governors who inhabit the discrete and deterritorialized space of global finance. Once we begin to recognize the significance of the restructuring of everyday practices to global finance and thereby begin to transcend the imaginary boundaries erected by the dominant representation of space, an understanding of governance is suggested that moves beyond an exclusive focus on transnational institutions and elites. The dynamics of governance extend through the everyday 'level' of global finance.

Multi-level governance (MLG) theory does much to draw attention to governance arrangements that span, cut across and overlap with the state. As such, the central kernel of MLG theory is suggestive of the flowering of an understanding of global financial governance that moves beyond transnational elites. In particular, it potentially draws attention to the very network qualities of global financial governance – collaboration without centralization, the complexity of dynamic interactions between interconnected and interdependent institutional and spatial nodes, a pattern of inclusion/exclusion, the prevalence of expert systems, and the integrative and communicative significance of a shared discourse (cf. Castells 1996: 61–2, 470–1) – that are largely overlooked by IPE commentators. Ultimately, however, the tendency in MLG theory to simply equate each 'level' that it considers with a discrete but interlinked set of institutions ensures that MLG theory, as it is presently constituted, simultaneously closes down some of the potentially fruitful avenues for inquiry that it opens up. The sets of authority relations that comprise governance networks may be more or less institutionalized, both formal and informal. The formal institutional face of global financial governance has been reasonably well explored by IPE scholars, and this work is taken further in this volume through MLG theory. What has been largely neglected to date, then, is the explicit incorporation of the informal or discursive face of the network into conceptualizations of global financial governance. A nuanced conceptualization of the authority relations of governance requires that discursive and institutional dynamics are recognized and combined. Discursive or 'epistemic authority' is found in the innumerable mechanisms that mould understandings of credit practices around prevailing norms, values and meanings as 'organizational principles' (Hewson and Sinclair 1999b: 10, 4). Organizational principles are important in terms of governance in the sense that they constitute shared meanings that become inherent in the social practices that they inform.

The significance of neo-liberal ideology to global finance is widely acknowledged in IPE research (e.g. Soederberg 2001b). What seems clear is that, while the appeal to reasoned and rational financial criteria has always been central in modern world finance, in the current neo-liberal era other forms of (e)valuation become de-legitimated to an unprecedented extent (de Goede 2001). The significance of neo-liberalism in the global financial order does not lie in its claimed capacity to describe and inform rational and objective credit practices. Instead, it provides a governance discourse to legitimate inherently subjective credit practices that are organized through hierarchical market institutional networks by reifying the façade of the market mechanism. Neo-liberal organizational principles of governance draw upon foundational beliefs in the role of the market mechanism as the fair and rational arbiter in society. Particularly as a consequence of the claims to universalism by neo-liberalism, made on the basis of assumptions about human nature, market institutions are deemed apolitical and become 'naturally' the only appropriate institutional loci for governance. Institutionalized practices take on a legitimate form once they are framed by market signals. The neo-liberal discourse also has implications for the orientation of the institutions of governance more broadly. For instance, within state institutions, practices become organized less according to bureaucratic professionalism and more according to a new public managerialism such that social and political issues become procedural matters, that is, matters to be managed. Amongst other changes, this manifests itself, for example, in the drive to render central banks 'independent' from government and politicians (see Baker, Chapter 6 of this volume).

The explicit incorporation of neo-liberalism into an account of global financial governance raises question-marks over the tendency in IPE to focus exclusively on transnational multilateralism. Conceptualized as an ideology, neo-liberalism becomes viewed as propagated by the elite 'epistemic communities' of transnational multilateralism centred, for instance, on the Bank of International Settlements (Kapstein 1994) and the G7 states (Soederberg 2001b). Once neoliberalism is conceptualized as dominant in the discursive face of contemporary authority relations, however, the problematic separation of the transnational multilateral 'governors' from the 'governed' comes into view. The (neo-liberal) governing principles inherent in those practices that create, allocate, buy, sell, regulate and restrict credit are not necessarily institutionally- or spatially-bounded, or propagated from 'out there'. As Robert Latham's (1999) illuminating work reminds us, IPE research into global financial governance tends to take the meaning of 'governance' for granted as 'what decision makers, administrators, or steering committees generate as they manage or administer the activities of their organizations or those of the people and things for which they assume responsibility' (p. 49). Such common sense arises, at least in part, from the treatment of 'governance' as an object of analysis rather than a theoretical concept (see Hudson, Chapter 4 of this volume). However, as Hewson and Sinclair (1999b: 7) have it, '[t]he global governance concept does not refer to any distinct sphere or level of global life. It is not monopolized in any special organizations.' They continue, suggesting that the

> ... most pervasive of all sorts of global governance emerges as if from the bottom up, from the increasing skills and capacities of individuals and from their altering horizons of identification in patterns of 'global life'. .... globalization is not just extensive, forming interconnections across space, but also intensive, reaching into the level of personal conduct ...
>
> (Hewson and Sinclair 1999b: 6–7)

Put differently, and following Palan (1999), what IPE scholars tend to label global financial governance (i.e. the institutions of transnational multilateralism) already and at once assumes and constructs the identity of the community that is to be governed.

Disintermediation, by way of example, has entailed an important shift in the predominant self-representation of everyday financial identity from 'the saver' to 'the investor'. The largely passive image of everyday saving and borrowing associated with intermediated finance has become increasingly challenged by the image of the active financial investor and consumer who engages with the disintermediated securities market. Savers entrust investment decisions to banks that hold their money, accepting that their collective savings became the basis for investment in the economy. Investors, meanwhile, make their own decisions as to, for instance, their choice of mutual fund, and the economy becomes the source of returns on their investments. The meaning of everyday saving/ investing practices in the economy is transformed and effectively turned on its head. This is supported by the information supplied by the growth of a specialized financial media, including the press and a range of dedicated websites, that in neo-liberal terms renders the disintermediated market transparent to the investor (cf. Leyshon *et al.* 1998). At its most extreme, this shift in financial identity is associated with the mythic profile of the so-called 'day trader' who, by virtue of the access to market information that is enabled by advances in information and communications technologies, can compete on a 'level playing-field' with the major financial institutions.

Foucauldians such as Aitken (2002) have begun the work to trace the legitimation and embedding of the identity of 'the investor' as a crucial feature of neo-liberal governmentality. Governmentality, as Foucault termed it, is 'the ensemble formed by the institutions, procedures, analyses and reflections, the calculations and tactics, that allow the exercise of this very specific albeit complex form of power, which has as its target population ... apparatuses of security' (1979: 20). The act of government, then, is not something simply undertaken by institutions and individuals holding authority over society. Rather, governmentality permits government from a distance, and thereby directly addresses the separation of 'governors' from 'governed' that is present in the vast majority of IPE accounts of global financial governance. As Dean (1999) identifies, the concept of governmentality is of particular utility in that (neo)liberal modes of government entail simultaneous attempts to respect the formal autonomy of rational subjects and govern within and through those autonomous actions. For Aitken (2002), then, neo-liberal governing principles that circulate in particular through media advertising are transforming the commitments of everyday actors as they self-govern their financial lives. More specifically, he argues that neo-liberalism has sought to overcome 'prudential masculinity'. This is one particular form of 'ethical' and masculinized financial identity and practice that, throughout the nineteenth and much of the twentieth century, has encouraged thrifty saving as an obligation to the household. In our terms, under neo-liberalism it is as an investor and not as a saver that individuals – especially male white individuals from the middle and upper echelons of Anglo-Saxon societies – are re-formulating their financial identities and practices.

Contemporary self-government by what we might call 'good financial citizens' is not limited to the saving/investment side of everyday credit practices. Disintermediated global finance has coincided with the intensification of a set of longer-standing developments in consumer credit practices. The recent boom in consumer borrowing across the G7 state–societies is typically viewed as entailing a further erosion of the virtues of Puritan thrift that first began to take hold in 1920s America (e.g. Tucker 1991; Clayton 2000). Here a further step-wise expansion in the hedonistic culture of consumption is blamed for the current borrowing binge, as individuals appear to have escaped from economic discipline. Such an interpretation sits uneasily with Gill's (1997b) work on the disciplinary features of consumer credit relations. He highlights that consumer credit practices have become subject to increased surveillance by networks of credit rating and marketing organizations that – as supermarkets, high street stores and specialist firms displace commercial banks in the provision of consumer credit – monitor, record, sort and evaluate their (electronic) traces.

Calder's (1999) inspirational analysis of the history of US consumer credit effectively builds on Gill's (1997b) intervention, furthering our understanding of everyday global financial governance. For Calder, the 'myth of lost economic virtue' (pp. 23–6) has reappeared during each period of rapid growth in consumer credit since the 1920s. Just as the 1920s and 1950s were characterized by fondness for the thriftiness of the late nineteenth century and 1930s respectively, so the contemporary era is marked by more than a backward glance to the post-war 'golden age' of Fordism. Calder couples his critical investigation of the myth of lost economic virtue with what he calls 'the myth of easy payments' (pp. 28–33), that is, the assumption that consumption on credit (as opposed to through saving) is an undemanding option. As he puts it,

> ... consumer credit has done for personal money management what Frederick W. Taylor's scientific management theories did for work routines in the factory. It has imposed strict, exogenous disciplines of money management on consumers ... Because 'easy payments' turned out to be not so easy – work and discipline were required to pay for them – consumer credit made ... the culture of consumption less a playground for hedonists than an extension of Max Weber's 'iron cage' of disciplined rationality.
>
> (Calder 1999: 28–9)

Obligations and repayments arising from consumer credit relations and practices ensure that consumption is necessarily 'disciplined hedonism' (Calder 1999: 31). Consider, for instance, the trials and tribulations detailed by Gill (1997b) of the North American consumer who seeks to re-establish his credit rating. Everyday self-government by the good financial citizen combines, then, the practices and identities of the investor and those of the disciplined borrower.

Concluding remarks

My starting point in this chapter was the contention that global finance is typically represented as a space unto itself, 'out there' somewhere and bounded from our everyday lives. I have highlighted the manner in which popular dichotomies drawn between the financial/'real' economies and the global/national economies are central to this representation. Significantly, the dichotomies are present in both neo-liberalism as the dominant mode of knowledge of global finance and in IPE accounts. The story of the emergence of global finance as a discrete tale of what is happening 'out there' was subsequently challenged. The restructuring of everyday credit practices has featured strongly in qualitative changes, such as disintermediation, that we associate with global finance. The explicit recognition that the emergence of global finance has been 'lived' in the changing everyday experiences of the superincluded in Anglo-Saxon state–societies has significant implications for IPE inquiry (Langley 2002b), not least for how global financial governance is understood.

Accounts of global financial governance in the IPE literature by and large follow from and further the dominant representation of the social space of global finance. Once global finance is imagined as bounded and differentiated 'out there', governance tends to be viewed as the preserve of the institutions and elites of what I have called 'transnational multilateralism'. After all, it is these governors who populate the discrete and deterritorialized space of global finance. However, once we revalue everyday life in our understanding of global finance and thereby begin to transcend the imaginary boundaries erected through the dichotomies that sustain the dominant representation of space, current IPE accounts of governance become inadequate. Features of governance that extend through the everyday 'level' of global finance appear worthy of further exploration. Conceptualized not as an ideology but as the discursive face of authority relations, neo-liberalism is less the preserve of the institutionally- and spatially-bounded governors 'out there', and more a set of organizational principles that become inherent in credit practices themselves. Indeed, neo-liberal principles can be seen as central to the discursive framing of a contemporary transformation in the identities and practices of everyday actors as they self-govern their financial lives. The everyday making of the identities and practices of the rational good financial citizen, the investor and disciplined borrower – prioritized and naturalized in the neo-liberal discourse – is, then, crucial to global financial governance.

Notes

1 Some notable exceptions in IPE include Adam Harmes (1998; 2001b), Stephen Gill (1997b) and Richard Minns (1996).
2 As highlighted by recent critique of these assumptions – see Martin (1999b) on the 'new geographical economics'.
3 This line of reasoning also draws upon a body of work concerned more broadly with overcoming the territorialist assumptions of IR (cf. Agnew and Corbridge 1995).
4 A focus on the everyday credit practices of those excluded from global credit relations in Anglo-Saxon state–societies would lead to a concern with, for instance, family networks, loan sharks, catalogue shopping, pawn-broking, money shops, and the risk assessment practices of commercial banks that manifest themselves in exclusion from all but the most basic financial services.
5 Elsewhere I have explored the constitutive importance of the restructuring of everyday credit practices to other qualitative changes (liberalization and financialization) that are widely regarded as crucial to the emergence of global finance (Langley 2002b).

6 The three-dimensional governance of macroeconomic policy in the advanced capitalist world

Andrew Baker[1]

Growing economic interdependence between states during the 1970s and 1980s meant that macroeconomic policy famously came to be conceived of as a two-level game, in which policy-makers had simultaneously to reconcile competing domestic and international pressures (Putnam 1988; Putnam and Henning 1989; Dyson 1994). While this two-level game metaphor may have captured the realities of intensifying interdependence, the intensification of large-scale instantaneous transborder financial transactions (often referred to as financial globalization) altered policy-makers' perceptions of macroeconomic policy and ultimately the macroeconomic governance process itself. Globalization is increasingly viewed as a re-configuration of social space (Scholte 2000). Such a view of globalization highlights the inadequacies of thinking solely in terms of the national–international intertwinements that are characteristic of interdependence (Cerny 1996). In this chapter I argue that, even in an area such as macroeconomic policy, which is still predominantly conducted at the national level, we need analytical frameworks that can grapple with the new geography of globalization and go beyond national–international interconnections to consider how transborder networks and social spaces overlay and intersect with traditional domestic and international levels of policy-making activity. The chapter makes the case for a modified and adjusted version of multi-level governance as such a framework.

During the 1990s macroeconomic policy was increasingly shaped by policy-makers' quest for 'credibility' with international investors. Most of the economics literature argues that macroeconomic credibility is enhanced by greater transparency (Balls 1998). The pursuit of macroeconomic credibility through greater transparency involves the social construction of an observable pattern of three-dimensional governance – consisting of three-way interactions between multilateral norms and exchanges, domestic policy-making, and scrutiny by a dispersed but globally networked audience of investors. These three-way interactions have in turn disciplined and restricted macroeconomic policy outcomes for most of the last decade. They have also produced, reinforced and maintained domestic macroeconomic institutional arrangements involving independent central banks with price stability mandates and fiscal rules that place limits on the size of fiscal deficits and state borrowing.

Three-dimensional governance is an observable pattern of interactive governance, but it can also be used as an analytical framework, albeit a simplified one, to explain the operation of macroeconomic governance across the G7, enabling us to understand where authority and influence is located in macroeconomic policy, and how these patterns of authority and influence are sustained through a series of politically constructed complex interactive social relationships. The response of policy-makers to market scrutiny, which in turn is aided by processes of multilateral surveillance, has been to represent and institutionalize the collective priorities of financial markets in domestic macroeconomic policy-making arrangements, while circumventing and largely ignoring the preferences of a broader range of domestic societal interests. Policy-makers have set specific targets for macroeconomic policy – inflation targets in monetary policy and deficit reduction or public borrowing targets in fiscal policy – as a means of signifying their good intentions to international investors, while conforming with accepted multilateral norms and notions of macroeconomic best practice. The net result of these moves has been the promotion of macroeconomic policy as a narrow technical matter revolving around the realization of stated and incontestable objectives, thus enhancing the authority of technocrats in finance ministries and central banks and insulating macroeconomic policy from wider political contestation. Yet macroeconomic policy debates are increasingly conducted on the terms and imperatives of financial markets, rather than those of a wider cross-section of society, and this itself is an inherently political state of affairs, sustained by political choices and political and social relationships.

This chapter begins with a discussion of how a modified version of the concept of multi-level governance can be usefully applied to macroeconomic policy. Three adjustments, or improvements, to the existing literature on multi-level governance are suggested. Then the concept of three-dimensional governance is introduced and its merits are discussed. The chapter goes on to discuss the variables evident in the three relevant spatial dimensions and how they interrelate to one another. There is also a demonstration of how three-dimensional macroeconomic governance operates in practice through a case study of the new multilateral codes of practice on monetary and fiscal policy, which effectively represent an institutionalization of the pattern of three-dimensional macroeconomic governance and the privileging of narrow conceptions of technical competence and authority over democratically responsive policy-making. The final part of the chapter introduces the notion of US exceptionalism in the context of three-dimensional governance. The conclusion summarizes the arguments of the chapter and considers their implications for issues of power, authority and democracy, arguing that macroeconomic policy has become more responsive to the views of non-citizens – foreign exchange traders, market analysts and the consensual views held by multilateral institutions and other finance ministries and central banks – than the democratically expressed preferences of citizens.

Three problems with multi-level governance

The literature on multi-level governance has identified the existence of overlapping competencies among multiple levels of governance activity and has examined the interactions of political actors across these 'levels' (Marks *et al.* 1996c). In one sense, therefore, multi-level governance is simply an expression of the increasingly diffuse and complex governance processes that are emerging in a more inter-connected and globalized world. As macroeconomic governance increasingly involves multilateral and transnational market scrutiny of national policies, multi-level governance, with its basic premise that it is possible to gain insights into policy processes by examining interaction between discrete social spaces, can be usefully applied to macroeconomic policy. However, first several adjustments or refinements need to be made to the existing literature.

First, multi-level governance has a predominantly descriptive character. There is a distinct absence of hypotheses emerging from the existing literature and there has been confusion over whether MLG is an object of analysis or a source of explanation (Buzan 1995). In its current applications the literature has said very little about the question of whose interests are served by various policy decisions, or how those interests sustain their dominant position in a given policy area.[2] There is also a conspicuous silence in the existing MLG literature on prescriptive and normative issues concerning the desirability of various types of multi-level governance, what multi-level governance does mean and should mean for democracy. This chapter intends to take some steps towards addressing these gaps. Multi-level governance does provide the opportunity to examine interactions between various discrete arenas and systems of social interaction without any preconceived assumptions or one-way determinism. It also offers the potential for analysis of the interactions between different forces, such as institutions, domestic interests, shared elite ideas and transnational structures.[3] Multi-levelled frameworks can consequently be used to identify relevant variables at different levels, structuring exploration of the interconnections between these variables, enabling us to achieve a better understanding of what drives a particular policy and the implication of this for patterns of authority and democratic governance.

The second shortcoming in existing notions of MLG is that they have viewed authority as something residing solely with public national, international, supranational or transgovernmental institutions. Yet a growing literature in IPE has pinpointed that international affairs is being characterized by a rise in private authority (Hall and Biersteker 2002; Higgott *et al.* 2000; Cutler *et al.* 1999; Strange 1996.) Multi-level governance has until now failed to factor in the private sphere, or market structures into multi-levelled frameworks and has therefore neglected the impact and power of markets as private decision-making arenas in their own right, including the characteristics these markets may possess and whether they have a structural impact on macroeconomic affairs (see chapters by Woodward and Hudson in this volume; Strange 1994; Webb 1991; Andrews 1994). Yet there is a well established tradition in the study of political economy that covers a range of perspectives, from the French physiocrats through to the work of Adam Smith, Karl Marx and Karl Polanyi, which has highlighted the importance of treating markets as arenas of governance and decision-making arenas in their own right (Underhill 2000). Moreover, financial markets increasingly transcend political frontiers and are defined by the extensity of the transactions and network relationships involved (spaces of flows). State territoriality is overlain by functional, sectional and socially oriented spatial forms. Macroeconomic policy, for example, has begun to revolve around a series of implicit and explicit communications with the de-territorialized spatial forms that are globally networked financial markets. If it is to realize its potential, therefore, MLG needs to loosen its fascination with, and attachment to, public authority and develop alternative understandings of geography that do not take the state, or the notions of territoriality associated with it, as their starting point or central coordinate. For example, Jan Aart Scholte has claimed that globalization is really a geographical term referring to a reconfiguration of space (Scholte 2000). Multi-level governance as a concept needs to come to terms with a new geographical reality that decision-making arenas and systems of social and political interaction are no longer defined solely by conventional senses of territory or space. Rather, we have seen the emergence of cross-border, transnational or de-territorialized social spaces that interact with traditional domestic (state–society) and international (interstate) levels in complex cross-cutting ways. Consequently, a conventional understanding of 'levels' as discrete hierarchically layered public spaces with pre-defined legal and institutional relationships is inadequate. If MLG is really to come to terms with contemporary governance processes it needs to be sensitive to the fluidity, complexity, interconnectedness and even informality of many of these governance processes and a range of spatial scales and forms.

The third problem that needs to be addressed concerns the language connected with multi-level governance and use of the term 'level'. Notably, the whole concept of a 'level' suffers from a boundary problem in the sense that it is susceptible to the allegation that it simply divides subject matter into convenient boxes (Amin and Palan 2001). The term 'multi-level' can be suggestive of some sort of club sandwich or multi-storey type of arrangement, with one level at the top, one level at the bottom, and subsequent levels in between. It can also construe hierarchy in both an empirical and an analytical sense. Empirically, 'level' can be suggestive of some sort of vertically ordered hierarchical command structure. Likewise, in an analytical sense, the whole notion of a 'level' might encourage the researcher to attribute primacy to one particular 'level'. Yet if we accept that globalization implies fluidity and interconnectedness as defining features of contemporary political economy, what Richard Woodward in this volume refers to as 'spaces of flows', that co-exist with more traditional 'spaces of places', we need a term that is more flexible, more sensitive to fluidity and to the array of spatial forms that comprise the current international political economy. For these reasons the term 'level' is dropped in favour of the term 'dimension' throughout the rest of this chapter, precisely because the latter construes a sense of interlocking, overlapping and inter-related spaces. In this respect, while financial markets can be viewed as distinct systems of social interaction (see Hudson, Chapter 5 this volume), it is not self evident that they comprise a level comparable to conventional domestic and international levels of analysis.

The notion of a dimension as a discrete, socially constructed space liberates us from this rigid attachment to 'levels' and the neo-realist ontology that underpins such an attachment. It also enables us to come to terms with the interconnectedness, fluidity and complexity of many contemporary governance processes and reflect the realities of the multiple interactions that characterize governance in a globalized world.

Multi-dimensional diplomacy, states and markets

In this chapter, the term 'dimension' will be used to refer to a specific locational or socially constructed space, which has its own distinct dynamic or logic. A dimension is constituted by a series of interactions between actors within specific locational parameters. In other words, a dimension is an identifiable series of interactions, deliberations and communications between actors that are clustered around specific 'focal points' or coordinating mechanisms, such as the state, a specific multilateral process, or even a particular marketplace. Understanding patterns of governance and policy-making requires that relevant locations/settings/dimensions and the variables and interactions specific to each 'dimension' are identified, followed by an examination of the interconnections between the various 'dimensions'.

Some of the more interesting contributions in IPE have noted the importance of abandoning notions of markets and political authorities as opposing logics, and thinking of them as part of the same integrated ensemble of governance – what Geoffrey Underhill has called a state–market *condominium* (Underhill 2000a; Strange 1971; Palan 2000; Amin and Palan 2001). Yet how do we integrate the market into analytical frameworks that can be applied to important empirical questions? Market interests obviously pursue their goals through national policy processes – the tradition IR question of how the national interest is arrived at, or, more specifically, in whose interest? But crucially, both in the popular imagination and in the imagination of policy-makers, markets such as the foreign exchange market are increasingly global in scope, operating as global cross-border spaces. The foreign exchange market, for example, simultaneously intersects with and exists within state territories, but it also operates outside of and beyond state territoriality through a series of computer networks and terminals that connect distant geographical locations and give the market a distinct dynamic as a form of social organization that cannot necessarily by captured by the conventional use of the term 'level'. Moreover, authorities increasingly communicate with this market on a range of macroeconomic matters, most especially exchange rate valuations, as if they were speaking to a world-wide audience of investors (i.e. the foreign exchange market as a single unified system) rather than operating through solely national channels. Likewise, market operators and analysts located in world financial centres express views about the future course of policy in terms of general market sentiment, and attempt to influence policy-makers' future decisions.

The three spatial dimensions of macroeconomic governance

In the making of macroeconomic policy – monetary, fiscal and exchange rate policy – finance ministries and central banks communicate with one other, with other domestic actors and interests, and with market operators. These multiple interactions are not straightforward, although analysis of them can be aided by creating a classificatory schema or analytical framework. Three dimensions or distinct social spaces relevant to the formulation of macroeconomic and exchange rate policy can be identified. Some of what follows takes Robert Putnam's earlier work on two-level games, which provided a framework for analysing the linkages betwen domestic politics and intergovermental bargaining, as a starting point (Putnam 1988).

Dimension I: multilateralism

Level I in Robert Putnam's two-level game model refers to interaction between national delegates in a multilateral setting, in which three or more states interact with one another in accordance with certain shared principles (Ruggie 1992; Cerny 1993: 30–3.) State–state or multilateral interactions take place in different settings and are shaped by different norms that give most multilateral processes their own distinct logic. Since the 1970s macroeconomic surveillance has become progressively institutionalized in a number of settings and the norms and social practices associated with this process play a key role in setting parameters for macroeconomic policy in the industrialized world. Dimension I variables are therefore those features specific to a particular multilateral process that give it a particular character and help to shape its relations with other dimensions, although the relationship will not be entirely one-way, as Dimension I variables will almost inevitably be shaped by variables in other dimensions.

Dimension II: the state and domestic politics

Level II in the two-level game model refers to domestic politics (Putnam 1988). Similarly, Dimension II here represents domestic state–society relations. Domestic politics remains central to macroeconomic policy because national (and macro-regional) central banks and national finance ministries continue to have responsibility for monetary, fiscal and exchange rate policies and have distinct national/macroregional mandates.[4] Domestic preferences and coalitions and domestic institutional arrangements, mandates and decision-making processes are key Dimension II variables. In a form of two-way second-dimensional diplomacy we can expect domestic interests to try to influence the agendas and priorities of macroeconomic policy-makers, in both the domestic and multilateral settings, while policy-makers will often use their multilateral meetings to produce collective statements and consensual positions designed to augment national policies and shape the expectations of national electorates and other bureaucracies in a form of transgovernmentalism (Keohane and Nye 1974).

Dimension III: networks of global investors and the foreign exchange market

Dimension III consists of the space occupied by networked financial markets. Most prominent here is the foreign exchange market as a transnational network that spans countries, continents and time zones. Financial markets increasingly operate as de-territorialized spaces operating across time zones 24 hours a day, in the context of what Richard Woodward refers to as spaces of flows (Cohen 1998; Leyshon and Thrift 1997; Martin 1999). This third dimension is also compatible with what Cerny refers to as a functional category – a distinct type of interaction that cuts across structural levels (Dimensions I and II outlined above) (Cerny 1993).

Dimension III variables in this instance are those features, which give a particular financial market a particular character and which determine its relations with other financial markets and with the state. They include the interactions between and the social practices and norms of traders, the process through which traders reach decisions on what to buy and sell, the role of any particular reserve currency, the infrastructure that enables the market to function, the volume of trades taking place in the market, the speed at which trades take place, the way in which this affects prices in a given market, and most crucially the channels of communication which enable the market to function and exert influence (see Hudson, Chapter 5 of this volume). Financial markets can consequently be seen as being constituted and reproduced by a series of social relations and practices (see Hudson and Langley, Chapters 4 and 5 of this volume respectively; Sinclair 1994; Harmes 1998).

The operation of three-dimensional governance

First-dimensional diplomacy: multilateral surveillance, elite social practices and shared normative and causal beliefs

Possibly the most significant feature of multilateral relations between G7 finance ministries and central banks over the last decade has been the existence of a shared, loose, multilateral consensus. This consensus is not a new or sudden creation, but has been evolving since the US government initiated the demise of the Bretton Woods exchange rate system and financial liberalization, and the subsequent failure of Keynesian reflationary macroeconomic strategies, most notably in France and the UK. By the 1990s the consensus had evolved to the point where it had five notable components. First, the delivery of low inflation was the principal objective of macroeconomic policy and continues to be seen as a prerequisite for economic growth. Second, central bank independence became accepted as the most reliable institutional fix for delivering low inflation. The thinking behind this was that central banks consisting of professional monetary economists (independent technocrats) were much less likely to be swayed by political considerations in making interest rate decisions, or to 'cheat' and dash for growth ahead of elections (Balls 1998; Alesina and Summers 1990). Third, it was accepted that monetary policy (interest rate policy) was most effective if it was used to target a measure of domestic (usually some sort of consumer index) prices, or a national inflation target. Fourth, fiscal consolidation and deficit reduction efforts were seen to contribute to economic expansion by reducing government debt, contributing to lower long-term interest rates and reducing government interest payments, freeing expenditure up for more productive uses. During the 1990s there were a number of attempts to introduce legal frameworks and legislation designed to stabilize debt-to-GDP ratios and limit the size of deficits any incoming government could run up. Finally, there is a view that exchange rates should reflect underlying domestic economic fundamentals and are something best determined by the market. The three major currencies in the international monetary system – the yen, the euro and the dollar – are left to float against one another, and the question of the most appropriate exchange rate is seen by officials as something that changes on a daily or even hourly basis.[5] In this context, exchange rates effectively represent the market's collective verdict on the performance of a particular national economy and the success of domestic monetary and fiscal policies. In other words, the current approach to exchange rates is an effective invitation for market operators to engage in a continuous ongoing referendum on national monetary and fiscal policies and the performance of national economies by buying and selling national currencies accordingly.

These broad beliefs have informed a multilateral surveillance exercise between the leading capitalist states which has set the parameters for the conduct of macroeconomic policy and monetary relations between these states over the last two or three decades. Multilateral surveillance consists of a series of frank and candid exchanges whereby national authorities expose their policies to collective scrutiny and comments (Wicks 1994). The surveillance exercise between the G7 countries is chaired by the managing director of the IMF, with the Fund reaching an independent view on each country. The world economic outlook is assessed, and comment is passed on individual national policies and economic conditions, by each participating country.

Surveillance has four principal purposes. First, it has the character of a form of peer review. It is intended to provide disincentives for countries to pursue reckless inflationary monetary and fiscal policies, by subjecting countries following such policies to peer criticism, although this does not preclude a collective verdict that a particular state has been pursuing macroeconomic policies that are too restrictive. Second, it is designed to reassure markets by providing an IMF-approved health check of the major economies. It also makes comparative data available on each of these economies, enhancing the information on which market operators can base their decisions. Third, an ongoing review of economic data enables finance ministries and central banks to identify any sustained and pronounced exchange rate misalignments. They can then convey their view that a certain currency is misaligned to the markets and call for a market-initiated correction. Finally, mutual exchanges of information are aimed at enhancing awareness of different national policies, so as to produce more informed and internationally sensitive national policy.[6] According to officials, discussions proceed on the basis of conversations along the lines of 'If you do such-and-such, do you realize the effect this will have on us?'[7]

Concerns over sovereignty and in particular central bank independence tend to prevent authorities from making precise demands of one another's macroeconomic policies in the context of the surveillance exercise.[8] That states do not bargain over, or make specific demands of, their counterparts' macroeconomic policies is widely accepted and indeed, over the last decade, has come to resemble what March and Olsen have termed a 'logic of appropriateness', whereby actors invoke a specific identity and match it to the particular social context they find themselves in, out of a sense of obligation and indeed 'appropriateness' (March and Olsen 1998). General views concerning the overall orientation of policy may be exchanged, but specific demands, or more conventional intergovernmental bargaining over macroeconomic policy, tend to be avoided. Exchanges between finance ministry and central bank officials also tend to have a highly technical character and assume the language of economics and finance, rather than that of politics. Political points are occasionally made but are usually done so within the terms of economic language (Wicks 2002). In this respect, a lot of discussion between the major powers on macroeconomic policy matters follows what Thomas Risse has called the 'logic of arguing', as the aim of discussion is to seek a reasoned consensus that sits comfortably with the technical ideas and causal beliefs the various protagonists hold about monetary and financial governance, while avoiding any serious breach of key domestic or national interests (Risse 2000). This is particularly apparent in the area of exchange rate policy, as the diagnosis and interpretation of exchange rates predominantly involves a process of constructing technical arguments on the basis of analyses of a range of economic data, and sometimes publicly presenting these arguments to the market in the form of collective public statements. While states clearly continue to have political preferences in relation to exchange rates, individual policy-makers know that their credibility, both with their peers and more significantly with the foreign exchange market, will be damaged if they try to advance spurious politically motivated positions without taking into account the economic data and the technical case for a particular exchange rate valuation. Exchange rate policy in particular, therefore, is characterized by an uneasy tension between political motivation and technical considerations.[9]

It is possible to trace the origins of the current macroeconomic regime back to the unilateral decision of the United States to abolish the Bretton Woods exchange rate system and to promote financial liberalization in the early 1970s. By the mid-1970s, despite some initial French opposition, the US had managed to secure a G6 agreement (G7 minus Canada) at head-of-state level (although the detailed work was done by finance ministry officials) for new articles of agreement for the IMF concerning a floating but 'stable' system of exchange rates (Pauly 1997).[10] This system of stable exchange rates was to be maintained by individual countries' efforts to deliver domestic price stability. At the same time, the mandate of the IMF was expanded and renewed so that the institution would exercise 'surveillance' over the international adjustment process. The new Article IV stated that IMF members had an obligation to pursue economic policies conducive to monetary stability as a means of producing exchange rate stability (Pauly 1997). It was believed that international market forces supplemented by peer pressure, exercised through the Fund, would discipline countries and foster domestic conditions conducive to international stability.[11] This process of peer and market scrutiny of national macroeconomic policies is referred to in this chapter as three-dimensional governance.

In short, the three-dimensional governance of macroeconomic policy involves a multilateral agreement between the advanced capitalist states, which lays the basis for an ongoing multilateral surveillance exercise that prioritizes monetary and price stability over other economic objectives, as a route to exchange rate stability. Surveillance consists of peer review, but it is also designed to facilitate enhanced market scrutiny of national policies, so as to create structural pressures on states to deliver domestic macroeconomic discipline. In other words, the obligations of multilateral surveillance also help to set domestic macroeconomic priorities, while the enhanced market scrutiny it facilitates contributes to the institutionalization of macroeconomic policy geared towards price stability.

Not coincidentally, as we shall see, the norms of the surveillance process have had the effect of improving the domestic standing and autonomy of those agencies most immediately involved in the surveillance exercise – finance ministries and central banks – enhancing their capacity to reach decisions on monetary and fiscal policies oriented towards domestic price stability, independently of other domestic agencies and wider societal interests. Far from being inevitable, therefore, the current macroeconomic regime involving independent central banks, fiscal rules, floating exchange rates and liberalized financial flows, has in part been socially and politically constructed by the multilateral decisions, agreements, consensus and social practices of advanced capitalist states (Pauly 1997).

Second-dimensional diplomacy: the de-nationalization of macroeconomic policy and the growing autonomy of finance ministries and central banks

Second-dimensional diplomacy refers to the relationships between the domestic institutions that make macroeconomic policy and participate in the Dimension I surveillance exercise and wider domestic societal interests. Relevant Dimension II variables include the mandates and decision-making procedures of finance ministries and central banks, and the interactions they have with a range of domestic societal interests. The main institutional features of macroeconomic policy in the advanced capitalist world over the last decade have been fiscal rules and independent central banks with inflation targets. Both are justified on the grounds that they enhance policy-makers' credibility with international investors by demonstrating their commitment to the overall delivery of price stability and low inflation, thus providing a reassurance to investors that a particular economy is soundly managed. In this respect prevailing macroeconomic policy-making arrangements reflect a narrow focus for macroeconomic policy and represent an attempt to communicate with and reassure international investors, while practically ignoring the preferences and interests of other domestic social groupings. Central bank independence involves the handing over of responsibility for interest rates to financial and monetary technocrats who are most sensitive to the requirements of money managers, traders and commercial bankers at any given time. This is a conscious political decision to conduct monetary policy that is more sensitive to the needs of the financial sector than to the needs of organized labour, the unemployed or manufacturing industry. Such moves are a demonstration of the structural power of financial markets and their capacity to determine and dictate macroeconomic objectives, albeit with the assistance of sympathetic technocratic elites in finance ministries and central banks (Gill and Law 1989). Trade unions, for example, will typically be more concerned with employment and wage levels than with inflation. Likewise, domestic manufacturers' greatest concern tends to be a competitively valued currency.[12] In other words, the very act of prioritizing inflation in monetary policy, or deficit reduction in fiscal policy, is a political act, simply because it prioritizes the interests of certain social groupings over others (Kirshner 2003). Prioritizing low inflation and institutionalizing it as the principal objective of macroeconomic policy is, as Matthew Watson has commented, 'a signal that a government will defend a social structure of accumulation based on monetary orthodoxy' (Watson 2002: 195) (the promotion of the interests of lenders and investors by placing the protection of the value of money ahead of all other economic and social concerns), and an indication 'that this particular way of organizing society is being constructed and defended against possible re-definition' (Watson 2002: 193).

Paradoxically, despite an increasingly inward-looking focus for macroeconomic policy in terms of national budget deficit and national (or, in the case of the euro, regional currency zone) inflation targets, these moves also represent a kind of de-nationalization of macroeconomic policy because such targets and objectives internalize and institutionalize in domestic institutional orders (Sassen 2002) the preferences of currency traders and international investors, who are most concerned that rising inflation might damage the value of their investments. In the case of macroeconomic policy this has seen finance ministries and central banks gain power relative to other parts of the state apparatus, enhancing their capacity to make decisions independently of other domestic actors. However, the principal constituents of finance ministries and central banks in this process, and the audience they are primarily trying to communicate with, are not domestic interests, but an audience of dispersed global investors. In other words, this process of denationalization involves endogenizing the global agendas of financial markets, particularly the foreign exchange market, in national policy-making processes (Sassen 2002). In this respect, moves to create independent central banks and institutionalize fiscal rules also conform with a widely accepted sense of multilateral best practice in the field of macroeconomic policy. This is the macroeconomic variant of the so-called Washington consensus endorsed by both the IMF and the G7, described earlier in the chapter. Current domestic macroeconomic institutional arrangements are a response to a prevailing international consensus as well as an attempt to communicate with financial markets, as global spaces, by signalling policy-makers' good intentions. In other words, the preferences of actors operating in Dimensions I and III are internalized in domestic Dimension II institutional arrangements, while scrutiny through surveillance also serves to maintain domestic macroeconomic discipline. The result is a series of mutually reinforcing interactive relationships between Dimensions I, II and III in macroeconomic policy that ensures that the current macroeconomic regime hangs together and is sustained as an integrated three-dimensional entity.

The practice of creating independent central banks and institutionalizing fiscal rules has also been referred to by Stephen Gill as a form of new constitutionalism – a legal and political strategy for separating economic forces from broad political accountability and securing management of the economy in the hands of technocrats who are responsive to transnational capital (Gill 1998). This has meant that finance ministries and central banks were much more insulated from societal preferences in the 1990s than they had been in earlier decades. For example, at the beginning of the 1990s only the US and Germany out of the G7 countries had independent central banks.[13] By the end of the decade Canada was the only G7 country without an independent central bank. The ECB has a euro-zone price stability mandate, the Bank of England has an inflation target, as does the Bank of Canada, and all of these central banks are pre-committed to these targets.[14] Similarly, legislation has been introduced to limit the size of budget deficits governments can run up. Increasingly, therefore, technocrats in finance ministries and central banks are able to conduct macroeconomic policy in a societal vacuum in accordance with their own technical concerns and considerations, insulated from political pressures. One of the consequences of this is that the ideas and social practices of elites become more important in determining macroeconomic policy than the demands of key domestic constituents.

To illustrate this further, there has traditionally been a divide between the Anglo-Saxon countries, the US and the UK, and Japan and Germany concerning exchange rate and monetary policy. In the US and the UK an arm's-length relationship between finance and manufacturing, and a well developed internationally active financial sector, resulted in a preference for a stronger currency as a means of protecting British and American investments abroad, as well as the all-important principle of shareholder value (Henning 1994; Dore 2002), whereas in Japan and Germany, close relationships between the banking and manufacturing sectors, evident in cross-shareholding practices, meant that there were strong societal preferences in favour of a competitively valued exchange rate in both countries (Henning 1994). However, it is becoming more difficult to have a proactive exchange rate policy for a number of reasons. First, the rise in the scope and speed of foreign exchange transactions has resulted in policy-makers downgrading foreign exchange market intervention as a policy instrument. As a result of this, and a shared multilateral understanding between the advanced capitalist states that they do not bargain over macroeconomic policies, or attempt to target specific exchange rate valuations for their currencies, any exchange rate policies have to be pursued primarily through declaratory policy. Finally, exchange-rate-attentive interest rate policy is off the agenda in the context of independent central banks with national or macroregional inflation targets. Consequently, the combination of a multilateral consensus, changing domestic/regional institutional monetary arrangements and the increase in private global financial transactions have made it more difficult for Japanese and German policy-makers to pursue a proactive, competitively-valued exchange rate policy, with the effect of circumventing traditionally strong societal preferences for such outcomes in these countries.[15] Therefore, while those who have worked on the politics of exchange rate policy such as Jeffrey Frieden (Frieden 1991) have pointed to increasing politicization as the number of sectional interests affected by and lobbying on exchange rate issues increases in tandem with economic integration, governments are less willing and less able to respond to interest groups' exchange rate demands, as they have increasingly privileged technocratic concerns in the conduct of their monetary and exchange rate affairs and generally appear less willing to contest market-determined outcomes.

Finally, domestic institutional mandates and decision-making procedures also influence the range of possibilities open to actors in a Dimension I setting. For example, it is difficult for central bank governors to bargain over interest rates with their counterparts at G7 meetings, precisely because they are committed to meeting specific national targets and because decisions are made collectively by national governing committees of experts such as the ECB's Governing Council, the US Federal Reserve's Open Market Committee, or the Bank of England's MPC. These national institutional factors reinforce the widely accepted consensual belief that there is little to be gained from coordinating interest rates, or using them to target exchange rates, as well as the accepted social practice that actors at Dimension I meetings should not make specific demands of one another's domestic macroeconomic policies.

Third-dimensional diplomacy: the socially-constructed supremacy of markets and the abdication of public purpose and authority

Third-dimensional diplomacy refers to the state–market interactions that characterize macroeconomic policy,[16] involving markets that operate as globally networked spaces, as if they were located in one place. As Paul Langley (Chapter 5 of this volume) demonstrates, global finance has come to be conceived of in the popular imagination as something that is 'out there', but so too this image of global finance, as an impersonal external force, appears to have permeated the mental maps of macroeconomic policy-makers. Policy-makers increasingly formulate decisions and adjust macroeconomic strategies as a consequence of their informal communications and dialogue with actors in financial markets, which are no longer contained within the territory of the nation-state. Public, but coded, communications are played out on the pages of global newspapers such as the *Financial Times*, which have become central intermediary mechanisms for the conduct of a form of communicative international monetary diplomacy between states and markets. Generally, market spokespeople attempt to articulate the mood of the market as a whole and express views on the implications of this for national policy in a variety of locations, while policy-makers attempt to pre-empt market movements by giving an analysis of prevailing economic conditions and how they think market movements should respond. Market actors are constantly judging what they perceive to be the quality of policy performance in individual economies. They are assisted in this activity by a range of increasingly sophisticated economic data sets and financial commentaries, many of them market-generated, and by private credit and bond rating agencies that similarly reach judgements and provide guidance to market actors on a government's creditworthiness (Sinclair 1994). Financial markets can consequently be viewed as 'a giant voting machine that records in real time, real world evaluations of policy' (Wriston 1998: 340), as operators in financial markets are engaged in a kind of 'perpetual opinion poll' (Cohen 2004b). The significance of this third-dimensional diplomacy[17] between markets and national authorities for macroeconomic policy is that it determines access to foreign credit. Access to private sources of credit enables national authorities to postpone macroeconomic adjustment and to run deficits – what Benjamin Cohen has called the 'power to delay' (Cohen 2004b). If markets reach a negative judgement on an economy, the cessation of lending can precipitate adjustment to address those deficits, through fiscal retrenchment, currency depreciation and/or interest rate adjustments. Ultimately, therefore, market judgements determine a state's 'power to delay' and to exercise macroeconomic freedom.

In one sense, financial globalization is a shorthand expression of the fact that financial flows take off and land at major urban world financial centres, which comprise the hubs of a global network (Budd 1999). Such flows respond to rapidly changing market signals about risk and return. Today's financial markets are characterized by electronic fund transfer systems that allow banks to movecapital around at a moment's notice, arbitraging interest rate differentials, taking advantage of favourable exchange rates and avoiding political unrest. Reuters, with 200,000 interconnected terminals world-wide, accounts for 40 per cent of the world's financial trades each day, through systems such as Instinet and Globex (Kurtzman 1993). Such networks mean that the average trade takes less than twenty-five seconds. Electronic money has therefore created a culture of transacting rather than investing, institutionalizing volatility and wild swings in prices in the process (Warf 1998). This in turn means that fortunes can be won and lost by staying micro-seconds ahead of the rest of the market. In this context information and communication, particularly on macroeconomic data and decisions, becomes all-important because access to important information can bring huge rewards if it is interpreted in a fashion that allows a dealer to predict market movements.

As the economic significance of financial market performance has increased, and global finance has permeated everyday life due to the spread of equity-linked mortgage, pension and investment plans, (Langley, Chapter 5 of this volume), so too has the social basis of central bank independence broadened (Watson 2003). For some observers central bank independence has created a structural dynamic of 'market followership', as central bankers respond to market movements by delivering an interest rate path that financial markets themselves have embedded in asset, or currency price movements (Blinder 1999). Market analysts continually comment and offer opinion on what different financial markets need in terms of interest rate policy. When central banks respond to market consensus, this rather tends to shed doubt over the realities and true extent of their independence, as formal independence from partisan politics and general public opinion does not appear to be accompanied by informal independence from those operating in financial markets (Watson 2002). In other words, the current macroeconomic regime also represents hard political choices as to which accumulation strategies should be prioritized and whose interests should be catered for in macroeconomic policy,[18] as macroeconomic policy is reflecting a trend of financialization and a general shift towards stock market capitalism (Dore 2002).

Moreover, current macroeconomic arrangements are in large part justified and sustained by specific socially constructed state–market relationships. Communications between global financial markets and macroeconomic policy-makers have taken three principal forms, but first we need to appreciate that these three forms of inter-communication are a direct product of the shared consensual beliefs held by finance ministry and central bank elites from leading states about the nature of this third-dimensional space and its organization. First, there is a view that greater capital mobility and increasing integration of world capital markets are good for the world economy and increase overall global welfare (Wicks 1994). Both are believed to lead to a greater realization of the efficiencies available from specialization, from more rapid technology transfer and more productive allocation of resources, from comparative advantage, and from the spur of competition. Second, financial markets are believed to behave rationally and consider all the information available to them, before using that information to maximize expected returns, whilst taking account of risk (Halifax Communiqué 1995). On this basis, macroeconomic policy-makers in the G7 countries expect markets to punish 'bad' policies and reward 'good' domestic policies. 'Therefore, if markets conclude that a country is pursuing poor economic policy they are likely to take their money elsewhere (Halifax Communiqué 1995).' Markets are therefore thought to behave most efficiently when the maximum amount of information is available to them. Third, the G7 finance ministries and central banks acknowledge that markets can occasionally overreact to macroeconomic data and behave in speculative fashion. Sustained exchange rate misalignments brought about by market overreaction are seen to result in resource misallocations both within and between economies. Consequently, finance ministries and central banks from the advanced capitalist states accept their responsibility to minimize such volatility, although their view of the limited utility of sustained public interventions, given the rise in private international capital flows, has meant that increasingly they rely on declaratory policy, or simple vocal persuasion and signalling.

Three basic forms of state–market communication, or what is referred to here as third-dimensional diplomacy, are identifiable in contemporary macroeconomic policy. The first form of communication between states and markets involves an ongoing form of symbolic signalling from states to markets. It is related to the concept of macroeconomic credibility. Credibility is the question of whether authorities' announced intentions are believable, given the dangers of 'time inconsistency', involving policy-makers' failure to keep to stated commitments, particularly in the lead-up to elections. Leading exponents of central bank independence claim that investors are inherently suspicious of authorities' intentions, which means they need to be reassured through institutional arrangements that pre-commit policy-makers to certain objectives such as low inflation, or prescribed limits for fiscal deficits (Balls 1998; King 1997). International investors clearly have an interest in low inflation as it protects the value of their investments. Furthermore, current inflation rates and projected fiscal deficits are also the economic indicators that are most monitored by currency traders, which possibly explains why policy-makers have chosen to target them as a means of maximizing market reassurance (Mosely 1997). Fiscal rules and independent central banks with inflation targets therefore constitute a kind of signalling to financial markets, indicating policy-makers' good long-term intentions to an audience of global investors in a symbolic fashion, by internalizing the interests of these market actors in the domestic macroeconomic policy-making apparatus.

The second form of third-dimensional diplomacy involves efforts to minimize the dangers of time inconsistency and, with it, investors' suspicions about public authorities' macroeconomic intentions. Policy-makers expect markets to react to news in a more rational fashion and revise prices accordingly if the information they receive is more accurate, timely and frequent. Moreover, countries prepared to provide more information about themselves are expected to have a lower risk premium and therefore cheaper access to world capital markets. Better information is believed to reduce the risk that wishful thinking and bandwagon enthusiasm might sustain the unsustainable. This in turn will minimize the intensity and scope of potential financial crises (Halifax Communiqué 1995). It is these beliefs that are at the root of recent G7 efforts to improve the quality of information available to market participants on countries' macroeconomic policies and the state of their financial sectors under the auspices of the banner of 'transparency'. Without such transparency and ready availability of data on the state of a country's public finances, the extent of foreign currency reserves, levels of consumer and corporate debt, balance of payments, national inflation, etc., there is an underlying assumption that financial markets will be prone to disruption, with heightened speculation against the national currency. The real impact of increased 'transparency', therefore, is market actors' enhanced capacity to effectively veto certain national macroeconomic policies, with national authorities being expected to engage in timely data release, so as to prevent unsustainable policies from being hidden from view, or else face market disruption and capital flight.

The third form of third-dimensional diplomacy is an ongoing public and two-way series of coded communications relating specifically to exchange rate valuations. This chapter has already identified how multilateral surveillance attempts to identify sustained and pronounced exchange rate misalignments. When such currency misalignments are identified, G7 policy-makers often move collectively to urge market correction through the issuing of public statements. Market actors, too, publicize their analyses of prevailing economic trends, rationalizing and explaining market movements and thinking, thereby attempting to bring pressure on policy-makers to respond to market movements. The words, analyses and discourses of market watchers (private and public sector), who have over time offered the most convincing interpretations of economic performance and market behaviour, can trigger market movements, giving those individuals a real form of communicative or discursive authority, precisely because the market as a whole moves and responds to their words (Soros 1989; Thrift and Leyshon 1994). As Peter Aykens has pointed out, whether or not an actor possesses authority is primarily a function of whether others believe his/her statements and actions to be truthful and credible, and this in turn means that authority must be continuously nurtured through personal performance (Aykens 2002). The 1990s revealed that, on exchange rate matters, policy-makers are increasingly relying on declaratory policy. This creates a strong disincentive for individual policy-makers to attempt to move exchange rates without a convincing technical case for such a movement. Such action, if repeated, will diminish the technical authority of that individual and possibly of declaratory policy more generally, because markets will simply dismiss the actions of such individuals as being politically motivated, with no foundation in either domestic policy or underlying economic fundamentals. In this respect, operators in financial markets seem increasingly willing to resist policy-makers' attempts at currency manipulation and to dispute their judgement of prevailing economic conditions (Baker forthcoming).

Over the last three decades the G7 countries have increasingly turned their backs on a proactive approach to exchange rates and adopted a reactive stance to market developments. Declaratory policy is the principal defining characteristic of this reactive approach. The G7 have downgraded collective exchange market interventions and exchange-rate-attentive interest rate policy has been rejected, due to their perceptions of the speed and scope of private financial transactions and the rise of independent central banks with inflation targets (second- and third-dimensional variables respectively). Consequently, financial globalization, symbolized by the growing ascendancy of private financial actors, is in large part a self-fulfilling prophecy. By its very nature declaratory policy is based on persuasion – an appeal to the better nature of market operators, or their rational decision-making capacities. This treats markets as authorities in their own right, capable of and willing to reach decisions that can be justified on the basis of the weight of economic evidence. It also allows them to dictate not only macroeconomic priorities, but also exchange rate outcomes. Unfortunately, such an approach suffers from two major flaws. First, market operators are often swept along by the exuberance of the market. Declaratory policy relies on some degree of self-awareness on behalf of market actors to acknowledge and correct excessive movements. Yet the experience of the last decade, involving repeated large gyrations between the major currencies, suggests faith in the foreign exchange market's capacity to behave 'reasonably' may be unwarranted. Second, markets can simply reject policy-makers' analyses, or arguments, on the grounds that prevailing market thinking is superior to that of public officials. Declaratory policy leaves policy-makers with no real response in such circumstances. When the markets refuse to respond to policy-makers' statements, the impotency of declaratory policy becomes all too apparent, and the belief that financial markets are all-powerful is further consolidated and augmented. Markets have this power because states are reluctant to intervene, or to attempt to direct them in a proactive fashion. In the absence of any feasible public sanction, market operators can offer alternative views to those of policy-makers, while claiming they have a better feel for market dynamics. As a consequence market operators become authorities in their own right because states allow them to. Clearly the state has not entirely retreated from the area of exchange rate policy. State authority has, however, declined on exchange rate matters, as the leading states willingly perform a minimal withdrawn function, allowing markets to determine exchange rates, while trying to contain excessively volatile movements. Yet even in this modest role states are not always successful because of their preference for presenting arguments to markets they assume to be rational, a faith which cannot always be justified.

Ultimately, with the notable exception of regional monetary union in Europe, states have chosen to resolve the Mundell Flemming dilemma by choosing national (or macro-regional in Europe's case) monetary policy autonomy ahead of wider international or global exchange rate stability (Pauly 2000). Unfortunately, this autonomy is increasingly an illusion because, although still national in name, macroeconomic priorities and targets are largely determined by international investors, rather than by domestic interests.

A further consequence of the reliance on declaratory policy is that technical authority has become just as important in determining the course of exchange rate policy as political motivation. An individual's technical credibility and competence, or their feel for the market, have become the most important features in determining capacity to influence market movements with spoken words. However, ultimate sanction in the state–market relationship that declaratory policy gives rise to, rests with the market. Therefore, exchange rate policy is becoming more technical, more market-determined, but less democratic. Actors in financial markets are by definition motivated by the maximization of returns. The opportunity for profit (and loss) is greatest when there are sudden shifts in prices. Market operators have much to gain from volatility and extreme movements, therefore, and as a consequence they are unlikely to have much in the way of a wider sense of public responsibility (Underhill 2001). Today, the G7 approach to exchange rate policy means that financial markets are judge and jury over the livelihood of millions of citizens (Story 2003). Finance ministry and central banking elites and the financial sectors of G7 countries may be happy with this, but increasingly it is questionable whether their own citizens are.[19] Exchange rates have real consequences on real peoples' lives, and arguments that they are simply technical issues will not wash. However, this pattern is not absolute. The United States, together with the G7, was successful in instigating an appreciation of the dollar in 1995; however, at other notable points during the decade it was less successful in influencing exchange rates (Baker forthcoming). More research is needed, not only on the record of market analysts and policy-makers in moving exchange rates, but also the circumstances in which policy-makers have been successful and unsuccessful in moving exchange rates.

Codes of practice and three-dimensional governance

Probably the best example of how three-dimensional governance functions is provided by the example of codes of good practice on monetary and fiscal policy that were formulated by the G7 countries after the Asian financial crises of 1997–98, in an effort to extend and institutionalize processes of peer and market scrutiny of national policies into emerging markets (Baker 2003). One of the principal conclusions the Western powers drew from the crises was that macroeconomic surveillance had not worked as well as it was supposed to, because of the requirement for countries to engage in voluntary data release.[20] One of the thrusts of the post-crises response, therefore, was an investigation of the ways of deepening, extending and institutionalizing surveillance, so as to place the current liberal financial order on a firmer institutional foundation. Under the banner of 'transparency', the British Treasury proposed introducing codes of practice on fiscal policy, monetary policy and corporate governance. These proposals were eventually accepted and endorsed by the rest of the G7, and the IMF was entrusted with the role of administering them. (For more on this, see Soederberg, Chapter 10 of this volume.)

The codes of practice essentially consist of clearly documented data standards with which national authorities are expected to comply in both monetary and fiscal policy, so as to maximize the information available to markets, while signalling policy-makers' good intentions (the first and second forms of third-dimensional diplomacy referred to earlier). The codes have no formal enforcement mechanism. Rather, they operate through the increased likelihood of a withdrawal of finance capital and higher interest rate premiums if countries fail to comply with the data standards spelt out in the codes. Moreover, a failure to comply with the data standards is likely to result in high-profile criticism from peers and multilateral institutions in Dimension I multilateral processes. In this respect, the new codes give both market actors and multilateral partners a clear standard by which to judge the efforts of other national authorities in macroeconomic policy.

The IMF's role in relation to the codes of practice is to publicize concerns about gaps in information disclosure. Multilateral approval acts as a stamp of approval, while criticism, or absence of such approval, can act as a catalyst for rapid exchange rate depreciation and currency crisis. In particular, the absence of multilateral endorsement increases currency traders' suspicions with regard to what data is being hidden concerning the state of public finances, balance of payments, monetary growth and inflation, and thereby reduces their willingness to hold a particular currency. In other words, the real effects of the codes of practice are two-fold. First, they increase the fear of capital flight in the international monetary system, if formulaic IMF/G7 prescriptions concerning tight monetary policy and public expenditure reductions are not followed. Second, by providing a uniform information standard, they threaten to heighten market suspicion if economic data is not forthcoming, forcing states to reveal as much macroeconomic data about their economies as possible. This effectively enhances the veto capacity of markets and their ability to dictate and determine macroeconomic priorities. In this context a range of competing domestic societal priorities and interests tends to get written out of the macroeconomic equation. The net result is the enhanced veto capacity of foreign investors where expansionary macroeconomic policies are concerned. Consequently countries in emerging markets have often been forced down the path of fiscal and monetary rectitude in the face of lingering recession because of an implicit threat of capital flight (the second form of third-dimensional diplomacy noted earlier). The most notable impact of the introduction of the new codes of practice, therefore, has been to place the pattern of three-dimensional governance consisting of peer and market scrutiny of national policies on a firmer institutional footing and extend into emerging markets, increasing the oversight capacity of market actors and various multilateral processes, with regard to national macroeconomic policies.

US macroeconomic exceptionalism and three-dimensional governance

Until now this chapter has said little about one of the key controversies in International Political Economy – US structural economic power; yet no discussion of macroeconomic governance is complete without some discussion of US exceptionalism (Strange 1994). The experience of the last three decades has revealed that three-dimensional governance has been least successful in disciplining the United States. In the 1980s, the US ran up record fiscal and balance of payments deficits, but was able to finance both deficits because of the reserve role of the dollar and the depth and liquidity of US financial markets made the United States an attractive location for foreign investors. Susan Strange made the point that this kind of structural power to attract foreign funds and the capacity to run such deficits were not representative of a power in decline (Strange 1994). However, the degree of discipline the US has demonstrated in macroeconomic policy has varied in accordance with the incumbent administration. Under the Clinton administration, the US ran its first fiscal surplus for thirty years. Deficit reduction under Clinton was based on the reasoning that it would lead to lower domestic interest rates, which would benefit Wall Street equities markets and act as an engine of growth for the economy more generally, but repeated international pressure from G7 partners added international support to deficit reduction attempts. The need to provide reassurance to Wall Street and to financial markets more generally seemed central to the administration's thinking. Certainly the evidence from the 1990s at least suggested that the US maybe had a reduced capacity to run fiscal deficits and that the financial forces unleashed during the 1980s were also beginning to discipline even the United States.

However, under the George W. Bush administration the United States has gone from fiscal surplus back to a position of deficit, at an amazingly rapid rate. Indeed, the current deficit is approaching 7 per cent of GDP. This has reflected the political pragmatism of an administration that on the whole has appeared to have had little interest in economic policy and has adopted the traditional Republican stance of lower taxes and higher military expenditure, with little thought for how this fits into a wider economic strategy. Nor has this strategy been concerned with any degree of wealth redistribution, because the principal beneficiaries of these lower taxes have been high earners. The change in US administration and in macroeconomic priorities does, however, demonstrate that the US continues to be the country least constrained by the prevailing international macroeconomic consensus and the pattern of three-dimensional governance. The administration has also been able to downgrade the Treasury Department with relative ease. Stimulus-oriented US macroeconomic policies have been engineered by White House advisors, but there has been no ringing endorsement of these from G7 partners. Rather, Japanese and European officials continue to express off-the-record reservations about the size of US budget and current account deficits as well as the falling dollar. Indeed, many at the Treasury Department, including former Treasury Secretary Paul O'Neil, appear to have had reservations about recent fiscal policies.

Of course, in the context of record trade and budget deficits, the strength of the US dollar inevitably came under market scrutiny, and it began to decline against other major currencies from the spring of 2001, with a sharp acceleration in that decline in the second half of 2003. What happens to the dollar in the context of large current account and budget deficits will be a good test of continuing US exceptionalism and the collective will of the G7 finance ministries and central banks to reassert their authority over financial markets. Some commentators have expressed concern about the real prospect of a dollar rout, which would undermine competitiveness in export-based economies in Europe and Asia and undermine foreign willingness to hold US bonds, with the resulting jump in long-term US interest rates choking off US growth, which in turn would have a detrimental impact on global growth prospects more generally.

In the past the US has largely been immune from investor fears over current account deficits because foreign investors have always been keen to accumulate foreign exchange reserves. The most secure way of doing this has been to invest surplus funds in the country with the world's biggest economy and most liquid capital markets. If and when foreigners can no longer be persuaded to finance the US, the dollar will decline. Between the end of January 2002, when the dollar began its decline, and October 2003, global foreign currency reserves rose by $831 billion. Of these, $611 billion were accumulated by Asian countries. Japan led the way with $219 billion, with China and Taiwan accounting for $184 billion and $73 billion respectively. These foreign currency reserves were predominantly invested in US official obligations and accounted for 4.5 per cent of US GDP. In other words, Asian countries have followed a strategy of exchange rate protectionism managing an undervalued exchange rate through sizeable exchange market interventions, accumulating reserves and encouraging export-led growth. The willingness of Asian countries to invest in these ways has helped keep both US bond prices and the dollar afloat, thus financing the borrowings of the US government and households. What has emerged is a *de facto* alliance or bargain between the US and Asian economies, in which the US has been quite happy to accept more interventionist Asian currency policies in an apparent breach of the G7 consensus, because these policies have effectively financed US payment imbalances by bringing inflows of foreign funds into the US financial system through the purchase of dollar-denominated US Treasury debt securities. However, these interventions have limited the extent of market-induced dollar adjustment, meaning that the dollar adjustment has fallen with full force on those currencies left to float, most notably the euro and sterling. This has caused great frustration within the euro-zone because the deterioration in net trade brought about by the appreciation of the euro, according to OECD forecasts, has reduced euro-zone growth from 1.2 per cent to 0.5 per cent. In these circumstances euro-zone states have struggled to emerge from a prolonged period of stagnation. The result has been rising tensions between the G7 powers concerning future exchange rate policy. The Europeans desire a more competitive currency, but the Asian–US bargain, which sees a tacit acceptance of Asian mercantilism in return for a source of financing for twin US deficits, has resulted in recent G7 statements having little or no impact on currency markets other than to further hasten the fall of the dollar against the euro.

For the time being at least the US capacity to delay macroeconomic adjustment remains intact, as does US exceptionalism, but voices on Wall Street are increasingly warning that the Bush tax cuts are a fiscal timebomb waiting to happen when baby-boom retirees lead to spiralling health and pension costs. If the US fiscal deficit continues to grow as expected, the US capacity to persuade foreigners to invest in US Treasury securities and in equities might well be squeezed. In this respect, the reckless fiscal policies of the Bush administration may well be hastening the decline of US exceptionalism.

Since the collapse of Bretton Woods, the strategic position of the US in the global financial system as the possessor of the world's leading reserve currency and the world's deepest most liquid financial markets has enabled it to avoid, or at least to minimize, the disciplinary impact of the three-dimensional macroeconomic governance process described in this chapter, thus delaying macroeconomic adjustment. Yet the continued capacity of the US to do this appears to be increasingly in question. There is a potential limit to the willingness of foreigners to go on lending to the US. Ultimately, the capacity of the US to postpone adjustment has been dependent on a perpetual opinion poll, involving the judgement of private financial market actors (and to a lesser extent foreign central banks) – the same kind of third-dimensional diplomacy all states have to engage in. To date the US has enjoyed structural advantages in playing this kind of third-dimensional diplomacy, stemming from the status of the dollar, but a loss of faith in the dollar and a shift in the opinions of market actors engaged in the continuous opinion poll of third-dimensional diplomacy will place great pressure on the US to reverse current deficits (Cohen 2004).

That the United States has largely managed to avoid the disciplinary affects of the three-dimensional governance dynamic described in this chapter has also been evident in the mandate of the Federal Reserve. The United States has been able to retain the Humphrey Hawkins act of 1977, which gives the Fed responsibility for delivering growth and employment as well as domestic price stability. In other words, the US central bank has not had to provide the same degree of symbolic reassurance to international investors as central banks in other industrialized states. At the end of the 1990s, legislation was drafted to give the Federal Reserve an inflation target and to provide a legal framework that compelled governments to run balanced budgets. However, as the record of the Bush administration in the United States demonstrates, fiscal legislation to curtail deficits amounts to little as long as the US has the 'power to delay' and postpone macroeconomic adjustment through a capacity to attract savings and investment from abroad, enabling it to finance twin deficits (Cohen 2004). If the US finds it increasingly difficult to finance widening deficits with foreign capital, it will be subject to the same three-dimensional disciplinary macroeconomic governance dynamic as other states. The real danger is that, if and when this happens, the world will lose its current principal engine of growth, as US expansionary capacity will be hugely curtailed, while it will become more difficult for US policy-makers to use macroeconomic policy in a growth-supportive role. The current economic outlook and macroeconomic regimes in Europe and Japan do not inspire confidence that there is another world locomotive to replace the United States in such circumstances.

Conclusions: Three-dimensional governance, power, authority and democracy

Three basic arguments have been made in this chapter. First, macroeconomic policy is characterized by an observable three-dimensional governance process consisting of market and multilateral scrutiny of national policies. Three-dimensional governance has its roots in the multilateral surveillance process instigated by the leading finance ministries and central banks following the collapse of the Bretton Woods exchange rate regime in the early 1970s, which from the outset prioritized price stability as a means to exchange rate stability. Market scrutiny in particular has intensified as barriers between national financial systems and divisions between previously separate market segments have broken down. Moreover, market scrutiny has been placed on a firmer institutional foundation by the formulation of recent codes of practice on monetary and fiscal transparency that obligate states to release data about their macroeconomic policies. Third-dimensional diplomacy is characterized by an ongoing market opinion poll (the most immediate in the global foreign exchange market, but also through global trading in equities and securities) amongst a worldwide audience of investors, about national policy performance that determines governments' access to foreign credit and their power to delay macroeconomic adjustment (Cohen 2004). To reassure international investors, to signal their good long-term intentions, and to enhance their 'credibility', policy-makers have moved to make central banks independent, and have introduced fiscal rules, thereby inserting financial market criteria and priorities into domestic institutional orders in an effective de-nationalization of national macroeconomic policy-making. Moreover, such institutional arrangements conform to a multilateral sense of best practice and the norms of multilateral surveillance. A dual pressure from the first-dimensional and third-dimensional spaces identified in this chapter has therefore pushed national policy-makers in the direction of independent central banks and fiscal rules. Moreover, the continuous nature of market scrutiny and multilateral surveillance ensure that there are ongoing, mutually reinforcing interactive relationships between these three spatial dimensions. This in turn means that the current macroeconomic regime hangs together, is sustained by and has to be understood as, an integrated three-dimensional entity.

Second, in this context three-dimensional governance can act as an analytical framework for examining the formulation of macroeconomic and exchange rate policy, facilitating more accurate assertions on the factors driving policy and multilateral cooperation. The application of the three-dimensional lens in this chapter has served to illustrate how contemporary macroeconomic policy-making arrangements emanate from a series of politically constructed social relationships between states and markets. The analysis here has demonstrated how, for the most part, current domestic institutional arrangements are the product of policy-makers' perceptions of how actors in financial markets operate, the nature of those markets and what this requires from policy-makers. Independent central banks with inflation targets and fiscal rules, therefore, represent conscious political choices about which economic objectives to prioritize in macroeconomic policy and the kind of wealth accumulation strategies most suitable for modern capitalist societies. Such macroeconomic choices privilege technocratic concerns and market stabilization in the formulation of macroeconomic policy, and represent an attempt to place macroeconomic decision-making outside of the traditional framework of partisan politics. The general pattern is that elites in finance ministries and central banks enjoy greater autonomy to conduct monetary and fiscal policies independently of other national agencies. Their own shared beliefs and social practices have become more important in driving macroeconomic and exchange rate policies than any obligation to respond to interests within their own domestic societies. It should be emphasized that these institutional and policy outcomes are the product of elite choices concerning the amount of freedom given to financial markets, the desirability of market-determined exchange rates and the need to prioritize stabilization and maintain confidence in a range of de-territorialized financial markets. Where macroeconomic policy is concerned, therefore, financial globalization is in large part a politically and socially constructed self-fulfilling prophecy. The application of the three-dimensional framework serves to illustrate how this self-fulfilling prophecy rests on a series of politically contestable social relationships, choices and communications that, in turn, serve to sustain the current macroeconomic regime. A three-dimensional approach does this by facilitating closer analysis of the linkages between shared elite causal/normative beliefs and social practices, domestic politics and policy-making, and the practices and priorities of operators in globally networked financial markets, thereby illuminating the mutually reinforcing interactive dynamic that characterizes the relationships between these discrete but interlocking social spaces.

Third, both of the conclusions above have implications for democratic governance and authority in the international monetary system. The 1990s saw a narrow series of technical and overtly financial considerations, themselves based on a series of quite distinct, yet contestable, intellectual assumptions, determine and dictate the public policy agenda. On the whole, three-dimensional governance brought government policies into conformity with transnational market preferences. Governments effectively became more responsive to non-citizens for their macroeconomic policies – international investors, foreign currency traders and other finance ministries and central banks and international organizations in various multilateral settings – than to their own electorates (see Thirkell-White and Soederberg, Chapters 8 and 10 respectively, in this volume). This was evident in a daily referendum on national policies in the foreign exchange market, and by regular multilateral surveillance exercises. In contrast, national electorates have had infrequent opportunities to exercise sanction at the ballot box. The result is that the financial markets, especially the foreign exchange market, have acted increasingly as judge and jury, both in terms of exchange rate valuations and in determining domestic macroeconomic institutional arrangements, long-term policy priorities and even short-term policy adjustments over the last decade.[21]

The one notable exception to this pattern of three-dimensional governance has been the United States. Continued privileged access to foreign credit has enabled the US to run up twin current account and fiscal deficits and to exercise its power to delay macroeconomic adjustment. Yet even for the United States this 'power to delay' is dependent on an ongoing opinion poll among private financial investors concerning their continuing confidence in the performance of the US economy – third-dimensional diplomacy. In other words, the United States can only continue to avoid the disciplinary affects of three-dimensional governance for as long as third-dimensional actors – foreign creditors – continue to accord the US special status. The ongoing opinion poll that characterizes the third dimension can shift in direction at any time. In other words, foreign creditors and investors can change their minds, and a sustained depreciation of the dollar might prove to be both a cause and an effect of this. The costs of this for world growth could be significant. Three-dimensional governance of macroeconomic policy is not a stable regime. It privileges technocratic knowledge and market authority over broader definitions of public interest. Most of all it represents the prioritization of rentier interests and the capacity of greed-obsessed and often unstable crisis-prone financial markets to determine public policy priorities.

Notes

1 An earlier version of this paper was presented at a conference on Multi-Level Governance at the University of Sheffield, 29 June 2001. I would like to thank the participants at that session and an anonymous reviewer of this volume for their helpful comments. Remaining shortcomings are my responsibility alone.
2 For one of the few exceptions see Hooghe and Marks (2001). They distinguish between a form of multi-level governance similar to federalism based on tightly defined jurisdictions and clearly delineated responsibilities (type I), and a form of multilevel governance popular with public choice economists concerned with efficient functional outcomes and based on a complex fluid patchwork overlapping jurisdictions (type II). Neither is strictly applicable to contemporary macroeconomic governance in advanced capitalist states, although the second is closest.
3 In IPE terms, therefore, MLG has a certain resonance with the neo-Gramscian perspective's focus on interactions between ideas, institutions and material capabilities and between world order, state–civil society complexes and systems of production (Cox 1981, 1983; see also Soederberg, Chapter 10 of this volume).
4 Even in the case of the new supranational and independent European Central Bank (ECB), the institution's mandate is to deliver price stability in the euro-zone on the basis of the consensual decisions of its governing council. The relatively limited opportunities for national lobbying of the ECB mean that the euro-zone practically operates as a monetary jurisdiction comparable to other national territories. Moreover, the euro is represented by the head of the ECB and his deputy in external forums such as the G7, as the ECB more or less acts as a substitute for national central banks in euro-zone states. This is not to deny that EMU has posed new fiscal

and labour market challenges and obligations for participating states that are being dealt with through the new euro group of finance ministers, which in turn is developing its own logic and system of meaning. The point here is that the ECB presides over the euro-zone as a whole, rather like national central banks preside over national territories, and there is little opportunity for national actors other than those individuals who are members of the ECB's governing council to influence ECB decision-making. This raises the whole question of the extent to which these individuals retain a national identity, or are in fact assuming a new supranational identity. Initial evidence seems to suggest the ECB is functioning on the basis of consensus and supranationalism, rather than intergovernmentalism or bargaining (Begg 2001).

5 Interview with a senior US official, Feburary 1998. There is some debate on the extent to which this view of exchange rates is accepted in Europe, particularly in France. In 1998 Oskar Lafontaine proposed a system of target zones for the yen, dollar and euro, but the French were quick to distance themselves from this proposal, pointing to a G7 consensus, while in Germany the chancellor's office rejected the proposals. Lafontaine resigned shortly afterwards.

6 Interview with officials, January 1998.

7 Interview with officials, January 1998.

8 Occasionally states will pressurize other states with regard to the general orientation of their policy. This was evident at the end of the 1990s when the rest of the G7 encouraged Japan to follow fiscal expansion. This is rather different from bargaining over national policies, however.

9 More conventional interest-based bargaining tends to come to the fore over the size of the national individual contributions to joint exchange market interventions needed to support a collective exchange rate stance.

10 Pauly has argued that this was a self-interested decision on behalf of the leading capitalist states, based on a calculation that it enhanced their room for manoeuvre.

11 France was prepared to accept this thinking, possibly overestimating the potential impact of such discipline on the US. The term 'surveillance' was chosen primarily because it had the right connotation for the US Congress, as it implied some sort of international oversight without deference to a higher international authority.

12 That is not to say that manufacturing has no interest in low inflation; but manufacturing would be unlikely to prioritize it in the making of monetary policy practically to the exclusion of all other objectives in the way authorities have done. The notable exception here, of course, is the Federal Reserve of the United States, which is mandated also to deliver growth and employment as well as price stability.

13 The ECB is a new supranational independent central bank (possibly the most independent), while the Bank of England and the Bank of Japan have gained operational independence.

14 There have also been debates and proposals for the Bank of Japan and the Federal Reserve to adopt inflation targets, but nothing has been formally adopted as yet.

15 This has been compounded by the fact that the traditional strong ties between manufacturing and finance in Germany and Japan are progressively, albeit slowly, weakening (Cerny 2000; Lutz 2000).

16 For the purposes of this framework, market–market interactions and inter-relationships are viewed as third-dimensional variables, rather than as a separate form of diplomacy.

17 Three-dimensional diplomacy raises the question, why three dimensions? The answer is that identifiable three-way interactions increasingly characterize macroeconomic and exchange rate policy. Other dimensions, or organizing categories, could be considered, but few have much of a role where macroeconomic and exchange rate policy is concerned. For example, we could consider the regional dimension as an additional dimension, separate from domestic state–society relations. However, so few regional authorities have an input into the determination of advanced capitalist coun-

tries' macroeconomic and exchange rate priorities that there is little case for inclusion. Moreover, if they do, it is solely through national institutions, just as other domestic interests would make representations, rather than through direct links with some supranational institution as is the case in some EU policy areas. Futhermore a macroregional monetary institution in the form of the ECB has emerged. However, the development of the Cologne process suggests that, as in a national monetary territory, trade unions and business interests in the euro-zone are forming direct communications and relations with the ECB, rather than moving through existing national institutions, and are attempting to articulate their concerns with one voice. Thus the ECB and its relations with wider society in the euro-zone can be considered part of the broader pattern of second-dimensional diplomacy.

18 It is true to say that the constituency benefiting from rentier-type activities has broadened, and an increasing number of individuals' wealth is bound up with the performance of financial markets. Over 53 per cent of Americans own stocks and shares. More generally, private pension provisions are increasingly linked to the performance of a range of financial markets. We have also seen the rise of various endowment investment plans and mortgages (Watson 2002; Langley, Chapter 5 of this volume).

19 There is some doubt about the Japanese position. There is a Japanese tradition of passivity in financial diplomacy, but they have a strong preference for a competitively valued yen and have been actively intervening in markets recently, in an effort to offset the detrimental trade effects of dollar depreciation.

20 Interview with official, March 1998.

21 Obviously this contradicts the findings of Garrett (1998), who has argued that fiscal activism persisted according to the political complexion of the governing party, but his work was based on data from the 1980s.

7 European banking policy

Between multi-level governance and Europeanization

Emiliano Grossman[1]

Regulatory policies in banking and finance have been profoundly transformed in the past fifteen or twenty years. National regulatory regimes have undergone radical change, putting an end to capital controls and all types of 'exceptional' regulation where it existed. At the same time, regulatory regimes have emerged at the international level (G10) as a response to the specific problems created by the internationalization of finance. For much of the time these regimes have taken the form of recommendations. More recently, in the context of European integration we have witnessed the emergence of much more formal arrangements. In June 2002 a European Securities Committee was created, with other areas such as insurance and banking set to follow. This chapter investigates the politics of regulatory integration in the European context.

The creation of a Single European Market has strongly affected a wide array of policy areas. The extent to which developments in EU policies upset or transform domestic policies and politics has become a primary concern of EU-related studies. Two separate lines of research have tried to address these types of question. Work on the emergence of 'multi-level governance' in Europe has usually tended to demonstrate the coexistence of European, national and sub-national levels in a complex web of permanent interactions. More recently, research on 'Europeanization' has focused mainly on the pressure for convergence generated by the emergence of a European level and domestic responses to it. Both lines of research share a lot of concerns and interests. They both contrast with traditional state-centred or supranationalist approaches to International Relations and European Studies. They bridge the gap between the two approaches without embracing the 'grand-theory' perspective of either. The major problem with multi-level governance (MLG) has been that it is under-theorized and is therefore imprecise about the dynamics of multi-level polities. Some authors show concern for the redistributive effects of MLG. Many underline the weakening of the role of the state (Eising and Kohler-Koch 1994; Hooghe and Marks 2001; Jachtenfuchs and Kohler-Koch 1996b; Marks *et al.* 1996c), while others see an opportunity for national governments to recover lost autonomy in the domestic arena (Grande 1996). Most work, however, shares Hooghe and Marks's (2001: 3) assertion that multi-level governance involves 'the dispersion of authority away from central government – upwards to the supranational level, downwards to subnational jurisdictions, and sideways to public/private networks'. For Hooghe and Marks, MLG fills efficiency gaps through the creation of multiple overlapping and complementary jurisdictions. European integration does not necessarily confirm this. Despite quite hierarchical and stable structures and jurisdictions, the European Union is characterized by strong tensions. Supranational authorities try to attract jurisdictional power, or to widen existing competencies. The Commission, and more recently the European Central Bank, have been trying to convince member states of the necessity to centralize, i.e. to integrate financial supervision and regulation. On the other hand, the path dependence of national regulatory systems (Hooghe and Marks 2001: 14–16) continues to mitigate against integration. This is due to persisting national identities, which are not particularly sensitive to efficiency. In fact, this chapter argues, in most countries finance remains an 'esoteric' topic with little or no publicly debated issues (cf. Coleman 1996: 9–10). It is usually dominated by stable and closed, or even, 'corporatist', policy communities, involving regulators, ministries and banks themselves (Moran 1991: 60ff). Consequently, national regulatory agencies and supervisory authorities are likely to oppose Europeanization on the grounds of 'bureaucratic' interests and efficiency-related arguments (see Woodward, Chapter 9 of this volume, on the City of London).

Unlike some of the contributors to this volume, I do not consider the market as a distinct level because the specific 'systemic risks' of banking markets mean that even the most radical free-marketeers have never advocated 'market-only regulation'. There is a consensus about the fact that market failure in the banking sector is too serious a matter to be left to market actors themselves. Consequently, debates centre around the appropriate extent of state intervention rather than whether state intervention is necessary.

The key question considered in this chapter is whether we are seeing 'more' multi-level governance in European banking, as a result of national-level institutions resisting further European integration, or 'less' multi-level governance, as national regulatory competencies are consolidated at the 'European' level. Overall this chapter suggests that policies related to the governance of finance have been integrated very slowly and with major resistance from key actors. However, increasingly the multi-level coexistence of national and European regulatory authorities is being progressively displaced by the complete integration of national regulatory authority. That is to say that European integration is gradually overcoming national resistance.

The emergence of multi-level governance in European banking

The emergence of multi-level governance in European banking regulation is the result of two parallel processes. On the one hand, national financial systems clearly retain differences. There has been some degree of convergence in the form of overall liberalization and the promotion of financial services. None the less the financial systems of the UK, France and Germany currently retain their essential characteristics. On the other hand, a distinctly European level has emerged. The Single Market Programme (SMP) has unleashed a process which will eventually lead to a more autonomous European level (though not necessarily to a level playing field). The specific characteristics of this European level are slowly emerging.

Building the single market for financial services

The European Community intervened in the process of financial liberalization at a rather advanced stage (Josselin 1996; Story and Walter 1997). Towards the end of the 1980s the European Community's Single Market Programme (SMP) engaged in building the 'Single Market for Financial Services'. Prior to this development, little had been done at Community level to integrate financial services. The only significant measure – the First Banking Directive – had been taken in 1977 and had had little impact. It simplified the opening of branches in other member states of EC banks and also created the Banking Advisory Committee, made up of representatives of national regulatory authorities and finance ministries.

The SMP contained three central elements in the area of finance. The first was the liberalization of capital movements achieved by the 1988 directive, designed finally to implement Article 67 of the Treaty of Rome. This was the precondition to the development of the Single Market for Financial Services. Though a number of leading European countries, including the UK and Germany, had already abolished capital controls, this measure was especially relevant to several southern European nations, such as Italy, where capital controls remained central to financial policy. The Second Banking Directive created the 'single passport' allowing banks, whether European or not, which obtained a licence in one EU country to open offices in other member states. The single passport rested upon the principles of 'mutual recognition' (whereby host countries recognize and accept foreign licences issued by other European member states) and 'home-country control' (whereby a bank licensed in any European member state is able to open branches in any other member state, but whose supervision remains the responsibility of the licensing or 'home' country). This development forced supervisory authorities to cooperate more closely and to develop a more elaborate regulatory framework.

Developments elsewhere also had ramifications for European banking policy. The decision by the US government in 1975 to eliminate capital controls sponsored the reintegration of national financial markets and fundamentally altered the competitive landscape for financial services and the necessary range of regulatory responses. The increasing interdependence of international banking markets prompted the Group of Ten to set up the Basle Committee. The latter is made up of central bank governors and representatives of national regulatory authorities of thirteen major countries.[2] After a first set of recommendations in 1975 – the Concordat – the Committee adopted the so-called 'Cook-ratio' in 1988. Despite criticism and objective shortcomings, the Cook-ratio has become an almost universal standard for minimum funds (see Herring and Litan 1995: 95ff). A much larger agreement, the 'McDonough-ratio' has been negotiated over the past few years. It is much more ambitious than its predecessor and seeks to introduce very detailed regulation by taking specific credit risks into account. To a large extent, European integration in the financial sector has been about 'translating' and unifying national interpretations of Basle recommendations. In that sense, one might add this 'global' level to the European one, with both initiatives pursuing the goal of an international 'level playing-field' in finance. However, with the Basle Committee increasingly preoccupied with negotiations between the EU and the US, the EU is becoming the main playing-field for most European actors. The Single Currency has further strengthened integration in Europe and as far as banking policy is concerned. Despite the fact that a European level of policy-making may no longer be adequate (McKenzie and Khalidi 1996), it is at this level that national authorities meet regularly.

The main conclusion to be drawn from the negotiations of the SMP for financial services is the clear intergovernmental character of the whole process. Tensions revolved around national coalitions. Story and Walter have stated that these negotiations revealed a 'battle of the systems', with the German and the French governments trying to safeguard and protect national arrangements that were in contradiction to the principles of the Single Market. The battle 'took shape because of the different responses of governments to the internationalization of the business of banking' (Story and Walter 1997: 275). Those coalitions included governments and, especially, finance ministries, supervisory authorities and banking associations. European associations at best served as an additional source of information, but were unable to build transnational policy consensus among banks (Josselin 1996: 175ff.). Moreover, the SMP deliberately left out a certain number of questions, which threatened to endanger the overall agreement. Faithful to the philosophy of 'mutual recognition', it limited itself to fixing rules and, where necessary, such as on capital adequacy or own funds, establishing minimum requirements. For example, the question of harmonizing supervisory arrangements, or creating a single regulator or supervisor, were not issues at this stage. Cooperation between national supervisors existed, but relied exclusively on bilateral agreements. A certain number of international forums did including the Contact group, the Banking Advisory Committee of the European Commission, the Federation of European Securities Comissions (FESCO) and the G10, but their role was largely limited to information exchange.

Financial systems between national traditions and globalization

The attitudes to finance vary strongly from country to country, but traditionally governments and public opinion in continental Europe have been more cautious about finance than in Britain. While monetary and financial business tends to be considered like trade in any other commodity in the UK, continental governments have until recently kept a tight grip on finance. These differing perspectives have proved something of an obstacle to European initiatives in this area, with governments, banks and their political representatives hesitating to support a unified European banking regime.

To a large extent, then, liberalization came as a response to extra-European developments (Moran 1991). Financial liberalization in Europe can be seen first as a response to the US measures that started in 1975 with the abolition of fixed fees at the New York Stock Exchange. This section will rapidly survey the changes that financial liberalization induced for three national financial systems and their fundamental characteristics: the UK, France and Germany.

The United Kingdom

In 1979 the UK followed the US in liberalizing capital controls and began the process of opening up its financial markets to international competition, culminating in the 'Big Bang' of 1986. This process put an end to 'gentlemanly capitalism' and 'esoteric policy-making' in the City of London (Augar 2000; Coleman 1996; Ingham 1984; Moran 1991). Until then, access to the City was restricted by a club-like network of old merchant banks. The reforms opened access to markets other than the already liberalized Euromarkets. By the mid-1980s the City had attracted very many of the most important continental European firms to London. On the banking side, the Building Societies Act of 1986 allowed building societies to become banks. The consequence has been the gradual fading of that sector, with the 'conversion' of its most significant members into banks. At the same time, the Banking Act abolished the remaining differences between deposit banks and investment banks, thus embracing a more German-style universal bank model. This measure has had little impact, though, since British clearing banks have limited their presence in the investment banking business, which is now dominated by foreign and, especially, US banks. In fact, as a consequence of the Big Bang, all of the major 'merchant' or investment banks of the City have now been absorbed by foreign banks, and only few significant firms remain in British hands in the area of investment banking (Augar 2000).

Political representation in the City has evolved, too. With the decline of the influence of the Bank of England, trade associations became more important. The British Bankers Association remains the most central one and represents all types of banks, even though it is said to be the voice of the British clearing banks. Only 16 per cent of its membership is actually British. The London Investment Banks Association (LIBA) is now entirely made up of foreign banks. The Treasury and the regulating authorities no longer make any distinction at all between British and foreign banks when it comes to consultations, hearings, working groups or others.

As a result of the Big Bang, the Single Market Programme (SMP) had only a minor impact on the City. The SMP, and especially the so-called 'single passport', probably led more continental European banks to open up branches in

London. Their continued presence in London, however, is above all due to the fact that the City remains for the time being the world's most important financial market. Banking policy has changed, in the sense that it has become more formal than it used to be before the reform. The state has intervened forcefully to render regulation and supervision more transparent and equally binding for everybody. The major recent change has been the creation in 1997 of the Financial Services Authority, a single regulator for banking, insurance and securities. The creation of this independent agency has put an end to the five self-regulatory organizations (SROs) which had worked under the overall supervision of the Securities and Investment Board (SIB) (Briault 2000). This change has been a deadly blow to the already declining influence of the Bank of England, which is now entirely excluded from supervision and regulation.[3]

What is most striking about the evolution of the British financial system is that it is largely independent from anything happening in Brussels or elsewhere on the European continent. By far the most open financial system in Europe, there is no indication of convergence towards any other model, remaining faithful to what Zysman (1983) called the model of 'capital-market based finance'. Changes in the overall architecture of the British financial system did not affect its foundations. Reforms, such as the creation of the FSA, have been the consequence of debates within the UK and discussions on regulatory techniques and the future of finance. Often, it is Britain's example that provokes debates in other European countries, as is the case with the creation of the FSA as a single regulator and supervisor.

France

As a consequence of British liberalization and its success, continental governments became increasingly receptive to domestic demands for more competitive financial markets. Most estimates stated that at least 20 per cent of the French wholesale market had moved to London by the mid-1980s (*Economist* 1988). Paris was the first to engage in profound reforms of its entire financial system.[4] Historically 'credit based and state-led' (Zysman 1983), it was again the state that initiated the reforms that were supposed to limit state interventionism in French finance (Coleman 1993). The 1984 Banking Act put an end to 77 different interest rate regimes, introduced an independent regulatory structure (Cerny 1989; Zerah 1993), brought French banks nearer to German-style universal banks and abolished the limitations applying to cooperative banks' activities. In 1986, the French futures market, MATIF, was created, and this was followed in 1988 by the liberalization of the French stock exchange. Moreover, France has privatized most public banks since 1986, including the controversial Crédit Lyonnais in 1999 (cf. Story and Walter 1997: 198–210). As a player, the state remains present through the powerful Caisse des dépôts et de consignations.

As to the representation of bank interests and their participation in the policy-making process, the state has always fixed the general guidelines and continues to do so. The 1984 Banking Act created a round table of financial services, the *Association française des établissement de crédits et des entreprises d'investissements* (AFECEI), to which all banks have to belong indirectly. This was confirmed in 2001 by the creation of the *Fédération française bancaire* (FFB), which is supposed to improve coherence and communication in French banking, especially with regard to Brussels. Once again, though, it appeared to be the Ministry of Finance that pushed for its creation.

On regulatory issues, the state remained central after the 1984–88 reforms through the Treasury and the Banque de France, which head or co-head all financial regulatory and supervisory committees (see Zerah 1993; Plihon 1999; Ruimy 2001). However, as a consequence of the Maastricht Treaty the Banque de France has obtained complete independence from the Treasury and the Ministry of Finance. Moreover, the Minister of Finance, who in principle heads the regulatory committees, hardly ever attends the meetings himself, leaving the chairmanship to the governor of the Banque de France. Hence, at the moment, it is the Banque de France which has the *de facto* lead responsibility in the regulation and supervision of finance in France. However, as Ruimy (2001) points out, the current discussions about the future of financial regulation and supervision tend to emphasize a strengthened role for the Treasury at the expense of the central bank. This could represent a reinforcement of the state's role in supervision and regulation at the expense of the central bank.[5] Hence, even though things have changed profoundly, the French financial system remains the tributary of years of *dirigisme* in banking policy. The state still has a close eye on finance and appears ready to intervene if necessary and to underline its authority over financial services. On the other hand, the system remains largely 'credit-based', with banks playing a central role. There is, therefore, a move towards a less activist role for the state, but at the same time no clear convergence towards self-regulation or more participation of banks and their representatives in the legislative process.

Germany

Germany was most reticent to open up (or to create) financial markets. While Germany's banks were strong and independent compared to the French, the specificity of the 'German industry–finance nexus' (Story 1997) appears to have acted as a brake to financial liberalization and the strengthening of German financial markets. In 1982 foreign banks operating in Germany set up their own association strongly supporting liberalization measures as a way of finally obtaining access to the German corporate finance market. Several of the bigger German players also realized they could not stay out of a general drive towards deeper and more diverse financial markets. With the support of finance minister Theo Waigel, several 'financial market promotion acts' (*Finanzmarktförderungsgesetze*) were formulated, introducing insider regulation, creating the legal base for derivatives markets in 1992 and the securities' equivalent of the powerful Credit Supervisory Authority in 1994. Furthermore, the German futures market, Eurex, has very rapidly overtaken the LIFFE (London) and the Chicago Futures Exchange.

With a public bank sector that still holds more than 35 per cent of overall market share, the German system represents a major exception in European banking. On the one hand there are the local savings banks, most of which are rather small and which continue to be one of the pillars of the German *Mittelstand* (in this context: SMEs). On the other hand there are the powerful *Landesbanks*, which have become major players in the international financial markets (Sinn 1999). Apart from public banks, there are the smaller but significant cooperative banks and the private banks. This 'three-tier system' was long supported by an overall consensus of public authorities and the major bank organizations.[6] Their voluntary round table, the *Zentraler Kreditausschuss* (ZKA), has worked efficiently for most of the post-war period and is systematically consulted by the ministry, the Bundesbank or BaKred, the supervision authority. This consensus may be breaking down, but the resistance of parts of government and of public banks to change shows that this system is deeply rooted. Tensions have arisen especially between private commercial banks and the larger public banks. Increasingly, the latter have become active in international financial markets. According to private banks they benefit from far too high ratings, thanks to the system of state guarantees.

Where regulatory issues are concerned, the German government has recently created a single regulator and supervisor: the '*Allfinanzaufsicht*'. This new agency is the supervisor for banking, insurance and securities, following the example of the British FSA. Unlike in Britain, though, the German central bank has managed to amend the project in a way that involves the central bank much more closely than is the case in the UK. Hence, even if there appears to be some policy convergence in regulatory policies, the outcome is strongly path-dependent. The strong position of the Bundesbank has not been questioned and its responsibility with regard to overall financial stability is acknowledged. As to overall evolution, the German 'model' is still stable, according to some observers (Deeg 1999). The financial system may be undergoing significant changes, but remains largely faithful to the tradition of 'credit-based' banking and 'managed capitalism' (Lutz 2000).

Towards which European level?

In spite of its limitations, and the persistence of distinctive national financial systems, the SMP led to the emergence of a distinctly European level. The structure of this European level is only just taking shape. There are now essentially two Directorate Generals (DGs) involved. DG Internal Market[7] initiates and coordinates regulatory policies in the area of financial services. Two out of six directorates handle financial institutions and markets. It is this DG which is primarily in charge of identifying remaining obstacles to the single market in financial services (and other areas) and initiating legislative proposals aimed at removing those obstacles. The other DG that is relevant to financial services is the powerful DG Competition. EU competition policy is subdivided into three relatively autonomous fields: restrictive practices, concentration control and state aids. One peculiar element of banking is the 'gentlemanly' behaviour of bankers. According to one official at DG Competition, this may explain why there are *no* complaints for restrictive practices in banking.[8] As to merger control, so far there have not been mergers leading to market shares comparable to those in cars, pharmaceuticals or aircraft. Hence, the main area of relevance is state aids, where investigation and complaints have developed throughout the 1980s leading to a certain number of significant decisions. In finance, this policy domain is even more recent, provided that the 'book case' has been Crédit Lyonnais, where a first decision was taken in 1995.

The European Parliament (EP) has played an increasingly significant role. The extension of the co-decision procedure to article 100a (now article 95, TCE) has transformed the EP into a major actor in single market policies. As for financial services, the Commission for Economic and Monetary Affairs (ECOM) has become a major target for financial lobbyists. An 'intergroup' made up of members of ECOM and the representatives of banks and bank associations organizes regular meetings on issues relating to financial policies. Christa Randzio-Plath, the German chair of ECOM, is repeatedly quoted by interviewees as a frequent contact at the EP.

The third component of the European level are the bank representatives and lobbyists themselves. Bank associations are quite numerous, but there are mainly three that are present on most topics, while most others are more limited in scope:[9] the European Banking Federation, the European Savings Banks Association and the European Co-operative Banks' Association. Apart from European associations, most German associations, as well as the biggest European banks, possess Brussels offices. Finally, there are a certain number of financial lobbyists working for several firms and there are the heads of the 'government relations departments' or 'European affairs departments' in the major Anglo-Saxon banks, who are not permanently in Brussels but who maintain high-level contacts with the Commission.

The emerging European level is developing several specific characteristics. It is clear that the whole purpose of the European Union, which for most of the past forty years has been essentially economic, favours certain types of governance over others. Unlike the national levels, it has no specific arrangements to resist liberalization. More important, its only *raison d'être* is the liberalization of capital movements and the distance-selling of financial services, since the legitimacy of its policies derive from the Treaty's provisions on the common (now single) market. If one limits the analysis to the governance of finance or even to regulatory policy in banking in Europe, this tendency towards a changed state–market balance in favour of markets is largely confirmed.

From this point of view, there has been, on the one hand, a tendency towards German-style universal banking, i.e. the possibility to sell all financial services from retail banking to consulting within the same bank. At the same time, opening up markets has meant liberalizing capital flows, making markets available to foreign competitors and rendering them more transparent. This means promoting common accounting standards, harmonizing fund requirements and other regulatory issues, and promoting international ratings. This has mainly favoured the development of financial markets and equity capital. The emerging European model is therefore clearly closest to what Zysman called the 'capital-market based' model of finance.

In spite of some progress, however, the European level has been limited in its expansion and efficiency by the reticence of the Council and certain member states to press forward on many issues considered vital for national financial systems. Even though something close to a policy community is emerging at this European level, for a long time it has been restrained by the power politics of the Council. Things are starting to change, though, as on the one hand regulatory activism in Europe coincides with tough negotiations within the G10 ('Basle 2'), and on the other state-aid policy becomes more and more aggressive towards certain types of national arrangement. Moreover, it has proved difficult to build up a working policy community in finance. Put differently, there has been no clear institutionalization of relationships between actors. While there have been attempts by the Commission to approach bankers, and by bankers to approach the European Parliament, this has not led to any sort of identifiable policy network. The main reason for this is the unpredictability of the European policy process. While 'trust' does play a role in specific relationships – Commission–bankers, bankers–Parliament – it is rather weak when it comes to the actual decision-making stage. The Council may at any point completely upset the policy process, due to a reversal in domestic public opinion or a new governing coalition. The resulting instability may act as an insurmountable brake to the policy process (cf. German opposition to the take-over directive).

In most such situations the Commission has followed a very opportunistic line of action. As a 'purposeful opportunist' (Cram 1997), it has always used privileged relationships with market actors to back its own positions. However, in case of conflict or agreement with the Council, it has always been quick to dissolve 'expert committees' and 'forum groups'. Another problem related to the Commission is its strong internal fragmentation. Different directorate-generals will pursue opposing policy objectives, and on some issues, such as consumer credit, opposition is strong.

These elements have undoubtedly created obstacles to the emergence of stable policy communities at the European level. The application of concepts from domestic politics to European politics is consequently difficult. Be it *'dirigiste'*, 'corporatist-esoteric' or 'industry–finance ties', none of the national 'models' applies to the European level, but partial validation can be found for any of these. A specific 'market–state' relationship may eventually emerge, but it is difficult to define it clearly at this stage. Recent developments may give some clues, and they will be discussed at the end of this chapter.

Towards a single European banking regime

The European level of banking regulation has increased its authority and competencies since the beginning of the Single Market Programme (SMP), over a decade and a half ago. It has repeatedly tried to revitalize the project of a single market in financial services. The kind of market that the Commission intends to build is very much in line with the most liberal demands of transnational financial firms. Moreover, the Commission has been able to offer support to liberalization through state-aid policy. Both examples clearly confirm continuing integration and the relative weakening of national institutions and arrangements. Thus, recent developments show that MLG in banking policy may be less stable and long-lasting than imagined. The inherent tensions and diversity of MLG, applied to a specific topic such as financial regulation, are eventually at the origin of outright conflicts, which are likely to lead to the relative strengthening of some level(s) at the expense of others.

European-level initiatives: how to achieve the single market in financial services

One of the priorities of the new single market strategy presented by the Commission in November 1999 aims at improving market efficiency.[10] Financial markets are to be paid special attention: the Financial Services Action Plan (FSAP) is to remedy the identified shortcomings of the Single Market in Financial Services. The FSAP was proposed by the Commission, following a demand made by the Cardiff European Council (15 and 16 June 1998). The survey launched by the Commission in 1996 to evaluate the impact of the SMP had shown the limits of European integration in financial services. While retail banking had been expected to resist integration, the evolution of other areas remained well below expectations (Commission of the European Communities 1997). The Commission has summarized the FSAP's objectives under four headings:

- Completing a single wholesale market;
- Developing open and secure markets for retail financial services;
- Ensuring the continued stability of EU financial markets;
- Eliminating tax obstacles to financial market integration.

All in all, forty-four measures are to be implemented by 2005 at the latest. In this context the Commission has launched an unprecedented consultation process with banks and financial firms in general. It has created six so-called 'forum groups' on different areas, made up of banking representatives, to discuss the necessary policy initiatives. First and foremost, these groups provide cheap expertise to the underfed Commission. It goes further, however, since the approval of new legislation by these actors is seen as a way of increasing the Commission's authority and legitimacy in this area. Yet, so far, consultations and auditions in the area of financial policy have tended to involve a limited number of 'experts', mostly from UK and US banks.

The 'public interest' clause in the Investment Services Directive has also limited the impact of the 'single passport' for investment services and maintained a high degree of host country control in most cases. The revision of this directive has been under way for several years, but no agreement has been found. In a similar fashion the much publicized Pension Funds Directive has not yet been approved. Both these measures are considered essential, though, for achieving the much-quoted 'most competitive and dynamic knowledge-based economy in the world, capable of sustainable economic growth with more and better jobs and greater social cohesion', called for by the Lisbon European Council (23 and 24 March 2000).

Priority in the FSAP is clearly given to capital markets aspects with the introduction of a single passport for issuers, the elimination of barriers to pension fund investment, the introduction of common accounting standards and the implementation of the risk capital action plan (Randzio-Plath 2000: 193). The European Parliament largely endorsed the plan in its resolution of 13 April 2000, but has emphasized the importance of consumer protection, more than the Commission's outline does. Since that time there has been some significant progress. The Commission has already set up the European Securities Committee (ESR), which will oversee the establishment of an 'integrated securities' market' by 2003. The ESR will produce legislation within the framework fixed by the Council. Only implementation is to be left to European and national administrations.

A second area worth examining is 'Basle 2'. To a large extent, the Commission limits itself to examining G10 guidelines, to turn them into directives. The omnipresent goal of creating a 'level playing-field' prevents officials and governments from pursuing different or stricter regulatory policies. Those would necessarily result in a competitive disadvantage for European banks compared to their US-American and Japanese competitors. The idea is that a level playing-field requires identical regulations and information requirements, and that any differences will disadvantage those that have to comply with stricter national regulations. There is no 'race to the bottom', however, in this area. Criticisms and comments on the currently negotiated 'Basle 2' agreement are attempting to emphasize its too demanding capital ratios (Genschel and Plumper 1997).

The European Parliament has underlined the necessity of intervening early on in the process in order to improve the democratic legitimacy of G10 decisions. The current draft has led to a lot of public debate, especially in Germany where the use of international rating agencies and strict capital ratios are said to threaten current structures of SME financing. On the whole, however, these developments tend to show that the European level is attracting increasing responsibilities and that member states' resistance to the transfer of these responsibilities is diminishing. The creation of the European Securities Committee in June 2002, moreover, is likely to accelerate integration in the area of securities markets. Other areas of finance may follow. It appears that the centralization of regulation and the maximum harmonization of national regulation are increasingly being accepted. In this respect, the European level is able to push national levels towards a more capital-market based model of financial governance.

The changing attitude of governments and changing multi-level alliances

European integration increasingly structures policy attitudes among economic actors. It is shaping the major divides and cleavages among European banks and financial services. While there was outright suspicion and defiance during the Single Market Initiative (see Josselin 1996), attitudes have begun to change. Many actors generally took 'pro-integration' stances, but they never had to be very precise about their exact content. Hence, for a long time, the very vagueness of such pro-European attitudes hid potential cleavages and opposition. Over the past few years, however, the consequences of European integration have been felt and sometimes resented by an increasing number of actors. Several factors have contributed to this strengthening of European integration. The first and main factor is the Single Currency. Monetary union has fundamentally transformed the economic environment of financial services. A process of profound restructuring in the banking sector started in the mid-1990s in anticipation of the consequences of monetary union. As a consequence, 'national champions' such as BNP in France or Deutsche Bank in Germany have adapted and 'Europeanized' their strategies. Most major international banks now openly support the majority of developments in European financial integration. A 'European Financial Services Round Table' was created in 2001 to promote the integration of retail markets in finance (European Financial Services Round Table 2002). The CEOs of most major financial groups are part of that round table.[11] Smaller banks are increasingly reluctant to support further integration and defend the principle of 'mutual recognition' against 'savage' harmonization. Even if there is nothing like a transnational anti-integration coalition, a transnational cleavage is increasingly visible, the main discriminatory factor being size. The FSAP and, especially, state aid policy have tended to strengthen the opposition of already sceptical actors to increased European financial integration.

At the same time, resistance from national regulators has diminished. With the changeover to the Single Currency, many central banks have obtained complete independence from the government. They therefore possess complete autonomy in the area of monetary policy and, arguably, a strong influence on economic policy in general. While this is not very new for the German Bundesbank, it is clearly revolutionary for the Banque de France. As explained earlier, the Bank of England has recently also received complete autonomy in the area of monetary policy, but has had to abandon all regulatory and supervisory power to the Financial Services Authority. The FSA is still very young, and its difficulties relate to reconciling three different 'cultures' – banking, insurance and investment. While Germany has adopted a similar scheme in the area of regulation and supervision, its new structure falls short of excluding the central bank from 'banking policy'. The Bundesbank will continue to have a say in this area. France is slightly different again, since all expertise in this area is concentrated in the *Commission bancaire*, which 'belongs' to the Banque de France, i.e. it is an administrative division of the Banque de France. Recent French attempts to increase the relative power of the Treasury have not had any impact so far.

With the emergence of 'truly European' financial conglomerates such as HSBC in the UK and Allianz-Dresdener in Germany, and others to come, many accept that stronger coordination is necessary. Even though most central bankers do not favour any strong integration, they do not appear to be strongly opposed to any of the current proposed measures, or to the European Securities Committee.[12] As for the European institutions, they have been 'naturally' favouring further integration. While efficiency-related arguments have been put forth again and again, it is clear that other, more 'bureaucratic', interests play a central role in European integration (see Cram 1997). In this area it has been mainly the European Commission and, to a lesser extent, the European Parliament and the European Central Bank which have tried to play a role.

The Commission and, more specifically, the DG Internal Market have favoured further integration ever since the Single Financial Market was implemented. Initially Commission activity was confined to attempts to bring financial integration back onto the agenda of the Council. Several hearings, expert groups and reports were designed to develop efficiency-related arguments, as well as to testify to the financial industry's approval of such measures. Interestingly, on some issues such as the prospectuses and market abuse directives, existing expert groups were not actually consulted, since Council approval in those areas was granted before expert groups produced any results. The market abuse directive provides an example of such an 'acceleration' which led to a comparatively short co-decision procedure. The Parliament, especially the parliamentary committee in charge of 'economic and monetary affairs', is known to be a strong supporter of harmonization. It is only since the Maastricht Treaty that the Parliament has actually been involved in 'European banking policy', and the action plan is the first major initiative it has had to deal with. Its position is overall more sensitive to SMEs and consumer protection than the Commission proposals, which are usually drafted by DG Internal Market.

The most significant and most influential change has taken place among member state governments. The reactions to the Lamfalussy Report clearly illustrate this. For years the Commission has used auditions and expert groups to favour further integration in the area of securities. The will to revise the Investment Services Directive dates back to the day the first directive was implemented, since the final draft had left many major players dissatisfied. It has taken just one European summit to put an end to years of discussions, auditions and expert groups. This is not the place to speculate about the reason of this major turn in the Council's position. However, it appears likely that the limits of the Single Market are being felt, as concentration processes in national financial systems are under way. States' regulatory capacity in this area has decreased and its main objective now is to allow national actors to compete on foreign markets.

Conclusion: only the temporary multi-level governance of European banking and finance?

In the light of the changes reported in this chapter, national levels are not merging or being replaced by the European level, at least not yet. None the less, the progress in the development of European banking policy calls into question the role of national policy-makers – to an ever increasing extent government ministries and regulatory agencies. Hooghe and Marks associate the European Union with 'type-1 MLG', which they see as being motivated by functional efficiency. This largely corresponds to the governance of finance in the European case. Backed by efficiency-related arguments, the regulation of finance is being progressively, albeit gradually, centralized at the European level, while 'local governments', i.e. national regulatory authorities, central banks or ministries, try to resist and to keep control of regulation.

This process is well known to federalist scholars, as Hooghe and Marks admit (Croisat and Quermonne 1999; Burgess 2000). Without going as far as to predict complete 'federalization', it is clear that type-1 MLG is hierarchical and likely to lead to centralization. The evolution of European financial regulation suggests that acceptance of the idea of a 'single market for financial services' back in 1986 actually implied further and more complete integration. The Single Currency has speeded things up as bank restructuring has proceeded in continental Europe, pushing policy-makers to set up clear rules and a 'level playing-field' in accordance with single market imperatives. Furthermore, progress on the FSAP and on state aid issues demonstrates that 'misfit' is increasingly difficult to sustain at the national level. Even member states such as France and Germany are finding they have to give in to the momentum of financial integration as national-level regulation is being challenged by community-level jurisdiction and the process of centralization in European Union banking policy.

In the meantime, national systems are increasingly 'hybridized' as they have to implement European directives that may sometimes contradict national rules and/or practices, such as high levels of state intervention. The two major member states, France and Germany, have repeatedly been in conflict with EU policies in the area of banking, usually at their own expense. One can assume that hybridization further supports European integration, since the contradictions of national systems appear to be reinforcing EU-level regulation and competencies.

Furthermore, there are signs that a restricted and tentative transnational financial policy community is emerging at the European level. Access to the European level is subject to several conditions. First of all, access is costly, thereby limiting the number of actors that may be present. In fact, as mentioned earlier, only about twenty of the major banks chose to be present in Brussels. Even fewer are actually able to 'lobby' Community institutions. The Commission carefully picks its allies in the private sector. Its main interest, however, remains to push its own agenda and to increase its own competencies. Expert committees, auditions and expertise are used in the political struggle over those competencies; and the Commission has shown repeatedly that it is able to make strategic use of these 'resources'. The Council, on the other hand, is sensitive to market participants' opinions, especially when they come from the member states. The Parliament appears to be less regarding when it comes to 'nationality', even if lobbies tend to contact 'national' parliamentarians. The emerging policy community is not stable and continues to shift, but cleavages are becoming visible. Most notably there is an implicit alliance between major European banks and the Commission, involving a desire to push integration. To some extent the Parliament feeds into that alliance. At the same time, smaller actors have a hard time getting heard and organized at the European level, although some German public banks have managed to play roles by using their vetos.

Consequently this chapter suggests that MLG in the area of finance is only temporary. The hierarchy between jurisdictions is leading, and will continue to do so, to a replacement of 'lower' national and subnational jurisidictions where they exist by European-level agencies and institutions. It has been argued that the focus on efficiency-related arguments in the most recent version of MLG (Hooghe and Marks 2001) may miss the politics and dynamics of MLG. Their efficiency argument makes premature judgements, effectively predicting outcomes before empirical research has been conducted. The quick survey of actors, interests and their evolution presented here shows that some of the issues just do not fit 'problem-solving' approaches. What we are witnessing in banking policy is two competing jurisdictions mobilizing strategies according to 'bureaucratic needs' involving survival and expansion. It is therefore necessary to focus on the *political dynamics* of multi-level governance and its material and distributive outcomes, rather than just its supposed 'superior problem-solving capacity'.

Notes

1 This chapter is an amended version of a paper presented at the conference 'Multi-level governance: interdisciplinary perspectives', University of Sheffield, June 2001. It draws on fieldwork undertaken for a recently completed PhD on banking interest groups in France, Germany and the UK.

2 The member countries are Belgium, Canada, France, Germany, Italy, Japan, Luxembourg, the Netherlands, Spain, Sweden, Switzerland, the United Kingdom and the United States

3 None the less, the Bank does possess a substantial 'financial stability' division, which *de facto* addresses issues related to 'macroprudential' supervision. This division clearly does play a role and the FSA and the Treasury do consult important issues with the Bank (various interviews).

4 Several interviewees have stressed the lead taken by the French state and, more particularly, by the French Treasury, sometimes in face of the lack of interest or outright reluctance of the concerned actors.

5 Private interview, 2001.

6 The organizations participating in the ZKA are the *Bundesverband Deutscher Banken* (private banks), the *Deutscher Sparkassen- und Giroverband* (savings banks), *Bundesverband der Volks- und Raiffeisenbanken* (cooperative banks), *Bundesverband der Hypothekenbanken* (mortgage banks) and the Bundesverband Öffentlicher Banken (*'Landesbanken'*).

Foreign banks ('*Auslandsbanken*') have long been excluded from the ZKA. Today they could join if they wanted to, but choose not to, according to the secretary-general of their association (interview, Frankfurt, 30 May 2001).

7 Formerly (i.e. before the Prodi Reform) DG 15, 'Internal Market and Financial Services'.

8 Interview, 2000.

9 Among these 'specialized' associations there are the European Mortgage Federation, the European federation of building societies (dominated by German and Austrian *Bausparkassen*) and the recently created European Association of Public Banks (dominated by German *Landesbanken*).

10 COM (1999) 624 final.

11 The following firms' CEOs are part of the EFSRT: AXA (France), Deutsche Bank (Germany), Nordea (Sweden), Assicurazioni Generali (Italy), ABN-AMRO Bank (Netherlands), CGNU (UK), ING Group (Netherlands), Royal Bank of Scotland (UK), BNP Paribas (France), UniCredito Italiano (Italy), BBVA (Spain), Münchener Rück (Germany), Allianz (Germany), AEGON (Netherlands), Fortis (Belgium).

12 Interviews at the Bundesbank, the Bank de France and the Bank of England, 2001.

8 The IMF, middle-income countries and the Asian financial crisis

Multi-level governance as adaptation

Ben Thirkell-White[1]

Introduction

The multi-level governance (MLG) literature has tended to be descriptive in character, drawing our attention to a number of shifts in the nature of governance, particularly within the EU. However, the literature has only just begun to pay attention to more general theoretical questions and to a wider range of institutions. In this chapter I want to determine how helpful the concept of MLG can be in exploring the international monetary regime that centres on the IMF – particularly in relation to conditionality in middle-income countries. I also want to provide some preliminary observations on the factors that have driven the IMF towards a system that resembles MLG and suggest some of the consequences the shift has had for IMF legitimacy.

My analysis is based on three trends that seem to me to be at the heart of the MLG literature:

1   The emergence of new flexible institutions whose jurisdictions are often defined in relation to emergent policy problems rather than pre-existing territorial boundaries.
2   The growing importance of non-state actors of various types: international institutions, regional and local government, NGOs and interest groups (both 'civil' and commercial), the markets, private-sector standard-setting bodies, etc.
3   A move from hierarchical rules-based systems of power centred on the nation-state towards less formal negotiated arrangements. Horizontal and vertical international linkages and relationships can be formed without the participation of nation-states opening up strategic struggles over forms of jurisdiction (so, for example, regional EU bodies may find it advantageous to deal with the EU directly without going through national governments).

In some cases the literature has simply been descriptive, documenting these changes and drawing out some of the detail. Here a key question has been how 'new' these developments really are. That will obviously depend on the institution concerned. In the case of the IMF, the degree of novelty varies, since some aspects (functional specificity and multiple actors) have been present for some time. However, I will argue that there are clear shifts along a continuum from an idealized, state-centred hierarchical system towards something more fluid and complex.

In other cases there has also been a more or less explicit normative enthusiasm for MLG. The emphasis is usually on flexibility and inclusiveness. The involvement of a wider range of actors within a less rigid framework provides the opportunity for more effective decision-making as more stakeholders are given a voice in the decision-making process. Working through negotiation rather than rules assists in producing flexible solutions to problems thrown up by a rapidly changing world. Institutional diversity may result in institutions that are better tailored to deal with specific circumstances, ensuring that issues are dealt with on the most appropriate scale for the problem concerned. For the most enthusiastic, it may even be possible to have competition between different institutions giving citizens choice over the mode of governance to which they are subjected.[2]

More recently, others are becoming more cautious.

> [W]e believe that multi-level governance, while tempting and attractive in its informality and orientation towards objectives and outcomes rather than focused on rules and formal arrangements, could be a 'Faustian bargain' in which core values of democratic government are traded for accommodation, consensus and the purported increase in efficiency in governance.
>
> (Peters and Pierre 2001b)

The concern is that rules-based frameworks are deliberately designed to clarify, and sometimes moderate, power relationships in the interest of broader social cohesion and perhaps various normative concerns. The danger of a more *ad hoc* fluid arrangement is that it will not be subject to these controls and, where there are conflicts of interest, will result in negotiations that favour more powerful actors. The sheer complexity of weakly institutionalized, multi-level relationships, and the opaque nature of negotiations relative to publicly established rules-based frameworks, may disguise power relationships or lead to anxiety that power relationships are being disguised.

One way to reconcile these perspectives is to acknowledge that there are degrees of movement away from a state-based system along a continuum. So, Hooghe and Marks make a distinction between Type I and Type II governance (Hooghe and Marks 2001). Type I governance is similar to federalism. Authority is dispersed in large packages to a limited number of non-overlapping jurisdictions. Type II governance is popular with economists and public-choice theorists. Here there are a far larger number of institutions designed to deal with particular problem areas: the picture is of:

> ... a complex and fluid patchwork of innumerable, overlapping jurisdictions. These jurisdictions are lean and flexible; they come and go as demands for governance change.
>
> (Hooghe and Marks 2001)

Hooghe and Marks suggest that Type II governance is most appropriate where jurisdictions are reasonably tightly defined and concern problems of coordination rather than distributive issues. Type I governance is less flexible, slower to adapt, and less able to deal with externalities and spill-overs across territorial jurisdictions, but it maintains the advantages of a more structured and transparent system of relationships. The two are not mutually exclusive. It is the relationship between them that is important. Ideally, one should try to create a mix of different kinds of governance depending on the policy areas that are being regulated. Type II governance has its place but should occur 'in the shadow of hierarchy' – within the context of a Type I structure. In very similar terms, Peters and Pierre conclude that:

> . . . multi-level governance embedded in a regulatory setting which enables weaker actors to define a legal basis for their action might be the best strategy to escape the Faustian bargain and to cheat the darker powers.
>
> (Peters and Pierre 2001b)

The analysis that follows will explore the way the IMF has tried to adapt to changes in the global economy with a particular focus on its relationship with middle-income countries. The first section of the paper will provide a historical overview, first of the way the IMF's role has adapted to changes in the global economy and then of the ways its institutional structures have evolved in response to that adaptation. In the second, more analytical, part of the paper, I will analyse these developments in terms of the three features of multi-level governance outlined on page 147. I will use some examples from the debates surrounding the Asian financial crisis that began in 1997 to illustrate the way the IMF's current institutions and mandate have functioned in practice. I will argue that the IMF's role has moved in a direction that means it has a greater need for Type I institutionalization, but that its institutional structure is in fact moving in a Type II direction. That seems to be the result of *ad hoc* adaptation in a context where there are distinct political difficulties in arriving at more deeply institutionalized bargains. This strategy has been successful in the short term but, following the Asian crisis, is increasingly being questioned.

From Breton Woods to the Asian crisis: adapting the IMF to a changing global economy

A changing role for the IMF

The IMF originally embodied a relationship between states. Multilateral rules were agreed for the governance of the international monetary system, the key obligations being a freely convertible currency and limits on exchange rate flexibility. To support these rules, the IMF would control a pot of funds contributed by the membership that could be used as a sort of insurance policy for openness:

lent to countries with balance-of-payments problems to ease adjustment. Together with the possibility of sanctioned devaluation, this provided countries with a 'double screen' to protect them from the socially damaging imperatives of gold standard adjustment (Cooper 1975).

The permanent, inclusive, legally binding, multilateral character of the institution that emerged was relatively novel (Burley 1993; Ruggie 1993b). However, it left few doubts about the continuing centrality of Westphalian sovereignty. Membership was voluntary, as was the decision to borrow (and therefore to accept conditionality). States were to remain solidly in control of the institution and its funds through their representatives on the Fund's two Boards. Relationships between the IMF and member countries were to be conducted solely through representatives of the financial arms of governments (Treasuries or central banks). Indeed the IMF regime, with its restrictions on capital flows, can be seen as an attempt to enhance states' collective sovereignty over international financial markets. It was a response to the social dislocations that had been so damaging during the Great Depression: an essential prerequisite for the postwar compromise of 'embedded liberalism' (Ruggie 1982).

In the early years, the central disputes within the Fund related to overall liquidity in the system and controversy over exchange rate changes (Ferguson 1988). Although resented, particularly in a Latin America committed to structuralist economics (Krasner 1968), the precise specification of conditionality (the focus of this chapter) was relatively uncontroversial (Finch 1989). Restrictions on capital flows limited the size of balance-of-payments crises, and resolution could be achieved by demand restraint. The Fund imposed ceilings on the money supply and fiscal spending but borrower governments had considerable freedom in how these were to be implemented. There was also reasonable technical consensus on the degree of restraint required (De Vries 1987; International Monetary Fund 2001c). In this context it was relatively easy to legitimate conditionality as simply the technical consequence of countries' pre-existing commitment to the Fund's code of conduct.

The relationships involved were relationships between states and had little impact on domestic societies.[3] They were, arguably at least, also reciprocal, in that all states (with the exception of a hegemonic US) were reasonably likely to find themselves needing to borrow from the Fund and therefore accepting its conditionality (though of course developing countries borrowed more often).

However, over time the situation has been transformed. For reasons that have been explored elsewhere (Eichengreen 1999), the Bretton Woods system broke down and states began to be more tolerant of capital flows. The return of international private sovereign (and later corporate) debt gradually resulted in a dramatic transformation of the IMF regime.

The rules-based regulatory framework evolved into one in which the Fund exercised 'firm surveillance' over member policies (Pauly 1997). The wide range of policies that might affect flexible exchange rates meant that the scope of surveillance expanded considerably. However, the limits of acceptable conduct were no longer clearly defined (Guitian 1992). In practice, non-borrowing countries were subject to a much looser discipline than in the past, exercised through negotiation and peer pressure – often outside the confines of the Fund – rather than through rules and enforcement (Baker, Chapter 6 of this volume).

In contrast, over the thirty years since the collapse of Bretton Woods the scope of conditionality has expanded dramatically, for a number of reasons (Polak 1991). Principally, the resurgence of private capital flows to developing countries in the 1970s allowed countries to leverage their balance-of-payments positions. When the debt crisis struck in the late 1970s and early 1980s, countries were therefore confronted by far larger crises than had been the case in the past. The sheer size of the problem ruled out a purely demand-side approach and the Fund was forced to try to help countries to grow as well as reduce spending. Without entering too deeply into debates about structural adjustment, it is important to note that supply-side measures are far more controversial and difficult to specify than the Fund's traditional policies had been. They also have a far more widespread and conspicuous domestic impact in developing countries.

This new type of crisis also initiated a new type of relationship between the IMF and other lenders. As crises became debt crises, the resources available for crisis resolution and the size of the funding gap depended on how much debt forgiveness or renegotiation other lenders were willing to undertake. IMF programmes became dependent on the actions of other lenders, and programmes would be more successful if the IMF could persuade them to be lenient. At the same time lenders could maximize the chances of repayment with the assistance of IMF conditionality (which it would be politically impossible for them to impose). There was some potential for a mutually advantageous arrangement under which IMF intervention would provide countries with better loan terms and the markets with greater security. However, tensions would remain since banks were still keen to minimize their losses at countries' expense. The way negotiations turned out in practice would be crucial (Finch 1989).

The second major change took place in the late 1990s as the Fund adopted a 'good governance' agenda. The Fund officially adopted governance policies quite late. The World Bank had begun to rediscover the importance of institutions in the late 1980s in response to the perceived failure of some of the market-centred excesses of its structural adjustment policies in Africa. The end of the Cold War then stimulated a far more political enthusiasm for democracy promotion and political conditionality amongst bilateral donors in the 1990s. Neither Bretton Woods institution is allowed to involve itself in the politics of member countries, but the Fund is particularly concerned to protect its neutral technocratic credentials. It was only in conjunction with a growing involvement with capital account issues that the Fund found a sufficiently technical reason to justify a more explicit involvement in governance issues. The central argument was that capital account stability is dependent on market confidence. Market confidence, in turn, is dependent on the transparency and predictability of domestic economic governance (Dhonte 1997). It was therefore alright for the Fund to become involved in governance issues where:

... poor governance would have a significant current or potential impact on macroeconomic performance in the short and medium term and on the ability of the government credibly to pursue policies aimed at external viability.

(International Monetary Fund 1997b: para. 9)

None the less, it is difficult to see the kinds of policies the IMF is involved in as purely 'technical' in their effects. So, for example, staff are to be concerned with

[l]imit[ing] the scope for ad hoc decision-making [and] rent seeking ... [through] liberalization of exchange, trade and price systems and the elimination of direct credit allocation.

(International Monetary Fund 1997b: para. 2)

... and to base their advice on the principles of 'transparency, simplicity, accountability and fairness'[4]

(International Monetary Fund 1997b: para 13).

Institutional adaptation

Despite significant changes in the IMF's role, there were surprisingly few changes in decision-making procedures and institutional form until the mid-1990s. The heart of the institution is the Executive Board, made up of twenty-four Executive Directors who represent the Fund's 192 member countries. Voting in the IMF is weighted, based on a country's 'quota' – the amount it is asked to contribute to Fund resources. Quotas, in turn, are officially determined on the basis of a complex formula designed to reflect a country's importance in the global economy. In fact, the issue of quota size has always been highly politicized and the main pre-1990 changes to Fund governance involved quota readjustments, first to reflect the power of oil producing countries as part of the NIEO movement, and later to recognize the growing importance of Japan.

When a country asks to borrow from the Fund, staff in Washington prepare a draft programme based on the relevant Area Department's information on the country concerned. A mission is then dispatched to the recipient country to gather further information and negotiate with government representatives (traditionally drawn from financial ministries and/or the central bank). The final programme is then moderated by the Fund's functional departments and submitted to the Executive Board for approval.

In practice the Executive Board invariably approves programmes so as not to undermine staff negotiating authority. However, if the Executive Board does not like measures that appear in a programme it makes its views clear during the approval process and the staff are requested not to include similar measures in the future. Staff wish to avoid provoking this reaction and are therefore tightly bound by Executive Board precedent. For complex or high-profile programmes, though, there may also be a high level of communication between the staff mission and the Executive Board or Managing Director during the negotiation process.

In keeping with the traditional conception of sovereignty, the IMF's Articles of Agreement make no stipulations about the way in which Executive Directors are to be held accountable to the countries they represent. They merely stipulate that EDs should be drawn from financial ministries or central banks. In fact, the Fund's architects, particularly Keynes, were concerned to limit the EDs' *political* accountability in the hope that they would identify with the institution and make decisions on the basis of a technical utilitarian conception of the common good rather than on narrow political criteria (Gardner 1980).

In practice, arrangements vary. Where EDs represent a number of countries, communication can be difficult. This situation is partly dealt with by appointing Alternate Executive Directors and research staff from a range of different countries but, by and large, EDs enjoy a great deal of freedom to make their own decisions.[5] At the other end of the spectrum, the Fund's location in Washington means that the US Treasury exercises considerable control over the US Executive Director. While discussing accountability with Congress, Thomas Dawson (a former US ED) suggested that Congress should 'lay it on Treasury not the poor US ED' (House Banking Oversight Subcommittee 1998).

Accountability is further complicated by the fact that decisions are largely made by 'consensus' rather than voting and, until recently, very little information was publicly available. This fits well with the Fund's vision of a technocratic institution partially insulated from political concerns offering a degree of representation of national interests, but is clearly problematic for accountability. Consensus is arrived at in the shadow of voting arrangements and need not imply anything like unanimous agreement. Since no vote takes place, it is difficult for domestic governments to determine whether their representatives are acting as instructed (Stiles 1991; Woods 2000). Since, originally, the arrangements agreed between governments and the Fund were also confidential it was very difficult for any outsider to monitor Fund operations.

It was only in the 1990s that this system began to change. Talk of a new world order based on liberal principles, combined with the Fund's own commitment to 'good governance' and 'transparency', inevitably led to pressure for institutional reform (Burnell 1994). The biggest change has been in the amount of information released about general Fund policy, decision-making and the specific details of particular Fund programmes. That development was particularly hard to avoid as the Fund's interest in policy credibility and the economics of information was fuelled by its growing involvement in capital account issues, particularly in the wake of the Mexican crisis (Kenen 1996).

More problematic, but potentially more significant over the longer term, have been moves towards more inclusive decision-making procedures. During the 1990s, there was mounting evidence that ever expanding IMF programmes were suffering from problems of non-implementation, and attention was turning to questions of 'ownership' (Killick 1995; Killick *et al.* 1998).

Traditionally the Fund had justified its rather narrow and secretive decision-making procedures on the ground that it carried out a tightly defined technical role and was seeking to minimize interference with domestic sovereignty. The Fund would calculate the overall size of necessary fiscal cuts, but it was up to governments (or more specifically to the financial technocrats that negotiated the programmes) whether they chose to make them by cutting back on military expenditure, civil service salaries or primary health care (Nowzad 1982).

As conditionality expanded to include poverty reduction and good governance, this position was increasingly untenable. The breadth of Fund programmes, now far more extensive than the narrow macroeconomic stipulations of the 1960s, made narrow technocratic representation seem highly anachronistic. Was the finance ministry really qualified to apportion funds in areas that increasingly covered the countries' entire development strategy? Even if it was qualified in technical terms, governments now needed far wider social cooperation to implement more intrusive programmes. Ownership would increasingly have to mean a broader public acceptance than narrow government consent could secure.

Although formal channels of representation have remained unchanged, informal procedures have been adapted. The IMF has increased the number of resident representatives in borrower countries and has encouraged them to make contacts with a wider range of political players and with broader social groups, including particularly trade unions and labour groups. NGOs, particularly those with a lobbying branch in Washington, have also had more access, and the IMF has run some high-level seminars on cooperation with 'civil society'.

The IMF and multi-level governance: evidence from the Asian financial crisis

The discussion so far has reviewed the evolution of the IMF's role and institutional structure up to the eve of the Asian crisis in 1997. The crisis provides a good test of the emergent middle-income country agenda that I have described, since it represents the culmination of a number of pre-existing trends. It was a pure capital account crisis, and IMF programmes were specifically designed to enhance market confidence. The new 'good governance' agenda played an important role, with governance featuring more extensively than ever before in the Asian programmes.

In this section I will use examples from the Asian crisis to analyse the changes in the IMF regime reviewed above in terms of the three core elements of the MLG literature that I identified at the beginning of the chapter. I will also discuss their relevance to the debates I reviewed there about the novelty of those changes and their normative evaluation.

Functionally driven, flexible problem-solving

The IMF's mandate was always specified in terms of a functional rather than a territorial jurisdiction, and that remains the case. However, the nature of the function that it serves has varied considerably over time. To some extent, flexibility and the ability to adapt are, as the MLG literature suggests, signs of institutional strength. However, rapid adaptation to changing circumstances implies considerable discretion as to how an institution's power is to be used, which can be problematic for institutional legitimacy.

In response to the capital account crises of the mid-to-late 1990s, the IMF extended its role in providing assistance for current account balance-of-payments crises into crises driven by the capital account. Rather than providing finance to cover what was essentially a 'cash flow' problem in the context of current account crises, the Fund's new role looked more like that of an international lender of last resort (LLR). The aim was to use a combination of lending and policy change to reverse an outflow of capital by enhancing market confidence in the economies concerned.

These crises struck very quickly and something clearly needed to be done: flexibility was an asset to the Fund. However, it also proved difficult to legitimate this new kind of intervention and the Fund's new role was the subject of considerable political controversy, particularly in Asia.

For many commentators, the IMF's emergent LLR function created moral hazard – bailing out imprudent lenders and borrowers. For some the problems should have been left to the markets to resolve (Calomiris 1998). For others, the IMF should have pursued a more interventionary course involving some kind of debt-workout procedure backed up with a temporary payment moratorium and perhaps capital controls (Radelet and Sachs 1998). Ultimately the LLR function will always involve complex political trade-offs between different interest groups as well as simply technical calculations, and it is this distributional aspect that led to legitimacy problems (Giannini 1999). If anything, flexibility therefore requires stronger mechanisms of accountability to reassure key stakeholders that adaptations are a genuine attempt to deal with events at hand rather than an unwarranted extension of institutional power.

Functional specificity also confers advantages, particularly in the context of an international institution that must be wary of infringing too deeply on jealously guarded state prerogatives. If narrow technical issues can be isolated, this may make it easier to establish institutional authority based on acquired expertise (broadly, the Type II model). I have already suggested that the relatively narrow scope of Bretton Woods-era conditionality meant that conditions were a less controversial issue than, for example, the overall level of liquidity in the international system. The problem is that, as we have seen, the boundaries between issues can be hard to maintain.

I have already shown that both the IMF's surveillance and its conditionality functions have expanded considerably over time. The Asian crisis marked a further extension with far deeper interventions into domestic systems of finance and corporate governance than the Fund has previously proposed. The most extreme case here is Indonesia, where letters of intent included legislation on corporate governance, central bank independence, bankruptcy, competition, prudential regulation, off-balance-sheet government financing, and financial and corporate sector restructuring (Government of Indonesia 1998).

This expansion into a much broader agenda caused considerable anxiety. Some felt that the IMF had become too involved in what should be domestic affairs (Feldstein 1998; International Financial Institution Advisory Commission 2000) Others, however, were principally concerned with the nature of what was included – provisions that (as they saw it) favoured financial and corporate interests – and argued that the Fund should also become involved in issues such as labour rights and the environment.[6]

Underlying both responses was the fact that it was increasingly difficult to see Fund interventions as part of an apolitical, technically-driven agenda. The fact that the economic consensus underpinning the adoption of structural adjustment in the 1980s had begun to fracture in relation to capital account crises added to the problems. The question was whether IMF legitimacy was better secured by limiting the IMF's role to a more narrow agenda or by broadening the scope of its interventions to achieve a wider social legitimation.

New actors

Here again, novelty could easily be exaggerated. IMF lending has always been a multi-level process. On the other hand it was originally confined to negotiations between states as representatives of their populations structured through the IMF's institutions. The transformation of the institution reviewed above clearly has created more important roles for a new series of actors, most noticeably other lenders and, more recently, a broader range of political actors.

Other lenders

The most fundamental change here is the increasing importance of other multilateral, bilateral and private finance providers in the negotiations surrounding IMF programmes. This was perhaps an inevitable development given the resurgence of capital flows. Once interest payments account for a significant part of the balance of payments on current account, dealing with capital account issues in the context of adjustment becomes unavoidable. None the less, the extent to which this has changed the character of IMF decision-making is important.

Under the Bretton Woods system, decisions about the level of resources available for adjustment and the conditions that would be attached rested with states. The influence that each state would have was formally delimited by the Articles of Agreement. Once debt negotiations began, some states were able to acquire additional influence through their position as bilateral lenders and their influence in the Paris Club.[7] More importantly, we saw that the IMF started to enter into a strategic relationship with private lenders when bargaining over the levels of resources that would be forthcoming.

With the development of the concept of a 'catalytic effect' the trend towards strategic interactions with the markets was pushed one step further. Instead of specific bargains with interested financial actors, the IMF has aimed to propose policies that 'enhance market confidence'.

The attempt to reverse capital flight in Asia provided the most extreme test of these attempts to date. Although there are obvious advantages in enhancing market confidence, the IMF's approach raised two key questions. The first concerns the costs of complying with market preferences, particularly when it appears that financial markets have been acting 'irrationally'. What policies are required and how much do they conflict with other state goals? The second problem concerns the extent to which those preferences can be identified and credibly implemented as part of IMF conditionality.

Both issues were raised in Asia. The structural parts of IMF programmes were justified in terms of both good governance (which I will discuss later) and 'market discipline'. A capital account crisis would tend to imply that capital had been misallocated before the crisis took hold. For the IMF, that was because companies were protected from proper market discipline as a result of limited transparency and moral hazard (International Monetary Fund 1997d).

The situation was different in different countries. So, for example, in Korea the principal problem was the capture of banks by large conglomerates – though a history of government involvement in strategic industrial policy played a role (Balino and Ubide 1999). In Indonesia, the main difficulty was the relationship between large Indonesian corporations (and indeed foreign joint ventures) and an extensive system of political patronage (International Monetary Fund 1997c; Robison 1997). In both cases the solution was the same. The state should be confined to a regulatory function, the central bank should be made independent, company reporting should be improved, corporate governance reformed to keep an arm's-length relationship between firms and banks, minority shareholder rights should be enhanced, and markets should be opened further so that foreign capital could discipline domestic policy (Balino and Ubide 1999; Government of Indonesia 1998). In short, the G7 market discipline agenda described by Baker (Chapter 6 of this volume) should be extended into Asia.

These interventions were highly controversial. First, were the policies really necessary to enhance market confidence, or did they in fact merely represent the preferences of the Fund's leading shareholders? After all, it is not as though they were negotiated as a result of any formal consultations with 'the markets'. Sceptics pointed out that Indonesian corruption had been a well-known feature of business in the country for several decades. The reforms may have been desirable but were they actually necessary or were they merely the price that had to be paid for IMF assistance (McLeod 1998)?

Second, even if we accept that the policies did reflect market preferences, what were the costs of compliance?[8] For some, even after the crisis, the Korean system of corporate governance remained a key reason for its economic success. Its deliberate purpose was to extend time horizons, limiting market discipline in the interests of long-term investment in technological innovation (Chang *et al.* 1998; Wade and Veneroso 1998). IMF-style policies would outlaw a variety of interventions such as the system of ethnic redistribution in Malaysia that was, arguably, central to ending the ethnic tensions of the 1960s (Mahathir 1998). There were fewer justifications for the Indonesian system but the social conse- quences of attempts to dismantle it (Mietzner 1999; Schwarz 1999) might at least give pause for thought.

In short, there is one set of questions about the limitations on state actions imposed by somewhat faceless financial markets. There is also a second set of questions about the extent to which the measures imposed by the IMF merely reflect those limitations, moderate them (as the IMF was originally intended to do), or enhance their restraining power. In terms of legitimacy the position of the IMF is more problematic because it represents a more concrete form of agency – a single institution actively making decisions with some power of enforcement.

These issues, relating to non-state financial actors, also clearly overlap with the questions about functional specificity and trade-offs reviewed earlier in the chapter. The IMF's relationship with the World Bank provides an interesting link. At one level, the tendency for World Bank lending to be tied to the signa- ture of a Fund programme seems to enhance IMF power, causing problems for IMF legitimacy. At another, the World Bank offers the potential for trade-offs and complementarities between the IMF's narrow role and the Bank's broader and perhaps more socially oriented agenda (Polak 1994). None the less, questions remain about which institution is in charge and which agenda will dominate – questions we will return to later in the chapter.

Government and civil society

The second development is an expansion in the number of political actors that are in some way involved in IMF decision-making. As we have seen, this is presented as a democratization of IMF decision-making in response to concerns that an increasingly intrusive domestic agenda required a broader legitimacy than consultations within the finance ministry could provide. As with the involve- ment of financial sector actors, this is clearly to be welcomed where there is a genuine common interest: where additional voices enable programmes to be better tailored to local needs. What is less clear, though, is what will happen when there are conflicts.

Figure 8.1 provides an indication of the complexity of the new model as it is discussed in IMF accounts. In the past, IMF missions negotiated with govern- ment officials on the basis that those officials were qualified to represent their populations and responsible for implementation of any agreement reached. Under the new model it appears that IMF staff teams should coordinate with other IFIs, particularly the World Bank and be aware of, perhaps even take into account, the views of both members of the other branches of government and NGOs of various kinds (International Monetary Fund 1998b). The sheer number of different actors would immediately suggest to any political scientist that conflicts were inevitable. The important questions then concern the priori- ties given to the views of different actors.

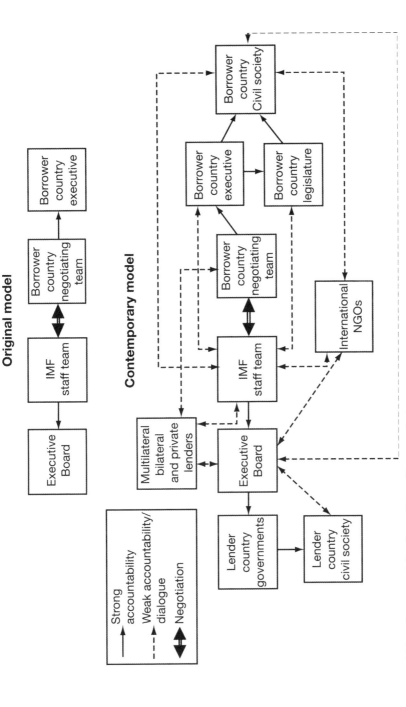

Figure 8.1 Old and new models of conditionality negotiations

The IMF's traditional utilitarian economic instincts would be to try to specify some optimum policy path based on maximizing aggregate (economic) welfare. Some versions of an emerging post-Washington consensus, based around an expanded technical agenda incorporating the importance of institutions, can perhaps be seen in this way.[9] The problem is that the wider this agenda gets, the more difficult it is to regard economists' prescriptions for the most efficient use of resources as an appropriate proxy for any comprehensive conception of aggregate utility.[10] Ultimately some kind of more political method of decision-making, where accountability as well as merely representation comes into play, would seem necessary.

Fewer rules, more negotiation, blurred hierarchy

The previous two sections have suggested that, where there is an extensive convergence of interests or the relevant policy issues are narrow, functionally specific institutions involving a wide number of actors can be a useful innovation. The problem is that, once conflicts need to be resolved in situations where utilitarian aggregation is not straightforward or is politically unacceptable, it remains necessary to establish a basis on which decisions can be made. In this section I will begin with the logic of the IMF's intergovernmental model, suggest some reasons why there has been pressure to include more actors, and move on to an analysis of the practical effects of this change based on the experience of IMF interventions in Korea and Indonesia.

Pre-Asia developments: MLG and hierarchy

This is the issue on which there is most danger that the novelty of multi-level governance could be exaggerated when talking about the IMF. It has never been correct to think about international institutions in the same terms as we have become accustomed to think about modern states since Hobbes. They have never been based, ultimately, on a single sovereign body which possesses the right to act as final arbiter in disputes and the coercive power to enforce its judgements (Hinsley 1986; Hobbes 1991). Instead, international institutions have always embodied more or less fragile bargains between states with varying degrees of institutionalization, enforced through peer pressure or, at best, various kinds of institutional sanction.

As I suggested in the section on IMF history, part of the novelty of the postwar international institutions was their degree of institutionalization. The IMF was considerably more than a treaty between states. It involved *multilateral* obligations and relative independence from individual states in some aspects of decision-making.

However, the Fund's legal framework also had its limits. Aspects of the Articles relating to Fund policy remained ambiguous and had to be negotiated in response to circumstances. Since the collapse of the Bretton Woods system, Fund policy has moved much further away from a rules-based framework. This is particularly noticeable in the content of conditionality, where the only meaningful guidance is Executive Board precedent, and even that is not binding on future Board decisions.[11]

The rules determining how decisions were made were originally rather clearer, but they too have begun to come under threat as the Fund's conditionality has expanded to encompass domestic issues that are harder to see simply in terms of negotiations between states. Under the original IMF vision, it was clear that states – and only states – were to represent the interest of their citizens (even if they were not always very good at doing so in practice). Accountability was clearly defined, if not always necessarily appropriate. Over time that system, though, has come under threat. As conditionality has expanded, states are finding it ever more difficult to agree to internationally acceptable policies that can also be legitimated at the domestic level. For a time, beginning in the late 1970s, the Fund was willing to assist states by participating (at least passively) in a scapegoating strategy. States would make internationalist agreements (more or less willingly) with the Fund while portraying them domestically as foreign impositions that they were powerless to avoid. So Pauly has argued that even more important than the Fund's role in global governance was its ability to act as a political 'buffer' between the logic of the international political economy and that of domestic systems (Pauly 1997).

Over time, though, the political stakes involved in Fund policy have got too high for the IMF to continue participating in this strategy. Citizens have become ever more sophisticated in scrutinizing their governments' relationships with the Fund. The global media has also made it more difficult to say one thing for an international audience and another for domestic consumption. So, for example, the US Commerce Department's attempts to persuade Congress that the IMF was a 'battering ram for US interests' during the crisis went down rather poorly with publics in Asia.

The IMF response has been to press governments to acknowledge ownership of programmes, while trying to take into account the views of a wider range of actors in both borrower and lender countries when it formulates policy. The advantage of including new actors is that it should encourage dialogue so as to arrive at a mutually satisfactory arrangement in which everyone gains. IMF accounts, not surprisingly, stress the welfare-maximizing aspects of the Fund's role. This is where much of the power of utilitarian arguments comes from in terms of legitimation. Dispute and resistance is portrayed as special pleading on the behalf of (often powerful) minorities, undermining the (democratic) level playing-field of the market (International Monetary Fund 1997b). What Fund accounts are more reluctant to talk about are situations that are not best thought of primarily as problems of coordination, and where utility calculations involve (relative or absolute) losers as well as winners. At that point, difficult decisions have to be made, and the question of how the calculation is arrived at, and therefore whose views are to be given priority and for what reason, becomes unavoidable. As the circle of actors involved in decision-making widens, these issues become both more important and more difficult.

Under the old model, policy decisions were regulated by pre-existing rules to some extent. Otherwise, where discretion was exercised, the ultimate answer was that states' interests would prevail in proportion to their voting rights. Under the new, looser, negotiated model the answers are less clear, at least in advance. Will developed country civil societies have more influence than developing country civil societies or even developing country states? Will the financial markets have more influence than either? How important will be the views of other bilateral and multilateral donors? The loose nature of current institutional arrangements makes those questions difficult to answer in advance, which is why I will now turn to a more thorough (if unavoidably still rather brief) look at the experiences of Korea and Indonesia during the Asian crisis.

The new system in practice

Success in Korea

The most politically and economically successful IMF programme, designed for South Korea, appears to provide some reasons for optimism. Kim Dae Jung was not a party to the negotiations for the first IMF programme and he campaigned against some aspects of it during the Presidential elections in late 1997. However, he was later converted and went on to campaign enthusiastically for implementation.[12] That seems to be because he felt the programmes provided an opportunity to pursue his long-standing political agenda of 'democratizing' the Korean economy by reducing the power of the Korean *chaebol* (Kim 1985).

A combination of direct IMF persuasion and Kim's radical credentials then enabled him to convince the Korean labour unions to enter into tripartite talks with government and the *chaebol*. The unions agreed to accept reduced job security and some redundancies in return for promises that business would also be made to suffer for its mistakes (Tripartite Commission 1998). There was clear popular support for the promise that the IMF programme would attack the authoritarian and often corrupt relationship between big business and big government, even if there was concern at high interest rates and less interest in internationalization (Shin and Rose 1998). The settlement, and the IMF programme more broadly, still proved difficult to implement. However, the positive initial contacts between the IMF and the labour movement were an important step in promoting programme ownership and the populist appeal of some aspects of the IMF's good governance agenda provided further assistance.

None the less, there was a strong current of minority opinion that saw the IMF programme as an imposition by the US and Japan designed to undermine Korea's industrial strength: 'A senior US Treasury official backhandedly manipulated IMF negotiations to push for market opening, while Japan used financial aid as a weapon to prop open the [Korean] domestic market for their goods' (*Dong a Ilbo*, 3 December 1997).

Particularly problematic in this respect was the secrecy with which initial negotiations were conducted. It was well known that the US had been pressing for market opening in Korea for many years – particularly in relation to inward direct investment and access to the market for financial services (Dobson and Jacquet 1998; Mo and Myers 1993). Two senior US Treasury figures arrived in Seoul at the same time as the first IMF mission, and it was widely reported in the press that Robert Rubin had personally held up negotiations for several hours pressing for more comprehensive standards for publication of *chaebol* accounts (Cumings 1998). The best available account draws out three agendas: an IMF staff agenda based around fiscal transparency; a US agenda centred on market access; and a Korean government agenda of labour market flexibility and corporate governance reform (Matthews 1998). However, the extent of overlap between the three agendas and the amount of controversy involved remains unclear.

The second big question mark concerns the reasoning behind an initial reluctance to address the debt problem directly, followed by an abrupt about-face at the end of December after the first programme failed to restore confidence. At this point, foreign banks (under pressure from their supervisory authorities, particularly the US Treasury) agreed to roll over loans in return for a government guarantee.

Overall, however, the broad political support it received makes it difficult to be too critical of the IMF programme, at least on political grounds.

Failure in Indonesia

There is a broad consensus that Indonesia was the least successful programme and that non-implementation and political difficulties were at the heart of the problems. What is in dispute are the implications of that analysis – could the situation have been handled better, or was disaster inevitable? Here the difficulties confronted by the new agenda in the face of significant disagreements are revealed.

Initial Indonesian responses to the crisis were widely praised. The *rupiah* was allowed to float, the government budget was cut and Suharto went to the IMF before the crisis got out of hand (World Bank 1998). However, it appears that Suharto was expecting to be able to resolve the crisis through his usual technique of sound macro-economic management compensating for patronage-driven micro-economic eccentricity (Reisenhuber 2001).

Unfortunately for Suharto, the IMF had other ideas. Fund staff seem to have decided that confidence would only be enhanced by a demonstrated commitment to tough reforms. The centrepiece, closing sixteen Indonesian banks, proved a disastrous mistake that triggered market panic. However, the problems were exacerbated when Suharto allowed two of the banks, owned by his relatives, to remain open, thus sending entirely the wrong messages to the markets (Enoch *et al.* 2001).

The second programme cut even deeper into the networks of patronage that were a key part of Suharto's power, directly damaging the interests of some of his longest-standing allies (Government of Indonesia 1998). Rather than implementing this programme, Suharto began to blame the crisis on ethnic Chinese Indonesians; criticized the IMF, calling for an 'IMF plus programme'; invited Johns Hopkins economist Stephen Hanke to discuss introducing a currency board; and argued that aspects of the IMF programme conflicted with the Indonesian constitution (Robison and Rosser 2000).

The political and economic situation deteriorated rapidly and, following bloody riots and demonstrations in Jakarta in May 1999, Suharto resigned, paving the way for the introduction of multi-party democracy in Indonesia. However, political uncertainty continued and the Indonesian economy has been slow to recover.

The IMF argued that its programmes would have worked if Suharto had implemented them. The fact that he did not was hardly its fault (Lane *et al.* 1999). Others have argued that it was clear from the start that the IMF programmes could not be implemented. Publishing that kind of agenda for reform was bound to *undermine* market confidence, as it suggested that, in the IMF's opinion, wide-ranging reforms (that could not in fact be implemented) were essential for Indonesian economic recovery. The IMF was screaming 'fire' in the theatre (Radelet and Sachs 1998).

Clearly, assessing the impact of IMF policy in Indonesia is controversial. At best, though, the Indonesian experience demonstrates how difficult it is to achieve IMF purposes without state support. One of the aims of the new IMF agenda would seem to be to use governance policies and wider social consultation to put pressure on states from below to implement policies that the IMF regards as being in the interests of their populations. The problem is that, if states completely refuse to play along, it is not clear what the IMF can do. This is reflected in IMF statements about the collapse of Suharto's New Order. The IMF is keen to claim some credit for standing up to Suharto's corruption while emphasizing that undermining Suharto's authority was never a deliberate intention of the IMF programme.

This is, of course, a difficult line to tread politically, and one that makes it all the more important that the IMF is able to justify its policies as the measures required to restore market confidence. If it cannot do so, its residual claim to be an apolitical technocratic institution falls apart and its interventions in Indonesia start to look about as political as they could possibly be. The problem is that, given the rather faceless nature of 'the markets' and the failure of the IMF programme (albeit in part because of non-implementation), this conclusive justification is hard to come by.

Analysis

In Korea, what we see (with some reservations) is an example of the way in which the new MLG agenda can work well. Key figures in the Executive were won over to the programme. The IMF's new-found willingness to talk to labour and the coincidence of IMF 'good governance' goals with the populist aspects of Kim Dae Jung's political programme (in the sense of being anti big business, rather than anti business *per se*) made implementation easier. There were some negotiations at the margins and there may have been more ambivalence about the IMF's market discipline agenda but, by and large, the programme can accurately be seen as a cooperative enterprise. In terms of developed-country opinion, the programme provided something for industrial interests (greater market access to Korea), financial interests (financial opening and an easier credit assessment environment in the future) and left-wing critics (the new-found willingness to negotiate with labour).

In Indonesia, in contrast, we see the limitations of the agenda when perceived interests are in stark conflict. In terms of hierarchy, the controversy surrounding the IMF programme could be reformulated as follows:

1   Was the IMF accurately expressing the choices faced by Suharto, given the will of the markets? Or was it expressing the desires of its leading shareholders and therefore exaggerating the restrictions on possible state action?
2   To what extent are the views of 'leading shareholders' to incorporate the views of transnational NGOs operating within their capitals, or business groups, or representatives of the financial markets?
3   Did Suharto have an alternative choice to following the IMF programme (such as instituting a currency board/capital controls) and (looking back to (1)), what market reaction (and therefore cost) would have attached to any such choice?
4   To what extent can popular Indonesian frustration with KKN (corruption collusion and nepotism) be seen to demonstrate a concurrence of interests between Indonesian civil society and the IMF's shareholders/the markets (question (1)) and therefore a justification for the overthrow of the Suharto regime on the grounds that it served no-one but itself? Who has the right to decide and (looking back to (3)) is the choice correctly seen as one between Suharto and complete agreement with the IMF?

What is problematic about the IMF's new role and institutional structure is the extent to which it reflects ambiguity and indeterminacy about how each of these questions is to be answered in terms of both process and outcome. When put in more general terms, the significance of the issues involved should be readily apparent.

1   To what extent can, should and do states collectively resist or accede to the will of the markets?
2   Where should the balance be struck between the need to resolve international coordination problems through collective agreement and the right of states to choose to take the individual consequences of derogation?

3   What say should the citizens of individual states or indeed civil society within those states have in the choices their states are to be allowed under (2)?

4   To what extent should states be allowed to appeal to other states' populations in an attempt to reinforce their (3) attempts to influence the outcome of choice (2)?

5   On what basis and through what institutions are the conflicts at each level to be sorted out?

The evidence of Indonesian experience suggests that, not only does the emergence of multi-level governance fail to propose solutions to these problems, it can serve to make it very difficult to identify the way that questions have been answered in practice.

> ... multi-level governance appears incapable of providing clear predictions or even explanations (other than the most general) of outcomes in the governance process ... It is very nice to say that a range of actors were involved and negotiated a solution but we would argue that a more definitive set of predictions are needed.
>
> (Peters and Pierre 2001b)

Indeed things are further complicated by the fact that there is no reason why different answers about whose voice is heard may not be found in relation to decisions on different substantive issues. If the answers are to be determined by a disparate set of non-transparent negotiations it is very difficult for anyone to know who is in charge, to hold them to account, and to organize political resistance to unacceptable decisions. It is also difficult to create the feeling of broad social trade-offs where losses on one issue are compensated for by gains on another, since it is never clear how independently different institutions are acting.

Here, even the Korean experience raises cause for concern. We do not actually know how far the US exceeded its official power as delimited by the IMF's Articles of Agreement. We do not know how much that mattered – how much Kim Dae Jung was a willing accomplice. For those who are concerned about the IMF's technical competence, it is also difficult to know how different IMF judgements were from those of the World Bank, the Asian Development Bank and most importantly Korean government policy-makers. It is therefore difficult to know who to hold to account and where efforts to advocate a different approach should be directed. The danger for IMF legitimacy here is that, even if decisions were made by a democratically elected and democratically accountable Korean president with no more than technical assistance from the IMF, it would still have been open to those who were disgruntled to portray the situation as an example of American and Japanese neo-colonialism with some degree of credibility.

A certain flexibility in Fund policy and an expansion of the number of actors involved in decision-making can, in some circumstances, confer advantages.

However, there are also genuine fears that a stress on flexibility and negotiation has more sinister effects. Qureshi points to

> . . . the deliberate cloaking and minimization of the role of law by States in monetary matters – especially in developed countries. This is manifest through the elaborate constructions of soft law rather than firm law that characterize IMF jurisprudence.
>
> (Qureshi 1999)

The complexity of the arrangements involved provides opportunities for blame-shifting. The blurring of hierarchy also allows for a blurring of accountability. While outcomes may be benign in some cases, we seem to be left with few guarantees.

Conclusions

I have suggested that moves towards a more multi-level model of IMF governance are an imperfect adaptation to changes in the global political economy. The IMF's flexible mandate has meant that its appropriate jurisdiction as well as its institutional structure are contested. Both the increasing complexity of the problems it has been asked to deal with (more financial actors, coordination with the World Bank) and attempts at legitimation (NGOs, interest groups and again coordination with the World Bank, etc.) have led it to involve more actors in its deliberations. If the IMF's role could still be seen in terms of resolving tightly defined coordination problems, the kind of issues that I suggested in the introduction were most appropriate for Type II governance, we might be happy to feel that new actors merely ensured that information flows were sufficient for tasks to be performed effectively. Indeed this can work reasonably well, as it did in Korea.

The problem is that Type II bargaining becomes less appropriate as issues become more political (concerned with issues of power and distribution). The IMF has to some extent attempted to maintain claims that it is involved in resolving technical issues. One way of interpreting the emergent post-Washington consensus is as a way of trying to extend the ambit of what is to count as technical economics. There are potential benefits, in that this offers opportunities for social scientists to enter into a dialogue with economists. However, the danger is that the outcome will be one in which an ever wider range of policies are classified as merely technical issues to be decided by experts (Fine 2000).

Evidence from Asia suggests that there is good reason to be cautious about the prospects for such an approach. It may be in various actors' interests to accept this technocratic story in certain contexts – for example Kim Dae Jung's strategic interests in attacking the *chaebol*. There is less evidence, though, that they actually believe it. So, for example, the Korean government's approach to corporate restructuring was clearly driven as much by political factors as by a wholehearted acceptance of the IMF's arguments about market discipline. Both academics and the IMF criticized the over-interventionary way that corporate restructuring was implemented in practice, underlining divergence from a market-based approach (Moon and Mo 2000).

If that is the case, IMF performance in Korea may have preserved Fund legitimacy enough to limit the present reform agenda. However, performance is only ever one part of legitimacy. Performance is vulnerable to mistakes or adverse circumstances and needs the support that a widely accepted institutional structure can give (Beetham 1991).[13] Here current attempts at multi-level governance just will not do.

This is the point about the importance of Type I governance that was made in the introduction. Bargains with significant political and social implications need to be struck within a broadly legitimate institutional framework that provides some kind of transparent and socially acceptable regulation of power relationships. The problem, of course, as international relations theorists are well aware, is that there is no such international framework outside the confines of the nation-state. That is why Type II models are so attractive as an idea in international relations (Keohane 1984). It is no accident that the IMF has historically legitimated itself as a technocratic institution resolving coordination problems within a framework defined by sovereign states.

Over time, though, that framework has become looser, technocratic arguments have become harder to sustain, and the bargains resolved within the IMF framework have had a more pronounced effect on a far wider and more diffuse range of actors. The Type II negotiations involved have become detached from their Type I moorings based around Westphalian sovereignty at the same time as the issues negotiated have become more fundamental and difficult to resolve.

Issues decided by the IMF are no longer issues between states. They are also domestic issues. It is not exactly that sovereignty has been undermined (at least in legal terms). State economic regulation (an exercise of sovereign power) is as important as ever. However, states are subject to increasing incentives to exercise their sovereignty in particular ways (Bromley 2000). At the same time, they also need to preserve their own legitimacy, which is dependent on their ability at least to appear to serve the interests of their populations (Dunn 2000). Where the freedom to act as a sovereign is diminished, there is a danger that states' domestic legitimacy will be undermined.

The solution would seem to be either retrenchment or some kind of more direct IMF legitimacy operating in parallel so that the restrictions the Fund imposes on states (in the form of incentives) can be seen genuinely to serve the interests of ordinary citizens. This is what optimists might see occurring in the context of the good governance agenda in its more political forms – particularly where it includes good governance within the Fund (transparency and wider consultation).

The problem is that there is very little in the way of an institutional (let alone legal) framework through which new actors have become involved and there is no guarantee whose interests they serve. So, for example, there is some evidence that an overdue scepticism about who exactly NGOs can claim to represent is emerging. After all, what kinds of organizations are to be categorized as NGOs? (Compare the Federation of Korean Industries, the American Bar Association, Greenpeace, the Grameen Bank, and a developing-country entrepreneur with an aid grant and a fax machine.) A situation where some Washington-based NGOs appear to have more influence than some African countries is clearly deeply unsatisfactory. The implications of greater IMF interaction with financial markets are more obviously problematic – everyone knows markets represent only themselves (although there may be genuine advantages in ensuring the IMF does at least accurately identify what will enhance 'market confidence'). That is not to say that consultation with NGOs is necessarily a bad thing; it is merely to point out that it simply cannot do the job of more formal political frameworks.

The current situation exists partly because of the elements of multi-level governance that were always present in the IMF model: a functionally-defined institution operating under relatively loose legal restraints without the discipline of any overarching sovereign power. The Fund has adapted over time to different tasks in the context of a transformed global economy. However, that adaptation has been gradual and *ad hoc*. The political difficulties in negotiating changes in the IMF's Articles have led to a tendency to work around what legal framework exists and negotiate reforms at the margins. This may be inevitable, but it is important to recognize the limits of this sort of process and the danger that, in the longer term, it could undermine the legitimacy both of states and of the IMF.

The IMF's flexibility means that there are a number of ways of dealing with the current situation. It is possible either to restrict the Fund's mandate or to enhance its legitimacy. There are some ways in which its institutional structure could be improved (Woods 1999; Woods 2000) but the difficulty of forging any system of broad social consensus at the international level, at least in the short term, would seem to imply that the IMF is nearing the limits of what it can legitimately achieve without fundamental reforms (probably only possible in the wake of another, more severe, global crisis).

In terms of the multi-level governance literature, the point is that the appropriateness of different forms of governance will depend on the issues being discussed. There are good reasons for thinking that it is important that we continue to experiment with novel ways of organizing political life (Unger 1995). However, that experimentation should remain subject to some form of overarching political control. It has often been remarked in the literature that multi-level governance does not signal the end of the state but rather the advent of a new kind of state whose role is more one of coordination and management and less one of action. What is sometimes less clear is that the state also embodies a particular set of rules for allocating power, and that this too remains indispensable for the future of legitimate politics at least until someone comes up with a better alternative.

Notes

1 I would like to acknowledge funding from the ESRC and the educational trust, and assistance from Simon Bromley and David Beetham.
2 This aspect of the literature is well discussed in Hooghe and Marks (2001).
3 Or, at least, little impact that was not largely inevitable given the existence of balance-of-payments difficulties.
4 For a fuller discussion of IMF governance policy see Thirkell-White (2003).
5 Interviews at the IMF, autumn 2000. See also Stiles (1991).
6 See, particularly, contributions by Congressmen Sanders and Frank in House Banking Oversight Subcommittee (1998).
7 The creation of the General Agreements to Borrow – additional Funds administered through the IMF but provided by a subset of the membership who retain an additional veto is the most clearly institutionalized example. Bilateral lending that takes place in conjunction with programmes, such as the commitments offered during the Asian crisis, has much the same effect on the relationships involved.
8 For some the very idea of the IMF enhancing market confidence was open to question (Bird and Rowlands 1997; Radelet and Sachs 1998).
9 The term 'post-Washington consensus' is usually attributed to Joseph Stiglitz (Stiglitz 1998). However, Stiglitz is clear that implementing these new interventions requires more than a narrow technocratic approach (Stiglitz 2000). For an interesting discussion of the post-Washington consensus as part of the colonization of social science by economists, see Fine (2000).
10 Although the fundamental principle of utilitarianism is relatively straightforward, issues become more complex as soon as questions are asked about what exactly utility is. See the different chapters in Sen and Williams (1982).
11 General guidelines on conditionality were published in 1979, but practical decisions soon breached them (Polak 1991). The Board has recently approved new guidelines, but it is too early to determine their practical impact.
12 See, for example, the speeches reproduced in Sohn and Yang (1998).
13 For a much fuller discussion of the concept of legitimacy and its application to the IMF, see Thirkell-White (2005).

9 Globalization and the City of London's financial markets

The emergence of multi-level governance in principal financial centres

Richard Woodward[1]

The recent history of the City of London epitomizes the difficulties of governing liberalized financial markets. In the last two decades the City has been engulfed by a series of financial scandals and crises deriving from inappropriate behaviour by City participants, coupled with the shortcomings of national regulatory structures that have failed to adjust adequately to the challenges posed by integrated financial markets. Indeed at the time of writing the City is once again embroiled in controversy, with the Financial Services Authority (FSA) and the House of Commons Treasury Select Committee investigating allegations regarding the mis-selling of split-capital investment trusts and imprudent business practices by a 'magic circle' of brokers, trust managers and directors. Already nineteen split-capital ventures have ceased trading, taking the savings of over 100,000 people with them (House of Commons Treasury Select Committee 2003).[2]

The central concern of this chapter is not to examine the efficacy of the arrangements for the regulation of the City's financial markets but to assess whether, and to what extent, it is accurate to refer to governance of the City of London's financial markets as a multi-level phenomenon. The chapter begins by tracing the changing contours of the City's regulatory structures since the late 1970s. Two trends are considered especially noteworthy. First, at what is tentatively labelled the national 'level', socially based networks of governance have been progressively displaced by state-backed regulatory authorities. Second, regional and international 'structures of authority' (Rosenau 1997) have assumed a more prominent role in the governance of the City of London's financial markets. The consolidation of national regulatory authority and the accompanying development of regional and international mechanisms of governance are, it will be argued, indicative of an emergent multi-level system of governance for the City's financial markets in a conventional 'spaces of places' sense. However, as Woodward (Chapter 3 of this volume) has observed, spaces of places models with their emphasis on public structures of authority offer only a partial understanding of contemporary governance structures. This chapter will use the case study of financial governance in the City of London to illustrate some of the flaws in the spaces of places literature. It then goes on to argue that, while the City is partly amenable to interpretation using a spaces of places approach, it represents a vast oversimplification of the bewildering array of authority structures governing financial markets in the City at the turn of the twenty-first century.

Governing the city in a global era

Regulating the City before 1979: the era of gentlemanly capitalism

Since 1979 financial regulation in the City of London has been radically over-hauled as successive governments have sought to grapple with the limitations of national regulation in an era of liberalized financial markets. However, prior to the late 1970s the state's involvement in City regulation was minimal. Instead, financial markets in the City were policed by senior members of the City hierarchy using an esoteric form of self-regulation. Banking supervision, for example, revolved around regular if somewhat casual meetings between high-ranking officials from the Bank of England and senior managers of the banks concerned. Usually the 'raised eyebrows' of the Governor of the Bank of England were sufficient to convince recalcitrant institutions to desist from unhelpful practices. The day-to-day responsibility for banking regulation was overseen by private associations such as the London Discount Market Association and the Accepting Houses Committee, whose primary role was to represent rather than to regulate the industry (Moran 1984). Two main factors made this system of self-regulation workable. The first was the peculiar social make-up of the City in this period. The City was a closed, self-perpetuating oligarchy drawing its leading participants from a narrow stratum of upper-class British society. The social homogeneity of the City's elite provided fertile ground for the cultivation of a system of shared rules, norms and values referred to by many commentators as 'gentlemanly capitalism' (Augar 2000; Cain and Hopkins 2001; Kynaston 1994; Michie 1998; Thompson 1997a, 1997b). At the heart of gentlemanly capitalism was the notion of trust learnt from repeated social interaction. There was a deeply ingrained assumption that one's social equals could be relied upon to act responsibly in their business dealings and that contractual obligations would be honoured as much to preserve the reputation of the parties concerned as in the knowledge that such obligations could be legally enforced.[3] Those who committed serious infractions of these informal norms and rules were ostracized. In the London Stock Exchange, for instance,

> . . . there was a very strict code of behaviour both formal and informal. The Stock Exchange rulebook set out clearly what was and what was not permitted and the system was operated in a meticulous manner. Disciplinary hearings did occur but the informal policing system was even more impressive. Word spread quickly when individuals or firms were consistently misbehaving and such parties suddenly found it hard to get liquidity or to be shown business.
>
> (Augar 2000: 20)

In short, the City 'was a place where a powerful, almost tribal elite maintained generally strict standards on those it was willing to do business with' (Kynaston 2001).

The second group of factors consisted of the international and domestic arrangements which cocooned the City from the exigencies of market competition, especially after the Second World War. In the international sphere the imposition of capital controls following the Bretton Woods agreement of 1944 checked the reintegration of financial markets, largely insulating the City and its institutions from cross-border competition and providing a modicum of international financial stability. Meanwhile, in the domestic context, competition was smothered by the continued application of rigid demarcation between different financial sectors. As a consequence the City's financial markets developed into a succession of self-contained cartels characterized by oligopolistic competition. These heavily circumscribed competitive conditions allowed financial activities to be neatly classified within specific spatial and sectoral parameters, obviating the need for draconian external regulation by state agencies (Goodhart 2000; McKenzie and Khalidi 1996).

Regulating the City 1979–97: self-regulation within a statutory framework

The conditions that had allowed self-regulation to prosper were abrogated in the 1970s by domestic and international upheavals, which once again exposed the City to financial instability and the rigours of competition. In the international sphere the relaxation of capital controls following the breakdown of Bretton Woods, the continued growth of the Eurocurrency markets, and the recycling of petrodollars ushered in a phase of sustained economic volatility and sponsored the reintegration of financial markets across national borders. In the UK, Edward Heath's Conservative government took the first hesitant steps towards deregulating financial services and began to dismantle the barriers separating different financial sectors. In 1979 the process of domestic deregulation received fresh impetus from the free market zeal of the newly-elected Thatcher administration. Under the aegis of the New Right, the incoming government believed that the limits placed on free competition by prevailing oligopolistic market structures inhibited innovation, enterprise and risk-taking, hindering the ability of the City and its institutions to compete on the global stage. They embarked on a strategy designed to subject the City to the uncompromising glare of market forces, in the expectation that this would instil a competitive ethos. This project involved, *inter alia*, the abolition of capital controls, accelerating the demolition of artificial barriers between financial sectors and the deregulation of the London Stock Exchange, an event known colloquially as the 'Big Bang'.[4]

These advances had serious repercussions for the established regulatory order predicated on gentlemanly capitalism. First, deregulation diluted the homogeneity of the City's social elite and weakened the dominant patterns of socialization and social reproduction. In 1964 there were just 98 branches of foreign banks in London. By 1985 this number had swelled to 490 (Michie 1998: 555). These institutions brought with them different preoccupations and attitudes to business conduct that stood in stark contrast to those presided over by the gentlemanly capitalists (Amin and Thrift 1992; Augar 2000; Moran 1991). The arrival of outsiders from overseas was compounded by the recruitment of more working-class men and women and ethnic minority groups into the City's 'Square Mile' (Augar 2000; Thrift and Leyshon 1994; Tickell 1996). Gentlemanly capitalists, while not extinct, were certainly an endangered species. Moreover, many felt that under conditions of heightened competition gentlemanly capitalism lacked sufficient strength to deliver adequate investor protection (Alcock 1992; Gower 1984; Lutz 1998; Strange 1998). The removal of impediments to competition threatened the viability of some corporations. In the past, companies had been reasonably sure of obtaining business through personal contacts and the prevalence of oligopolistic price setting. New entrants and more intense price competition raised the spectre of companies resorting to improper business practices to protect and enhance market share, especially as the ties that previously bound the gentlemanly capitalists unravelled.

The government decided a more stringent system of regulation was required to meet the challenges of the competitive market forces they had unleashed. Through the 1980s and 1990s the cosy networks of self-regulation were replaced with a state-based regulatory framework that is more 'codified, juridified and institutionalized' (Moran 1991: 13). The transition began with the Banking Acts of 1979 and 1987, which formalized the Bank of England's supervisory responsibilities and conferred upon it legal sanctions to punish disobedient institutions. Beyond the banking sector, the main regulatory reforms were instigated by the Financial Services Act 1986. This legislation provided for the creation of a new state regulator, the Securities and Investments Board (SIB), which in turn delegated its powers to a phalanx of Self-Regulatory Organizations (SROs), each responsible for a discrete arena of the City's activities. By the end of the 1980s surveillance of the City was administered by a veritable alphabet soup of regulatory agencies (see Figure 9.1). However, this reorganization represented a half-way house. Out of the chrysalis of self-regulation emerged a system of self-regulation within a statutory framework. Though their activities were more tightly prescribed by statute, practitioners retained both their customary role in generating rules and considerable discretion over how those rules were enforced. For instance the Bank of England Acts allowed the Bank of England significant latitude in interpreting and implementing its powers regarding the liquidity and solvency of the institutions it regulated.

From the beginning, the new regulatory edifice was beset by problems. Notwithstanding the imposition of a more elaborate statutory framework, the Bank of England, the practitioner-based SIB and its offspring, all too frequently relied upon the informal, trust-based form of supervision which hitherto had pervaded the City. The failure to banish the last vestiges of gentlemanly regulation were widely cited as important contributory factors in the collapse of Johnson Matthey Bank in 1984 and Barings Bank in 1995 (House of Commons

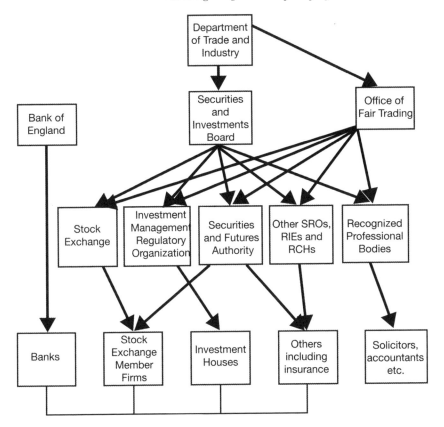

Figure 9.1 Control of the securities industry after the 'Big Bang'
Source: Alcock (1992).

Treasury Select Committee 1996), and in allowing an employee of the Sumitomo Corporation, Yasuo Hamanaka, to manipulate the global copper market via the London Metal Exchange throughout the early 1990s (Thomson 1999). The crises of Barings and Sumitomo were symptomatic of the broader problems confronting London's regulatory authorities. The jurisdiction of the City's regulatory organizations was limited by national and sectoral boundaries at a time when financial markets were treating such borders with impunity.

Governing the City into the twenty-first century

The Financial Services Authority

Throughout the early 1990s a number of cosmetic changes were made to the City's regulatory structures. New SROs emerged and others amalgamated as the state endeavoured to match the pace of change in the provision of financial services. However, it was not until the election of the Labour government in 1997 that any major restructuring came about. Shortly after their election the Chancellor, Gordon Brown, announced the creation of a new, all-encompassing regulator, the Financial Services Authority (FSA).[5] The FSA was designed to knit together the existing patchwork of regulatory authorities into a seamless regulatory behemoth fully backed by statutory powers. The FSA would subsume the duties previously discharged by the SIB and the SROs. In addition, the FSA would take charge of the prudential supervision of the banking sector, a task relinquished by the Bank of England following the passage of the Bank of England Act 1998.[6] Moreover the FSA would have less scope for varying the extent and purpose of their activities. The Financial Services and Markets Act 2000 explicitly states that the FSA will have four statutory objectives; to maintain confidence in the UK financial system; to promote public understanding of the financial system; to protect consumers; and to reduce financial crime (see Financial Services Authority 2000b).

The birth of the FSA marks the final stage of the metamorphosis of the City's domestic regulatory regime from the informal networks and conventions intrinsic to gentlemanly capitalism to a framework of rules assembled and backed by state authority. As one analyst has commented:

> [T]hree decades ago it was impossible to find a financial market which was not governed by the traditional British version of self-regulation; now it is impossible to find a significant City market which is not subjected to elaborate state regulation.
>
> (Moran 2001: 110)

International and regional dimensions

The majority of the literature on the City of London has focused exclusively on the 'revolution' (Moran 1991) in domestic regulatory structures. In so doing, the development and importance of international and regional mechanisms of governance has been overlooked. The re-integration of financial markets and the growing porosity of state borders engender new hazards for nationally-based regulatory authorities. In particular they are vulnerable to destabilizing events and activities occurring outside of, but crucially linked to, their jurisdiction. This problem is especially acute for regulators in the City of London, owing to the extraordinarily transnationalized nature of its markets, institutions and transactions.

The City of London is distinguished from other large financial centres such as New York and Tokyo because it specializes in offering services to international capital (Baker 1999; Roberts and Kynaston 2001: Chapter 5). The international interconnectedness of the City is reflected across the financial spectrum. Presently the City plays host to 478 foreign banking institutions, 50 per cent more than any other single financial centre (Financial Times 2002a).[7] More German and American banks operate in London than in their own domestic financial centres in

Frankfurt and New York. In August 2003, 52 per cent of the assets held in the UK banking system belonged to foreign owned banks (International Financial Services London 2003: 7) compared to one-fifth in Japan and one-tenth in the United States (Coleman and Porter 1994: 192). In total, 81 per cent of the UK's external lending originates from foreign-owned banks (Corporation of London 2002) and London is the world's foremost centre for cross-border bank lending, with 19 per cent of all such business being conducted by City institutions (International Financial Services London 2003: 2). The City's pre-eminence in cross-border finance is further underscored by the foreign exchange and securities markets. With 31 per cent of the global market share and a daily turnover of $504 billion the City of London is the world's leading centre for foreign exchange transactions (International Financial Services London 2003: 2).[8] Furthermore, in 2001, a mere 13 per cent of foreign exchange transactions involved sterling (International Financial Services London 2003: 23), while other leading currencies are routinely traded more in London than in their native countries. The City's dominance is even more pronounced in the international equities markets. City-based firms issue 60 per cent of the world's international bonds and execute 70 per cent of the trades undertaken in the secondary market. In the first eight months of 2002 the City's official stock exchanges accounted for 45 per cent of the global turnover in foreign equities (International Financial Services London 2003: 2) and the total of 376 foreign companies listed on the London Stock Exchange as of January 2004 is second only in number and proportion to the New York Stock Exchange (World Federation of Exchanges 2004).

The density of the City's interlinkages exposes its regulatory immune system to the full gamut of viruses, which stalk the global financial system. As Howard Davies, the Chairman of the Financial Services Authority from 1997 to 2003, has remarked, 'there is no possible way, in this current environment, of hoping to police all investment activity on a host-state basis' (Davies 2000b; Financial Services Authority 2000a). Constraints upon domestic regulatory efforts have compelled British financial regulators to collaborate more intensively with their counterparts in other jurisdictions, through conventional international organizations and what Slaughter (1997, 2000) terms transgovernmental networks.

Transgovernmental networks assist in the governance of the City's markets in a number of ways. They provide a forum in which regulators from different countries can meet and share experiences, they foster and formalize international cooperation and the exchange of information in supervisory matters, and they promulgate global standards and codes of practice to which national regulatory bodies should aspire. These regulatory networks have no prescribed sanctions or independent mechanism for monitoring compliance. Consequently, the exchange of information and the implementation and enforcement of international codes of practice rely upon peer pressure arising from the mutual recognition that effective domestic regulation is critically dependent on the rigorous application of globally-agreed standards in other jurisdictions (Basle Committee on Banking Supervision 2002; International Organization of Securities Commissions 2002; International Association of Insurance Supervisors 2002).

This type of international collaboration began to grow in importance from the mid-1970s and, at the outset, the City's regulators were among the most wholehearted adherents to the enterprise. In 1974 the Bank of England was one of the founding members of the Basle Committee on Banking Supervision (BCBS) whose remit was to endorse and strengthen cooperative ties between banking regulators in different countries. The BCBS was instrumental in establishing the principle of 'international co-operation based on home country control' (Kapstein 1994), which became the blueprint for subsequent transgovernmental undertakings. The doctrine of international cooperation based on home-country control holds that, while international cooperation has spawned a number of agreements designed to enhance the supervision of cross-border financial activities and minimize the threat of crises, it remains the duty of the home country to authorize and oversee the activities of domestic institutions operating abroad. The 1980s and 1990s saw transgovernmental networks expand their remit beyond the banking sector into the realm of securities (through the International Organization of Securities Commissions (IOSCO)) and insurance (via the International Association of Insurance Supervisors (IAIS)).

The City's regulatory bodies dutifully joined the appropriate regulatory hub, but by the early 1990s the SIB's relations with its overseas counterparts were, according to the then SIB Chairman Andrew Large, at a 'low ebb'. However, the chastening experience of the Barings and Sumitomo scandals rekindled enthusiasm for international cooperation (*Financial Times* 1997). The resurrection of international cooperation has gathered momentum under the FSA. The Financial Services and Markets Act formalizes transnational collaboration, stipulating guidelines for reciprocal cooperation and stating that the FSA must act in accordance with its international obligations.[9] The FSA inherited membership of over 70 international committees from the bodies it subsumed (Davies 1999a), and has since expanded and fortified these links. In the first four years of its existence the FSA has more than doubled its membership of international committees to 144, and can boast a total of 168 bi-lateral and multilateral Memoranda of Understanding with its overseas brethren (Woodward 2001). The importance accorded to international concerns is now reflected in the FSA's organizational structure. In early 2001 the FSA created the International Policy Committee to ensure that international matters receive the necessary attention (Davies 2001).•Similarly, the Bank of England, though shorn of its role of prudential supervision of the banking sector, has renewed its pledge to international dialogue in pursuit of maintaining the stability of the UK financial system (Bank of England 2002, 2003).

Networks of international regulators represent just one aspect of the international dimension of City governance. Official diagnoses of the financial meltdowns in Mexico and East and Southeast Asia assigned a prominent role to weaknesses in the governance of domestic financial markets. Concomitantly, the development of well-regulated, transparent financial markets in the domestic context has become an integral part of subsequent efforts to renovate the international financial architecture, and the tentacles of international financial institutions have become ever more intrusive in the governance of domestic financial markets. The City's regulators are expected to monitor and enforce codes of practice set down by, *inter alia*, the International Monetary Fund (IMF) and the Organization for Economic Co-operation and Development (OECD). Furthermore there is evidence of greater collaboration among differing international-level mechanisms of governance. One of the problems associated with transgovernmental networks is that they lack the resources and the powerful sanctions required to monitor compliance and enforce standards. Self-assessment and peer review are now acknowledged to have achieved only modest success in assuring fulfilment of key standards. This was vividly demonstrated by the Asian financial crises, in which many of the affected countries were in principle signed up to the BCBS's *Core Principles of Banking Supervision* and IOSCO's *Principles of Securities Regulation* but in practice they were paid scant attention by national regulators (Davies 1999b, 2000a; Key 1999: 71). The proposed solution to this problem has been to marry the surveillance and compliance capacities of international financial institutions to the standard-setting expertise of the transgovernmental regulatory networks. In 1999 the IMF and the World Bank launched the Financial Sector Assessment Program (FSAP) to help promote the goal of developing sound financial systems among member countries. A key part of this assessment process are the Reports on the Observance of Standards and Codes (ROSCs). ROSCs evaluate the degree to which members observe internationally-agreed standards and codes in eleven areas. These include areas such as banking, securities and insurance supervision, the resilience of the payments and settlements systems, corporate governance and accounting and auditing where standards have principally been developed by transgovernmental networks (see International Monetary Fund 2001a, 2002). As Soederberg reflects in Chapter 10 of this volume, ROSCs represent powerful disciplinary devices because failure to act in accordance with them will invariably result in less permissive access to financial markets.

The ongoing process of political and economic integration within the European Union (EU) has given the City's governance structures an extra dimension. The quest to create a single market for financial services has resulted in a seemingly unquenchable stream of Directives from the EU evoking the need for compliance among member states. Like the international dimension of governance, the European Union's Directives initially focused on the banking sector (starting with the First Banking Directive of 1977) before spreading into the regulation of the securities and insurance industries (Moran 1994). The significance of EU-level governance is set to grow both qualitatively and quantitatively following the inauguration, at the Cardiff European Council in June 1998, of what later became known as the Financial Services Action Plan (European Union 1998). This plan was designed to ensure the stability and competitiveness of EU financial markets by replacing the labyrinth of national regulations with harmonized EU standards (Commission of the European Communities 1999). To date the European Commission has approved 36 of the

42 pieces of legislation needed to unify EU regulatory practices (European Union 2003), but progress on many issues continues to be hindered by the intransigence of vested national interests and the difficulties of reconciling the widely divergent financial markets of the fifteen member states (*Financial Times* 2002b). Arguably, the harmonization of EU financial standards is being more effectively advanced by regionally-based transgovernmental networks such as the Committee of European Securities Regulators (CESR) (formerly the Federation of European Securities Commissions (FESCO)). The CESR is constituted by the seventeen statutory securities regulators of the European Economic Area (EEA). Its primary task has been to improve coordination among European securities regulators and to disseminate guidelines, recommendations and standards to facilitate the uniform implementation of EU law in the domestic context (Committee of European Securities Regulators 2002).

Multi-level governance in the City of London?

The previous section intimates that financial markets in the City of London are now governed by an embryonic framework of multi-level governance in a conventional spaces of places sense. That is to say that governance is undertaken by structures of authority distinguished and defined by territorial scales of varying extensity. The four levels of governance operating in the City of London are detailed in Figure 9.2. The national level of governance is dominated by the FSA and the Bank of England. This is complemented by regional-level governance, in the form of the EU and the CESR, and international-level governance through adherence to rules, codes and standards promulgated by international organizations and international regulatory networks. Within the international level the Financial Stability Forum (FSF) brings together the various national and international supervisory agencies in an attempt to promote stability in the international financial system. Finally, at the global level the Group of 7 has an indirect bearing on governance in the City by choreographing the work of international institutions and defining their ideological parameters (Baker 2000).

The remainder of this section assesses the applicability of this framework of multi-level governance with particular reference to the governance of financial markets in the City of London. First the advantages of this configuration of multi-level governance will be outlined. This is followed by an examination of the potential and actual pitfalls of such an approach. It is suggested that the main problems associated with this model of multi-level governance revolve around the conceptualization of 'level', what one might refer to as the 'L' in MLG. Some of these problems are more practical and descriptive, whereas others are more theoretical and analytical. Nevertheless, each of these obstacles needs to be considered in the light of the same question, namely, does the framework outlined in Figure 9.2 correspond to reality of governance in the City of London's financial markets?

The framework of multi-level governance sketched in Figure 9.2 is a useful point of departure when examining contemporary structures of governance in

Group 7	'Global' level
International Organizations (IMF, WTO, OECD)	
Financial Stability Forum	
International Regulatory Networks (IOSCO, IAIS, BCBS)	International level
European Union	
Committee of European Securities Regulators (CESR)	Regional level
Financial Services Authority Bank of England	National level

Figure 9.2 Multi-level governance in the City of London: the spaces of places approach

the City. First, and in contrast to some leading commentators on financial globalization (see for example Greider 1997; Friedman 2000; Strange 1998), it asserts a prime role for the state in governing financial markets. Second, it alerts us to the fact that states are but one of many structures of authority responsible for governing global finance. States, as the chapter has already demonstrated, 'have increasingly adopted strategies of multilateral management of transworld finance, through a host of interstate, transstate and suprastate mechanisms' (Scholte 2002b: 193). Third, it highlights some interesting features about the construction of governance in the City and the way in which the roles of certain authority structures vary in different contexts. For example, the FSA and the Bank of England might be said to belong to more than one level of governance. Though they are both ostensibly national-level institutions they also operate at the international level through their participation in international networks, and at the regional level in the course of discharging their obligations to the EU. However, their roles at these levels differ markedly. At the international and regional levels the FSA and the Bank of England contribute to the governance of the City of London by framing international standards and cooperating with their counterparts in other jurisdictions. In contrast, in the national context the FSA and the Bank of England are charged with the task of ensuring international rules are implemented and enforced, and with the smooth running of international cooperation.

Despite these advantages, the multi-level governance framework outlined in Figure 9.2 has a number of limitations. The appearance of the same actors at different levels indicates a considerable amount of imbrication between the levels. This raises the question of whether discrete territorial levels of authority can in fact be identified. The example of the FSA and the Bank of England and their appearance at the national, regional and international levels is pertinent here. One could question whether international bodies such as IOSCO and the IAIS deserve to be designated as a distinct 'level' of governance. They are international in the sense that their membership consists of agencies from many different states and their rules are commonly applicable to several different national jurisdictions. Nevertheless these rules are debated and arrived at by bodies deriving their authority from national sources. Moreover, international rules can only be operationalized by incorporation into the body of rules and regulatory practices governing the City and their subsequent enforcement as part of the national-level regulatory process. Putting the responsibility for implementation and enforcement of international regulatory standards in the hands of national regulators means that the effectiveness of international-level governance is critically dependent upon the national-level regulatory apparatus. The notion that international bodies constitute a discrete level of authority and governance is contestable. International regulatory networks may not be separate sources of authority but instead represent the reconstitution of state authority and the pursuit of state-level governance by other means. This raises a further issue, namely, whether it may be necessary to distinguish between sources and sites of authority when looking at multi-level governance. This acknowledges Hudson's (Chapter 4 of this volume) observation that everything must happen somewhere. Though the source of authority may originate from the global, international or regional level, the actual site where that authority impacts and is exercised is in the national level, i.e. within the City. This suggests that the best analogy for multi-level governance is not a layer cake or a club sandwich (see Baker, Chapter 6 of this volume) as exemplified by Figure 9.2, but more like a concertina that collapses or expands depending on the circumstances.

A second issue that arises in connection with the distinctiveness of these various levels of authority is whether or not the regional and international spheres should be analysed separately. This reflects the fierce debate about the significance of the EU for established concepts in political science, in particular whether the EU should be seen as a genuinely novel form of political organization (Ruggie 1993c) or whether, as the neo-functionalist and liberal intergovernmentalist approaches suggest, it is merely a glorified form of international organization, a 'Europe of the nations' (Benz 2000). The truth lies somewhere between the two. Integration in the EU is inherently international. Equally, it is true to say that the unique political imperatives driving political and economic integration within the EU give it a distinctive character, and arguably the separation of the two levels is justified. Similarly the international and global levels in Figure 9.2 are problematic. The G7 could conceivably be included in the international level; justification for the global level is difficult to sustain, given that membership of the G7 is neither universal, nor representative of the world as a whole.[10]

A further issue related to the identification of levels is that the framework presented in Figure 9.2 is too simplified. It implies levels composed of actors displaying similar characteristics and executing the same tasks. Normally theories of multi-level governance start from this position and then seek to analyse the relationship between levels (see, for example, Hirst and Thompson 1999) and the way in which all the various levels may eventually coalesce to govern globalization. This is without doubt a central issue, but it fails to address the prior question of whether coherent and stable levels exist in order to conduct these analyses. Before looking at the relationships *between* levels, it is necessary to ascertain whether such a 'level' can be said to exist by looking at relationships between actors *within* particular territorial contexts. Already it has been shown that international regulatory networks set standards whose success depends upon the muscle and legitimization of international institutions and the implementation powers of national authorities. The appearance of hybrid institutions such as the FSF complicates the picture still further. The international level presented in Figure 9.2 may in fact consist of many international 'levels'. In addition to these vertical fissures in the multi-level model, it is also possible that these levels might be fractured horizontally. In this chapter, financial markets in the City have been presented as an undifferentiated whole. In reality, financial markets in the City are hugely diverse. At the national level the governance of all these different markets now falls within the purview of a single regulator, the FSA. Nevertheless, at the international level, governance is still organized along functional lines (Woodward 2001), with separate bodies dealing with securities, banking and insurance. This raises the possibility that the governance of certain areas may be more 'multi-level' than that of others. For instance the international level of governance in the arena of insurance is far less well developed than that of international banking and securities. Figure 9.2 may not be universally applicable to the City of London although it may provide an overall framework through which governance in the City can be assessed.

Despite the utility of the spaces of places model in revealing the multi-level nature of governance in the City's financial markets, closer scrutiny suggests that it reveals only one part of a much broader regulatory canvas. Most significantly, it ignores those mechanisms of governance whose authority is neither delimited by, nor derives from, control over territorial space. This oversight is especially egregious in the City because it conceals both the historical and the contemporary significance of non-territorial structures of authority. The private associations that once bestrode the City have now been stripped of their regulatory functions, as state-backed regulatory institutions have come to prevail. This does not mean, however, that these private associations have ceased to play a role in the governance of the City. They continue to promulgate industry standards policed by their own members and they are critical in ensuring that the City's payments and clearing systems operate effectively. The various financial markets and exchanges still maintain their own rulebooks and codes of conduct, but these rules and regulations must now be compatible with the exigencies of the FSA. The growth of state-based authority has curtailed the impact of some of the domestic private governance structures in the City. However, many industry associations are now international in character and have been instrumental in harmonizing standards and the manufacture of self-regulatory codes of practice across a wide range of financial markets (Scholte 2002b; see also Chapter 1 of this volume) including securities (Filipovic 1997), auditing, accounting and derivatives (Tsingou 2003).

The dilemma for multi-level governance is how to fit these private structures of authority into the model. On the one hand it might be argued that there is a clear territorial dimension to these bodies. In the previous paragraph these bodies were variously described as national and international. Indeed some are national to the extent that they exist in specific national centres and others are international in the sense that they operate across state boundaries, but terms such as national and international fail to capture their intricacies. Why is it that institutions in the City of London are willing to submit themselves to the standards of these bodies, when their codes and standards are not necessarily blessed or backed by official authority? This suggests that private authority continues to rest on a form of gentlemanly capitalism and self-regulation, governed by authority over a given social rather than territorial space.

The rehabilitation of the belief in free markets has further complicated the terrain for multi-level governance. The orthodox view after 1945 proclaimed that markets were imbued with innate pathologies which made them prone to 'manias, panics, and crashes' (Kindleberger 1996; Soros 1998). Concomitantly markets were manacled by a plethora of regulatory restrictions to assuage their deleterious impact on society. The breakdown of the post-war economic settlement led many to question this orthodoxy. Free market economists argued that markets are spontaneous, self-governing orders that only dysfunction when imperfections exist. From this perspective the task of government is not to restrict the operation of markets but to ensure a propitious climate in which the free interplay of market forces is possible. In other words, markets were increasingly seen not only as an object to be governed but as a *mechanism of governance* (Cohen 1998). Nowhere is the almost messianic faith in free markets better demonstrated than in the City of London.

The state-based regulators of the 1980s and 1990s have unashamedly promoted market arbitration in the City of London. The philosophy underpinning the FSA's regulatory approach is that market discipline is more effective than state regulation at producing desired outcomes. For example, it is felt that exposing financial institutions to the gaze of the market is more likely to result in firms adopting more effective internal risk management procedures than pressure from a state regulator. This is because those pursuing sound business practices will gain a reputation for probity and soundness and will be rewarded with more business from rational market actors. Conversely those who fail to implement comprehensive controls or follow risky or malfeasant strategies are liable to lose business. As a former Chief Secretary to the Treasury, Alan Milburn, commented, 'we look to the financial services industry as a whole to manage its affairs properly. Those firms that do will gain competitive advantage' (House of Commons 1999: Col 40). Milburn's successor, Andrew Smith, argued in a similar vein that 'governments have a responsibility to ensure the right kind of regulatory environment for the capital markets. Regulation must allow for the free play of competition and innovation' (HM Treasury 2000). In other words it is the duty of the government to ensure that markets are fair and transparent in order that participants can respond most effectively to the price signals of the market. As Baker (1999: 86) presciently observes, 'overall, the trend is [towards] preference for more market freedom and less state intervention, with the state providing the residual framework required for efficient market operations'.

Markets are an intrinsic part of governance in the City of London. The dilemma for theories of multi-level governance is how to incorporate the market as a structure of authority into the framework. The problem of modelling market-oriented governance comes back to the core pursuit of those engaged in the discipline of international political economy (IPE), namely, specifying the relationship between states and markets. One of the unifying features of the IPE literature is the recognition of the interdependence of states and markets. Unfortunately a lot of this work casts the state–market relationship as one of 'interdependent antagonism' (Underhill 2000a: 818). States and markets are portrayed as competing and incompatible forms of social organization engaged in a battle to rein supreme over the global economy. This dichotomy between states and markets means that

> [O]ne of the difficulties in discussing economic governance is the assumption that the economy belongs to the private sphere and governance to the public, and that economic governance is therefore concerned with the relationship between the economy and state, how the state *governs* the economy.
> (Gamble 2000: 110; emphasis in original)

The market is viewed as an object to be governed rather than as an authoritative mechanism of governance. The spaces of places model exemplifies these deficiencies. It provides satisfactory coverage of the structures of authority from the public domain but offers no insight into private or market 'spaces of flows' structures of authority. Notions such as the 'state–market condominium' (Underhill 2000a) and the 'authoritative domain' (Cohen 1998) offer potential solutions to the conundrum of how spaces of places and spaces of flows could fit together into an integrated model of governance. Nevertheless, one is immediately confronted with a series of analytical and practical considerations, perhaps the most important of which is whether to retain the territorial levels and to assess state–market relations against a territorial backdrop or whether it might be better to jettison the rigid hierarchy of levels in favour of more fluid arrangements which more accurately reflect the complexities of governing the City of London in a global era.

Conclusion

Today, governance of the City of London's financial markets is unrecognizable from that which existed some twenty-five years ago. Until 1979 the state's role in financial regulation was restricted to a handful of antiquated statutes. Governance was the preserve of private industry associations operating through a nexus of personal relationships. However, at the turn of the twenty-first century the City is 'a club no more' (Kynaston 2002). Liberalization has destroyed the limited competitive conditions upon which self-regulation was predicated, necessitating the development of state-backed regulatory authorities that are more systematic and intrusive. Liberalization also helped to cement the City's pre-eminence in the field of international financial services. Unfortunately the intensity and extensity of the City's interlinkages make it impossible for national regulators to protect it against crises and instability from exogenous sources. To overcome these deficiencies City regulators have intensified international cooperation and agreed to abide by international standards. In addition, tighter European integration has led to the incorporation of vast swathes of EU law into the City's governance regime. The presence of national, regional and international mechanisms of governance suggests that financial markets in the City are governed by a rudimentary framework of multi-level governance.

The notion of multi-level governance is useful in the City context because it signposts the existence of sites and structures of authority which include, but are not limited to, the state. Furthermore it highlights some of the subtleties of City governance with the same actors dispensing different functions in different contexts. Nevertheless, the basic template relying on the spaces of places conception of political authority exhibits many of the drawbacks of multi-level governance discussed elsewhere in this volume (see Introduction, and Chapters 6 and 3). Many of the problems revolve around the notion of levels. From a practical and descriptive standpoint there are a number of unresolved questions. Can distinct territorial levels be identified? Is there any real and objective difference between regional and international levels of governance? How are these levels organized? How do they interact? Is the simple and permanent hierarchy of territorial scales accurate or justified? Even if convincing answers to these questions are forthcoming, a number of theoretical and analytical shortcomings with the spaces of places model still need to be addressed. Most seriously the spaces of places model disregards sources of authority that are not defined by territorial space. It is incapable of recognizing private and market-oriented governance structures that have been and remain an indispensable element of City governance, and as a result it offers a vastly oversimplified account of the prevailing structures of governance in the City of London. The evidence regarding the importance of private authority in the City is mixed. Unquestionably the importance of the long-established private industry associations has waned as state authority has waxed. By contrast, in the international sphere, there is a large and growing body of private standards and codes of practice that impinge upon City markets. The case for the increased significance of market forces in the governance of the City of London is more clear-cut. In the post-war period, states generally sought to restrain and control financial markets by imposing a panoply of restrictions upon them. However, the restoration of the belief that markets constitute spontaneous, self-regulating orders was the catalyst for a dramatic change in the state's role in regulating financial markets. Now state regulation aims to provide the conditions for efficient market operation in the conviction that participants will respond to price signals and the market will effectively be a self-regulating mechanism. Governance by markets is now preferred to governance of the market by state institutions. The problem with these structures of governance is that their authority is not derived from, or delimited by, the territorial coordinates imposed by the spaces of places model. They exist in functional and social spaces more easily identifiable with the notion of spaces of flows. This gives rise to what is perhaps the ultimate question for theories of multi-level governance, namely, to what extent can 'levels' be identified at all? While territorial levels make sense when we are referring to public forms of authority, they seem less compatible with private and market forms of authority. Indeed Baker's (Chapter 6 of this volume) notion of 'dimension' appears more apposite for these non-territorial structures of authority.

It seems, therefore, that multi-level governance is a step in the right direction. The recognition that governance is undertaken by actors deriving authority from a number of different spatial scales is valuable. The problem is that, in its present incarnation, multi-level governance tends to focus exclusively on public and territorial structures of authority to the detriment of private and market forms of authority. The tentative conclusion of this chapter is that the multi-'level', territorial model of governance interacts, intersects and overlaps with the multi-'dimensional', non-territorial model to form an overarching system of governance within the City of London. The next task is systematically to evaluate these relationships, both in the City and in other contexts, in order to develop models of governance (whether labelled multi-level or not) capable of interpreting and understanding financial regulation in a global era.

Notes

1   This chapter is based upon the theoretical component of an earlier paper entitled '"Spaces of places", "spaces of flows" and "authoritative domains": Multi-level governance in the City of London's financial markets', presented to the conference on Multi-level Governance Interdisciplinary Perspectives, hosted by the Political Economy Research Centre, University of Sheffield, 28–30 June 2001. I am grateful to the conference participants for their comments and criticisms. The usual caveats apply.

2   Other notorious incidents from the last twenty years include the collapse and subsequent bail-out of Johnson Matthey Bank (1984), the fraudulent activities of Barlow Clowes (1988) and Roger Levitt (1993), the collapse of the Bank for Credit and Commerce International (1991) and Barings Bank (1995), the insolvency of Equitable Life (2001) and the ongoing saga of mis-sold pensions and mortgage endowments.

3   Hence the phrase 'my word is my bond'.

4   Lawson (1992: 626) details a more comprehensive list of measures undertaken by the Thatcher governments with regard to financial liberalization.

5   Although the FSA was formally constituted in 1997, it did not receive its full powers until November 2001 after the protracted passage through Parliament of the Financial Services and Markets Bill and the necessary secondary legislation.

6 Other new responsibilities for the FSA included a new authorization and disclosure scheme for mortgage lending, the supervision of the Society of Lloyd's, money laundering, credit unions and insider dealing.

7 The number of foreign banks in the City of London has fallen from a peak of 537 in 1999 (Corporation of London 2000; Davies 2000c). This 11 per cent slide is the result of mergers in the banking sector and retrenchment in banking activity, linked to problems in emerging markets and, more recently, the global economic slowdown and dwindling merger and acquisition activity (Roberts and Kynaston 2001). More worryingly for the City, the number of foreign banks locating in other European financial centres has risen sharply in the last few years. Since 1998 the number of foreign banks in Frankfurt has increased by 39 per cent to 320. Similarly, Paris has experienced a 14 per cent expansion in the number of foreign banks. These trends and the choice of Frankfurt as the home for the European Central Bank suggest that the City's pre-eminence among European financial centres is not assured.

8 The figure of $504 billion reflects a substantial drop from the $637 billion reported in 1998 (Bank of England 1998: 1). This downturn reflects the introduction of the euro and the concomitant elimination of trading of the twelve currencies in the euro area and the appreciating value of the dollar over the same period.

9 The conditions for assisting an overseas regulator are set out in section 47 of the Financial Services and Markets Act. They are: '(a) whether in the territory of the regulator concerned, corresponding assistance would be given to a United Kingdom regulatory authority; (b) whether the case concerns the breach of law, or other requirement, which has no close parallel in the United Kingdom or involves the assertion of a jurisdiction not recognized by the United Kingdom; (c) the seriousness of the case and its importance to persons in the United Kingdom; and (d) whether it is otherwise appropriate in the public interest to give the assistance sought.'

10 I am grateful to Andrew Baker for this point.

10 The New International Financial Architecture (NIFA)

An emerging multi-level structure of neo-liberal discipline

Susanne Soederberg[1]

Introduction: NIFA and the problems with multi-level governance

The litany of crises in emerging markets over the past decade exposed the Achilles' Heel of the existing global financial system: free capital mobility does not lead to stable growth regimes in the South, but instead, to bubble-led (inflated asset prices) growth. In response to the growing turmoil in the international financial system, leaders from the G7 countries established a series of formal and informal networks and policies that cut across various institutions and organizations in the hope of strengthening the existing international financial system, or what has been referred to as the New International Financial Architecture (or the NIFA). Despite its novel form, the NIFA does not, I suggest, represent a radical altering of the underlying neo-liberal premise upon which the existing international financial system has been based since the demise of the Bretton Woods system (1944–71), namely, the norm of free capital mobility (Soederberg 2004).

Before outlining the objectives and arguments of this chapter, it is helpful to sketch briefly the various 'levels of governance' that will be examined. First, the chapter explores the relationship of the United States to the global political economy. Next, we look at the Financial Stability Forum (FSF) – which brings together senior representatives of national financial authorities (e.g. central banks, supervisory authorities and treasury departments) largely from the developed world, international financial institutions, international regulatory and supervisory groupings, committees of central bank experts and the European Central Bank. Briefly, the main objective of the FSF is to achieve systemic stability by ensuring that all countries – especially those that are seen by the G7 as the main source of instability, namely, emerging market economies – adopt the rules and standards of the global capital markets and G7 countries through adherence to free market principles. At the core of this stabilization strategy lie twelve standards and codes that are collectively known as the Reports on Observances of Standards and Codes (ROSCs). These 'universal' standards and codes are aimed at regulating the economic activity in both private and public sectors. The ROSCs encompass twelve areas, such as transparency, corporate governance, securities, insurance, payment systems and so forth. Our discussion, however, will limit its focus to the corporate governance ROSC.

While many scholars have contributed greatly to our understanding of various features of the NIFA, the analyses have been limited in two ways. First, owing to the predominant economic analyses, its inner functions are usually glossed over in highly technical terms whilst evading the NIFA's political nature by the use of sanitized language (cf. Eichengreen 1999; Akyüz 2002; Cartapanis and Herland 2002). Second, analysts of international political economy have tended to focus primarily on the institutional framework of the NIFA, and thereby ignore the social relations of power imbued in the global capitalist system, including the role played by the United States (Armijo 1999a, 2002; Germain 2002; Cerny 1993d). Because of these insouciances, concepts such as authority and multi-level governance have been treated in a pluralist framework (Dahl 1956), which, while useful in describing and explaining how the NIFA functions, does little to shed light on either the underlying contradictions from which the NIFA emerged, or the relations of power inherent in this new building.

In contrast to the above approaches, our frame for understanding the NIFA may be described as critical political economy. The latter does not suggest a new paradigm, but rather an analytical sketch plan based upon an historical materialist perspective (Marx 1990; Harvey 1999; Cox 1987) through which we will be able to make sense of terms such as multi-level governance. Before doing so, let us revisit the guiding definition of a 'level' in this volume. According to the editors of this volume, levels are socially constructed spaces, or systems of social interaction, that have their own logic and are distinct from other social spaces and systems of social interaction, but may be influenced by them (see Chapter 1 of this volume). While I agree with the need to rethink the term 'levels' (national, sub-national, international, and global spaces), I also believe that we need to reflect on the limitations of the pluralist undertones far too often associated with terms such as multi-level (or global) governance. For example, global economic governance is said to be about 'steering or control mechanisms' initiated at multiple spaces of political organization with no single centre of global economic governance (cf. Commission on Global Governance 1995; Rosenau 1995). Drawing on Philip Schmitter, pluralism, as it is understood here,

> . . . can be defined as a system of interest representation in which the constituent units are organized into an unspecified number of multiple, voluntary, competitive, nonhierarchically ordered and self-determined (as to type or scope of interest) categories which are not specifically licensed, recognized, subsidized, created or otherwise controlled in leadership selection or interest articulation by the state and which do not exercise a monopoly of representative activity within their respective categories.
>
> (Quoted in Carnoy 1984: 37)

Before proceeding with our discussion, I should like to mention that my specific contention with pluralist understandings of multi-level governance does not lie in their utility in describing and analysing the role of financial, political and social actors and their differentiated interactions within variegated spaces that constitute the NIFA. Instead, my dissatisfaction with a pluralist perspective lies in my own predilection towards critical as opposed to problem-solving theory. As Robert Cox suggested, problem-solving theories assume that the basic elements of the international system are not subject to fundamental transformation. Therein, with regard to the NIFA, for problem-solvers it is the action, structures and processes within the parameters of this new building that are the object of study. The analytical focus is demarcated by the institutional components of the new edifice. It is within this bounded framework that these theorists seek to observe and explain action, without questioning the limits of the system. As such, questions of who benefits and why from the construction of the NIFA remain unanswered. Cox goes on to suggest that critical theory is central to anyone who 'abhor[s] the social and political implications of the [neo-liberal-led] globalization project [and they] must study its contradictions in order to work for its eventual replacement' (1996: 297).

Viewed through the lens of a critical perspective, the conceptualizations of multi-level governance have all too often been seen as devoid of disciplinary power of capital (including both capitalists and capital-in-general) (cf. Latham 1999; Bakker and Gill 2003; Soederberg forthcoming). Specifically, these understandings of multi-level governance seem to conceal the increasingly intrusive and coercive influence to which the South (or what the G7 refers to as strategically important emerging markets) is currently being subjected in the form of private and official financial flows (Soederberg 2004). For example, according to Philip Cerny this power of finance is diffusive in that it resides in a highly complex *multi-level structure* 'which is increasingly likely to constrain, channel and shape the actions of the most significant participants in international and transnational politics, from powerful political and economic elites, to "autonomous" state structures, and to the mass of ordinary people in all their diversity' (1993d: 27). While finance is indeed dominant, its power (e.g. the norm of free capital mobility) does not derive merely from actors, but from the wider crisis within capital accumulation, which in turn renders profitability in the productive sphere less attractive than speculative investment in the global casino. Take for example the foreign exchange markets (forex), which constitute a larger market than global trade in goods and services. The mammoth size of forex markets is not simply a result of economic and political decisions, but the inner contradiction within capital accumulation – accumulation that has been global in nature since its inception (Marx 1990; Arrighi 1994). Seen from this angle, the dominance of finance over production is the result of what Marxists refer to as the crisis of over-accumulation. According to David Harvey, '[s]uch crises are registered as surpluses of capital and of labour power side by side without there apparently being any means to bring them profitably together to accomplish socially useful tasks' (2003: 61). For Harvey, one way to absorb these surpluses is through spatial and temporal reorganization (1999). In whichever manner capitals seek to deal with the surplus of capital and labour, however, given the inherent nature of capitalism, it will emerge from a highly conflictual process of class-based struggle.

Because this common denominator of the inner contradictions of global capitalism runs through each level of governance, the latter may possess different expressions of reorganization to overcome the surplus of capital and labour, largely due to the specific class configuration at each space of social interaction, but they are not, nor have they ever been, self-contained units. For instance, while governance at the level of the Fund's International Monetary and Finance Committee is distinct in terms of its actors and policy outcomes from, say, the level of a European macro-hedge fund and the US Treasury Department, they all have vested interests in recreating the dominance of neo-liberalism as the only manner in which states and markets should be organized throughout the world, or what Peter Gowan refers to as the 'Dollar–Wall Street Regime' (1999). Put another way, in a Marxian framework, power is not merely the ability for actor A to impose her will on actor B, but instead it is derived from the position of that actor in the overall exploitative social relations that comprise global capitalism, including the inter-state system. It follows that power is not only class-based but is also derived from social relations of production, as opposed to 'structures' or 'levels' *per se*. In the parlance of this volume, levels or spaces of governance are both constituted by and rooted in capitalist social relations of production. As such, power within these spaces is not only highly fluid in nature but also contradictory. In other words, we draw on a class-based analysis, which views both society and states, as well as international organizations (such as the FSF) as capitalist in nature. This implies that, unlike a pluralist understanding, multi-level governance is neither neutral nor a logical 'steering mechanism' (Rosenau 1995); but is instead infused with the contradictions inherent in the wider capital accumulation process. It follows from this that a more apt phrase to describe these relations is 'multi-level domination'.

Multi-level domination, as represented by the NIFA, is a class-based strategy aimed at imposing new forms of disciplinary neo-liberalism (Gill 2000) at various spaces in order to overcome the current crisis, or more specifically, the various financial crises manifesting themselves in the 'strategically important emerging markets'. This implies that the informal and formal rules promoted by, for example, the FSF and the ROSCs are aimed at strengthening and reproducing the existing neo-liberal tenets found in the Washington Consensus (WC). It follows that the NIFA serves those interests who benefit the most from reproducing and embedding norms of liberalized cross-border financial movements: highly mobile international capitalists, and the United States (Soederberg 2001a, 2003). The need to reinvent the WC emerges not simply as a reaction to the spate of crises in emerging markets, but more fundamentally from the inherent contradictions associated with the ever-increasing power of finance vis-à-vis production – indeed a power that has been evolving over the past quarter of a century (cf. Helleiner 1994; Strange 1986).

Before exploring the various levels or spaces of domination inherent in the NIFA, we begin our discussion with an examination of the power structures in the global political economy. Concentrating our analysis along the North–South axis of US structural power, which includes the WC, we are able to identify relations of domination involving states and multilateral lending institutions. Next we turn our attention to the underlying motivation of the US government's attempt to universalize the imperative of free capital mobility via the multilateral lending institutions, such as the IMF. This discussion is useful as it helps us to understand the contradictions of global capitalism from which the NIFA emerged, as well as how the power of international finance increased over time.

The overarching space of domination: the United States and global capitalism

American structural power and the Washington consensus

Although many countries have prospered from ongoing financial liberalization, the Dollar–Wall Street nexus is clearly the largest beneficiary and the most dominant centre of financial activity in the world. The vested interest of the United States in promoting financial liberalization lies in its low level of domestic savings and therefore the need to obtain a constant stream of funds from abroad to feed its ever-growing trade and budget deficits (Gowan 1999: 125ff). Owing to its ability freely to decide the price of the world's trading and reserve currency, the United States has been able to exercise structural power[2] over other states by influencing the international monetary and financial arrangements in the global economy (Baker forthcoming).

In the absence of an interstate consensus, or what Louis Pauly refers to as a 'putative consensus' among its leading members (1999), the United States has flexed its powerful muscles to unilaterally pursue, *inter alia*, a development agenda for the Third World that has been to promote its interests (cf. Soederberg 2001a). Generally speaking, this development agenda is known as the Washington Consensus. The WC, a term made famous by John Williamson (1990a), basically holds that the three keys to prosperity were macro-stability, liberalization (lowering tariff barriers and market deregulation), and privatization: in short, market-led growth.[3] Largely through the means of 'conditionality' (policy reforms in exchange for the money that the IMF and World Bank lend), which was inherent in the market-led 'structural adjustment programmes' (SAPs), this development philosophy is transmitted to debtor countries in Latin America, Asia and Africa by strongly encouraging governments to lift barriers to imports and exports to both outside investment and to foreign currency transactions if full economic expansion is to be achieved.

The WC is an important element of US structural power, not only because of the role it played in expanding markets for US goods, but also because it assisted in stabilizing and universalizing the norms and values of global financial capital, which in turn strengthens the position of the United States in the global economy. The orthodoxy of the consensus is based on the assumption that progress will be brought about via free trade, free capital mobility and a non-interventionist state. The political and ideological complement to this has been the neo-liberal supposition that globalization is not only an inevitable and natural progression that emanates from external forces, but also that governments and societies are required to embrace globalization if they wish to share in increased prosperity (Bhagwati 1998). These assumptions assist in reproducing the power of both finance and those capitalist states who benefit the most from re-legitimating free capital mobility and free trade as conditions arising from the market, whilst drawing attention away from the active role states are playing in ensuring that these conditions are not only met but also recreated (Panitch 2000; Soederberg 2001a).

Within the wider context of financialization, the WC has had at least two important consequences for the South. First, through its policies, the WC has assisted in increasing the dependency of emerging market economies on short-term flows as their primary source of credit. In 1981, for example, while bank loans comprised 77 per cent of the foreign investment in such emerging markets as Mexico, Brazil, Chile, Argentina and Sri Lanka, by 1993 74 per cent of private foreign investment received by these five countries came in the form of mutual funds, hedge funds and pension funds (Dillon 1997: 70). Second, this move has led to the concentration of power in an increasingly smaller number of institutional investors, which, in effect, has led to a situation where decisions relating to capital allocation have become more and more centralized. Ten hedge funds, which operate entirely unregulated, dominate the largest segment of financial markets, namely, foreign exchange derivatives. The majority of the trading activity is what is known as 'over the counter' as opposed to within exchange institutions, and therefore is entirely unregulated (Gowan 1999). Taken together, the strike force (e.g. capital flight and investment strike) of powerful institutional investors has grown exponentially in the South.

Contradictions underpinning American structural power

Given the nature of global capitalism, there are some inherent contradictions in the seeming win-win relationship between Wall Street and the global financial markets. For instance, the viability of international financial markets has become increasingly dependent on the health and stability of the financial markets regardless of their location. As the former Secretary of the US Treasury department, Robert Rubin, stated in reaction to Indonesia's economic woes in 1997, it was more than the stock market shocks and fluctuating currencies that were at stake; so too was financial stability. 'Financial stability around the world is critical to the national security and economic interest of the United States' (*New York Times* 1 November 1997). Thus, with each debacle in the emerging markets, the neo-classical premises upon which the Washington consensus rests – especially the equation between free capital mobility and sustained prosperity – become gradually more and more difficult to legitimate. To illustrate, the Mexico peso crash of 1994–95 not only brought down what was widely regarded as the IMF's Golden Boy, but its contagion (the so-called 'Tequila effect') was also felt not only in the developing but also the industrialized world. According to some observers, as a result of the financial liberalization that took place over the six years of President Salinas's rule, international speculators increased the nominal value of their portfolios by some US$100 billion by buying and selling the shares of privatized firms on the Mexican Stock Exchange. As I have argued elsewhere (Soederberg 2001a), foreign portfolio investment (FPI) has not led to any improvement in economic growth (the productive sphere), but instead largely serves to fuel 'jobless growth', primarily based on transfer of ownership. In fact, the International Labour Office has recently noted that more than 80 per cent of new jobs created in Latin America have been in the informal economy (Altvater 2002). John Dillon (1997) argues that, while Mexico's downfall included corruption and mismanagement in both public and private spheres, its financial liberalization strategies, which were encouraged through its dependency on IMF loans particularly since the 1982 debt crisis, not to mention the legal framework of the North American Free Trade Agreement (NAFTA) and especially its guarantees against any form of capital controls, also played a contributing factor.

The timing of the crisis could not have been worse. The US electorate was deeply divided over whether their country should be entering into a legal trade agreement with a developing country such as Mexico. Luckily for the US institutional investors tied up with the debacle, and the Mexican government, the Clinton administration was not only determined to go through with the NAFTA negotiations, but was also willing to demonstrate the viability of such a project. Thus, failing to get Congressional approval for a $20 billion loan from the Exchange Stabilization Fund, President Clinton used his executive powers and extended a line of credit to Mexico, which was used not only to bail out wealthy investors but also to allow the US government to earn a healthy sum of interest – more than it would have collected had it lent the money to its own citizens (Dillon 1997). Alongside high-profile financial crises such as the 1992–93 Exchange Rate Mechanism (ERM) breakdown, the Mexican peso crisis fuelled concern over the stability of the international financial system. In 1995, policy-makers and pundits began to discuss how they should reform the international financial system at the G7 summit in Halifax, Nova Scotia. Nevertheless, it was not re-regulation of global financial flows that was on the table, but instead how policy-makers could strike a balance between continued financial deregulation and stability. Blind faith in the power of market rationality came to rule the day. The question that surfaces at this point is, for how long?

A few short years after this meeting, and prior to the Asian crash, the Interim Committee of the IMF – under the auspices of its largest shareholder, the US government – attempted to revise the Fund's charter by imposing a legal obligation of open capital accounts on its members (International Monetary Fund 1997a: 8). As Benjamin J. Cohen notes, this was the high-water mark of the attempt to consecrate 'free market mobility as a universal norm' (2002). The Asian crisis of 1997 placed this strategy in serious question, however. Unsurprisingly the US Congress baulked when the Clinton Administration attempt to contribute $57 billion to the IMF for a bail-out for South Korea, $17 billion for Thailand, and $34 billion for Indonesia. The following year, Russia was to receive $16 billion and Brazil $42 billion (and another $30 billion in 2002). The Asian crisis, and its contagion, constituted a turning point regarding the unabashed acceptance of many policy-makers and pundits of the neo-liberal assumptions driving the WC.[4] For instance, government regulation over cross-border financial flows would become a serious issue in the face of the growing demands for reform of the international financial system. It is to this debate that the discussion now turns.

Cracks in the norm of free capital mobility

The Asian crash

The Asian crisis shook the foundations upon which neo-classicism rested. In 1996, a publication arising from a conference sponsored by the IMF held in high praise the region's strong macroeconomic fundamentals in the Association of Southeast Asian Nations (ASEAN). These same paragons were quickly trans-formed into pariahs as the IFIs and the US government blamed the crisis on crony Asian capitalism (International Monetary Fund 1999), as opposed to the reckless and excessive behaviour of speculators. The IMF 'made reforms of corporate governance and related institutions a condition for its bail-outs in the region' (*Economist* 2001a). There is far from a consensus on this issue, however. High-profile US policy-makers and economic pundits, such as former Federal Reserve Chairman Paul Volcker (Greider 1997), former Chief Economist of the World Bank, and Joseph Stiglitz (2002), have begun to question not only the wealth-creating properties of free capital mobility, but also the lack of structural coherence for continued capital accumulation. The events in the so-called IMF-3 (South Korea, Indonesia and Thailand) made painfully clear that the underlying tenets of the WC were more than faulty.

Some observers have argued that liberalized financial markets will not 'consis-tently price capital assets correctly in line with future supply and demand trends, and that the correct asset pricing of liberated capital markets will, in turn, provide a continually reliable guide to saving and investment decisions . . . and to the efficient allocation of their economic resources' (Felix 2002). Other organic intellectuals tend to agree with this position. The highly reputed MIT economist, Paul Krugman, for example, has stated that 'most economists today believe foreign exchange markets behave more like the unstable and irrational asset markets described by Keynes than the efficient markets described by modern finance theory'. Jagdish Bhagwati, an eminent defender of free trade, reinforced this claim by stating that short-term, speculative capital flows are not productive, but rather are characterized by panics and manias, which will continue to be 'a source of considerable economic difficulty' (1998).

The significance of these debates lies in the fact that they represent an ideological renewal of capital controls as a necessary mechanism to reduce market volatility by seeking to curb short-term speculation. One popular way of achieving this is by imposing a steep tax on short-term inflows, such as the Tobin tax (Dillon 1997: 95). The tax, ranging from 0.1 to 0.5 per cent, would be applied to all foreign exchange transactions as a way of reducing currency speculation. In the process, enhancing the efficacy of macroeconomic policy whilst encouraging longer-term investment and raising some tax as a by-product could circumvent the unholy trinity (Tobin 1978). Nevertheless, to be effective it must be implemented both uniformly and universally in conjunction with other reforms to deter speculation, such as a domestic financial transaction tax, and, more fundamentally, within a new international system of stable relationships between major currencies, or what some have called a new Bretton Woods system (cf. Bretton Woods Commission 1994).[5] This solution drives a stake through the heart of the Washington Consensus, for a new Bretton Woods system necessitates an interstate system based on serious political and economic compromises, which could serve to weaken the position of the US by limiting the immense flows of finance,which act to buoy up its ever-increasing twin deficits.

Those opposed to the implementation of universal controls have argued that the Tobin tax is unfeasible due to technical and administrative barriers. Yet Tobin himself has countered this claim by arguing that 'while the implementation of the tax may appear complex, it is not any more complicated, probably much less so, than the detailed provisions of many existing taxes . . . Indeed if the standards of what is feasible employed here had been used before imposing income tax or value added tax (VAT) they would never have been introduced! The dominant feature in the introduction of new taxation has always been the political will rather than administrative feasibility' (Arestis and Sawyer 1999: 163). As Cohen (2002) observes, of the possible reasons why governments may hesitate in implementing capital controls, the political opposition of the United States appears to be the most decisive. Despite the fact that the burden of proof has shifted from those advocating capital controls to those in favour of capital mobility, this debate has not received much attention. However, it has not, as some writers have observed, been ignored. International bourgeoisie and the caretakers of the global economy have been painfully aware of the concerns raised by these organic intellectuals as well as the general sustainability of global capitalism in the developing world.

The United States, and the G7 countries, faced some serious problems. On the one hand, there was a need to legitimate to the electorate that the continuation of free capital mobility was both viable and desirable. On the other hand, the G7 had to gain the cooperation of the political elites in emerging markets, which were important investment sites for their powerful capitalist interests. Gaining universal acceptance of free capital mobility based on the principles dictated by the United States was becoming increasingly difficult, especially in the East Asian region. This was particularly true after the IMF stormed – wrongly, some have argued – into these countries with a long list of demands, including the shutting-down of private banks. The reaction to the US government and the IMF in the region has been far from cooperative. Indeed the growing popularity in East Asia for increased policy autonomy via closing-off of capital accounts posed a serious threat to the Washington Consensus. Japan's attempt to revive the older notion of an Asian Monetary Fund (AMF) at the height of the crisis is a case in point. The AMF was 'to serve as a pool for the foreign exchange reserves of the reserve-rich Asian countries that would repel speculative attacks on Asian currencies' (Bello *et al.* 2000: 18). Unsurprisingly Washington categorically rejected this, largely on the grounds that it could nurture policy choices, such as regional controls, that would be contrary to free capital mobility.

The NIFA should be seen as a political reaction to these manifestations of the underlying paradoxes of global capital accumulation based on free capital mobility. In short, the NIFA was an attempt to revise the rules and standards so as to reproduce, as opposed to radically alter, the nature of the WC. The following sections take a closer look at two key components of the multi-level structure of the NIFA: the FSF and the ROSCs.

The FSF and the ROSCs: emerging spaces of dominance in the NIFA

The FSF

On 3 October 1998, the Finance Ministers and Central Bank Governors of the G7 countries commissioned Hans Tietmeyer, President of the Deutsche Bundesbank, to consult with various public and private international bodies and recommend ways for enhancing the cooperation among national and international supervisory bodies and the International Financial Institutions (IFIs) in order to achieve stability in the international financial system. The main recommendation of the Tietmeyer's (1999) report, more formally known as the report on International Co-operation and Co-ordination in the Area of Financial Market Supervision and Surveillance, was to establish a Financial Stability Forum (the FSF). First convened in April 1999, the FSF was established to promote international financial stability 'by facilitating better-informed lending and investment decisions, improving market integrity, and reducing the risks of financial distress and contagion' (Akyüz 2002: 29).

The FSF's membership is confined to a total of forty members from G7 countries. The Forum, which is a political body that reports to and is supervised jointly by the G7 leaders, represents a multi-level structure of neo-liberal governance. For instance, the FSF emerged as a response to financial capitals to establish a regulatory regime to assist in the continued expansion of global capital accumulation in an interstate system characterized by increasing forms of competition for, and dependency upon, private, short-term financial inflows. Specifically the FSF's membership is comprised of one chairman, twenty-five national authorities (three from each of the G7 countries: from the Treasury,

Central Bank and Supervisory Agency), six members from the international financial institutions: two members from the IMF, two from the World Bank, one from the Bank for International Settlements, and one from the Organization of Economic Co-operation and Development. There are six members from International Regulatory and Supervisory Groupings: two from each of the Basle Committee on Banking Supervision, the International Organization of Securities Commissions and the International Association of Insurance Supervisors. And, finally, two Committees of Central Bank Experts: the Committee on the Global Financial System and the Committee on Payment and Settlement Systems.[6]

The FSF is defined by closed policy communities of industrialized countries 'wherein an elite group works out the management of its own vital interests without wider public involvement' (Underhill, 1997b: 31). Stephen Gill's term *new constitutionalism* (1992) captures this attempt to remove or substantially insulate the new economic institutions from democratic accountability or popular scrutiny in order to increase and centralize bourgeois power and authority in the attempts not only to guarantee the freedom of entry and exit of internationally mobile capital in different socio-economic spaces, but also to universalize rules across national spaces. One way this has been achieved is through the FSF's 'Compendium of Standards' (2000), which 'provides a common reference for the various economic and financial standards that are internationally accepted as relevant to sound, stable and well-functioning financial systems'.

By focusing on one international standard – corporate governance – the next sections explore how the nature of the multi-level structures of the NIFA is moving towards the political construction of universal norms and rules (cf. Cerny 1993a, 2002) to ensure that all countries, and the emerging markets in particular, adhere to neo-liberal management of their capital accounts.

A complementary space of domination: the ROSCs and the case of corporate governance

One of the manifold strategies underpinning the NIFA has been the restructuring of the IFIs. Specifically there has been a concerted effort to reinforce the technical assistance provided for in the IMF's Article IV consultations, whereby the Fund is able to scrutinize the degree to which the terms of conditionality have been adhered to by the debtor nation. To enforce the FSF's objective of creating a more stable international financial system, and to complement the above-mentioned compendium of standards, both the World Bank and the IMF have recently systematized 'eleven areas where standards are important for the institutional underpinning of macroeconomic and financial stability, and hence useful for the operational work of the two institutions' (International Monetary Fund 2001a: 105). Specifically there are eleven modules which constitute what the IFIs refer to as the ROSCs: data dissemination, fiscal practices, monetary and financial policy transparency, banking supervision, insurance supervision, securities market regulation, payments systems, corporate governance, accounting, auditing, insolvency regimes, and creditor rights (International Monetary Fund 2000). Each unit represents an 'internationally agreed standard', which is then benchmarked against country practices in a given area of state policy or market behaviour. The primary aim of this exercise is to promote the 'proper management' of financial liberalization in the developing world. Moreover, the member countries of the FSF voluntarily participate in the assessments of the twelve international units that comprise the ROSCs. Thus, through various multi-level consultations with appropriate and relevant international bodies such as the IMF and World Bank, and with private sector actors such as credit-rating agencies, it is believed that the integrity of the international financial system may be strengthened.

Although internationally agreed standards are not new, the ROSCs are novel in that they have not only developed many-tentacled surveillance in the public sector, but they have also moved into the private spheres of emerging market economies. The module of corporate governance, for example, falls under the 'official' responsibility of the World Bank and its regional satellites such as the Asian Development Bank (ADB), the Organization of Economic Co-operation and Development (OECD), and, implicitly, the US-based credit-rating agency Standard and Poor's (S&P). In this way the international standard of corporate governance is inspected more frequently and intensely than simply on an annual basis via the Fund's Article IV consultations.

Despite the absence of a consensus, the OECD describes corporate governance as '[t]he structure through which shareholders, directors and managers set the board objectives of the company, the means of attaining those objectives and monitoring performance' (Organization for Economic Co-operation and Development 1998; 1999). The ultimate aim of adapting good corporate governance measures is to ensure that investors (suppliers of finance, shareholders or creditors) get a return on their money (cf. Blair and MacLaury 1995; Shleifer and Vishny 1986; Van den Berghe and De Ridder 1999; Vives 2000b; Zhuang *et al.* 2000; Johnson *et al.* 2000). This imposed standardization of corporate governance serves two overlapping goals. First, it attempts to stabilize the international financial system by ensuring that emerging markets adapt to the exigencies of the neo-liberal open market economy. Second, by placing greater emphasis on 'shareholder value' rather than on other variants of corporate governance, the interests of foreign capitals are protected. Both these aims converge on a wider disciplinary strategy imbued in the corporate governance module of the ROSCs, namely, a class-based attempt not only to establish comprehensive webs of surveillance in order better to police the behaviour of economies and states in the emerging markets, but also to legitimize the subjective meaning of these codes by insisting that the ROSCs represent 'common values' across national spaces – despite the fact that they clearly serve the interests of Western institutional investors (e.g. public and private pension funds, insurance companies, bank trusts, and mutual funds) who are closely tied to the relatively more powerful world financial centres, such as Wall Street and Main Street. Taken together, this two-pronged strategy serves to construct a reality in which no other alternative but the principle of free capital mobility is permitted to exist.

As the former General Manager of the Bank for International Settlements (BIS), Alexandre Lamfalussy, puts it:

> [T]o correct mismanaged liberalization there is a need to change the existing institutions, the 'management culture', in particular in risk-assessment and risk-control procedures; an appropriate institutional framework has been set up that allows for the creation of new institutions, for instance, mutual funds or other institutional investors needed for a well-functioning capital market
>
> (Lamfalussy 2000: 90–1; cf. O'Sullivan 2000)

Many powerful policy-makers seem to agree with Lamfalussy. For example, to promote a 'correct' management culture in the global South the IMF aggressively sought the revision of Article 1 of its charter, which would effectively charge the Fund with the responsibility of promoting the 'orderly' liberalization of capital accounts in its member states. Likewise, in 1998, President Bill Clinton and Prime Minister Tony Blair encouraged the G7 to set out a plan for the IMF to extend short-term credit lines to any government that implements IMF-approved reforms, drawing from the recently approved $90 billion increase in the Fund's lendable resources. As George Soros observes: '[t]he G7 ministers also called for increased collaboration between private-sector creditors and national author-ities and the adoption by the IMF member nations of a code of financial transparency enforcement by annual IMF audits' – what are known as Article IV consultations (Soros 1998/99: 63). This decision was subsequently reinforced at the 1999 Köln summit, where the G7 leaders urged the IMF to coordinate surveillance of the degree to which countries comply with international standards and codes of conduct.

These concerns to construct a framework whereby developing countries may properly managed financial liberalization have also been reflected in the way in which the Fund's new Managing Director, Horst Köhler, has approached his core mission: maintaining macroeconomic stability. 'In [Köhler's] mind, going back to basics requires a greater emphasis on capital markets and financial flows; a bigger effort to prevent crises, rather than simply to manage them; and a streamlining of the conditions the Fund attaches to its loans' (*Economist* 2001b). Within the wider frame of neo-liberal institutionalism, the codification of norms and rules presupposes a convergence of expectations, which in turn assumes that participants in the international system have similar ideas about what rules will govern their mutual participation: *everyone expects to play by the same rules*. From this perspective, the IMF's push for international standards and codes, such as corpo-rate governance, are seen as reducing cheating or free riding because all states know what the others are doing. Through the ROSCs, alongside other policing activities such as the Data Dissemination Standard that is policed by the IMF through its instruments of the Special Data Dissemination Standard General

(SDDS) and the General Data Dissemination System (GDDS) (cf. Soederberg 2001a), the IMF and the World Bank are able to pursue surveillance activities not only in the public but also the private sphere of the developing world. In its 2001 Annual Report, the Fund noted that its surveillance 'now devotes more attention to factors that make countries vulnerable to financial crises, including financial system, capital account developments, poor governance, and public and external debt management'. It is clear that these efforts to strengthen the financial system are aimed at reproducing the status quo by incorporating 'the views of and developments in international financial markets into its surveillance activities . . . As a result of these efforts, surveillance has become more focused and candid' (International Monetary Fund 2001d).

All told, the international standard of corporate governance is a more specific expression of the ascent disciplinary strategy that not only subjects emerging markets to more direct influence of the exigencies of ever-increasing short-term horizons of major players in the world market, such as pension and mutual funds, but also legitimates and reproduces a single version of reality that serves this same constituency, as well as the interests of the United States. Thus the version of corporate governance put forward by IFIs, and the economic backlash that results from following anything but 'good' corporate governance, are part of a larger objective to construct a loose regime around the sentiment of free capital mobility, an outlook not shared by all political elites.

The form of imposing corporate governance

The surveillance and disciplinary characteristics of the institutions responsible for the corporate governance module are intended to replace conditionality by fortifying the IMF's Article IV consultations. For its part, the World Bank is able to police the implementation of what is considered 'good' corporate governance practices in debtor countries on a regular basis by essentially making them an integral part of its anti-poverty and growth strategies, and withholding funds as the ultimate act of punishment. The function of the OECD, on the other hand, lacks this coercive characteristic. None the less, in the capacity of a well respected international think-tank for the wealthier nation states, the OECD serves an important role not only in manufacturing the meaning of good corporate governance, but also of legitimizing this social construct through the appearance of consensus formation. In its attempts to formulate the principals of corporate governance, for example, the OECD went out of its way to invite not only the usual suspects of government officials, international policy-makers and powerful international financial groups, but also trade unions and non-governmental organizations. In this way, the 'imagined community' of international civil society was suggested as being adequately represented in the creation of the 'universal principals' governing corporate governance, a factor that we will discuss further.

Unlike the above two institutions involved in the wider disciplinary strategy of corporate governance, the third actor is a non-governmental regulatory body, namely, S&P. The significance of S&P arises when viewed in concert with the OECD and the World Bank. The latter have effectively granted S&P *de facto* policing rights vis-à-vis corporate governance. Similar to the IFIs, the authority of S&P derives from its specialized knowledge upon which their judgements are based, and the fact that capital markets defer to and behave according to their ratings. The rating agency's appearance as a partisan institution, devoid of political affiliation and thus of motive, also conceals its disciplinary nature in terms of ideologically reproducing the 'international' standard of corporate governance. Aside from its powers of moral suasion, S&P wields coercive power as well. Its ability to inflict potentially great economic harm to a country by downgrading a country's debt rating has serious ramifications for governments and markets alike, the most obvious reason being a negative signal to international creditors, institutional investors and traders, which is usually followed by capital flight and/or investment strikes. To take a recent example: in order to punish Japan for its slow progress on structural reform, S&P recently downgraded the country's long-term debt rating, putting Japan on par with Italy, the only other G7 country with a rating below the top-grade AAA (*Financial Times* 2001). Upon the release of this news, institutional investors engaged in the so-called 'Wall Street Walk' out of Japan, while other investors stayed away from the country (investment strike).

Specifically, the linkages between these three regulatory institutions are discernible in the following manner. The ADB advertises its use of S&P's version of corporate governance directly on its website. The meaning of corporate governance that S&P draws on is none other than the definition provided by the OECD, upon which the World Bank also appears to base its meaning of this standard. In its efforts to rate (to quantify) corporate governance, S&P has transformed the OECD definition into a veritable disciplinary mechanism, sytematizing it in the form of a corporate governance score (CGS).[7] Interestingly, CGS is comprised of scores derived from corporate governance ratings at both country and company levels. *Company governance* measures the effectiveness of the interaction among a company's management, board, shareholders and other stakeholders by focusing on what a company does rather than on the minimum required by local laws and regulations; *country governance* on the other hand measures the effectiveness of legal, regulatory and informational infrastructure. This focuses on how external forces at a macro level can influence the quality of a company's corporate governance. Taken together, the CGSs not only aim effectively to police both the political and the economic spaces of an emerging market, but also to expose both spheres more directly to the discipline of international finance.

The basic aim of the ROSCs and their respective intergovernmental and nongovernmental organizations was to erect a regulatory scaffolding around both states and markets in the developing world so as to ensure compliance through constant and vigilant surveillance at the national, regional and global levels. However, to grasp 'who benefits' from this institutional reconfiguration, it is important to remain critical of motives underpinning this supposed 'new' international financial architecture, by resisting mainstream explanations which focus on either the US government's desire for a more equitable and democratic international regulatory structure governing finance, or a move to signal a new multilateralism. Despite the appearance of institutional change, the power structures that underscore this project remain firmly entrenched in the parameters of what Stephen Gill refers to as the class-based '*G7 nexus*' (Gill 1994). This nexus embraces not only the political elite tied to the G7, but also their frequent interactions with powerful international capitals in highly clandestine meetings and institutions such as the Trilateral Commission, World Economic Forum, Mont Pelerin Society, the OECD, and so forth These high-level social and business dealings also take place in key regulatory agencies such as credit rating agencies, the two largest being the US-based Moody's and S&P, as well as those distant, yet highly powerful, UN cousins, the IMF and the World Bank. As Gill rightly emphasizes, the agenda-setting and policy-making processes of the G7 nexus revolve around the dominant interests of the US. Suffice it to say here that the G7 nexus of international regulatory institutions, such as the one that is involved in constructing and policing good corporate governance in the global South, resemble closed-policy (epistemic) communities of industrialized countries, marked by an elite group of like-minded individuals which promotes its own interests without involving the wider public. This clandestine global management effectively depoliticizes the class-based attempt to strengthen the existing system marked by tighter communicative lines and increased cooperation – largely by legitimating and stabilizing it as opposed to reforming it via democratization processes.

As such, the creation of common values, which underlies the formulation of the ROSCs, is not a procedural and technical exercise based on a pre-existing consensus. Instead it is highly political attempt to construct an imagined community between states. The establishment of universal values is part and parcel of this disciplinary strategy, of which corporate governance is said to be a moment. Although the OECD Principles of Corporate Governance (1999) are quite general, and stress that there is no single model of good corporate governance, e.g. the Anglo-American model or the bank-oriented model of Japan, Yilmaz Akyüz points out two problems with such a form of multi-levelled governance. First, the international code of corporate governance neglects to comment on more political issues like the 'relations between companies and their lenders and investors, such as appropriate levels of leverage. They also avoid more detailed rules for the market for corporate control.' Second, and more important, there is a real danger that the technical assistance and assessment exercises with the transmission of the OECD Principles through the webs of governance involving other international organizations such as the World Bank and S&P 'will contain features that reflect biases in favour of concepts linked to particular models of corporate governance' (Akyüz 2002: 48), such as those associated with the United States (Soederberg 2004; cf. Ackoff 1994; Lazonick and O'Sullivan 2000).

Yet it should be underlined that there is more to the dominance of the Anglo-American model of corporate governance than the preference of one ideal-type over the other. The option to model an alleged 'international standard' on

Anglo-American codes and best practices is rooted in the wider power relations in the global political economy. Specifically, this model of corporate governance reflects the interests of Western institutional investors, most of whom profit from a market-centric system of the United States where they are able to operate in a less restricted fashion, as opposed to the bank-centric systems found in Western Europe and Japan. This should raise some questions regarding the links between stabilizing the international financial system by attempting to impose 'internationally agreed standards' in the developing world and thereby protecting Western institutional investors by creating an environment that suits the interests of these powerful international actors.

The neo-liberal disciplinary nature of the multi-level of the NIFA (FSF and ROSCs) needs to be highlighted here, since it serves to reinforce the commitment of governments of emerging market economies to continue to comply with the tenets of free capital mobility, in three overlapping ways. First, it reinforces the view that increased volatility in the international financial system is due to home-grown policy errors in emerging markets – not so much those of profligate governments, which have been largely 'corrected' by SAPs, but those resulting from bad structures of corporate governance (relatedly, this presupposes that the regulatory structures of the advanced industrialized countries, especially those of the US, do not need reform). Second, it shifts the blame for the crises onto the emerging markets and absolves the international financial markets, which thus need not be subject to reform. Third, it induces the governments of emerging market countries to endorse the status quo by means of inclusionary politics. As the G7 made clear during the Köln summit, the key objective of this interstate initiative was to integrate emerging market economies more fully and flexibly with the world economy. This move is not an attempt to shift the balance of power between the developing and developed world but to strengthen the existing system through collective surveillance. Yet, as Underhill (1997b) notes, these closed international communities provide only *ad hoc* and patchy regulation and supervision of the markets, which in turn greatly facilitates the growth of capital volatility and mobility. At the same time, the highly technical economistic language used by these institutions evokes value-neutral sentiments which often tend to depoliticize the activities of powerful financial actors, such as hedge funds, by establishing a scientific element to what are usually self-interested political decisions by powerful capitals.

The question that arises at this point is, does the NIFA mitigate or aggravate the paradox of economic growth fuelled by financial liberalization and increasing volatility in the emerging markets? It is to this question that the concluding section now turns.

The multi-leveled governance structure of the NIFA: stability or straightjacket for 'systematically important' emerging markets?

The NIFA may, at least temporarily, subdue deep-seated contradictions of global capitalism based on free capital mobility. However, upon closer inspection, this multi-leveled building appears to aggravate more than it placates the underlying paradox of global capitalism. Specifically, there are at least two important tendencies that can be identified. First, there appears to be a greater vulnerability to the economy to risk, financial volatility and crisis of emerging markets. Second, there is a growing imposition of restrictions on policy autonomy (Grabel 1996; cf. Armijo 1999a), which may result in increased economic problems and higher levels of repression in the Third World. To elaborate on the first point, as governments of emerging markets embrace portfolio investment (stock and bond purchases) as a source of financing, their exposure to the risks of capital flight increases. As mentioned above, the Asian crisis has clearly demonstrated that even sound economic fundamentals (e.g. low inflation, high savings rates, falling unemployment numbers) no longer provide a guarantee that mammoth amounts of highly mobile capital would not choose to flee a country in a nanosecond. Despite the robust macroeconomic equilibria and high rate of domestic savings, for instance, these 'miracle economies' buckled under the quick exit of foreign funds. Indeed, the changing nature of financial flows to emerging markets have made it increasingly difficult to protect the domestic economy against the devastating effects of contagion and capital flight. There is another downside to this new financial openness: the increased likelihood of a cross-border contagion. Similarly, during panics investors and lenders see developing countries in an undifferentiated fashion, or what Ilene Grabel refers to as the principle of 'guilt by association' (1999).

On the second and related point, the need continuously to signal creditworthiness to global financial markets has not only limited the scope of policy autonomy of states in emerging markets, but has made policy-makers more accountable to the needs of international capitals than to those people it governs. To attract what appears to be the main source of public financing, governments enter into a 'pact with the devil' whereby market credibility assumes a central position in policy-making in such areas as exchange and interest rates as well as tight fiscality – all of which must take precedence over other domestic concerns, especially the needs of powerless segments of the population such as labour unions and the poor. In more substantive terms, policy-making is constrained in two ways. On the one hand, in the current era of a flexible exchange rate regime, a large amount of capital inflows would lead to an appreciation of a country's domestic currency. For developing countries, most of which are dependent on exports, currency appreciation implies cheaper imports and more expensive exports, which could bring about an increase in the country's current account deficit, as well as inflation. On the other hand, for a country to attract FPI, the domestic interest rates have to exceed the international rate of interest (i.e. US rates) by at least the expected rate of depreciation of the domestic currency. These high interest rates can have harmful effects on productive investment as well as making the servicing of public debt more expensive, which could in turn limit the already low levels of welfare expenditures (Damodaran 2000).

Finally, there exists another issue brought about by free capital mobility for developing countries. Institutional investors (pension and mutual funds) appear to value political stability and a consistency in policies that favour the interests of foreign investors over democracy. Mary Ann Haley suggests that investors, attracted to those countries that rapidly implement and maintain intense economic reforms while simultaneously controlling political opposition to these measures, may continue to find political democracy not only unnecessary, but also perhaps even contrary to their interests (2001). Above all, and especially during times of crisis, the government is required to maintain political stability. This has led to increased authoritarian tendencies aimed at quelling social discontent, so as to attract and maintain capital inflows, which can in turn limit the democratization process within and beyond the national borders. For example, the limits placed on policy autonomy and the priority given to international finance in terms of neo-liberal policies (liberalization, flexibilization, privatization) make it increasingly difficult for other voices (labour unions and the poor – those largely associated with the vibrant informal economy) to be heard, let alone their demands responded to. As the cases of Thailand, South Korea and Malaysia make clear, the popular protests and struggles that ensue from these constraints on state intervention are usually accompanied with increased forms of political repression and national populism by the government to protect one of the most coveted features of a good investment site or creditworthy nation, namely, political stability.

This is not easy in current times, especially given the waning levels of broad public support for the neo-liberal project in the wake of ever-widening income polarization and increased poverty rates in many 'systematically important' emerging countries such as Indonesia, Russia, India, South Africa and Turkey (cf. World Bank 2000; Soederberg 2001a). The corollary of this is that the political and social effects of the vicious cycle of crisis-and-bailout over the past two decades are making the neo-classical stance of free capital mobility difficult to sustain and to legitimate to those who pay the costs whenever short-term indebtedness falls due and asset price bubbles implode. The flood of 'second generation' policies of the IFIs, which are aimed at issues of social justice and anti-poverty through the establishment of partnership and ownership, may be viewed as an attempt to address the waning levels of legitimacy for the existing neo-liberal reforms that the G7 believe must be adopted if these countries are to become economically viable.

It remains to be seen how long the NIFA, despite its novel form of multi-level structure of neo-liberal governance, can continue to legitimate and stabilize the political constructed imperative of free capital mobility, whilst these paradoxes in global capitalism continue to place pressure on the crumbling foundations upon which its scaffolding has been built, namely, the neo-liberal virtues of the Washington Consensus. There are at least three developments that cast doubt on the ability of the NIFA to roll back the increased volatility of an already volatile world economy. The first is the weakening economic situation of the largest and most important economy in Latin America, Brazil; the deterioration of an already gloomy situation in Argentina; and the impending default of Uruguay. Second, the IMF, which acts as the lynchpin of the NIFA, is experiencing growing internal dissent regarding its competence as crisis manager (lender of last resort) and its ability to prevent crises in the South. Indeed, these concerns were at the centre of discussion during the 2002 Annual Meeting of the Boards of Governors of the World Bank Group and IMF (*Economist* 2002). Third, the ongoing scandals in the US corporate world, involving the likes of Enron, Adelphia Communications, Arthur Andersen, Tyco, WorldCom, Global Crossing and so forth, have seriously damaged the legitimacy of the United States to set the standard of good governance for the 'systematically important' emerging markets.

It would seem, for the time being, that the interests of powerful international capitals and hegemonic concerns of the United States – both of which are expressed in the neo-liberal-driven norms of the NIFA – have been able to wield their dominance over all aspects of social and political life. However, given the conflict-led nature of capital accumulation, particularly the struggles inherent in the strategies to overcome the surpluses of capital and labour, the ability of the NIFA, and the relations of power therein, to achieve its objectives of stabilizing increasingly volatile forms of capital accumulation, under the rubric of the norm of free capital mobility, will ultimately depend upon the outcome of the struggles between relations of power within various spaces of domination. It will also be contingent on the ability of those class interests, which are represented in the NIFA, to re-legitimate the common sense assumption that neo-liberalism is the only viable form of organizing social relations of production.

Notes

1   The argument presented here draws heavily on my forthcoming book, *The Politics of the New International Financial Architecture: Reimposing Neoliberal Dominance in the Global South* (London: Zed Books, 2004).
2   Strange defines structural power as 'the power to shape and determine the structures of the global political economy within which other states, their political institutions, their economic enterprises and (not least) their scientists and other professional people [such as economists] have to operate' (1994: 24–5).
3   Williamson originally proposed ten policy prescriptions for developing countries: fiscal discipline, redirect public expenditure, reform taxation, liberalize finance, adopt a single competitive exchange rate, liberalize trade, eliminate barriers to foreign direct investment, privatize state-owned enterprises, deregulate market entry and competition, ensure secure property rights (1990a).
4   The vote surrounding the release of this huge sum of money played a major role in setting up the International Financial Institutions Advisory Commission (IFIAC), and the subsequent publication of the Meltzer Commission Report, which was released in March 2000.
5   This was the result of a private conference of forty-seven international financial experts called the Bretton Woods Commission in 1994, chaired by Paul Volcker. See, for example, Bretton Woods Commission, *Bretton Woods: Looking to the Future* (Washington, DC: Bretton Woods Commission, 1994).

6   See the FSF website, www.fsforum.org (accessed 15 July 2004).
7   The key components of S&P's Corporate Governance Scores are as follows:

---

1. Ownership
- Transparency of ownership
- Concentration and influence of ownership

2. Financial Stakeholder Relations
- Regularity of, ease of, access to, and information on shareholder meetings
- Voting and shareholder meeting procedures
- Ownership rights (registration and transferability, equality or ownership rights)

3. Financial Transparency and Information Disclosure
- Type of public disclosure standards adopted
- Timing of, and access to, public disclosure
- Independence and standard of auditor

4. Board and Management Structure and Process
- Board structure and composition
- Role and effectiveness of board
- Role and independence of outsider directors
- Board and executive compensation, evaluation and succession policies

---

Source: www.standardandpoors.com/ResourceCenter/RatingsCriteria/CorpGovScores/index.html

Part III

11 Conclusions

Financial globalization, multi-level governance and IPE

Andrew Baker, David Hudson
and Richard Woodward

The phenomenon of globalization is challenging conventional approaches to the study and analysis of authority and governance in IPE. In particular, it has been suggested that there has been an 'unbundling' (Ruggie 1993c: 171) of the exclusive relationship between authority, statehood and territoriality that has alerted scholars to a much broader set of authoritative actors and structures operating in the global economy. This necessitates new analytical frameworks which recognize that the state and other territorially defined actors are just one of the many structures of authority responsible for the governance of money and finance. This volume has suggested that multi-level governance, despite its many faults, goes some of the way towards surmounting the difficulties associated with conventional state-centred frameworks, further illuminating our understanding of monetary and financial governance. That said, many of the contributors to this volume have highlighted methodological, practical and analytical limitations associated with the existing literature and its applicability to financial and monetary issues and to IPE more generally. In this regard, this concluding chapter proposes some tentative answers to the questions posed at the outset:

- Is multi-level governance a suitable analytical lens through which to view contemporary structures of financial and monetary governance?
- Why does there appear to be 'more' multi-level governance in recent years and will this trend be sustained?
- Are overlapping multi-level governance structures enhancing market power and interests at the expense of public interests, and is this contributing to a 'democratic deficit' in the exercise of governance in the contemporary world?
- Can multi-level governance ever be a genuine explanatory theory or is it destined to remain a descriptive analytical device?

The analytical merits of multi-level governance in an era of financial globalization

The first task in assessing the potential contribution of the multi-level governance framework is to ask whether it accurately portrays the patterns of power and authority responsible for governing global finance. In other words, to what extent is the governance of money and finance 'multi-level', and what do we mean by this? Virtually all of the case study chapters have suggested that it is possible to conceive of the governance of money and finance in terms of levels, and that therefore some analytical purchase can be obtained from the application of the multi-level governance framework. In most cases levels are understood in a conventional 'spaces of places' sense. That is to say they recognize the existence of authoritative actors at any number of spatial scales or 'levels' of varying territorial extensity. Though the importance of these various levels differs from case to case, most contributors continue to assign considerable importance to the level of the nation-state and the power and authority vested in state institutions, including central banks, finance ministries and regulatory bodies, when it comes to the governance of money and finance (see chapters by Baker, Thirkell-White, Soederberg and Woodward). Nevertheless, while power and authority at the level of the nation-state are taken as the starting point, it is recognized, first, that the power and authority used to execute the governance of money and finance is dispersed across a host of other territorial levels from the global to the local; and second, that while it might be theoretically possible to identify discrete levels of authoritative actors, these various levels crosscut, intersect and overlap.

This formulation of multi-level governance as a hierarchy of authoritative actors arranged at various territorial scales is useful to the extent that it generates a neat, parsimonious model that imposes a modicum of order on an increasingly complex world and is more nuanced than analytical frameworks equating power and authority solely with the state. The downside is that this representation of multi-level governance is still too simplified and insufficiently nuanced. In particular, it assumes that the governance of global money and finance is administered by actors and structures deriving their power and authority from control over a given territorial space. However, the broader literature on global financial governance and several of the contributions to this volume drive a bulldozer through this assumption by demonstrating the centrality of private and market actors to governance of money and finance (see chapters by Cerny, Hudson, Baker, Woodward, Thirkell-White and Soederberg). Despite this, the existing multi-level governance literature has had remarkably little to say about these non-territorial sources of power and authority, how they might fit into governing arrangements or how they might be conceived as part of a multi-level framework. Instead, the existing literature has concentrated on public power and authority, effectively conflating multi-level governance with multi-level government. Until this problem can be remedied, multi-level governance will remain only a partially descriptive analytical framework.

A fruitful line of enquiry posited by a number of contributors to this volume, is to reformulate the idea of a level, the 'L' in MLG, in such a way that enables it better to reflect the prevailing patterns of power and authority in global money and finance. The dilemma is that, as soon as non-territorial sources of power and authority are introduced, the idea of a level quickly mutates into something else. In trying to incorporate non-territorial actors into his analysis, Baker prefers the concept of a dimension, which he defines as a discrete, socially constructed space consisting of a series of interactions, deliberations and communications between actors clustered around specific locational 'focal points' or coordinating mechanisms. Woodward's attempt to reconcile non-territorial structures of authority with the multi-level model sees him adopt the idea of 'domains'. Elsewhere, other commentators have argued that levels should be discarded in favour of concentric circles (Smith 1997) and layers (Held *et al.* 1999). While dimensions, domains, layers and concentric models may more accurately reflect the more sedimentary and fluid set of arrangements now associated with governing global money and finance, it appears that there is some agreement that, in order to incorporate non-territorial structures of authority into the analysis, we must also move away from the notion of a level. It is almost as though we have become so accustomed to seeing levels as territorial entities that we find it practically impossible to conceive of them in any other way.

Finally, Paul Langley has highlighted the as yet unrecognized potential of multi-level governance to move our understanding of global financial governance beyond the activities of transnational elites to the very network qualities of global finance that produce a complexity of dynamic interactions between interconnected and interdependent institutional and spatial nodes, some of which remain overlooked in IPE. What Langley has in mind is the problematic separation of transnational multilateral 'governors' from the 'governed' that pervades existing studies of global financial governance. If multi-level governance is to realize its potential analytical purchase in the study of global financial governance, Langley argues, it has to operate as a holistic framework and draw attention to the fact that global finance and global financial governance are 'lived' in the changing everyday experiences of a range of citizens, consumers, investors, debtors and creditors, because neo-liberalism is not just the preserve of institutionally and spatially bound governors 'out there'. It is equally a set of organizational practices that become inherent in everyday credit practices themselves. Multi-level governance needs not only to draw attention to the role of globalizing elites, but also to focus on the linkages and relationships between these activities and the everyday making of the identities and practices of the rational good financial citizen – the investor and the disciplined borrower – associated with the rise of disintermediation, as practices which are equally crucial to global financial governance.

The growing phenomenon of multi-level governance

With the exception of Grossman and his case study of banking regulation in the EU, all of the empirical contributions to this volume have suggested that multi-level governance has become more prevalent in recent decades. The leading explanation for this phenomenon, advanced and explored by several contributors, is that multi-level governance is a response to the globalization of financial activity. That is to say, multi-level governance is a reaction to the widespread liberalization of financial markets and the emergence of new technologies that have sponsored an explosive growth in the intensity, extensity, velocity and impact (Held *et al.* 1999) of cross-border financial activity. As a store of value, a unit of account and a medium of exchange, finance and money are by definition fungible and fluid (see Cerny, Chapter 2 of this volume) and, as Richard Woodward points out in Chapter 3, finance operates in the context of spaces of flows. Financial and monetary flows interconnect economies and territorial locations, while various financial markets develop a systemic dynamic of their own. In Cerny's memorable phrase, finance is the 'infrastructure of the infrastructure' (Cerny 1994), linking but also transcending a variety of spatial locations and scales. Global finance, Paul Langley reminds us, is not something that is 'out there'. Through processes such as disintermediation, global finance is also represented and its disciplinary affects reproduced in the everyday saving and investing practices of the good financial citizen, as a crucial important component of global financial governance. Therefore, as finance is an inherently multi-spatial phenomenon, the governance of finance also has to have multi-spatial characteristics if systemic stability is to be aspired to, and if the disciplinary effects of global finance are to be reproduced. In a globalized era, in which there are increasingly few barriers to financial flows, one might even say that financial governance has to have a multi-levelled or multi-spatial character if financial globalization is to be governed. In this respect, financial globalization is a multi- or even a trans-spatial process that is challenging established political and socio-cultural structures, most notably the state, leading to a complex combination of resistance, promotion and accommodation. Authority to govern becomes dispersed across networks, markets and hierarchies that are linked in an increasingly complex fashion, creating composite structures of governance linking states, transnational social movements, multinational corporations, financial markets, sub-national, cross-national and policy-oriented coalitions of actors. Financial governance is becoming poly-centric, characterized by co-existing and overlapping functional authorities (Cerny 1999b, and Chapter 2 of this volume).

In order to unpack this discussion a little further, the effects of financial liberalization will be briefly considered. As Cerny (1991: 178–9) explains, liberalization and deregulation 'transform the structural context of deregulation itself, shifting the problem – and the necessary range of policy alternatives – to different levels, requiring quantitatively or qualitatively different approaches to deal with the consequences, such as new international regulatory regimes'. This process is exemplified in Woodward's narrative on the changing context of regulation in the City of London. The liberalization of financial markets, both within the UK and among its major competitors, necessitated a radical overhaul of domestic regulatory structures, including in the UK the consolidation of most regulatory functions into a single body, the Financial Services Authority (FSA). Nevertheless, the FSA is founded upon the explicit recognition of the limitations associated with national-level regulation in an era of global financial markets. The FSA maintains that the effective governance of the City's financial markets depends critically on international- and regional-level bodies that have augmented national-level authority in recent decades. Similarly, in his chapter on the IMF, Thirkell-White concludes that, while IMF lending programmes have always had a multi-level character, this has become more pronounced as international capital mobility has intensified the frequency and severity of financial crisis. The IMF's growing reliance on supply-side rather than demand-side measures has meant that lending programmes have become more intrusive in domestic systems of governance, resulting in more diffuse multi-level negotiating processes involving a greater number of actors.

The hypothesis that the globalization of financial markets has or will result in more multi-level governance is contradicted by Grossman's analysis of European banking regulation. He suggests that, as a result of the expansion of the EU's legal competencies, we are witnessing the progressive Europeanization, or centralization, of banking regulation. This process is leading to the gradual erosion of national banking regulatory competencies, reducing the degree of multi-level governance in this policy area. However, three caveats should be entered with regard to these arguments. First, these findings are considerably at odds with the seemingly endless stream of studies pointing to the growing importance of multi-level governance in European policy-making (see, for example, Marks *et al.* 1996c; Risse-Kappen 1996; Smith 1997; Martin and Pearce 1999; Brugue *et al.* 2000). Second, formidable obstacles remain to anyone seeking to build a pan-European regulatory apparatus, not least the opposition from existing national regulators. Though the UK's FSA is a leading advocate of international and regional regulatory cooperation (see Woodward, Chapter 9 of this volume), it remains implacably opposed to the idea of a pan-European regulator. This stems not only from a desire to maintain its operational independence, but from a belief that the City's competitiveness would inevitably suffer from a 'levelling-up' of European regulations, and that specialized local knowledge and well-developed relationships with the financial sector in any given country leave national regulators in the best position to deliver effective supervision (*Economist* 1999; Financial Services Authority 2000c, 2001). Given the City of London's significance, it is inconceivable that there could be an effective and authoritative EU-wide regulator without UK participation, and therefore it seems likely that national regulatory bodies will persist for the foreseeable future. In accordance with this, Grossman highlights the current trend of what he calls hybridization, involving dynamic interactions between national traditions and EU-level developments, producing a mixture of Europeanization and multi-level governance. Finally, multi-level governance in the context of the EU may be better explained by the unique political dynamics associated with European integration rather than by globalization. In short, the case study of EU banking regulation provides a useful counterweight to some of the other contributions to this volume, and points to the need to differentiate between regionally distinct patterns. Nevertheless it should not detract from the overall pattern which points towards the growing salience of multi-level governance in money and finance.

The implications of multi-level governance for authority and democracy

The introductory chapter noted that one of the main deficiencies with existing literature on global governance was that all too often its prime concern was with whether globalization could be governed rather than with who governs, the values underpinning governance and the interests that governing institutions represent. The central question for many of those investigating global governance came to revolve around how to govern an increasingly globalized economy at a time when the political authority required to do so remained limited by territorial boundaries. One obvious solution to this spatial mismatch was a multi-level framework whereby political authority was dispersed to 'higher levels' that better corresponded to the global economy. Thus multi-level governance came to be seen as a *solution* to the *problem* of whether we could govern globalization. The drawback was that this relegated normative concerns about the implications of multi-levelled systems of governance for democratic accountability to a secondary issue behind a concern with efficient problem-solving (see chapters by Soederberg and Thirkell-White). Indeed, it is noticeable that the EU, the region where the theory and practice of multi-level governing is most developed, continues to be plagued by allegations that it suffers from a 'democratic deficit'. A recurring concern in this volume has been that the growth and development of multi-level governance means that democratic solutions are giving way to technocratic solutions that privilege special interests and prevent the vast majority of citizens from influencing decisions in the financial domain (Stiglitz 2002).

This process gains much of its momentum from finance's increasingly complex, specialized and rarefied character. For the majority of citizens who are not versed in its arcane language and rocket-science equations, democratic participation becomes extremely difficult indeed. More and more decisions on the governance of finance are being taken outside the nation-state – the traditional space of democratic politics. Whether that be through the definition of norms, good practice and acceptable ideas in multilateral technocratic settings (see the chapters by Baker, Soederberg and Thirkell-White), or through the pressure markets can exercise by the threat of capital flight and through the scrutiny of national policies, which is in turn advocated by concepts such as transparency and 'credibility' (see chapters by Cerny, Baker, Thirkell-White and Soederberg). Either way, a key trend identified in this volume is that democratically elected governments appear to be becoming more accountable to markets and multilateral/transnational institutions, or standard-setting bodies, than they are to their own citizens. This may be just about palatable if the markets worked as their champions would have – rationally and efficiently – but the evidence is that market dynamics have a tendency to be speculative and damaging (see Hudson, Chapter 4 of this volume; Keynes 1936; Kindleberger 1996; Chancellor 1999).

Soederberg's analysis of the FSF and ROSCs is instructive in this regard. The Financial Stability Forum (FSF) is in many respects a microcosm of multi-level governance. Here, national finance ministries, central banks and regulators meet with representatives from suprastate bureaucracies such as the IMF, from transnational policy communities such as IOSCO, and from interstate, albeit relatively independent, bodies such as the Basle Committee, creating a complex overlapping patchwork of agencies. The stated aim of the FSF is to improve information exchange between these bodies, but bringing the various bodies together also has more profound effects. Notably, additional legitimacy and authority are secured for the technocratic and predominantly neo-classically oriented findings and reports of the FSF. The consensus and endorsement of all of these actors make it difficult for outsiders to penetrate or contest the technocratic discourse that is produced. In this respect, the FSF can be viewed as a multi-level body designed to monopolize technocratic expertise so as to legitimate and endorse the agendas of the G7 finance ministries and central banks, particularly in the United States, as evidenced in the FSF's recent report on Highly Leveraged Institutions and Hedge Funds (FSF 2002). For Soederberg, the NIFA represents a form of 'multi-level' domination, as a class-based strategy aimed at imposing new forms of disciplinary neo-liberalism (Gill 2000) across various spaces and to prevent financial crises manifesting themselves in systemically important emerging markets.

In a pattern not dissimilar to the processes described by Thirkell-White, in the case of the IMF, and Baker in the case of G7 surveillance, ROSCs are intended to facilitate a joint multilateral and market monitoring process of national data and information release standards, as well as more general financial governance practices. In the case of the ROSCs on corporate governance, Standard & Poors, a private credit rating agency, is responsible for creating credit scorecards on states' corporate governance practices. A poor score on the S&P rating increases the likelihood of investor mistrust and capital flight. Moreover, S&P use the OECD's definition of good corporate governance, demonstrating the circularity and mutually reinforcing nature of the combination of multilateral and market scrutiny that is serving to bring national policy and practice into conformity with the standards set by the ROSCs. Soederberg argues that something approximating a public–private system of neo-liberal disciplinary governance, or a disciplinary ensemble of integrated state-market governance, is the most immediate outcome of the NIFA.

In a similar but more general fashion, Philip Cerny identifies a transfer of the role of 'ideal collective capitalist' from the state to a neo-medieval collection of overlapping and competing authorities, loyal above all to the stabilization of markets, the protection of property rights and the extension of capitalist practices. Grossman also demonstrates how the European Commission has used market opening and other EU policy instruments to discriminate in favour of large transnational banks that operate in global markets at the expense of small local banks and public banks concerned with public infrastructure investment.

Thirkell-White raised perhaps one of the most interesting questions concerning the democratic implications of multi-level governance in the field of money and finance, in his chapter on the IMF. He argued that, in practice, more multi-levelled governance implies an increase in informal communications and divisions of responsibility between a wider range of actors, but that this has also led to a 'Faustian bargain' whereby core values of democratic government are traded for accommodation, consensus and increased efficiency in governance (Peters and Pierre 2001b). In such circumstances, Thirkell-White follows Peters and Pierre's lead in suggesting that weaker actors need a tightly defined legal basis that secures their participation in governance process. Thirkell-White's point is that, in the case of IMF involvement in middle-income countries, processes of consultation and decision-making appear to have become more informal, despite a need for democratic reasons for greater institutionalization of certain actors' roles. More informality, Thirkell-White contended, is inappropriate, as the kind of governance issues the IMF has become involved in are more intrusive and have implications for the distribution of power and wealth. The danger of this, Thirkell-White argued, is that it has resulted in the extension of the ambit of technocratic economics, because the range of issues classified as technical issues to be decided by Fund economists is expanding.

Finally, in his analysis of macroeconomic policy, Baker drew attention to various emerging forms of third-dimensional or state–market symbolic diplomacy that have resulted in market preferences and priorities being internalized in domestic institutional orders, in the form of independent central banks with inflation targets and fiscal rules. These institutional arrangements are in turn designed to provide reassurance to international investors concerning national policy-makers' good intentions. Macroeconomic discipline has on the whole been further reinforced by the norms associated with multilateral surveillance exercises, which have a mutually reinforcing and interdependent relationship with domestic policy-making arrangements and also facilitate further market scrutiny of national policies, producing a continuous market opinion poll on national macroeconomic policies. Similarly, in exchange rate policy, policy-makers have increasingly come to rely on declaratory policy, or the release of statements that are an effort to collectively communicate national authorities' analyses of prevailing economic conditions to the foreign exchange market and how this should affect price movements. Unfortunately, market operators are showing an increasing willingness to contest the verdicts of public policy-makers on exchange rate matters and have often rejected policy-makers' analysis over the last decade. In other words, policy-makers have often resorted to little more than persuasion in an effort to influence exchange rates, while markets have more often than not refused to respond to these statements, ensuring that policy-makers themselves have effectively had little option other than to suspend their own judgement. The general trend is that the authority of leading market analysts and spokespeople is increasing at the expense of public authority on macroeconomic and exchange rate matters. This places an enormous faith in the rational decision-making capacity of financial markets, yet these markets, particularly the foreign exchange market, have shown themselves susceptible to repeated disruptions and dislocations over the last decade.

In short, there is deepening concern that the delegation of political authority away from the nation-state to regional, international and global levels facilitates decision-making on financial issues to be taken outside of the democratic process. Moreover, this process is entrenching neo-liberal ideology beholden to special financial interests. Yet, at the same time, Cerny also points to a potential upside resulting from more multi-level governance of increased flexibility that results in a greater range of access points to complex political and economic processes, with new possibilities for expanding the 'public good' of financial stability and liquidity across the world and capturing the benefits of globalization for a wider range of constituencies. Therefore, as well as constraints stemming from the complexity, messiness and broad lack of accountability of multi-level financial governance, there are also new potential opportunities in terms of flexibility and growth. Unfortunately, there is little evidence in this volume to suggest that those opportunities are being realized, or harnessed in fruitful and emancipatory ways. How these opportunities may be realized and harnessed is a crucially important future research agenda for IPE.

Multi-level governance as an explanatory theory?

The final question to be considered by this concluding chapter concerns whether multi-level governance can make the leap from being a descriptive analytical framework into a theory capable of making explanations and predictions. The dilemma is that such a theory would require an understanding of how levels are constituted – the endogenous characteristics of each level, the constellation of levels outside – the exogenous environment in which that level exists, how different levels interact and cut across one another (see Cerny, Chapter 2 of this volume), how they evolve and which interests they serve. Multi-level governance can act as an analytical framework for structuring such analysis, but alone it has limited capacity to generate explanatory hypotheses. In other words, MLG needs to be accompanied by the operationalization of other theoretical frameworks, for example Hudson's ethnographic lens in the case of financial markets in this volume, and Soederberg's neo-Gramscian, or Coxian, framework. We hope therefore that this volume has signposted some of the useful ways in which multi-level governance might be applied to global financial governance and combined with existing frameworks, both within and outside of IPE, as well as some of the future challenges multi-level governance faces if it is to find a permanent place in the interdisciplinary analytical toolkit of IPE.

A further contribution this volume has made is that it has highlighted that even getting baseline agreement on precisely what constitutes a 'level' can be difficult. On the one hand, we could accept the established notion of levels predicated on territorial coordinates. But this conceptualization of multi-level governance is imperfect because it ignores many of the most important structures of power and authority in contemporary financial governance. On the other hand, we could begin the search for a new conception of levels. Here the problem is that incorporating new sources of power and authority may require abandonment of the idea of 'levels' in favour of another related concept, such as spatial dimensions or domains.

Some final reflections

In the introduction to this volume it was noted how multi-level governance was frequently invoked as a shorthand description for patterns of power and authority in the emergent global epoch, but that little work had been done to examine whether this was an accurate representation of global governance. The systematic application of the multi-level governance framework to the arena of money and finance has revealed both the advantages and disadvantages of such an approach. In particular it has sensitized us to the changing nature and distribution of public authority and has provided us with some insights into the changing role of the state under conditions of globalization. Indeed it might be accurate to state that this volume has in part charted the rise of multi-level government of money and finance, but it has also identified some of the spaces that are absent from existing multi-level accounts and it has begun the task of demonstrating how multi-level governance can be adapted and developed to illustrate how these spaces are politically and socially constructed and how they interact with other spaces. Nevertheless, key problems remain. Like all analytical frameworks, multi-level governance is imperfect and has greater or lesser relevance depending on the reality it is seeking to describe. The observation that levels are insufficiently nuanced and need to be refined in order to recognize structures of authority from beyond the public sphere remains just that: an observation. Precisely how this might be achieved remains to be established. Certainly, one of the most urgent tasks confronting IPE is to understand better how territorially- and publicly-based sources of authority interact and coalesce with private, market and non-territorial sources of authority. One of the more controversial suggestions arising from this volume is that perhaps it is time for IPE, and the social sciences more generally, to rethink, or even jettison, their obsession with hierarchically informed analyses that attempt to establish the primacy of any one level, attributing causal significance to developments at that level, and instead focus on the interactive and mutually reinforcing relationships between different levels, as well as the net consequences and outcomes of those interactions. Multi-level governance, and multi-spatial frameworks, potentially at least, provide a means of approaching this task, and we hope that this volume has suggested as much.

Bibliography

Abbott, J.P (2002) 'The internet and the digital divide: representational space or representation of space?', in J.P. Abbott and O. Worth (eds) *Critical Perspectives on International Political Economy*, Basingstoke: Palgrave.

Abbott, J.P. and Worth, O. (eds) (2002) *Critical Perspectives on International Political Economy*, Basingstoke: Palgrave.

Abolafia, M.Y. (1996) *Making Markets: Opportunism and Restraint on Wall Street*, London: Harvard University Press.

Ackoff, R.L. (1994) The Democratic Corporation: A Radical Prescription for Recreating Corporate America and Rediscovering Success, New York: Oxford University Press.

Adler, P.A. and Adler, P. (eds) (1984) *The Social Dynamics of Financial Markets*, London: JAI Press.

Agnew, J.A. (1994) 'The territorial trap: the geographical assumptions of international relations theory', *Review of International Political Economy* 1, 1: 53–80.

—— (1996) 'Spacelessness versus timeless space in state-centred social science', *Environment and Planning A* 28, 11: 1929–32.

—— (1998) *Geopolitics: Re-visioning World Politics*, London: Routledge.

—— (1999) 'Mapping political power beyond state boundaries: territory, identity, and movement in world politics', *Millennium* 28, 3: 499–521.

—— (2000) 'Global political geography beyond geopolitics', *International Studies Review* 2, 1: 91–9.

Agnew, J. and Corbridge, S. (1995) *Mastering Space: Hegemony, Territory and International Political Economy*, New York: Routledge.

Aitken, R. (2002) 'The (re)making of prudential masculinity: culture, discourse and financial identity', Paper presented at the International Studies Association Annual Convention, New Orleans, March.

Akyüz, Y. (2002) *Reforming the Global Financial Architecture: Issues and Proposals*, London: Zed Books.

Albert, M. (1991) *Capitalisme Contre Capitalisme*, Paris: Points Seuil.

Albrow, M. (1990) 'Introduction', in M. Albrow and E. King (eds) *Globalisation, Knowledge and Society*, London: Sage.

Albrow, M. and King, E. (eds) (1990) *Globalisation, Knowledge and Society*, London: Sage.

Alcock, A. (1992) *Dealing in UK Equities*, Bristol: Jordan and Sons.

Alesina, A. and Summers, L. (1990) 'Central Bank independence and macroeconomic performance: some empirical evidence', *Harvard International Economic Research Discussion Paper* 1496, May.

Allen, R.E. (1994) *Financial Crises and Recession in the Global Economy*, Aldershot: Elgar.

Altvater, E. (1997) 'Financial crises on the threshold of the 21st Century', in L. Panitch (ed.) *Socialist Register – Ruthless Criticism of All That Exists*, Suffolk: Merlin.

—— (2002) 'The growth obsession', in L. Panitch and C. Leys (eds) *Socialist Register*, London: Merlin Press.

Amin, A. and Palan, R. (2001) 'Towards a non-rationalist international political economy', *Review of International Political Economy* 8, 4: 559–77.

Amin, A. and Thrift, N. (1992) 'Neo-Marshallian nodes in global networks', *International Journal of Urban and Regional Research* 16, 4: 571–87.

Amin, S. (1996) 'The challenge of globalization', *Review of International Political Economy* 3, 2: 216–59.

Amoore, L. *et al.* (1997) 'Overturning "Globalisation": resisting the teleological, reclaiming the "Political" ', *New Political Economy* 2, 1: 179–95.

Anderson, J. (1996) 'The shifting stage of politics: new medieval and postmodern territorialities', *Environment and Planning D* 14, 2: 133–53.

Andrews, D. (1994) 'Capital mobility and state autonomy: towards a structural theory of international monetary relations', *International Studies Quarterly* 38, 2: 193–218.

Andrews, D.M., Henning, C.R. and Pauly, L.W. (eds) (2002) *Governing the World's Money*, Ithaca: Cornell University Press.

Arestis, P. and Sawyer, M. (1999) 'What role for the Tobin tax in world economic governance?', in J. Michie and J. Grieve Smith (eds) *Global Instability: The Political Economy of World Economic Governance*, London: Routledge.

Armijo, L.E. (1999a) 'Mixed blessing: expectations about foreign capital flows and democracy in emerging markets', in L.E. Armijo (ed.) *Financial Globalization and Democracy in Emerging Markets*, London: Macmillan.

—— (ed.) (1999b) *Financial Globalization and Democracy in Emerging Markets*, London: Macmillan.

—— (ed.) (2002) *Debating the Global Financial Architecture*, Albany: State University of New York Press.

Arrighi, G. (1994) *The Long Twentieth Century: Money, Power, and the Origins of Our Times*, London: Verso.

Ashley, R.K. (1988) 'Untying the sovereign state: a double reading of the anarchy problematique', *Millennium*, 17, 2: 227–62.

Augar, P. (2000) *The Death of Gentlemanly Capitalism*, London: Penguin.

Aykens, P. (2002) 'Conflicting authorities: states, currency markets and the ERM crisis of 1992–93', *Review of International Studies* 28, 2: 359–80.

Bache, I. and Flinders, M. (eds) (2004) *Multi-level Governance*, Oxford: Oxford University Press.

Baker, A. (1999) 'Nebuleuse and the "internationalization of the state" in the UK? The case of HM Treasury and the Bank of England', *Review of International Political Economy* 6, 1: 79–100.

—— (2000a) 'The G7 as a global "ginger group": plurilateralism and four-dimensional diplomacy', *Global Governance* 6, 2: 165–89.

—— (2000b) 'Globalisation and the British "Residual State" ', in R. Stubbs and G.R.D. Underhill (eds) *Political Economy and the Changing Global Order*, Oxford: Oxford University Press.

—— (2003) 'The G7 and architecture debates: norms, authority and global financial governance', in G.R.D. Underhill and X. Zhang (eds) *International Financial Governance Under Stress: Global Structures Versus National Imperatives*, Cambridge: Cambridge University Press.

—— (forthcoming) *The Group of Seven: Finance Ministries, Central Banks and the Politics of Global Financial Governance*, London: Routledge.

Baker, W. (1984) 'The social structure of a national securities market', *American Journal of Sociology* 89, 4: 775–811.

Bakker, I. and Gill, S. (eds) (2003) *Power, Production and Social Reproduction*, London: Palgrave.

Balino, J.T. and Ubide, A. (1999) *The Korean Financial Crisis of 1997 – A Strategy of Financial Sector Reform*, IMF Working Paper, Washington DC.

Balls, E. (1998) 'Open macroeconomics in an open economy', *Scottish Journal of Political Economy* 45, 2: 113–32.

Bank of England (1998) *The UK foreign exchange and over-the-counter derivatives markets in April 1998*. Available online at http://www.bankofengland.co.uk/fxotcsum.pdf (1 December 2002).

—— (2002) *Annual Report 2002*, London: Bank of England.

—— (2003) *Annual Report 2003*, London: Bank of England.

Basle Committee on Banking Supervision (2002) 'The Basle Committee on Banking Supervision'. Available online at http://www.bis.org/bcbs/aboutbcbs.htm (12 December 2002).

Bauman, Z. (1998) *Globalization: The Human Consequences*, Cambridge: Polity Press.

Baylis, J. and Smith, S. (eds) (1997) *The Globalisation of World Politics: An Introduction to International Relations*, Oxford: Oxford University Press.

Bayne, N. (2000) 'The G7 summit's contribution: past, present, and prospective', in K. Kaiser, J.J. Kirton and J.P. Daniels (eds) *Shaping a New International Financial System: Challenges of Governance in a Globalizing World*, Aldershot: Ashgate.

Bayne, N. and Woolcock, S. (eds) (2003) *The New Economic Diplomacy: Decision Making and Negotiations in International Economic Relations*, Aldershot: Ashgate.

Beaverstock, J.V., Smith, R.G. and Taylor P.J. (2000) 'World-city network: a new metageography', *Annals of the Association of American Geographers* 90, 1: 123–34.

Beetham, D. (1991) *The Legitimation of Power*, London, Macmillan.

Begg, I. (2001) 'The euro? A success against the odds', Paper presented at the Institute of European Studies, Queen's University of Belfast, Queen's seminars on Europeanization, 9 May.

Bello, W., Bullard, N. and Malhotra, K. (eds) (2000) *Global Finance: New Thinking on Regulating Speculative Capital Markets*, London: Zed Books.

Bello, W. *et al.* (2000) 'Notes on the ascendancy and regulation of speculative capital', in W. Bello, N. Bullard and K. Malhotra (eds) *Global Finance: New Thinking on Regulating Speculative Capital Markets*, London: Zed Books.

Bennett, P. (2000) 'Environmental governance and private actors: enrolling insurers in international maritime regulation', *Political Geography* 19, 7: 875–99.

Benz, A. (2000) 'Two types of multi-level governance: intergovernmental relations in German and EU regional policy', *Regional and Federal Studies* 10, 3: 21–44.

Berger, S. and Dore, R. (eds) (1996) *National Diversity and Global Capitalism*, Ithaca: Cornell University Press.

Berle, A.A. and Means, G.C. (1932) *The Modern Corporation and Private Property*, New York: Macmillan.

Bhagwati, J. (1998) 'The capital myth: the differences between trade in widgets and dollars', *Foreign Affairs* 77, 3: 7–13.

Birchfield, V. (1999) 'Contesting the hegemony of market ideology: Gramsci's good sense and Polanyi's double movement', *Review of International Political Economy* 6, 1: 27–54.

Bird, G. and Rowlands, D. (1997) 'The catalytic effect of lending by the international financial institutions', *World Economy* 20, 7: 967–91.

Blackburn, R. (2002) *Banking on Death or, Investing in Life: The History and Future of Pensions*, London: Verso.

Blair, M.M. and MacLaury, B.K. (1995) *Ownership and Control: Rethinking Corporate Governance for the Twenty-First Century*, Washington DC: Brookings Institute.

Blinder, A. (1999) *Central Banking in Theory and Practice*, Cambridge, Mass.: MIT Press.

Block, F.L. (1977) *The Origins of International Economic Disorder: A Study of United States International Monetary Policy from World War II to the Present*, Berkeley and Los Angeles: University of California Press.

—— (1990) *Postindustrial Possibilities: A Critique of Economic Discourse*, London: University of California Press.

Booth, K. and Smith, S. (eds) (1995) *International Relations Theory Today*, Cambridge: Polity Press.

Boyer, R. and Drache, D. (eds) (1996) *States Against Markets: the Limits of Globalization*, London: Routledge.

Brancato, C. (1997) *Institutional Investors and Corporate Governance: Best Practices for Increasing Corporate Value*, Chicago: Irwin.

Brenner, N. (1998) 'Glocal cities, glocal states: global city formation and state territorial restructuring in contemporary Europe', *Review of International Political Economy* 5, 1: 1–37.

—— (1999) 'Beyond state-centrism? Space, territoriality, and geographical scale in globalisation studies', *Theory and Society* 28, 1: 39–78.

Brenner, R. (2001) 'The world economy at the turn of the millennium: toward boom or crisis?', *Review of International Political Economy* 8, 1: 6–44.

Bretton Woods Commission (1994) *Bretton Woods: Looking to the Future*, Washington DC: Bretton Woods Commission.

Brewer, A. (1980) *Marxist Theories of Imperialism: A Critical Survey*, London: Routledge and Kegan Paul.

Briault, C. (2000) 'FSA revisited and some issues for European securities markets regulation', paper presented at the conference 'Financial supervision of banks in the EU', Florence, 15 December.

Bromley, S. (2000) 'The logic of liberal sovereignty', in D. Marsh and C. Hay (eds) *Globalisation, Welfare Retrenchment and the State*, London, Macmillan.

Broughton, J.M. (2000) 'From Suez to Tequila: the IMF as crisis manager', *The Economic Journal* 110: 273–91.

Bruck, C. (1989) *The Predators' Ball*, London: Penguin.

Brugue, Q., Goma, R. and Subirats, J. (2000) 'Multilevel governance and Europeanization: the case of Catalonia', *South European Society and Politics* 5, 2: 95–118.

Bryant, R. (2003) *Turbulent Waters: Cross-Border Finance and International Governance*, Washington DC: Brookings Institute.

Budd, L. (1999) 'Globalisation and the crisis of territorial embeddedness of international financial markets', in R. Martin (ed.) *Money and the Space Economy*, Colchester: Wiley.

Bull, H. (1977) *The Anarchical Society: A Study of Order in World Politics*, London: Macmillan.

Burgess, M. (2000) *Federalism and European Union: The Building of Europe, 1950–2000*, London: Routledge.

Burley, A.-M. (1993) 'Regulating the world: multilateralism, international law, and the projection of the new deal regulatory state', in J. Ruggie (ed.) *Multilateralism Matters: The Theory and Praxis of an Institutional Form*, New York and Chichester, Columbia University Press.

Burnell, P. (1994) 'Good government and democratization: a sideways look at aid and political conditionality', *Democratization* 11, 3: 485–503.

Busch, A. (2000) 'Unpacking the globalisation debate: approaches, evidence and data', in C. Hay and D. Marsh (eds) *Demystifying Globalisation*, London: Macmillan.

Buzan, B. (1995) 'The levels of analysis problem in international relations reconsidered', in K. Booth and S. Smith (eds) *International Relations Theory Today*, Cambridge: Polity Press.

Byers, M. (ed.) (2000) *The Role of Law in International Politics*, Oxford: Oxford University Press.

Cain, P.J. and Hopkins, A.G. (2001) *British Imperialism 1688–2000* (2nd edition), London: Longman.

Calder, L. (1999) *Financing the American Dream: A Cultural History of Consumer Credit*, Princeton: Princeton University Press.

Calomiris, C. (1998) 'The IMF's imprudent role as lender of last resort', *Cato Journal* 17, 3: 275–95.

CalPERS, California Public Employee Retirement System (1998) *Corporate Governance Principals and Guidelines*, Sacramento: CalPERS.

Cameron, A. and Palan, R. (1999) 'The imagined economy: mapping transformations in the contemporary state', *Millennium* 28, 2: 267–88.

Camilleri, J.A., Jarvis, A.P. and Paolini, A.J. (eds) (1995) *The State in Transition: Reimagining Political Space*, Boulder: Lynne Rienner.

Carlnaes, W., Risse, T. and Simmons, B.A. (eds) *Handbook of International Relations*, London: Sage.

Carnoy, M. (1984) *The State and Political Theory*, Princeton: Princeton University Press.

Carr, E.H. (1981) *The Twenty Years' Crisis, 1919–39: An Introduction to the Study of International Relations* (3rd edition), London: Macmillan.

Cartapanis, A. and Herland, M. (2002) 'The reconstruction of the international financial architecture: Keynes' revenge?', *Review of International Political Economy* 9, 2: 271–97.

Castells, M. (1996) *The Information Age: Economy, Society and Culture, Volume 1 – The Rise of the Network Society*, Oxford: Blackwell.

Cerny, P.G. (1989) 'The "Little Big Bang" in Paris: financial market deregulation in a dirigiste system', *European Journal of Political Research* 17, 2: 169–92.

—— (1990) *The Changing Architecture of Politics: Structure, Agency and the Future of the State*, London: Sage.

—— (1991) 'The limits of deregulation: transnational interpenetration and policy change', *European Journal of Political Research* 19, 2–3: 173–96.

—— (ed.) (1993a) *Finance and World Politics: Markets, Regimes and States in the Post-Hegemonic Era*, Aldershot: Edward Elgar.

—— (1993b) 'American decline and the emergence of embedded financial orthodoxy', in P.G. Cerny (ed.) *Finance and World Politics: Markets, Regimes and States in the Post-Hegemonic Era*, Aldershot: Edward Elgar.

—— (1993c) 'The deregulation and re-regulation of financial markets in a more open world', in P.G. Cerny (ed.) *Finance and World Politics: Markets, Regimes and States in the Post-Hegemonic Era*, Aldershot: Edward Elgar.

—— (1993d) 'Plurilateralism: structural differentiation and functional conflict in the post-Cold War world order', *Millennium* 22, 1: 27–51.

—— (1994a) 'Money and finance in international political economy: structural change and paradigmatic muddle', *Review of International Political Economy* 1, 3: 587–92.

—— (1994b) 'The infrastructure of the infrastructure? Toward "embedded financial orthodoxy" in the international political economy', in R.P. Palan and B.K. Gills (eds) *Transcending the State–Global Divide: A Neostructuralist Agenda in International Relations*, Boulder: Lynne Rienner.

—— (1996) 'Globalization and other stories: the search for a new paradigm for international relations', *International Journal* 50, 4: 617–37.

—— (1997) 'Paradoxes of the competition state: the dynamics of political globalization', *Government and Opposition* 32, 2: 251–74.

—— (1998a) 'Politicising international finance', *Millennium* 27, 2: 353–61.

—— (1998b) 'Neomedievalism, civil war and the new security dilemma: globalisation as durable disorder', *Civil Wars* 1, 1: 36–64.

—— (1999a) 'Globalization and the erosion of democracy', *European Journal of Political Research* 36, 1: 1–26.

—— (1999b) 'Globalising the political and politicising the global: concluding reflections on international political economy as a vocation', *New Political Economy* 4, 1: 147–62.

—— (2000a) 'Political agency in a globalizing world: toward a structurational approach', *European Journal of International Relations* 6, 4: 147–62.

—— (2000b) 'Embedding global financial markets: securitization and the emerging web of governance', in K. Ronit and V. Schneider (eds) *Private Organizations in Global Politics*, London: Routledge.

—— (2000c) 'Money and power: the American financial system from free banking to global competition', in G. Thompson (ed.) *Markets*, vol. 2 of *The United States in the Twentieth Century* (2nd edition), London: Hodder and Stoughton.

—— (2000d) 'The big bang in Tokyo, financial globalization and the unravelling of the Japanese model', in H.Harukiyo and G.Hook (eds) *The Political Economy of Japanese Globalization*, London: Routledge.

—— (2001) 'Privatizing transnational governance: markets, networks and authority in international finance', *Manchester Papers in Politics* 7/01.

—— (2002) 'Webs of governance: the privatization of transnational regulation', in D.M. Andrews, C.R. Henning and L.W. Pauly (eds) *Governing the World's Money*, Ithaca: Cornell University Press.

—— (2004) 'Governance, globalization and the Japanese financial system: resistance or restructuring?', in G. Hook (ed.) *Contested Governance in Japan*, London: Routledge.

Chancellor, E. (1999) *Devil Take the Hindmost: A History of Financial Speculation*, London: Macmillan.

Chandler, A.D. Jr. (1992) *Scale and Scope: The Dynamics of Industrial Capitalism*, Cambridge, Mass.: Harvard University Press.

Chang, H.J., Park, J.-J. and Yoo, C.G. (1998) 'Interpreting the Korean crisis – financial liberalisation, industrial policy and corporate governance', *Cambridge Journal of Economics* 22, 6: 735–46.

Cini, M. (2000) 'From soft law to hard law? Discretion and rule-making in the Commission's state aid regime', *Robert Schuman Centre Working Paper*, 2000/35.

Cini, M. and McGowan, L. (1998) *Competition Policy in the European Union*, London: Routledge.

Clark, G.L. (2000) *Pension Fund Capitalism*, Oxford: Oxford University Press.

Clark, G.L. and O'Connor, K. (1997) 'Informational content of financial products and the spatial structure of the global finance industry', in K.R. Cox (ed.) *Spaces of Globalization: Reasserting the Power of the Local*, London: Guildford.

Clark, I. (1999) *Globalization and International Relations Theory*, Oxford: Oxford University Press.

Clayton, J.L. (2000) *The Global Debt Bomb*, New York: M.E. Sharpe.

Coase, R. (1988) *The Firm, the Market and the Law*, Chicago: Chicago University Press.

Cohen, B.J. (1996) 'Phoenix risen: the resurrection of global finance', *World Politics* 48, 2: 268–96.

—— (1998) *The Geography of Money*, Ithaca: Cornell University Press.

—— (2000) 'Taming the phoenix? Monetary governance after the crisis', in G.W. Noble and J. Ravenhill (eds) *The Asian Financial Crisis and the Architecture of Global Finance*, Cambridge: Cambridge University Press.

—— (2001) 'Electronic money: new day or false dawn?', *Review of International Political Economy* 8, 2: 197–225.

—— (2002) 'International finance', in W. Carlnaes, T. Risse and B.A. Simmons (eds) *Handbook of International Relations*, London: Sage.

—— (2004a) *The Future of Money*, Princeton: Princeton University Press.

—— (2004b) 'The meaning of monetary power', Paper presented at the International Studies Association Annual Convention, Montreal, March.

—— (2003) 'Capital controls: the neglected option', in G.R.D. Underhill and X Xiaoke (eds.) *International Financial Governance Under Stress: National imperatives versus global structures*, Cambridge: Cambridge University Press, 60–76

Cohen, E.S. (2001) 'Globalization and the boundaries of the state: a framework for analysing the changing practice of sovereignty', *Governance* 14, 1: 75–97.

Coleman, W.D. (1993) 'Reforming corporatism: the French banking policy community, 1941–1990', *West European Politics* 16, 2: 123–43.

—— (1994) 'Policy convergence in banking: a comparative study', *Political Studies* 42, 2: 274–92.

—— (1996) *Financial Services, Globalization and Domestic Policy Change*, London: Macmillan.

Coleman, W.D. and Porter, T. (1994) 'Regulating international banking and securities: emerging co-operation among national authorities', in R. Stubbs and G.R.D. Underhill (eds) *Political Economy and the Changing Global Order*, Basingstoke: Macmillan.

Commission of the European Communities (1997) *Single Market Review, Series II (Services), Vol. 11: Financial Services*, Luxemburg, Office of Publications of the European Union.

—— (1999) *Implementing the Framework for Financial Markets: Action Plan*, COM (1999) 232 final.

Commission on Global Governance (1995) *Our Global Neighbourhood: The Report of the Commission on Global Governance*, Oxford: Oxford University Press.

Committee of European Securities Regulators (2002) 'Presentation of CESR'. Available online at http://www.europefesco.org/v1/Presentation_of_CESR.htm (19 December 2002).

Cooper, R.N. (1975) 'Prolegoma to the choice of an international monetary system', *International Organization* 29, 1: 63–97.

Cooper, R.N. *et al.* (eds) (1989) *Can Nations Agree? Issues in International Economic Co-operation*, Washington DC: Brookings Institution.

Corbridge, S., Martin, R. and Thrift, N. (eds) (1994) *Money, Power and Space*, London: Blackwell.

Corporation of London (2000, 2002) *The Global Powerhouse: The City of London*.

Cox, K.R. (ed.) (1997) *Spaces of Globalization: Reasserting the Power of the Local*, London: Guildford.

Cox, R.W. (1981) 'Social forces, states and world orders: beyond international relations theory', *Millennium* 10, 2: 126–55.

—— (1983) 'Gramsci, hegemony and international relations: an essay in method', *Millennium* 12, 2: 162–75.

—— (1986) 'Social forces, states and world orders: beyond international relations theory' (with a postscript), in R.O. Keohane (ed.) *Neorealism and its Critics*, New York: Columbia University Press.

—— (1987) *Production, Power, and World Order: Social Forces in the Making of History*, New York: Columbia University Press.

—— (1992) 'Multilateralism and world order', *Review of International Studies* 18, 2: 161–80.

—— (2000) 'Political economy and world order: problems of power and knowledge at the turn of the millennium', in R. Stubbs and G.R.D. Underhill (eds) *Political Economy and the Changing Global Order*, Oxford: Oxford University Press.

Cox, R.W. with Sinclair, T.J. (1996) *Approaches to World Order*, Cambridge: Cambridge University Press.

Cram, L. (1997) *Policy-Making in the European Union*, London: Routledge.

Croisat, M. and Quermonne, J.-L. (1999) *L'Europe et le Fédéralisme: Contribution à L'Emergence d'un Fédéralisme Intergouvernemental*, Paris: Montchrestien.

Crouch, C. and Streeck, W. (eds) (1997) *The Political Economy of Modern Capitalism: Mapping Convergence and Diversity*, London: Sage.

Culpeper, R. (2000) 'Systemic reform at a standstill: a flock of "Gs" in search of global financial stability'. Available online at http://www.g7.utoronto.ca/g7/scholar/culpeper2000/index.html. (4 April 2004).

Cumings, B. (1998) 'The Korean crisis and the end of late development', *New Left Review* 231: 43–72.

Cutler, A.C. (1995) 'Global capitalism and liberal myths: dispute settlement in private trade relations', *Millennium* 24, 3: 377–97.

—— (1999a) 'Locating authority in the global political economy', *International Studies Quarterly* 43, 1: 59–81.

—— (1999b) 'Private authority in international trade relations: the case of maritime transport', in A.C. Cutler, V. Haufler and T. Porter (eds) *Private Authority and International Affairs*, Albany: State University of New York Press.

Cutler, A.C., Haufler, V. and Porter, T. (eds) (1999a) *Private Authority and International Affairs*, Albany: State University of New York Press.

—— (1999b) 'The contours and significance of private authority in international affairs', in A.C. Cutler, V. Haufler and T. Porter (eds) *Private Authority and International Affairs*, Albany: State University of New York Press.

Cutler, T. and Waine, B. (2001) 'Social insecurity and the retreat from social democracy: occupational welfare in the long boom and financialization', *Review of International Political Economy* 8, 1: 96–117.

Dahl, R. (1956) *A Preface to Democratic Theory*, Chicago: University of Chicago Press.

Damodaran, S. (2000) 'Capital account convertibility: theoretical issues and policy options', in W. Bello, N. Bullard and K. Malhotra (eds) *Global Finance: New Thinking on Regulating Speculative Capital Markets*, London: Zed Books.

Daniels, P.W. and Lever, W.F. (eds) (1996) *The Global Economy in Transition*, Essex: Addison Wesley Longman.

Davies, H. (1999a) 'A forum for stability', *Financial Times* 14 April: 18.

—— (1999b) 'The changing face of international financial regulation', Speech by Howard Davies, Chairman, UK Financial Services Authority to the Japan Bankers Federation, Tokyo, 11 November. Available online at http://www.fsa.gov.uk/pubs/speeches/sp34.html (13 December 2002).

—— (2000a) 'C D Deshmukh memorial lecture', Speech by Howard Davies, Chairman, UK Financial Services Authority, Mumbai, 7 February. Available online at http://www.fsa.gov.uk/pubs/speeches/sp39.html (13 December 2002).

—— (2000b) 'Global markets, global regulation', Speech by Howard Davies, Chairman, UK Financial Services Authority to the IOSCO Annual Conference, 17 May. Available online at http://www.fsa.gov.uk/pubs/speeches/sp45.html (29 November 2002).

—— (2000c) 'Eurofi conference', Speech by Howard Davies, Chairman, UK Financial Services Authority to the Eurofi Conference, Paris, 15 September. Available online at http://www.fsa.gov.uk/pubs/speeches/sp57.htm (29 November 2002).

—— (2001) 'The role of financial regulators in promoting financial stability', Speech by Howard Davies, Chairman, UK Financial Services Authority to IOSCO Conference, Stockholm, 27 June. Available online at http://www.fsa.gov.uk/pubs/speeches/sp81. html (29 November 2002).

Dean, M. (1999) *Governmentality: Power and Rule in Modern Society*, London: Sage.

Deeg, R. (1999) *Finance Capitalism Unveiled. Banks and the German Political Economy*, Ann Arbor: University of Michigan Press.

Deeg, R. and Perez, S. (2000) 'International capital mobility and domestic institutions: corporate governance and finance in four European cases', *Governance* 13, 2: 119–53.

Degen, R.A. (1987) *The American Monetary System: A Concise Survey of Its Evolution Since 1896*, Lexington: D.C. Heath.

Deprez, J. and Harvey, J.T. (eds) (1999) *Foundations of International Economics: Post Keynesian Perspectives*, London: Routledge.

De Vries, M.G. (1987) *Balance of Payments Adjustment 1945–1986: The IMF Experience*, Washington DC: IMF.

Dhonte, P. (1997) *Conditionality as an Instrument of Borrower Credibility*, IMF papers on policy analysis and assessment, PPAA/97/2.

Dillon, J. (1997) *Turning the Tide: Confronting the Money Traders*, Ottawa: Canadian Centre for Policy Alternatives.

Dobson, W. and Jacquet, P. (1998) *Financial Services Liberalization in the WTO*, Washington DC: Institute for International Economics.

Dombrowski, P. (1998) 'Haute finance and high theory: recent scholarship on global financial relations', *Mershon International Studies Review* 42, 1: 1–28.

Dore, R. (2002) 'Stock market capitalism and its diffusion', *New Political Economy* 7, 1: 115–27.

Doremus, P.N. *et al.* (1998) *The Myth of the Global Corporation*, Princeton: Princeton University Press.

Dunn, J. (2000) *The Cunning of Unreason: Making Sense of Politics*, London: Harper Collins.

Dyson, K. (1994) *Elusive Union: The Process of Economic and Monetary Union in Europe*, London: Longman.

Easton, D. (1953) *The Political System*, New York: Knopf.

Eatwell, J. and Taylor, L. (2000) *Global Finance at Risk: The Case for International Regulation*, New York: The Free Press.

Economist (1988) 'La grande boom', 1–7 October: 111–12

—— (1999) 'No SECs please, we're European', 21–27 August: 70–1.

—— (2001a) 'A survey of Asian business: in praise of rules', 7–13 April.

—— (2001b) 'Kohler's new crew', 16 June: 77.

—— (2002) 'Doubts inside the barricades', 26 September–2 October: 89–91.

Eichengreen, B. (1996) *Globalizing Capital: A History of the International Monetary System*, Princeton: Princeton University Press.

—— (1999) *Towards a New International Financial Architecture*, Washington: Institute for International Economics.

Eising, R. and Kohler-Koch, B. (1994) '*Inflation und zerfaserung: trends der interessenvermittlung in der Europ$ischen gemeinschaft*', *Politische Vierteljahresschrift* 25, 25: 175–206.

Ekengren, M. and Jacobsson, K. (2000) 'Explaining the constitutionalization of EU governance – the case of European employment cooperation', *Stockholm Centre for Organizational Research (SCORE) Working Paper* 2000–8. Available online at http://www.score.su.se/pdfs/2000–8.pdf (3 March 2001).

Enoch, C. *et al.* (2001) 'Indonesia: anatomy of a banking crisis two years of living dangerously, 1997–1999', *IMF Working Paper* WP/01/52.

European Financial Services Round Table (2002) *The Benefits of a Working European Retail Market for Financial Services Report to European Financial Services Round Table*, Berlin: Institut für Europäische Politik/Europa Union Verlag

European Union (1998) *Financial Services: Building a Framework for Action*. Available online at http://europa.eu.int/comm/internal_market/en/finances/general/fsen.pdf (14 December 2002).

—— (2003) 'Progress on the Financial Services Action Plan – Annex'. Available online at http://europa.eu.int/comm/internal_market/en/finances/actionplan/#annex (20 February 2003).

Evans, P. (1997) 'The eclipse of the state?: Reflections on stateness in an era of globalization', *World Politics* 50, 1: 62–87.

Fama, E. (1970) 'Efficient capital markets: a review of theory and empirical work', *Journal of Finance* 25, 2: 383–417.

Fama, E. and Jensen, M. (1983) 'Separation of ownership and control', *Journal of Law and Economics* 26, 2: 301–25.

Feldstein, M. (1998) 'Refocusing the IMF', *Foreign Affairs* 77, 2: 20–33.

Felix, D. (2002) 'The economic case against free capital mobility', in L.E. Armijo (ed.) *Debating the Global Financial Architecture*, New York: State University of New York Press.

Ferguson, T. (1988) *The Third World and Decision Making in the International Monetary Fund: The Quest for Full and Effective Participation*, New York: Pinter.

Ferguson, Y.H. and Barry Jones, R.J. (eds) (2002) *Political Space: Frontiers of Change and Governance in a Globalizing World*, New York: State University of New York Press.

Ferguson, Y.H. and Mansbach, R.W. (1996) *Polities: Authority, Identities, and Change*, Columbia: University of South Carolina Press.

Filipovic, M. (1997) *Governments, Banks and Global Capital: Securities Markets in Global Politics*, Aldershot: Ashgate.

Financial Services Authority (2000a) *Financial Services Authority Annual Report*. Available online at http://www.fsa.gov.uk/pubs/annual/ar1999_00.pdf (29 November 2002).

—— (2000b) *A New Regulator for the New Millennium*. Available online at http://www.fsa.gov.uk/pubs/policy/p29/pdf (29 November 2002).

—— (2000c) *Financial Services Authority Plan and Budget 2000/01*. Available online at http://www.fsa.gov.uk/pubs/management/pb2000_01.pdf (8 May 2001).

—— (2001) *Financial Services Authority Plan and Budget 2001/02*. Available online at http://www.fsa.gov.uk/pubs/management/pb2001_02.pdf (8 May 2001).

Financial Stability Forum (2000) *12 Key Standards for Sound Financial Systems*. Available online at http://www.fsforum.org/compendium/key_standards_for_sound_financial_system.html (10 April 2004).

—— (2002) *Report of the Working Group on Highly Leveraged Institutions*. Available online at http://www.fsforum.org/publications/Rep_WG_HLI00.pdf. (6 April 2004).

Financial Times (1997) '"Planning blight" in the City', 20 May: 23.

—— (2001) 'Japan suffers fresh blow with S&P downgrade', 28 November.

—— (2002a) 'Capital keeps its prominence as European finance centre', 8 February: 3.

—— (2002b) 'How politics, protectionism and cultural clashes could dash Europe's dreams of a single financial market', 4 December: 17.

Finch, D. (1989) 'The IMF: the record and the prospect', *Essays in International Finance*, 175.

Fine, B. (2000) *Social Capital Versus Social Theory: Political Economy and Social Science at the Turn of the Millennium*, London, Routledge.

Forrester, G. (ed.) (1999) *Post-Soeharto Indonesia. Renewal or chaos?*, Singapore: Institute for Southeast Asian Studies.

Foucault, M. (1979) 'On governmentality', *Ideology and Consciousness* 6: 5–22.

Frankel, J. (1996) 'How well do markets work: might a Tobin Tax help?', in M. ul Haq, I. Kaul and I. Grunberg (eds) *The Tobin Tax: Coping with Financial Volatility*, Oxford: Oxford University Press.

Frieden, J. (1991) 'Invested interests: the politics of national economic policies in a world of global finance', *International Organization* 45, 4: 125–48.

Friedman, M. (1953) *Essays in Positive Economics*, Chicago: University of Chicago Press.

Friedman, T.L. (2000) *The Lexus and the Olive Tree: Understanding Globalization*, London: Harper Collins.

Fukao, M. (1995) *Financial Integration, Corporate Governance, and the Performance of Multinational Companies*, Washington DC: Brookings Institution.

Galbraith, J.K. (1967) *The New Industrial State*, London: Hamish Hamilton.

Gamble, A. (2000) 'Economic governance', in J. Pierre (ed.) *Debating Governance: Authority, Steering and Democracy*, Oxford: Oxford University Press.

Gardner, L.C. (1964) *Economic Aspects of New Deal Diplomacy*, Boston: Beacon Press.

—— (1976) *Imperial America: American Foreign Policy Since 1898*, New York: Harcourt Brace Jovanovich.

—— (1980) *Sterling–Dollar Diplomacy in Historical Perspective* (3rd edition), New York: Columbia University Press.

Garrett, G (1998) *Partisan Politics in the Global Economy*, Cambridge: Cambridge University Press.

Geertz, C. (1975) 'Thick description: toward an interpretative theory of culture', in C. Geertz, *The Interpretation of Cultures: Selected Essays*, London: Fontana.

Germain, R. (1997) *The International Organisation of Credit: States and Global Finance in the World-Economy*, Cambridge: Cambridge University Press.

—— (ed.) (2000) *Globalization and its Critics*, London: Macmillan.

—— (2001) 'Global financial governance and the problem of inclusion', *Global Governance* 7, 4: 411–26.

—— (2002) 'Reforming the international financial architecture: the new political agenda', in R. Wilkinson and S. Hughes (eds) *Global Governance: Critical Perspectives*, New York: Routledge.

Ghosh, D.K. and Ortiz, E. (eds) (1997) *The Global Structure of Financial Markets: An Overview*, London: Routledge.

Giannini, C. (1999) 'An enemy to none but a common friend to all? An international perspective on the lender of last resort function', *Essays in International Finance*, 214.

—— (2000) 'The role of the International Monetary Fund as lender of last resort', in K. Kaiser, J.J. Kirton and J.P. Daniels (eds) *Shaping a New International Financial System: Challenges of Governance in a Globalizing World*, Aldershot: Ashgate.

Giddens, A. (1999) *Globalisation*, 1999 BBC Reith Lecture. Available online at http://www.lse.ac.uk/Giddens/reith_99/week1/week1.htm (6 April 2004).

Gill, S. (1992) 'The emerging world order and European change: the political economy of the European Union', in L. Panitch and R. Miliband (eds) *Socialist Register*, London: Merlin Press.

—— (1994) 'The global political economy and structural change: globalising elites in the emerging world order', in Y. Sakamoto (ed.) *Global Transformation*, Tokyo: United Nations University Press.

—— (1995) 'Globalisation, market civilisation and disciplinary neo-liberalism', *Millennium* 24, 3: 399–423.

—— (ed.) (1997a) *Globalization, Democratization and Multilateralism*, London: Macmillan.

—— (1997b) 'Finance, production and panopticism: inequality, risk and resistance in an era of disciplinary neo-liberalism', in S. Gill (ed.) *Globalization, Democratization and Multilateralism*, London: Macmillan.

—— (1998) 'European governance and new constitutionalism: Economic and Monetary Union and alternatives to disciplinary neo-liberalism in Europe', *New Political Economy* 3, 1: 5–26.

—— (2000) 'The constitution of global capitalism'. Available online at http://www.theglobalsite.ac.uk/global-library/ (6 April 2004).

—— (2003) *Power and Resistance in the New World Order*, New York: Palgrave.

Gill, S. and Law, D. (1988) *The Global Political Economy: Perspectives, Problems and Policies*, Hemel Hempstead: Harvester Wheatsheaf.

—— (1989) 'Global hegemony and the structural power of capital', *International Studies Quarterly* 33, 4: 475–99.

Gills, B. (2001) 'Re-orienting the new (international) political economy', *New Political Economy* 6, 2: 233–45.

Gilpin, R. (1987) *The Political Economy of International Relations*, Princeton: Princeton University Press.

—— (2002) 'The evolution of political economy', in D.M. Andrews, C.R. Henning and L.W. Pauly (eds) *Governing the World's Money*, Ithaca: Cornell University Press.

de Goede, M. (2001) 'Discourses of scientific finance and the failure of long-term capital management', *New Political Economy* 6, 2: 149–70.

Goodhart, C.A.E. (2000) 'The organisational structure of banking supervision', *LSE Financial Markets Group Special Paper* No.127. Available online at http://fmg.lse.ac.uk/pdfs/sp0127.pdf (18 November 2002).

Goodman, J.B. and Pauly, L.W. (1993) 'The obsolescence of capital controls: economic management in an age of global markets', *World Politics* 46, 1: 50–82.

Government of Indonesia (1998) *Memorandum of economic and financial policies*, 15 January 1998, Jakarta.

Gowa, J. (1983) *Closing the Gold Window: Domestic Politics and the End of Bretton Woods*, Ithaca: Cornell University Press.

Gowan, P. (1999) *The Global Gamble: Washington's Faustian Bid for World Dominance*, London: Verso.

Gower, L.C.B. (1984) *Review of Investor Protection Part I*, House of Commons Command Paper Cm-9125, London: HMSO.

Grabel, I. (1996) 'Marketing the third world: the contradictions of portfolio investment in the global economy', *World Development* 24, 11: 1761–76.

—— (1999) 'Mexico redux? Making sense of the financial crisis of 1997–98', *Journal of Economic Issues* XXXIII, 2: 375–81.

Gramsci, A. (1971) *Selections from the 'Prison Notebooks'*, trans. Q. Hoare and G. Nowell-Smith, London: Lawrence and Wishart.

Grande, E. (1996) 'The state and interest groups in a framework of multilevel decision-making: the case of the European Union', *Journal of European Public Policy* 3, 3: 318–38.

Gray, J. (1999) *False Dawn: The Delusions of Global Capitalism*, London: Granta Books.

Greider, W. (1997) *One World Ready or Not: The Manic Logic of Global Capitalism*, London: Penguin.

Group of Seven (1995) *The G7 Finance Ministers Report to the Heads of State and Government at the Halifax Summit*.

Guitian, M. (1992) 'The unique nature and responsibilities of the International Monetary Fund', *International Monetary Fund Pamphlet Series*, 31.

Guttmann, R. (1994) *How Credit-Money Shapes the Economy: The United States in a Global System*, New York: M.E. Sharpe.

Guzzini, S. (1998) *Realism in International Relations and International Political Economy: The Continuing Story of a Death Foretold*, London: Routledge.

Haley, M.A. (2001) *Freedom and Finance: Democratization and Institutional Investors in Developing Countries*, London: Palgrave.

Hall, P.A. and Soskice, D. (2001) *Varieties of Capitalism: The Institutional Foundations of Comparative Advantage*, Oxford: Oxford University Press.

Hall, P.A. and Taylor, R.C.M. (1996) 'Political science and the three new institutionalisms', *Political Studies* 44, 4: 936–57.

Hall, R.B. and Biersteker, T.J. (eds) (2002) *The Emergence of Private Authority in Global Governance*, Cambridge: Cambridge University Press.

Handelsblatt (2000) 'Landesbanken sorgen in Brüssel in Wirbel', 27 July.

—— (2001) 'Schröder verspricht sparkassen unterstützung im streit mit Brüüssel', 16 May.

Harmes, A. (1998) 'Institutional investors and the reproduction of neoliberalism', *Review of International Political Economy* 5, 1: 92–121.

—— (2001a) 'Institutional investors and Polanyi's double movement: a model of contemporary currency crises' *Review of International Political Economy* 8, 3: 389–437.

—— (2001b) 'Mass investment culture', *New Left Review* 9: 103–24.

Harukiyo, H. and Hook, G. (eds) *The Political Economy of Japanese Globalization*, London: Routledge.

Harvey, D. (1999) *The Limits to Capital*, London: Verso.

—— (2003) 'The "new" imperialism: accumulation by dispossession', in L. Panitch and C. Leys (eds) *Socialist Register*, London: Merlin Press.

Harvey, J.T. (1999) 'Volatility and misalignment in the post-Bretton Woods era', in J. Deprez and J.T. Harvey (eds) *Foundations of International Economics: Post Keynesian Perspectives*, London: Routledge.

Haslam, P. (1999) 'Globalization and effective sovereignty: a theoretical approach to the state in international political economy', *Studies in Political Economy* 58: 41–68.

Hasselström, A. (2003) *On and Off the Trading Floor: An Inquiry into the Everyday Fashioning of Financial Market Knowledge*, Doctoral Dissertation: Department of Social Anthropology, Stockholm University.

Haufler, V. (1999) 'Self-regulation and business norms: political risk, political activism', in A.C. Cutler, V. Haufler and T. Porter (eds) *Private Authority and International Affairs*, Albany: State University of New York Press.

—— (2000) 'Private sector international regimes', in R. Higgott, G.R.D. Underhill and A. Bieler (eds) *Non-State Actors and Authority in the Global System*, London: Routledge.

Hay, C. (2002) 'Globalisation as a problem of political analysis: restoring agents to a "process without a subject" and politics to a logic of economic compulsion', *Cambridge Review of International Affairs* 15, 3: 379–92.

Hay, C. and Marsh, D. (eds) (2000a) *Demystifying Globalization*, Basingstoke: Macmillan.

—— (2000b) 'Introduction: demystifying globalization', in C. Hay and D. Marsh (eds) *Demystifying Globalization*, Basingstoke: Macmillan.

Hay, C. and Rosamond, B. (2002) 'Globalisation, European integration and the discursive construction of economic imperatives', *Journal of European Public Policy* 9, 2: 147–67.

Held, D. and McGrew, A. (eds) (2002) *Governing Globalisation: Power, Authority and Global Governance*, Cambridge: Polity Press.

Held, D. *et al.* (1999) *Global Transformations: Politics, Economics and Culture*, Cambridge: Polity Press.

Helleiner, E.N. (1993) 'When finance was the servant: international capital movements in the Bretton Woods order', in P.G. Cerny (ed.) *Finance and World Politics: Markets, Regimes and States in the Post-Hegemonic Era*, Aldershot: Edward Elgar.

—— (1994) *States and the Re-emergence of Global Finance*, New York: Cornell University Press.

Henning, R. (1994) *Currencies and Politics in the United States, Japan and Germany*, Washington: Institute for International Economics.

Henning, R. and Destler, I. (1988) 'From neglect to activism: American politics and the 1985 Plaza Accord', *Journal of Public Policy* 8, 3/4: 317–33.

Henwood, D. (1998) *Wall Street: How it Works and for Whom* (2nd edition), New York: Verso.

Herring, R. and Litan, R. (1995) *Financial Regulation in the Global Economy*, Washington DC: Brookings Institution.

Herz, J.H. (1957) 'Rise and demise of the territorial state', *World Politics* 9, 4: 473–93.

—— (1976) *The Nation State and the Crisis of World Politics*, New York: McKay.

Hewson, M. and Sinclair, T.J. (eds) (1999a) *Approaches to Global Governance Theory*, Albany: State University of New York Press.

—— (1999b) 'The emergence of global governance theory', in M. Hewson and T.J. Sinclair (eds) *Approaches to Global Governance Theory*, New York: State University of New York Press.

Higgott, R. and Reich, S. (1998) 'Globalisation and sites of conflict: towards definition and taxonomy', *Centre for the Study of Globalisation and Regionalisation Working Paper* 1/98. Available online at http://www.warwick.ac.uk/fac/soc/CSGR/wpapers/wp0198.pdf (6 April 2004).

Higgott, R.A., Underhill, G.R.D. and Bieler, A. (eds) (2000) *Non-State Actors and Authority in the Global System*, London: Routledge.

Hinsley, F. (1986) *Sovereignty* (2nd edition), Cambridge, Cambridge University Press.

Hirsch, J. (1978) 'The state apparatus and social reproduction: elements of a theory of the bourgeois state', in J. Holloway and S. Picciotto (eds) *State and Capital: A Marxist Analysis*, London: Edward Arnold.

Hirst, P. (1997) *From Statism to Pluralism: Democracy, Civil Society and Global Politics*, London: UCL Press.

—— (2001) 'Politics: territorial or non-territorial?'. Available online at www.theglobalsite. ac.uk (30 October 2002).

Hirst, P. and Thompson, G. (1999) *Globalization in Question: The International Economy and the Possibilities of Governance* (2nd edition), Cambridge: Polity Press.

HM Treasury (2000) Speech by Chief Secretary to the Treasury, Andrew Smith At The World's Stock Exchanges Conference. Available online at http://www.hm-treasury. gov.uk/Newsroom_and_Speeches/speeches/ChiefSecSpeeches/speech_cst_70200.cfm (29th December 2002)

Hobbes, T. (1991) *Leviathan*, ed. Richard Tuck, Cambridge: Cambridge University Press.

Hobsbawm, E.J. (1969) *Industry and Empire*, Harmondsworth: Penguin.

Holloway, J. and Picciotto, S. (eds) (1978) *State and Capital: A Marxist Analysis*, London: Edward Arnold.

Hooghe, L. and Marks, G. (2001) 'Types of Multi-Level Governance', *European Integration online Papers (EIoP)* 5, 11. Available online at http://eiop.or.at/eiop/texte/2001–011a. htm (7 April 2004).

Hook, G. (ed.) (2004) *Contested Governance in Japan*, London: Routledge.

House Banking Oversight Subcommittee (1998) *Transcript of a Hearing to Review the Operation of the IMF*, 21 April.

House of Commons (1999) *Hansard: House of Commons Official Report Sixth Series*, Vol.334 28 June–8 July.

House of Commons Treasury Select Committee (1996) *Barings Bank and International Regulation Volume I*, Cm 65–i 1996–97.

—— (2003) *Split Capital Investment Trusts*, Cm-HC 418–ii 2002–2003.

Hudson, A.C. (1998) 'Reshaping the regulatory landscape: border skirmishes around the Bahamas and Cayman offshore financial centres', *Review of International Political Economy* 5, 3: 534–64.

Hülsemeyer, A. (ed.) (2003) *Globalization: Convergence and Divergence*, London: Palgrave.

Hurd, I. (1999) 'Legitimacy and authority in international politics', *International Organization* 53, 2: 379–408.

Ingham, G. (1984) *Capitalism Divided? The City and Industry in British Social History*, London: Macmillan.

—— (1996) 'Money as a social relation', *Review of Social Economy* 54, 4: 507–29.

International Association of Insurance Supervisors (2002) 'About IAIS'. Available online at http://www.iaisweb.org/framesets/about.html (12 December 2002).

International Financial Institution Advisory Commission (2000) *Report*, Washington DC.

International Financial Services London (2003) *International Financial Markets in the UK November 2003*. Available online at http://www.ifsl.org.uk/uploads/RP_IFM_2003_11.pdf. (22 February 2004).

International Monetary Fund (1997a) 'IMF responds to globalisation's challenges on many fronts in 1996/97', *IMF Survey* 26, 17: 277–9.

—— (1997b) *Good Governance: The IMF's Role*, Washington DC: IMF.

—— (1997c) 'IMF approves stand-by credit for Indonesia', *IMF Press Release*, 97/50.

—— (1997d) *World Economic Outlook Supplement: Interim Assessment*, Washington DC: IMF.

—— (1998a) *International Capital Markets: Developments, Prospects and Key Policy Issues*, World Economic and Financial Surveys, Washington DC: IMF.

—— (1998b) *External Evaluation of the ESAF: Report by a Group of Independent Experts*, Washington DC: IMF.

—— (1999) *IMF-Supported Programs in Indonesia, Korea, and Thailand: A Preliminary Assessment*. Occasional Paper 178. Washington DC: IMF.

—— (2000) *Reports on the Observances of Standards and Codes – Canada*. Available online at http://www.imf.org/external/np/rosc/can/securities.htm (6 April 2004).

—— (2001a) 'Assessing the implementation of standards – an IMF review of experience and next steps'. Available online at http://www.imf.org/external/np/sec/pn/2001/pn0117.htm#attI (13 December 2002).

—— (2001b) 'Widespread participation, cooperation are key in developing, implementing standards', *IMF Survey* 30, 7: 101–5.

—— (2001c) *Structural Conditionality in Fund Supported Programmes*, Washington DC: IMF.

—— (2001d) 'Reports on observance of standards and codes (ROSCs): Republic of Korea, Fiscal Transparency, January 23, 2001'. Available online at http://www.imf.org/external/np/rosc/rosc/asp (13 December 2002).

—— (2002) 'Reports on the observance of standards and codes (ROSCs)'. Available online at http://www.imf.org/external/np/rosc/rosc.asp (13 December 2002).

International Organisation of Securities Commissions (2002) 'General information on IOSCO'. Available online at http://www.iosco.org/gen-info.html (12 December 2002).

Iqbal, F. and You, J.-I. (eds) (2001) *Democracy, Market Economics and Development: An Asian Perspective*, Washington DC: World Bank.

Jachtenfuchs, M. and Kohler-Koch, B. (eds) (1996a) *Europäische Integration*, Opladen: UTB/Leske and Budrich.

—— (1996b) 'Regieren im dynamischen mehrebenensystem', in M. Jachtenfuchs and B. Kohler-Koch (eds) *Europäische Integration*, Opladen: UTB/Leske and Budrich.

Jacobs, J. (1984) *Cities and the Wealth of Nations*, Harmondsworth: Penguin.

Jang, H.-s.J. (2001) 'Corporate governance and economic development: the Korean experience', in F. Iqbal and J.-I. You (eds) *Democracy, Market Economics and Development: An Asian Perspective*, Washington DC: World Bank.

Jayasuriya, K. (1999) 'Globalization, law, and the transformation of sovereignty: the emergence of global regulatory governance', *Indiana Journal of Global Legal Studies* 6, 2: 425–55.

—— (2001) 'Globalization and the changing architecture of the state: the regulatory state and the politics of negative co-ordination', *Journal of European Public Policy* 8, 1: 101–23.

Jensen, M.C. (1978) 'Some anomalous evidence regarding market efficiency', *Journal of Financial Economics* 6, 2/3: 95–101.

Jessop, B. (1999) 'The dynamics of partnership and governance failure'. Available online at http://www.comp.lancs.ac.uk/sociology/soc015rj.html (4 December 2000).

Johnson S. *et al.* (2000) 'Corporate governance in the Asian financial crisis', *Journal of Financial Economics* 58, 1/2: 141–86.

Johnston, R. (2001) 'Out of the "moribund backwater": territory and territoriality in political geography', *Political Geography* 20, 6: 677–93.

Johnston, R.J., Taylor, P.J. and Watts, M.J. (eds) (1995) *Geographies of Global Change: Remapping the World in the Late Twentieth Century*, Oxford: Blackwell.

Jordan, A. (2001) 'The European Union: an evolving system of multi-level governance . . . or government?', *Policy and Politics* 29, 2: 193–208.

Josselin, D. (1996) *Les Réseaux en Action. Paris, Londres et la Construction du Marché Unique Financier*, Paris: L'Harmattan.

Kaiser, K., Kirton, J.J. and Daniels, J.P. (eds) (2000) *Shaping a New International Financial System: Challenges of Governance in a Globalizing World*, Aldershot: Ashgate.

Kalthoff, H., Rottenburg, R. and Wagener, H.-J. (eds) (2000) *Ökonomie und Geschellschaft. Facts and Figures: Economic Representations and Practices*, Marburg: Metropolis Verlag.

Kapstein, E.B. (1994) *Governing the Global Economy: International Finance and the State*, London: Harvard University Press.

Kenen, P. (1996) 'From Halifax to Lyon: what has been done about crisis management?', *Essays in International Finance*, 200.

Keohane, R.O. (1984) *After Hegemony: Cooperation and Discord in the World Political Economy*, Princeton: Princeton University Press.

—— (ed.) (1986) *Neorealism and its Critics*, New York: Columbia University Press.

Keohane, R.O. and Nye, J.S. (eds) (1972) *Transnational Relations and World Politics*, Cambridge: Harvard University Press.

—— (1974) 'Transgovernmental relations and international organizations', *World Politics* 27, 1: 39–62.

—— (1977) *Power and Interdependence: World Politics in Transition*, Boston: Little, Brown and Company.

Key, S.J. (1999) 'Trade liberalization and prudential regulation: the international framework for financial services', *International Affairs* 75, 1: 61–75.

Keynes, J.M. (1936 [1997]) *The General Theory of Employment, Interest and Money*, New York: Prometheus Books.

Killick, T. (1995) *IMF Programmes in Developing Countries*, London: Routledge.

Killick, T., Marr, A. and Gunatilaka, R. (1998) *Aid and the Political Economy of Policy Change*, London: Routledge.

Kim, D.-j. (1985) *Mass Participatory Economy: A Democratic Alternative for Korea*, Boston: Centre for International Affairs, Harvard University and University Press of America.

Kindleberger, C.P. (1973) *The World in Depression, 1929–1939*, Berkeley: University of California Press.

—— (1984) *A Financial History of Western Europe*, Oxford: Oxford University Press.

—— (1996) *Manias, Panics, and Crashes: A History of Financial Crises* (3rd edition), New York: John Wiley.

King, M. (1997) 'The inflation target five years on', *LSE Financial Markets Group Lecture*.

King, M.R. and Sinclair, T.J. (2001) 'Grasping at straws: a ratings downgrade for the emerging international financial architecture', *Centre for the Study of Globalisation and Regionalisation Working Paper* 82/01. Available online at http://www.warwick.ac.uk/fac/soc/CSGR/wpapers/wp8201.pdf (6 April 2004).

Kirshner, J. (1999) 'Keynes, capital mobility and the crisis of embedded liberalism', *Review of International Political Economy* 6, 3: 313–37.

—— (2003) 'Money is politics', *Review of International Political Economy* 10, 4: 645–60.

Kobrin, S.J. (1998) 'Back to the future: neomedievalism and the postmodern digital world economy', *Journal of International Affairs* 51, 2: 361–86.

—— (2002) 'Economic governance in an electronically networked global economy', in R.B. Hall and T.J. Biersteker (eds) *The Emergence of Private Authority in Global Governance*, Cambridge: Cambridge University Press.

Kofman, E. and Youngs, G. (eds) (1996) *Globalisation: Theory and Practice*, London: Pinter.

Kohler-Koch, B. (1997) 'Organized interests in European integration: the evolution of a new type of governance?', in H. Wallace and A. Young (eds) *Participation and Policy-Making in the European Union*, Oxford: Oxford University Press.

Kooiman, J. (1993) *Modern Governance: New Government–Society Interaction*, London: Sage.

Krasner, S.D. (1968) 'The IMF and the third world', *International Organization* 22, 3: 670–88.

—— (1983) *International Regimes*, Ithaca: Cornell University Press.

—— (1999) *Sovereignty: Organized Hypocrisy*, Princeton: Princeton University Press.

—— (2001) 'Sovereignty', *Foreign Affairs* 122: 20–9.

Kratochwil, F. (1986) 'Of systems, boundaries, and territoriality: an inquiry into the formation of the state system', *World Politics* 39, 1: 27–52.

Kratochwil, F. and Ruggie, J.G. (1986) 'International organization: a state of the art on an art of the state', *International Organization* 40, 4: 753–75.

Kurtzman, J. (1993) *The Death of Money*, Boston: Little, Brown and Company.

Kynaston, D. (1994) *The City of London: Vol. II, Golden Years 1890–1914*, London: Chatto and Windus.

—— (2001) 'Servants of an unholy financial empire', *Financial Times* 30 March, 21.

—— (2002) *The City of London: Vol. IV, A Club No More 1945–2000*, London: Pimlico.

Lamfalussy, A. (2000) *An Essay on Financial Globalisation and Fragility: Financial Crises in Emerging Markets*, New Haven: Yale University.

Lane, T. *et al.* (1999) *IMF Supported Programs in Indonesia, Korea and Thailand: A Preliminary Assessment*, Washington DC: IMF.

Langley, P. (2002a) *World Financial Orders: An Historical International Political Economy*, London: Routledge.

—— (2002b) 'The everyday life of global finance', Paper presented to the British International Studies Association Annual Conference, London School of Economics, December.

—— (2004) '(Re)politicising global financial governance: what's "new" about the "new international financial architecture"?', *Global Networks* 4, 1: 69–87.

Langley, P. and Mellor, M. (2002) ' "Economy", sustainability, and sites of transformative space', *New Political Economy* 7, 1: 49–66.

Latham, R. (1999) 'Politics in a floating world: toward a critique of global governance', in M. Hewson and T.J. Sinclair (eds) *Approaches to Global Governance Theory*, New York: State University of New York Press.

Lawson, N. (1992) *The View From No. 11: Memoirs of a Tory Radical*, London: Bantam Press.

Lawton, T.C., Rosenau, J.N. and Verdun, A.C. (eds) (2000) *Strange Power: Shaping the Parameters of International Relations and International Political Economy*, Aldershot: Ashgate.

Lazonick, W. and O'Sullivan, M. (2000) 'Maximizing shareholder value: a new ideology for corporate governance', *Economy and Society* 29, 1: 13–35.

Lefebvre, H. (1991) *The Production of Space*, Oxford: Blackwell.

Levi-Faur, D. (1997) 'Economic nationalism: from Friedrich List to Robert Reich', *Review of International Studies* 23, 3: 359–70.

Levitt, A. (2002) *Take on the Street: What Wall Street and Corporate America Don't Want You to Know, What You Can Do to Fight Back*, New York: Pantheon.

Leyshon, A. (1996) 'Dissolving difference? Money, disembedding and the creation of "global financial space" ', in P.W. Daniels and W.F. Lever (eds) *The Global Economy in Transition*, Essex: Addison Wesley Longman.

Leyshon, A. and Thrift, N. (1995) 'Geographies of financial exclusion: financial abandonment in Britain and the United States', *Transactions of the Institute of British Geographers* 20, 3: 312–41.

—— (1996) 'Financial exclusion and the shifting boundaries of the financial system', *Environment and Planning A* 28, 7: 1150–6.

—— (1997) *Money/Space: Geographies of Monetary Transformation*, London: Routledge.

Leyshon, A., Thrift, N. and Pratt, J. (1998) 'Reading financial services: texts, consumers and financial literacy', *Environment and Planning D* 16, 1: 29–55.

Lukes, S. (1974) *Power: A Radical View*, London: Macmillan.

—— (1987) 'Perspectives on authority', in R.J. Pennock and J. Chapman (eds) *Authority Revisited*, New York: New York University Press.

Lütz, S. (1998) 'The revival of the nation-state? Stock exchange regulation in an era of globalized financial markets', *Journal of European Public Policy* 5, 1: 153–68.

—— (2000) 'From managed to market capitalism? German finance in transition', *MPIfG Discussion Paper* 00–2.

—— (2002) 'Convergence within national diversity: a comparative perspective on the regulatory state in finance', Paper presented to the Annual Meeting of the British International Studies Association, London School of Economics, 17–19 December.

McKenzie, G. and Khalidi, M. (1996) 'The globalization of banking and financial markets: the challenge for European regulators', *Journal of European Public Policy* 3, 4: 629–46.

McLeod, R. (1998) 'From crisis to cataclysm? The mismanagement of Indonesia's economic ailments', *World Economy* 21, 7: 913–30.

Mahathir, M. (1998) 'The exchange control policy of Malaysia', Speech given at a meeting organized by Nikkei, Tokyo, 16 October.

Malpas, J. and Wickham, G. (1995) 'Governance and failure: on the limits of sociology', *The Australian and New Zealand Journal of Sociology* 31, 3: 37–50.

March, J. and Olsen, J. (1998) 'The institutional dynamics of international political orders', *International Organization* 52, 4: 943–69.

Marks, G. *et al.* (eds) (1996) *Governance in the European Union*, London: Sage.

Marks, G. *et al.* (1996) 'Competencies, cracks and conflicts: regional mobilisation in the European Union', in G. Marks *et al.* (eds) *Governance in the European Union*, London: Sage.

Marks, G. *et al.* (1996) 'European integration from the 1980s: state-centric v. multi-level governance', *Journal of Common Market Studies* 34, 3: 341–78.

Marsh, D. and Hay, C. (eds) (2000) *Globalisation, Welfare Retrenchment and the State*, London, Macmillan.

Martin, R. (1994) 'Stateless monies, global financial integration and national economic autonomy: the end of geography', S. Corbridge, R. Martin and N. Thrift (eds) *Money, Power and Space*, Cambridge: Blackwell.

—— (ed.) (1999a) *Money and the Space Economy*, Colchester: Wiley.

—— (1999b) 'The new "geographical turn" in economics: some critical reflections', *Cambridge Journal of Economics* 23, 1: 65–91.

Martin, S. and Pearce, G. (1999) 'Differentiated multi-level governance? The response of British sub-national governments to European integration', *Regional and Federal Studies* 9, 2: 32–52.

Marx, K. (1990) *Capital. Volume 1*, London: Penguin Classics.

Mathiason, J.R. (1998) 'Managing global governance'. Available online at http://www.intlmgt.com/pastprojects/Mangov.html (30 June 2000).

Matthews, J. (1998) 'Fashioning a new Korean model out of the crisis: the rebuilding of institutional capabilities', *Cambridge Journal of Economics* 22, 6: 747–59.

Michie, J. (ed.) (2003) *The Handbook of Globalization*, London: Edward Elgar.

Michie, J. and Grieve Smith, J. (eds) (1999) *Global Instability: The Political Economy of World Economic Governance*, London: Routledge.

Michie, R.C. (1998) 'Insiders, outsiders and the dynamics of change in the city of London since 1900', *Journal of Contemporary History* 33, 4: 547–71.

Mietzner, M. (1999) 'From Soeharto to Habibe: the Indonesian armed forces and political Islam during the transition', in G. Forrester (ed.) *Post-Soeharto Indonesia. Renewal or chaos?*, Singapore: Institute for Southeast Asian Studies.

Minc, A. (1993) *Le nouveau Moyen Age*, Paris: Gallimard.

Minns, R. (1996) 'The social ownership of capital', *New Left Review* 219: 42–61.

Mo, J. and Myers, R.H. (eds) (1993) *Shaping a New Economic Relationship: The Republic of Korea and the United States*, Stanford: Stanford University Press.

Moon, C.I. and Mo, J. (2000) Economic Crisis and Structural Reforms in South Korea: Assessments and Implications, Washington DC: Economic Strategy Institute.

Moran, M. (1984) *The Politics of Banking: The Strange Case of Competition and Credit Control*, London: Macmillan.

—— (1991) *The Politics of the Financial Services Revolution: The USA, UK and Japan*, London: Macmillan.

—— (1994) 'The state and the financial services revolution: a comparative analysis', *West European Politics* 17, 3: 158–77.

—— (2001) 'The new regulatory state in Britain', *Talking Politics* 13, 2: 109–12.

—— (2002) 'Understanding the regulatory state', *British Journal of Political Science* 32, 2: 391–413.

Mosley, L. (1997) 'International financial markets and government economic policy: the importance of financial market operations', Paper presented at the Annual Meeting of the American Political Science Association, Duke University.

Murphy, C.N. (1994) *Organization and Industrial Change: Global Governance Since 1850*, Oxford: Oxford University Press.

—— (2000) 'Global governance: poorly done and poorly understood', *International Affairs* 76, 4: 789–803.

Murphy, C.N. and Tooze, R. (eds) (1991a) *The New International Political Economy*, Boulder: Lynne Rienner.

—— (1991b) 'Getting beyond the "common sense" of the IPE orthodoxy', in C.N. Murphy and R. Tooze (eds) *The New International Political Economy*, Boulder: Lynne Rienner.

New York Times (1997) 'The economic stakes in Asia', 1 November.

Noble, G.W. and Ravenhill, J. (eds) (2000) *The Asian Financial Crisis and the Architecture of Global Finance*, Cambridge: Cambridge University Press.

North, D.C. (1977) 'Markets and other allocation systems in history: the challenge of Karl Polanyi', *Journal of European Economic History* 6, 3: 703–16.

Nowzad, B. (1982) 'The IMF and its critics', *Essays in International Finance*, 146.

O'Brien, Richard (1992) *Global Financial Integration: The End of Geography*, London: Royal Institute of International Affairs.

O'Brien, Robert (2000) 'Labour and IPE: rediscovering agency', in R. Palan (ed.) *Global Political Economy: Contemporary Theories*, London: Routledge.

—— (2002) 'The nuances of multilevel and global governance', Paper presented to the conference Globalization, Multilevel Governance and Democracy: Continental, Comparative and Global Perspectives, Queen's University Belfast, 3–4 May.

O'Brien, Robert *et al.* (2000) *Contesting Global Governance: Multilateral Economic Institutions and Global Social Movements*, Cambridge: Cambridge University Press.

Odell, J.S. (1982) *U.S. International Monetary Policy*, Princeton: Princeton University Press.

Ohmae, K. (1990) *The Borderless World: Power and Strategy in the Interlinked Economy*, London: Collins.

—— (1995) *The End of the Nation State: The Rise of Regional Economies*, London: Harper Collins.

Organisation for Economic Co-operation and Development (1998) *OECD Corporate Governance Guidelines*, Paris: OECD.

—— (1999) *OECD Principles of Corporate Governance*, Paris: OECD.

O'Sullivan, M. (2000) *Contests for Corporate Control: Corporate Governance and Economic Performance in the United States and Germany*, Oxford: Oxford University Press.

Painter, M. (2001) 'Multi-level governance and the emergence of collaborative federal institutions in Australia', *Policy and Politics* 29, 2: 137–50.

Palan, R. (1999) 'Global governance and social closure or who is to be governed in the era of global governance', in M. Hewson and T.J. Sinclair (eds) *Approaches to Global Governance Theory*, Albany: State University of New York Press.

—— (ed.) (2000a) *Global Political Economy: Contemporary Theories*, London: Routledge.

—— (2000b) 'New trends in the global political economy', in R. Palan (ed.) *Global Political Economy: Contemporary Theories*, London: Routledge.

Palan, R. and Abbott, J. (1996) *State Strategies in the Global Political Economy*, London: Pinter.

Palan, R.P. and Gills, B. (eds) (1994) *Transcending the State–Global Divide: A Neostructuralist Agenda in International Relations*, Boulder: Lynne Rienner.

Panitch, L. (ed.) (1997) *Socialist Register – Ruthless Criticism of All That Exists*, Suffolk: Merlin.

—— (2000) 'The new imperial state', *New Left Review* 2: 5–20.

Panitch, L. and Leys, C. (eds) (2002) *Socialist Register*, London: Merlin.

—— (eds) (2003) *Socialist Register*, London: Merlin.

Panitch, L. and Miliband, R. (eds) (1992) *Socialist Register*, London: Merlin.

Pauly, L.W. (1997) *Who Elected the Bankers? Surveillance and Control in the World Economy*, Ithaca: Cornell University Press.

—— (1999) 'Good governance and bad policy: the perils of international organizational overextension', *Review of International Political Economy* 6, 4: 401–24.

—— (2000) 'Capital mobility and the new global order', in R. Stubbs and G.R.D. Underhill (eds) *Political Economy and the Changing Global Order*, Oxford: Oxford University Press.

Payne, A. (forthcoming) 'The study of governance in a global political economy', in N. Phillips (ed.) *Globalizing Political Economy*, London: Palgrave.

Peck, J. (2001) 'Neoliberalizing states: thin policies/hard outcomes', *Progress in Human Geography* 25, 3: 445–55.

Pennock, R.J. and Chapman, J. (eds) (1987) *Authority Revisited*, New York: New York University Press.

Pesaresi, N. and de la Rochefordière, C. (2000) '*Crises bancaires: un bilan de l'application des règles de concurrence en matière d'aides d'Etat. Leçons de la crise du Crédit Lyonnais*', *Competition Policy Newsletter* (European Commission) 3: 12–26.

Peters, B.G. and Pierre, J. (2001a) 'Developments in intergovernmental relations: towards multi-level governance', *Policy and Politics* 29, 2: 131–5.

—— (2001b) 'Multi-level governance: a Faustian bargain?', Paper presented at the PERC conference on multi-level governance, Sheffield, June.

Phillips, N. (forthcoming) *Globalizing Political Economy*, London: Palgrave.

Pierre, J. (ed.) (2000a) *Debating Governance: Authority, Steering and Democracy*, Oxford: Oxford University Press.

—— (2000b) 'Introduction: understanding governance', in J. Pierre (ed.) *Debating Governance: Authority, Steering and Democracy*, Oxford: Oxford University Press.

Plihon, D. (1999) *Les Banques. Nouveaux Enjeux, Nouvelles Stratégies*, Paris: La Documentation française.

Polak, J. (1991) 'The changing nature of IMF conditionality', *Essays in International Finance*, 184.

—— (1994) *The World Bank and the IMF A Changing Relationship*, Washington DC: Brookings Institute.

Polanyi, K. (1944) *The Great Transformation: The Political and Economic Origins of Our Time*, Boston: Beacon Hill.

Pomeranz, K. and Topik, P. (1999) *The World That Trade Created: Society, Culture, and the World Economy 1400 to the Present*, London: M.E. Sharpe.

Porter, T. (1993) *States, Markets and Regimes in Global Finance*, Basingstoke: Macmillan.

—— (2001a) 'The Democratic deficit in the institutional arrangements for regulating global finance', *Global Governance* 7, 4: 427–39.

—— (2001b) 'Negotiating the structure of capital mobility', in T.J. Sinclair and K.P. Thomas (eds) *Structure and Agency in International Capital Mobility*, Basingstoke: Palgrave.

—— (2002) 'Multilevel governance and democracy in global financial regulation', Paper presented to the conference Globalization, Multilevel Governance and Democracy: Continental, Comparative and Global Perspectives, Queen's University Belfast, 3–4 May.

Porter, T. with Schnabel, A. (2002) *Civil Society and Global Finance*, London: Routledge.

Przeworski, A. (1985) *Capitalism and Social Democracy*, Cambridge: Cambridge University Press.

Putnam, R.D. (1988) 'Diplomacy and domestic politics: the logic of two-level games', *International Organization* 42, 3: 427–60.

Putnam, R. and Henning, R. (1989) 'The Bonn Summit of 1978: A case study in co-ordination', in R.N. Cooper *et al.* (eds) *Can Nations Agree? Issues in International Economic Co-operation*, Washington DC: Brookings Institution.

Qureshi, A. (1999) *International Economic Law*, London: Sweet and Maxwell.

Radelet, S. and Sachs, J. (1998) *The East Asian Financial Crisis: Diagnosis, Remedies, Prospects*, mimeo.

Randzio-Plath, C. (2000) 'Challenges and perspectives for a Single Market for financial services in Europe', *Intereconomics* 35, 4: 192–7.

Reich, R.B. (1983) *The Next American Frontier*, New York: Times Books.

Reigner, H. (2001) 'Multi-level governance or co-administration? Transformation and continuity in French local government', *Policy and Politics* 29, 2: 181–92.

Reisenhuber, E. (2001) *The International Monetary Fund Under Constraint: Legitimacy of its Crisis Management*, The Hague: Kluwer Law International.

Rhodes, R.A.W. (1996) 'The new governance: governing without government', *Political Studies* 44, 4: 652–67.

Risse-Kappen, T. (1996) 'Exploring the nature of the beast: international relations theory and comparative policy analysis meet the European Union', *Journal of Common Market Studies* 34, 1: 53–80.

Risse, T. (2000) 'Let's argue!: communicative action in world politics', *International Organization* 54, 1: 1–28.

Roberts, R. and Kynaston, D. (2001) *City State EC2: How the Markets Came to Rule Our World*, London: Profile Books.

Robison, R. (1997) 'Politics and markets in Indonesia's post-oil era', in G. Rodan, K. Hewison and R. Robison (eds) *The Political Economy of Southeast Asia*, Oxford: Oxford University Press.

Robison, R. and Rosser, A. (2000) 'Surviving the meltdown: liberal reform and political oligarchy in Indonesia', in R. Robison *et al.* (eds) *Politics and Markets in the Wake of the Asian Crisis*, London, Routledge.

Robison, R. *et al.* (eds) (2000) *Politics and Markets in the Wake of the Asian Crisis*, London, Routledge.

Rodan, G., Hewison, K. and Robison, R. (eds) (1997) *The Political Economy of Southeast Asia*, Oxford: Oxford University Press.

Ronit, K. and Schneider, V. (1999) 'Global governance through private organizations', *Governance* 12, 3: 243–66.

—— (eds) (2001) *Private Organisations in Global Politics*, London: Routledge.

Rosamond, B. (2003) 'Babylon and on? Globalisation and international political economy', *Review of International Political Economy* 10, 4: 661–71.

Rosenau, J.N. (1969) *Linkage Politics: Essays on the Convergence of National and International Systems*, New York: The Free Press.

—— (1990) *Turbulence in World Politics: A Theory of Change and Continuity*, Princeton: Princeton University Press.

—— (1992) 'Governance, order, and change in world politics', in J.N. Rosenau and E.-O. Czempiel (eds) *Governance Without Government: Order and Change in World Politics*, Cambridge: Cambridge University Press.

—— (1995) 'Governance in the twenty-first century', *Global Governance* 1, 1: 13–43.

—— (1997) *Along the Domestic–Foreign Frontier: Exploring Governance in a Turbulent World*, Cambridge: Cambridge University Press.

—— (2000) 'Change, complexity and governance in a globalizing space', in J. Pierre (ed.) *Debating Governance: Authority, Steering and Democracy*, Oxford: Oxford University Press.

—— (2004) 'Strong demand, huge supply: governance in an emergent epoch', in I. Bache and M. Flinders (eds) *Multi-level Governance*, Oxford: Oxford University Press.

Rosenau, J.N. and Czempiel, E.-O. (eds) (1992) *Governance Without Government: Order and Change in World Politics*, Cambridge: Cambridge University Press.

Rosenberg, J. (2000) *The Follies of Globalization Theory: Polemical Essays*, London: Verso.

Rosow, S.J. (1994) 'Introduction: boundaries crossing – critical theories of global economy', in S.J. Rosow, N. Inayatullah and M. Rupert (eds) *The Global Economy as Political Space*, Boulder: Lynne Rienner.

Rosow, S.J., Inayatullah, N. and Rupert, M. (eds) (1994) *The Global Economy as Political Space*, Boulder: Lynne Rienner.

Ruggie, J.G. (1982) 'International regimes, transactions, and change: embedded liberalism in the post-war order', *International Organization* 36, 3: 379–415.

—— (1992) 'Multilateralism: an anatomy of an institution', *International Organization* 46, 3: 561–83.

—— (ed.) (1993a) *Multilateralism Matters: The Theory and Praxis of an Institutional Form*, New York: Columbia University Press.

—— (1993b) 'Multilateralism: the anatomy of an institution', in J. Ruggie (ed.) *Multilateralism Matters: The Theory and Practice of an Institutional Form*, New York: Columbia University Press.

—— (1993c) 'Territoriality and beyond: problematizing modernity in international relations', *International Organization* 47, 1: 139–74.

Ruimy, M. (2001) '*La Bourse en France*', *Cahiers français* 301: 3–14.

Sakamoto, Y. (ed.) (1994) *Global Transformation*, Tokyo: United Nations University Press.

Sassen, S. (1991) *The Global City: New York, London and Tokyo*, Princeton: Princeton University Press.

—— (1996) *Losing Control? Sovereignty in an Age of Globalization*, New York: Columbia University Press.

—— (1999) 'Global financial centres', *Foreign Affairs* 78, 1: 75–87.

—— (2000) *Cities in a World Economy* (2nd Edition), London: Sage.

—— (2002) 'Globalization and the state', in R.B. Hall and T. Biersteker (eds) *The Emergence of Private Authority in Global Governance*, Cambridge: Cambridge University Press.

—— (2003) 'Globalization or denationalization?', *Review of International Political Economy* 10, 1: 1–22.

Scharfstein, D. (1988) 'The disciplinary role of takeovers', *Review of Economic Studies* 55: 185–99.

Scharpf, F.W. (1997) 'Introduction: the problem solving capacity of multi-level governance', *Journal of European Public Policy* 4, 4: 520–38.

—— (2001) 'Notes toward a theory of multi-level governing in Europe', *Scandinavian Political Studies* 24, 1: 1–26.

Schmidt, V. (2002) *The Futures of European Capitalism*, Oxford: Oxford University Press.

Scholte, J.A. (1997) 'The globalization of world politics', in J.A. Baylis and S. Smith (eds) *The Globalisation of World Politics: An Introduction to International Relations*, Oxford: Oxford University Press.

—— (2000) *Globalization: A Critical Introduction*, Basingstoke: Palgrave.

—— (2002a) 'Governing global finance', Centre for the Study of Globalisation and Regionalisation Working Paper 82/02. Available online at http://www.warwick.ac.uk/fac/soc/CSGR/wpapers/wp8802.pdf (6 April 2004).

—— (2002b) 'Governing global finance', in D. Held and A. McGrew (eds) *Governing Globalization: Power, Authority and Governance*, Polity: Cambridge.

Schwarz, A. (1999) *A Nation in Waiting: Indonesia's Search for Stability* (2nd edition), Boulder, Westview.

Seabrooke, L. (2001) *US Power in International Finance: The Victory of Dividends*, London: Palgrave.

Sen, A. and Williams B. (eds) (1982) *Utilitarianism and Beyond*, Cambridge: Cambridge University Press.

Shin, D.-c. and Rose, R. (1998) *Responding to Economic Crisis: The 1998 New Korea Barometer Survey*, Glasgow: University of Strathclyde.

Shliefer, A. and Vishny, R.W. (1986) 'Large Shareholders and Corporate Control', *Journal of Political Economy* 94, 3: 461–88.

Shonfield, A. (1965) *Modern Capitalism: The Changing Balance of Public and Private Power*, London: Oxford University Press.

Simmons, B. (1994) *Who Adjusts? Domestic Sources of Foreign Economic Policy During the Interwar Years*, Princeton: Princeton University Press.

Sinclair, T.J. (1994a) 'Between state and market: hegemony and institutions of collective action under conditions of international capital mobility', *Policy Sciences* 27, 4: 447–66.

—— (1994b) 'Passing judgement: credit rating process as regulatory mechanisms of governance in the emerging world order', *Review of International Political Economy* 1, 1: 133–59.

—— (1999) 'Bond-rating agencies and coordination in the global political economy', in A.C. Cutler, V. Haufler and T. Porter (eds) *Private Authority and International Affairs*, Albany: State University of New York Press.

—— (2000a) 'Reinventing authority: embedded knowledge networks and the new global finance', *Environment and Planning C* 18, 4: 487–502.

—— (2000b) 'Deficit discourse: the social construction of fiscal rectitude', in R. Germain (ed.) *Globalization and its Critics*, London: Macmillan.

Sinclair, T.J. and Thomas, K.P. (eds) (2001) *Structure and Agency in International Capital Mobility*, Basingstoke: Palgrave.

Singer, J.D. (1961) 'The level-of-analysis problem in international relations', *World Politics* 14, 1: 77–92.

Sinn, H.-W. (1999) *The German State Banks. Global Players in the International Financial Markets*, Cheltenham: Edward Elgar.

Slaughter, A.M. (1997) 'The real new world order', *Foreign Affairs* 76, 5: 183–97.

—— (2000) 'Governing the global economy through government networks', in M. Byers (ed.) *The Role of Law in International Politics*, Oxford: Oxford University Press.

Smelser, N.J. and Swedberg, R. (eds) (1994) *The Handbook of Economic Sociology*, Princeton: Princeton University Press.

Smith, A. (1997) 'Studying multi-level governance. Examples from French translations of the structural funds', *Public Administration* 75, 4: 711–29.

Soederberg, S. (2001a) 'Grafting stability onto globalisation? Deconstructing the IMF's recent bid for transparency', *Third World Quarterly* 22, 5: 849–64.

—— (2001b) 'The emperor's new suit: the new international financial architecture as a reinvention of the Washington consensus', *Global Governance* 7, 4: 453–67.

—— (2003) 'The promotion of Anglo-American corporate governance in the South: who benefits from the new international standard?', *Third World Quarterly* 24, 1: 7–28.

—— (2004) *The Politics of the New International Financial Architecture: Reimposing Neoliberal Domination in the Global South*, London and New York: Zed Books.

—— (forthcoming) *Contesting Global Governance*, London: Pluto Press.

Soederberg, S., Menz, G. and Cerny, P.G. (eds) (forthcoming) *Internalizing Globalization: The Rise of Neoliberalism and the Erosion of National Models of Capitalism*, London: Routledge.

Sohn, C.-H. and Yang, J. (eds) (1998) *Korea's Economic Reform Measures under the IMF Program: Government Measures in the Critical First Six Months of the Korean Economic Crisis*, Korea Institute for International Economic Policy, Seoul.

Solow, R. (1999a) 'The amateur: making billions and misunderstanding the market', *The New Republic*, 8 February.

—— (1999b) 'Sound economics', *The New Republic*, 12 April.

Soros, G. (1988) *The Alchemy of Finance*, New York: Wiley.

—— (1998) *The Crisis of Global Capitalism: Open Society Endangered*, London: Little, Brown and Company.

—— (1998/99) 'Capitalism's last chance?', *Foreign Policy* 113: 55–72.

—— (1999) 'Irrational expectations', *The New Republic*, 12 April.

Spar, D. (2001) *Pirates, Prophets and Pioneers: Business and Politics Along the Technological Frontier*, London: Random House.

Spero, J.E. (1977) *The Politics of International Economic Relations*, London: Routledge.

Spruyt, H. (1994) *The Sovereign State and Its Competitors: An Analysis of Systems Change*, Princeton: Princeton University Press.

Stiglitz, J. (1998) 'More instruments and broader goals: moving towards the post-Washington consensus', *WIDER Annual Lectures*, 2.

—— (2000) 'What I learned at the world economic crisis', *The New Republic*, 17 April.

—— (2002) *Globalization and Its Discontents*, London: Penguin.

Stiles, K. (1991) *Negotiating Debt: The IMF Lending Process*, Boulder, Westview.

Stilwell, F. and Troy, P. (2000) 'Multilevel governance and urban development in Australia', *Urban Studies* 37, 5–6: 909–30.

Stoker, G. (1998) 'Governance as theory: five propositions', *International Social Science Journal* 50, 155: 17–28.

Stopford, J. and Strange, S. (1991) *Rival States, Rival Firms: Competition for World Market Shares*, Cambridge: Cambridge University Press.

Story, J. (1997) 'Globalisation, the European Union and German financial reform: the political economy of 'Finanzplatz Deutschland'', in G.R.D. Underhill (ed.) *The New World Order in International Finance*, Basingstoke: Macmillan.

—— (2000) 'The emerging world financial order and different forms of capitalism', in R. Stubbs and G.R.D. Underhill (eds) *Political Economy and the Changing Global Order*, Oxford: Oxford University Press.

—— (2003) 'Reform of the international financial architecture: what has been written?', in G.R.D. Underhill and X. Zhang (eds) *International Financial Governance Under Stress: Global Structures Versus National Imperatives*, Cambridge: Cambridge University Press.

Story, J. and Walter, I. (1997) *Political Economy of Financial Integration in Europe: The Battle of the Systems*, Cambridge, Mass.: MIT Press.

Strange, S. (1970) 'International economies and international relations: a case of mutual neglect', *International Affairs* 46, 2: 304–15.

—— (1976) 'The study of transnational relations', *International Affairs* 52, 3: 333–45.

—— (ed.) (1984) *Paths to International Political Economy*, London: George Allen and Unwin.

—— (1986) *Casino Capitalism*, Oxford: Blackwell.

—— (1988) *States and Markets*, London: Pinter.

—— (1994) *States and Markets* (2nd edition), London: Pinter.

—— (1996a) *The Retreat of the State: The Diffusion of Power in the World Economy*, Cambridge: Cambridge University Press.

—— (1996b) 'The defective state', *Daedalus* 24, 2: 55–74.

—— (1998) *Mad Money*, Manchester: Manchester University Press.

Stremlau, J. (1994/95) 'Clinton's dollar diplomacy', *Foreign Policy* 97: 18–36.

Stubbs, R. and Underhill, G.R.D. (eds) (1994) *Political Economy and the Changing Global Order*, Basingstoke: Macmillan.

—— (eds) (2000) *Political Economy and the Changing Global Order* (2nd edition), Oxford: Oxford University Press.

Summers, L. (1996) 'US policy towards the international monetary system on the eve of the Lyon Summit', *Remarks to Emerging Markets Traders Association*, 24 June.

Sutcliffe, J.B. (2000) 'The 1999 reforms of the structural fund regulations: multi-level governance or renationalization?', *Journal of European Public Policy* 7, 2: 290–309.

Swedberg, R. (1994) 'Markets as social structures', in N.J. Smelser and R. Swedberg (eds) *The Handbook of Economic Sociology*, Princeton: Princeton University Press.

Taylor, P.J. (1994) 'The state as container: territoriality in the modern world-system', *Progress in Human Geography* 18, 2: 151–62.

—— (1995) 'Beyond containers: internationality, interstateness, interterritoriality', *Progress in Human Geography* 19, 1: 1–15.

—— (1996) 'Embedded statism and the social sciences: opening up to new spaces', *Environment and Planning A* 28, 11: 1917–28.

—— (2000) 'Embedded statism and the social sciences 2: geographies (and metageographies) in globalization', *Environment and Planning A* 32, 6: 1105–14.

Taylor, P.J., Watts, M.J. and Johnston, R.J. (1995) 'Remapping the world: What sort of map? What sort of world?', in R.J. Johnston, P.J. Taylor and M.J. Watts (eds) *Geographies of Global Change: Remapping the World in the Late Twentieth Century*, Oxford: Blackwell.

Thirkell-White, B. (2003) 'The IMF, good governance and middle-income countries', *European Journal of Development Research* 15, 1: 91–125.

—— (2005) *The IMF and the Politics of Financial Globalisation: From the Asian Crisis to a New International Financial Architecture?*, Basingstoke: Palgrave.

Thompson, G. (ed.) (2000) *Markets*, volume 2 of *The United States in the Twentieth Century* (2nd edition), London: Hodder and Stoughton.

Thompson, P. (1997a) 'The pyrrhic victory of gentlemanly capitalism: the financial elite of the city of London, 1945–90', *Journal of Contemporary History* 32, 3: 283–304.

—— (1997b) 'The pyrrhic victory of gentlemanly capitalism: the financial elite of the city of London, 1945–90, Part 2', *Journal of Contemporary History* 32, 4: 427–40.

Thomson, R. (1999) *Apocalypse Roulette: The Lethal World of Derivatives*, London: Macmillan.

Thrift, N. (1994) 'On the social and cultural determinants of international financial centres: the case of the city of London', in S. Corbridge, R. Martin and N. Thrift (eds) *Money, Power and Space*, London: Blackwell.

Thrift, N. and Leyshon, A. (1994) 'A phantom state? The de-traditionalization of money, the international financial system and international financial centres', in *Political Geography* 13, 4: 299–327.

Tickell, A. (1996) 'Making a melodrama out of a crises: reinterpreting the collapse of Barings Bank', *Environment and Planning D* 14, 1: 5–33.

Tietmeyer, H. (1999) *International Cooperation and Coordination in the Area of Financial Market Supervision and Surveillance.* Available online at http://www.fsforum.org/publications/Tietmeyerreport.pdf (10 April 2004).

Tobin, J. (1978) 'A proposal for international monetary reform', *Eastern Economic Journal* 4, 3–4: 153–9.

Tooze, R. (1984) 'Perspectives and theory: a consumers' guide', in S. Strange (ed.) *Paths to International Political Economy*, London: George Allen and Unwin.

Tripartite Commission (1998) 'Second statement by the tripartite commission', in C.-H. Sohn and J. Yang (eds) *Korea's Economic Reform Measures Under the IMF Program: Government Measures in the Critical First Six Months of the Crisis*, Seoul: Korea Institute for International Economic Policy.

Tsingou, E. (2003) 'Transnational policy communities and financial governance: the role of private actors in derivatives regulation', *Centre for the Study of Globalisation and Regionalisation Working Paper* No.111/03. Available online at http://www.warwick.ac.uk/fac/soc/CSGR/abwp11103.html (9 April 2004).

Tucker, D. (1991) *The Decline of Thrift in America*, New York: Praeger.

ul Haq, M., Inge, K. and Grunberg, I. (eds) (1996) *The Tobin Tax: Coping with Financial Volatility*, Oxford: Oxford University Press.

Underhill, G.R.D. (ed.) (1997a) *The New World Order in International Finance*, Basingstoke: Macmillan.

—— (1997b) 'Private markets and public responsibility in a global system: conflict and co-operation in transnational banking and securities regulation', in G.R.D. Underhill (ed.) *The New World Order in International Finance*, Basingstoke: Macmillan.

—— (2000a) 'State, market, and global political economy: genealogy of an (inter?) discipline', *International Affairs* 76, 4: 805–24.

—— (2000b) 'Conceptualising the changing global order', in R. Stubbs and G.R.D. Underhill (eds) *Political Economy and the Changing Global Order*, Oxford: Oxford University Press.

—— (2000c) 'Global money and the decline of state power', in T.C. Lawton, J.N. Rosenau and A.C. Verdun (eds) *Strange Power: Shaping the Parameters of International Relations and International Political Economy*, Aldershot: Ashgate.

—— (2001) 'States, markets and governance: private interests, the public good and the democratic process', Inaugural Lecture, University of Amsterdam, 21 September.

Underhill, G.R.D. and Zhang, X. (eds) (2003) *International Financial Governance Under Stress: Global Structures Versus National Imperatives*, Cambridge: Cambridge University Press.

Unger, R.M. (1995) *Democracy Realized*, London, Verso.

Van den Berghe, L. and De Ridder, L. (1999) *International Standardisation of Good Corporate Governance: Best Practices for the Board of Directors*, Dordrecht: Kluwer.

Vives, X. (ed.) (2000a) *Corporate Governance: Theoretical and Empirical Perspectives*, Cambridge: Cambridge University Press.

Vives, X. (2000b) 'Corporate governance: does it matter?', in X. Vives (ed.) *Corporate Governance: Theoretical and Empirical Perspectives*, Cambridge: Cambridge University Press.

Vogel, D. (1995) *Trading Up: Consumer and Environmental Regulation in a Global Economy*, Cambridge, Mass.: Harvard University Press.

Vogel, S.K. (1996) *Freer Markets, More Rules: Regulatory Reform in Advanced Industrial Countries*, Ithaca: Cornell University Press.

Wade, R. and Veneroso, F. (1998) 'The Asian crisis: the high debt model versus the Wall Street–Treasury–IMF complex', *New Left Review* 228: 3–23.

Walker, R.B.J. (1993) *Inside/Outside: International Relations Theory as Political Theory*, Cambridge: Cambridge University Press.

—— (1995) 'From international relations to world politics', in J.A. Camilleri, A.P. Jarvis and A.J. Paolini (eds) *The State in Transition: Reimagining Political Space*, Boulder: Lynne Rienner.

Wallace, H. and Young, A. (eds) (1997) *Participation and Policy-Making in the European Union*, Oxford: Oxford University Press.

Walter, G., Dreher, S. and Beisheim, S. (1999) 'Globalisation processes in the G7', *Global Society* 13, 3: 229–55.

Waltz, K.N. (1959) *Man, the State and War: A Theoretical Analysis*, New York: Columbia University Press.

—— (1979) *Theory of International Politics*, Reading, MA: Addison-Wesley.

Warf, B. (1999) 'The hypermobility of capital and the collapse of the Keynesian state', in R. Martin (ed.) *Money and the Space Economy*, Chichester: Wiley.

Watson, M. (1999) 'Rethinking capital mobility, re-regulating financial markets', *New Political Economy* 4, 1: 55–75.

—— (2002) 'The institutional paradoxes of monetary orthodoxy: reflections on the political economy of central bank independence', *Review of International Political Economy* 9, 1: 183–96.

Webb, M.C. (1991) 'International economic structures, government interests and international co-ordination of macroeconomic adjustment policies', *International Organization* 45, 3: 309–42.

—— (2000) 'The group of seven and political management of the global economy', in R. Stubbs and G.R.D. Underhill (eds) *Political Economy and the Changing Global Order*, Oxford: Oxford University Press.

Weber, M. (1968) *Economy and Society: An Outline of Interpretive Sociology*, New York: Bedminster Press.

Weiss, L. (1998) *The Myth of the Powerless State: Governing the Economy in a Global Era*, Cambridge: Polity Press.

Wendt, A.E. (1992) 'Anarchy is what states make of it: the social construction of power politics', *International Organization* 46, 2: 391–425.

Wicks, N. (1994) 'The development of international financial institutions and the G7 co-ordination process', Speech at the Groucho Club, London, December.

—— (2003) 'Governments, the international financial institutions and international co-operation', in N. Bayne and S. Woolcock (eds) *The New Economic Diplomacy: Decision Making and Negotiations in International Economic Relations*, Aldershot: Ashgate.

Wilkinson, R. and Hughes, S. (eds) *Global Governance: Critical Perspectives*, New York: Routledge.

Williams, K. (2000) 'From shareholder value to present day capitalism', in *Economy and Society* 29, 1: 1–12.

Williams, W.A. (1972) *The Tragedy of American Diplomacy* (2nd edition), New York: Dell.

Williamson, J. (ed.) (1990a) *Latin American Adjustment: How Much Has Happened?*, Washington: Institute for International Economics.

—— (1990b) 'What Washington means by policy reform', in J. Williamson (ed.) *Latin American Adjustment: How Much Has Happened?*, Washington: Institute for International Economics.

Woodruff, D. (1999) *Money Unmade: Barter and the Fate of Russian Capitalism*, Ithaca: Cornell University Press.

Woods, N. (1999) 'Good governance in international organisations', *Global Governance* 5, 1: 39–61.

—— (2000) 'The challenge of good governance for the IMF and the World Bank themselves', *World Development* 28, 5: 823–41.

—— (2001) 'Who should govern the world economy? The challenges of globalisation and governance', *Renewal* 9, 2–3: 73–82.

Woodward, R. (2001) ' "Slaughtering" the British state? Transgovernmental networks and the governance of financial markets in the city of London', Paper presented to the Global Studies Association Inaugural Conference, 'Networks and Transformations', Manchester Metropolitan University, 2–4 July.

—— (2003) 'An "ation" not a "nation": the globalization of world politics', in J. Michie (ed.) *The Handbook of Globalization*, London: Edward Elgar.

World Bank (1998) *Indonesia in Crisis: A Macro-Economic Update*, Washington DC: World Bank.

—— (2000) *World Development Report 2000/2001: Attacking Poverty*, Oxford: Oxford University Press.

World Federation of Exchanges (2004) *World Federation of Exchanges Focus*, No. 132 February. Available online at http://www.world-exchanges.org/publications/Focus0204web.pdf (22 February 2004).

Wriston, W (1998) 'Dumb Networks and Smart Capital,' *Cato Journal*, 17:3, 333–44

Yarborough, B.V. and Yarborough, R.M. (1994) 'Regionalism and layered governance: the choice of trade institutions', *Journal of International Affairs* 48, 1: 95–117.

Yergin, D. (1977) *Shattered Peace: The Origins of the Cold War and the National Security State*, Harmondsworth: Penguin.

Youngs, G. (1999) *International Relations in a Global Age: A Conceptual Challenge*, Cambridge: Polity.

Zerah, D. (1993) *Le Système Financier Français. Dix Ans de Mutations*, Paris: Les études de la Documentation française.

Zhuang, J., Edwards, D. and Webb, D. (2000) *Corporate Governance and Finance in East Asia: A Study of Indonesia, Republic of Korea, Malaysia, Philippines and Thailand, Volume 1*. Manila: Asian Development Bank.

Zysman, J. (1983) *Governments, Markets and Growth: Financial Systems and the Politics of Industrial Change*, Ithaca: Cornell University Press.

Index